The Dangerous God

The Dangerous God

Christianity and the Soviet Experiment

EDITED BY DOMINIC ERDOZAIN

NIU Press / DeKalb, IL

Northern Illinois University Press, DeKalb 60115
© 2017 by Northern Illinois University Press
All rights reserved

26 25 24 23 22 21 20 19 18 17   1 2 3 4 5
978-0-87580-770-6 (paper)
978-1-60909-228-3 (e-book)
Book and cover design by Yuni Dorr

Library of Congress Cataloging-in-Publication Data
is available online at http://catalog.loc.gov

To the "holy fools"

CONTENTS

Acknowledgments ix

INTRODUCTION 3
The Rhythm of the Saints
Dominic Erdozain

1 EMPOWERING THE FAITHFUL 12
The Unintended Consequences of Bolshevik Religious Policies
Scott Lingenfelter

2 COMBATING GOD AND GRANDMA 32
The Soviet Antireligious Campaigns and the Battle for Childhood
Julie deGraffenried

3 PERSECUTION, COLLUSION, AND LIBERATION 51
The Russian Orthodox Church, from Stalin to Gorbachev
Michael Bourdeaux

4 "I AM A FIGHTER BY NATURE" 74
Fr. Gleb Iakunin and the Defense of Religious Liberty
Wallace Daniel

5 "AN INWARD MUSIC" 97
Revolution and Resurrection in *Doctor Zhivago*
Dominic Erdozain

6 "THE PEARL OF AN UNREASONABLE THOUGHT" 117
   Religion and the Poetic Imagination
   Josephine von Zitzewitz

7 "I HASTEN TO ESTABLISH A COMMON LANGUAGE WITH YOU" 138
   Orthodox Christian Dissidents and the Human Rights Movement
   Lauren Tapley

8 THE ORTHODOX LITURGY AS POLITICAL RESISTANCE 158
   John P. Burgess

9 "AND I WILL TELL OF THE BEST PEOPLE IN ALL THE EARTH" 170
   Faith and Resilience in the Gulag
   Xenia Dennen

10 "THERE ARE THINGS IN HISTORY THAT SHOULD BE CALLED BY THEIR PROPER NAMES" 187
   Evaluating Russian Orthodox Collaboration with the Soviet State
   Geraldine Fagan

11 THE USEFUL GOD 210
   Religion and Public Authority in Post-Soviet Russia
   James W. Warhola

AFTERWORD 226
   Whether in Words or Deeds, Known and Unknown
   Roy R. Robson

Contributors 229
Notes 231
Index 269

ACKNOWLEDGMENTS

On August 7, 2012, I scampered from my office on the Strand to catch a train from London to Preston in the northwest of England. The Olympics were in full flow and Euston Station was awash with volunteers, brimming with good will and bottled water. A little late to the Olympic party, I had booked myself into the first-class carriage, planning to do some work. My pile of books caught the attention of my distinguished looking co-passenger, and there began one of the most remarkable conversations of my life. Both of us had studied at Oxford, a mere fifty-five years apart, we had both played a bit of rugby. But there the comparisons ended. My co-traveler was Hugh Lunghi, one of the last surviving participants of the "Big Three" meetings between Allied leaders at Tehran, Yalta, and Potsdam, who had translated for Winston Churchill, brokered meetings with Stalin, and had been the first British soldier to enter Hitler's bunker in Berlin in 1945. Only some of this came out as we rattled along the West Coast line in unusual comfort, Hugh preferring to quiz me on my work rather than talk about his own.

I told him that I was writing a book on the great critics of Christendom, including Karl Marx, interpreting his atheism as a kind of prophetic revolt. He agreed that Marxism is inherently religious, but in a dangerous way, and he talked about Lenin as one who radicalized Marx's philosophy to create a "religion of hate." Hugh had been involved in setting up the BBC World Service behind the Iron Curtain, and later worked for an organization that served to resist Soviet infiltration of a variety of British institutions, and he left me in no doubt of the degree to which the Cold War was a battle of ideas. Much of his work had been to persuade a somnambulant British establishment of the reality of KGB energies within its corridors of power—something that we now understand but a position that invited the unflattering label of "cold warrior" at the time.

Hugh offered to continue the conversation, and I later visited him at his home in Hampshire, where he showed me the original typescript of a meeting he had arranged between Stalin and Lord Mountbatten, among other treasures of his military career. We talked about Christianity in the Soviet Union, and the degree to which Christians had been ahead of the game in grasping the destruction inherent in Soviet ideology. Religion was *a* factor in the collapse of the regime, Hugh agreed, but not the central cause. He sent me on my way with a handful of books, many of them energetically annotated, including Aleksandr Iakovlev's *A Century of Violence in Soviet Russia*, and two books on religion and dissent in the USSR by Michael Bourdeaux. It was here that this project began.

Reading Iakovlev's insider's account of disenchantment with Soviet ideology alongside Bourdeaux's Christian analysis was exhilarating. I began to think of a book that could tell the story of Christian survival under the Soviet regime while also touching upon the wider and more elusive question of demystification. It was an in-house joke that Stalin's minister for religious affairs was known as *Narkomopium*—"people's commissar for opium"—but what of the role of religion in unseating the mythology of dialectical materialism? Was there a link between the deeply ethical critique of Marxism developed by party members such as Iakovlev and the openly theological dissidence of a figure such as Father Gleb Iakunin? Could a turbulent priest like Father Iakunin fall within the same narrative of liberation as the writer Alexander Solzhenitsyn or the nuclear physicist and human rights activist Andrei Sakharov? These were, I soon discovered, questions that others, and others more qualified than me, were already asking.

I had the pleasure of meeting Michael Bourdeaux at Baylor University in November 2013. He remembered being "briefed" by Hugh Lunghi as he prepared to make his first visit to the USSR as a student in the 1950s. I also met Wallace Daniel, Julie deGraffenried, Lauren Tapley, and James Warhola, all of whom subsequently agreed to contribute to this book. Profound thanks to all of them. The event was sponsored by the Keston Center at Baylor, which now houses the extensive archive on religion in communist territories amassed by Keston College in the late Soviet period. Keston College (now the Keston Institute) was founded by Michael Bourdeaux and John Lawrence in 1969 to promote understanding of religion and religious freedom in communist countries, a brave, truth-telling operation that was rarely far from the attentions of the KGB. Bringing the struggles of persecuted believers and prisoners of conscience before Western media and leaders such as Margaret Thatcher, Keston became a significant player in Cold War diplomacy, serving at times as an informal source of intelligence on the USSR for the Thatcher government. The Keston story is one that substantiates the link between faith, democracy, and freedom, and it is central to the story told here. I am grateful to Xenia Dennen, who chairs the Keston Institute, for her contribution to the book, and to the Keston Council for generously supporting this project. I would also like to thank Kathy Hillman, director of the Keston Center for Religion, Politics, and Society at Baylor, for her support and encouragement, and Larisa

Seago, archivist at the Keston Library, for kind assistance at various stages of the research process.

Thanks are also due to John Burgess, Geraldine Fagan, Scott Lingenfelter, and Josephine von Zitzewitz for their lively and penetrating contributions, reminding me that there is a difference between the specialist and the enthusiast—and it is occasionally possible to be both. Most of the writers in this book come from outside the Russian Orthodox tradition, but all, I think, have come to a profound appreciation of the depth and creativity of Christian thought in Russia. It has been a privilege working with each of them. I am also grateful to Philip Boobbyer and Lee Congdon for their generous and judicious appraisal of the project, to Roy Robson for steering me toward Northern Illinois University Press, and to Amy Farranto and Nathan Holmes for taking on the book and guiding it toward publication. As ever, thanks to my family for encouragement and support. Finally, I would like to thank Aleksandr Ogorodnikov for the use of the image on the cover of this book: a cross made for him by fellow prisoners during one of his many internments.

In March 2014 I received an email from Hugh Lunghi's daughter, Diana, telling me that he had died at the age of ninety-three, and mentioning how much he had enjoyed our conversations. My meeting with Hugh is in some ways a microcosm of the life of the historian: the honor of entering the company of extraordinary people. We dedicate this book to the people who lived the history we are fortunate enough to write.

Dominic Erdozain
Atlanta, Georgia,
February, 2017

"But don't you see, this is just the point—what has for centuries raised man above the beast is not the cudgel but an inward music: the irresistible power of unarmed truth, the powerful attraction of its example. It has always been assumed that the most important things in the Gospels are the ethical maxims and commandments. But for me the most important thing is that Christ speaks in parables taken from life, that He explains the truth in terms of everyday reality. The idea that underlies this is that communion between mortals is immortal, and that the whole of life is symbolic because it is meaningful."

"I haven't understood a word. You should write a book about it!"

—Boris Pasternak, *Doctor Zhivago*

INTRODUCTION

The Rhythm of the Saints

Dominic Erdozain

Measured in the currency of human life and suffering, the October Revolution of 1917 was the most significant event of the twentieth century. At the beginning of the century, Aleksandr Blok predicted that the coming era would introduce changes in the very structure of humankind.[1] The Russian Revolution was that change: a breathtaking experiment in the reordering of a civilization. Lavish in promise, and ruthless in execution, the Russian Revolution was that rare thing in history: an idea translated into power.

Central to the ambitions of a socialist state was the remolding of consciousness: the construction of a revolutionary mind, with eyes only for the future. History would be made, not written. Ethics would be negotiated, not assumed. And souls—in Stalin's chilling formulation—would be "engineered." It was an ambition destined to collide with the ancient rhythms of religion, faith, and conscience. The resulting conflict may stand as the harshest episode of religious persecution in human history. Never before or since the "seventy-year civil war" of Soviet rule have men and women of faith faced a more formidable adversary. Churches were destroyed, desecrated, or turned into museums of atheism. Priests were murdered in numbers that defy belief and with methods that haunt the imagination.[2] Ordinary believers faced anything from ridicule and ostracism to forced psychiatric treatment, imprisonment, or martyrdom. Religion mattered to the Soviet state. It vexed and angered the revolutionary mind. And the failure of a totalitarian state to engineer souls to order was one of the seeds of its demise. It was dangerous to be a Christian, or a Muslim, or a Jew in the Soviet Union. But it was also dangerous to be an atheist, dancing on the grave of an imagined deity. "The production of souls is more important than the production of tanks," Stalin told a gathering of writers in 1932.[3] It ultimately proved more difficult. Disturbingly thorough as the attempt to burn faith out of the Russian soul was, it remained a project unfinished, and the intensity of the treatment sometimes excited the patient. This book is the story of the survival of the Christian faith under communist rule, a survival that evolved into something like resistance.

This is not to suggest that the encounter between Christianity and Soviet ideology respected conventional boundaries between "religion" and the "secular." Far from it. Building upon groundbreaking scholarship in history and political science,[4] these essays describe the interpenetration of religious ideas within a hostile Soviet culture—and, it must be said, the permeation of Soviet ideology within the Russian Orthodox Church. The picture that emerges is not of a religious community rising up against a secular state, but a series of subtle subversions. Insofar as there was a theology of resistance, it was diffuse, eclectic, and hungry in its appropriation of materials historically alien to the churches. As Wallace Daniel writes in his article on leading Christian dissident Father Gleb Iakunin (1934–2014), the theology that sustained a dissident movement could not afford to be inward-looking or otherworldly. The misanthropic outlook portrayed by Fedor Dostoevsky in the monk "Ferrapont" in the *Brothers Karamazov* was foreign to the dissident mind. Rather, it was the urge to escape what Iakunin termed the "sin" of "hating the world" that characterized a spiritual resistance.

Indeed, a refusal to hate a gray, and graying, Soviet culture, even as it descended to barbaric modes of persecution, is one of the most remarkable features of the material assembled here. The Soviet concentration camps, wrote the Christian poet Irina Ratushinskaia, were "so hostile to the idea of the individual" that they were "in the process of creating a new anthropological type."[5] The Christian response, insofar as it may be summarized, was not intellectual critique but a resolute and radiant humanity. "We greeted all notices about deprivations of various kinds with jokes," wrote Ratushinskaia, in a stunning memoir of life in the Gulag. "We could go on strike or hunger strike—but we did it with a smile. And we smiled when they marched us off to punishment cells."[6] In such circumstances, faith was existential rather than intellectual—though invariably underscored by a profound theology of the human person. The result was a spirituality that moved easily with secular or non-believing dissidence—an ecumenism of dissent movingly portrayed in

Ratushinskaia's memoir and neatly delineated by Lauren Tapley in her chapter on Orthodox Christian dissidents and the human rights movement. The female dissident who protested the Soviet invasion of Czechoslovakia in 1968 with the assertion that, "the whole nation minus one person is no longer the whole nation," happened to be a Christian, Natalia Gorbanevskaia. But her conviction that religious belief, Enlightenment ideas, and human rights were forces in tandem was typical of the energetic ecumenism that connected the scattered worlds of Soviet dissidence.[7] No attempt is made here to blend these elements into a single story, yet there are continuities and shared convictions that together begin to justify Nicolas Zernov's claim that "the struggle between the Christians and the Marxists in Russia raises a number of problems concerning not only the future of the Church in Russia but also the destiny of Christianity in the modern world."[8] Among them was an ability to expose the cultic dimensions of a so-called secular modernity. In the Soviet Union, faith was a way of seeing.

Aleksandr Iakovlev, disillusioned Marxist and architect of perestroika, regarded the Bolshevik seizure of power in October 1917 as a "counterrevolution" and a step back into servitude—albeit on a larger scale than anything conjured by the tsars. Others have interpreted Bolshevism as the self-destruction of the Russian intelligentsia, a brutal philistinism that savaged the noble aspirations of the Russian Enlightenment. Lenin is not the terminus of a raging Enlightenment, in this school of thought; still less is Joseph Stalin. Both were, to a disillusioned Iakovlev, the bloody emissaries of "a pseudoscientific neoreligion."[9] Yet no one could deny that ideas mattered to the creators of the Gulag. And one of the most unsettling facts about this "century of violence" is the degree to which it was tethered to a clear and distinct ideology. Bolshevism was Marxism, toughened for action. The "anthropological catastrophe" of the Soviet era is traceable to an audacious project of Western modernity. The Soviet Union was, in one scholar's phrase, an "ideocratic state," in which extreme measures were justified within a fiercely historical political vision.[10] Intellectual certitude, maintained Boris Pasternak, was the original sin of a bloodletting superstate.[11] As Iakovlev himself affirmed in a piercing narrative of repentance: aggression toward your political enemy becomes an awful lot easier "if from the very beginning you are firmly convinced that the observed object is sentenced to death, and the collisions and conflicts you witness are only spasms of the expiring life." The violence of the Soviet experiment could not be separated from its intellectual roots and a Marxist philosophy that "idolized the gross physical clash between the proletariat and the ruling classes."[12] "In romanticizing violence," wrote the dissident journalist Raissa Lert, "we gave it added life, we preserved it even when it became absolutely superfluous, when it became an absolute evil."[13] Against all of this, Christianity brought suspicion, humanity, and occasionally heroic charity. Faith was doubt in the USSR: a cautionary brake on an engine of reform that knew no harmony of means and ends. It was, in the phrase of Aleksandr Ogorodnikov and Vladimir Poresh—founders of an influential "Christian Seminar" in the 1970s—"a culture within the culture."[14]

Religious faith, and the artistic creativity that it so often inspired, did not propose a rival system of ideas so much as a doctrine of life. Christianity offered humanism to what Pasternak termed "the inhuman reign of the lie." It spoke for the person against the machine. Against a deadening materialist philosophy, it helped to proclaim—in Iakovlev's blunt riposte—that "no ... the individual's free will is not a tale told by idiots."[15] Faith was movement, energy, and dynamism beneath the crushing rigor of an imperious worldview. It was, to borrow an image from Pasternak, like the quiet flow of water below the marbled rivers of a Russian winter. It was a stubborn asterisk to what Albert Weinberg has termed "the grim romanticism of the totalitarian state."[16] And if the compromises of frightened clergy, as described by Wallace Daniel, Michael Bourdeaux, and Geraldine Fagan below, recall some of the more sobering episodes of Christianity's long dance with power, the heroism and dignity of those who held firm against persecution invites loftier comparisons. "Christian obedience," wrote Diarmaid MacCulloch of the martyrs of late antiquity, "repeatedly plays a troubling wild card."[17] No phrase could better capture the peaceable anarchy created by Christianity in the USSR.

The essays below aim to reflect some of that intellectual anarchy. Dissident piety produced thinkers, not followers, and biting individuality was often the result. Not everyone thought the same way. Father Gleb Iakunin and Aleksandr Ogorodnikov, two of the greatest dissidents of the late Soviet era, did not get on. And it can be no surprise that persecuted Christians, who displayed enormous courage and dignity in refusing to hate their oppressors, sometimes failed to extend the same charity to the ecclesiastical superiors who acquiesced in their struggles. The Christianity explored here is no uniform phenomenon but it perhaps contains one, profound division: between those who suffered for their faith and those who did not. Part of the value of such a history, for several of the authors below, is to contribute to processes of reconciliation and healing that can only proceed with historical honesty. Such is the tenor of Geraldine Fagan's searching analysis of Russian Orthodox collaboration with the Soviet state, with its frank evaluation of one archbishop's claim that "there are in our church real KGB men who have pursued meteoric careers." Fagan's recognition that clerical willingness to submit to the state predated the Soviet regime provides vital context for this sensitive matter, and it helps to contextualize the wider problem of Soviet persecution as a continuing reaction against a symbol of tsarist autocracy. The persecutions unleashed in 1918 had their origins in the politics of "Caesaropapism," a problem as old as Christendom. The task facing the leaders of a beleaguered underground church was to nourish faith and freedom of conscience without succumbing to either a new politics of resentment or a detached, apolitical spirituality.

Such dilemmas are deftly explored in John Burgess's essay on "The Orthodox Liturgy as Political Resistance," which relates Alexander Solzhenitsyn's concern that "a Church 'above politics' merely becomes a tool of the state." Indeed, the clerical bromide that the church must be concerned for eternity, not time, was a position that arguably substantiated the Marxist complaint that religion is simply the oil on the wheels of power: an "ideology." As Ludwig Feuerbach was the first to argue, with Marx following in the famous "opium of the people" passage, an apolitical spirituality is sometimes the most political religiosity of all.[18] Part of the genius of the Christian response to Soviet rule, as developed by figures such as Nikolai Berdiaev (in exile), Father Aleksandr Men (theological mentor to the late-Soviet Christian movement), and Solzhenitsyn himself, was a capacity to hold spiritual and secular concerns in tension. Indeed, for people forced to nurture their faith on fragments of conversation, a smuggled Eucharist, or the play of sunlight on the wall of a prison cell—as described in Xenia Dennen's chapter on "Faith and Resilience in the Gulag"—boundaries between the sacred and the profane were ever-negotiable. For someone like Irina Ratushinskaia, it was the ability to reconceive and transfigure the secular that gave her faith such emotional resonance and critical potential. The result was often a direct repudiation of the faith-as-opium thesis, occasionally signaling respect from the Soviet authorities. When Aleksandr Ogorodnikov met a highly placed KGB official after the collapse of the Soviet Union in 1992, a man who had only recently presided over his tortures now saluted his endurance: "You ... never made concessions," he acknowledged, before asking if Ogorodnikov would serve as his "spiritual father."[19] The story of Christianity in the USSR is not the triumph of a church over a secular state but the triumph of inner freedom over external compulsion.

Four further themes serve to connect these stories of survival and resistance. The first is an overriding concern for human dignity, against an ideology that began with a crudely instrumental estimate of human value and descended into cruelty, pure and simple. Part of the attraction of Christian thought—both for those who held on to their faith, and those who were drawn toward it, such as Pasternak—was the importance it invested in ordinary human life. A related commitment was to values of compassion, mercy and non-violence. Such was the regime's distaste for the saintly do-goodery of pious babushkas, even the word for mercy—*miloserdie*—fell out of official usage, marked as "obsolete" in dictionaries until recovered and reinvented during glasnost.[20] Rubashov's icy summary of the Soviet project in Arthur Koestler's *Darkness at Noon*—"We have replaced decency by reason"— became literal reality.[21] Christians were not the exclusive guardians of this endangered virtue but they possessed an anthropology of human sanctity and an often startling capacity to realize it. Irina Ratushinskaia's smiles were not sarcastic. "Happy are the downtrodden. They have something to tell about themselves," muttered Pasternak's heroine, Lara, in *Doctor Zhivago*. Resistance to a superstate sometimes took the form of caring for its most vulnerable. This was not the dashing counterattack of a Iakunin or a Solzhenitsyn, but it helped to prevent a crumbling society from dissolving altogether, and it dramatized the gap between the realities of Soviet culture and its improbable claims. In the prisons, hospitals, and orphanages of the USSR, Christian believers brought their faith to bear with an unspoken eloquence. It may be that in the drama of faith and cruelty in the Gulag the Soviet Union suffered its profoundest embarrassment.

A second, related theme was truth-telling: a resolute, almost fevered commitment to truthfulness in all situations, against the casual, programmatic mendacity of an ideological superpower. More than ten years after the collapse of the regime, Aleksandr Iakovlev shuddered to recall Bolshevik directives that sanctioned "repressive measures of various kinds"—including "capital punishment"—for "anti-Soviet parties, *even when we have no concrete evidence against them*." As he protested: "Only a government criminal in nature would 'take repressive measures' without having 'concrete evidence.' Essentially, it was on such principles that the entire 'legal system' of Bolshevism was built."[22] Again: Christian reaction was both revealing and redemptive. The refusal of people like Aleksandr Ogorodnikov or Irina Ratushinskaia to tell lies, pay bribes, or even to wrong foot their prison guards when the opportunity arose, opened for other prisoners a window on an alternative mental universe. Prisoners of conscience spoke of the freedom found in escaping the coded duplicities of a Soviet culture in which, as Iakovlev recalled: "We thought one thing, said another, and did a third."[23] It was in search of an absolute purity of expression that Pasternak invited the charge of philistinism with his odes to honesty, honest toil, and unaffected simplicity in *Doctor Zhivago*. For Pasternak, weary of a revolutionary outlook long addicted to "the glittering phrase," even eloquence became a suspect commodity—savoring of artifice, evasion, and a refusal to face facts. It was better to be plain than elegantly delusional.

Once again, Christians did not monopolize a vogue for unflinching candor that, for Daniil Granin, reached unhealthy extremes in the era of glasnost, when he playfully objected that "ordinary human life cannot be cruel in its demand for absolute truth."[24] But as Philip Boobbyer has shown, the zeal for truthfulness apparent in the late Soviet period owed much to the resurfacing of Christian concepts of sin, conscience, and repentance.[25] And as several of the contributors demonstrate below, it was through poetry, art, and literature that such values were often transmitted from their religious sources to the wider culture. The arts were integral to what Zernov has termed the "Russian religious renaissance of the twentieth century," and religion was central to that frontier of creativity and soulcraft so coveted by the regime but never claimed.

Artistic creativity—the "concrete freedom to create," in Vladimir Bukovskii's marvelous phrase—was a dimension of truth-telling, but one that transcended all didacticism and thudding utility. It was, in the words of the poet Elena Shvarts, a form of "holy madness," "the pearl of an unreasonable thought." As Josephine von Zitzewitz writes below, poets like Shvarts "explicitly invoked the cultural stereotype of the poet-as-holy-fool." "The holy fool is a truth-teller," she explains, "but the truth they proclaim is often, literally, 'ugly.'" The poetry of the literary underground was saturated with Christian imagery, metaphysical speculation, and playful caprice, bringing "festive news" to a parched intellectual landscape. It suggested, for one writer, "that our world is open and permeable to a different kind of power." And as such it constituted, for Olga Sedakova, a form of "aesthetic and spiritual resistance" to the Soviet project. Playful, heterodox, and daring in its picturing of a Christ mingling effortlessly with the reprobates of the Leningrad underground, this poetry "of spiritual adventure" was a powerful expression of Christianity's subversive potential. And it symbolized a fourth theme of the Christian resistance to Soviet hegemony: the power of the laity.

Although many of the Leningrad poets became interested in Christianity only in the 1970s, others, such as Olga Sedakova, "had been familiar with the Russian Orthodox tradition since childhood, through the example of her much-loved grandmother, a practicing believer." Revival is often another word for survival. The centrality of such figures in preserving a Christian tradition robbed of an ordained priesthood is richly documented by Scott Lingenfelter and Julie deGraffenried in their essays on parochial and domestic responses to state-imposed secularization. Both show that the effect of persecution was often to energize faith, recentering religious authority on the private sphere of the home and the elusive ground of conscience. Julie deGraffenried explores the migration of religious education from the Church to the family circle, where pious grandmothers formed the last line of defense of an embattled

Orthodox tradition. In the demonization of the pious grandma the Soviet state mixed severity with absurdity, but as deGraffenried suggests, the Bolsheviks were right to worry about what children were learning at bedtime. Children learned to "speak Bolshevik" when required, and to drop the mask of conformity when the opportunity arose, moving smoothly between different worlds. Faith and religious identity was, for Muslims and Jews as well as Christians, an enduring corrective against ideological assimilation. Indeed, as de Graffenried demonstrates, secular indoctrination sometimes enhanced the credentials of faith.

None of this is to minimize the destruction and dislocation visited upon ordinary life by a crusading socialist state. Scott Lingenfelter recognizes the scale of a persecution that saw 85 percent of Russian clergy and monastics arrested, killed, or forcibly removed from their posts between 1917 and 1939. Of the fifty thousand plus churches operating in the prerevolutionary era, only two to three hundred remained in 1939. Lenin's injunction to "shoot" reactionary clergy was embraced with disturbing alacrity. But as Lingenfelter delicately argues, there was vulnerability in ferocity, and a parallel impulse of Bolshevik religious policy was simply to leave the churches alone. He quotes Lenin twice, at the Eighth and Tenth Party Congresses (in 1919 and 1921) urging that "we must give absolutely no offense to religion," since to offend "the religious susceptibilities of believers" leads only to "the strengthening of religious fanaticism." Once the Church had been disestablished, education would do the work. This was Lenin, urging restraint in the handling of faith. The party "vacillated," Lingenfelter writes, "unleashing terror," on one hand, and an almost respectful pragmatism, on the other. The indecision created opportunities at the parish level, and positive freedom for "the various Protestant sects, some of whom saw the 1920s as a golden decade." Real history does not flow in straight lines.

The heaviest blows against religious believers were delivered by Stalin, the ex-seminarian, though even he, as Michael Bourdeaux writes, was forced to make concessions to the Russian Orthodox Church during the Second World War. The old socialist bravado resurfaced under Nikita Khrushchev, who boasted that his grandchildren would see the last believing *babushka* visiting the Soviet Union's last open church. But once again, the facts of this historic encounter reveal the fragility of both parties. The state was never as powerful as it seemed, and the Russian Orthodox Church remained a complex and troubled institution. Bourdeaux, writing as both witness and participant in the drama, remains indignant at the degree to which the Kremlin succeeded in manipulating international opinion and deceiving the World Council of Churches as to the realities of religious freedom in the USSR. But he also shows what could be achieved by a single, dissident priest, prepared to defy both the state and his clerical superiors. It is in memory of such people that this book has been written.

Finally, the political scientist, James Warhola, takes us into the era of Vladimir Putin and the ambiguities of a renewed and, one could say, rearmed Russian Orthodox Church, which has reclaimed some of the political presence that was lost in 1917. Whether the Church has traded leverage for prestige is a question he approaches with admirable indeterminacy. If the Soviet experience teaches anything it is that appearances are no guide to inner dynamics. But there is no doubt that after the millennial fervor of glasnost and perestroika, and the collapse of a militantly secular state, the current status of religion in the Russian Federation is a cause for concern and disappointment. At the time of writing, President Putin has affirmed a raft of measures curtailing "missionary activity"—including the sharing of faith in "residential buildings" or an email invitation to attend a service of worship.[26] Religion is once again useful to an authoritarian state, as well as dangerous.

Yet history is not a closed circuit, a leaden pattern of reprisal. To explore the past is to unsettle the present. "History," wrote Iurii Afanas'ev, one of the progenitors of perestroika, "is self-awareness."[27] These essays are confined to Russia and the Russian experience of communism. The material is inevitably fragmentary. But I hope they convey some of the energy and vision of the people they describe.

1

EMPOWERING THE FAITHFUL

The Unintended Consequences of Bolshevik Religious Policies

Scott Lingenfelter

By 1921, Russia had run the gauntlet of world war, two revolutions, famine, severe economic and demographic dislocation, and a brutal civil war that claimed the lives of some 10 million people. The world's first socialist regime also began engineering a complete transformation of state, society, economy, and culture. The Bolsheviks attempted to reconstitute the old Russian Empire on a new ideological footing, one that included something no other modern regime had ever attempted: to eliminate religion itself. Beyond disestablishing the Russian Orthodox Church—the oldest and most basic of all Russian institutions—churches by the thousands were destroyed, treasured icons were burned, priests were summarily executed, and leading theological academies were shuttered. By 1941, it seemed that the comrades had dutifully eradicated all but the remnants of Russia's celebrated spiritual traditions, and the faithful were given to understand that they stood on the wrong side of history.

This chapter offers an ecumenical, contextualized account of the formative years (1917–1925) of the Soviet regime's approach to its Christian communities. Ecumenical because excellent work published since the collapse of the Soviet Union on Russian Christianity demands an avoidance of confessional niches. Contextualized because Soviet religious policies involved much more than commissars and clerics. They entailed resolving internal (often socialist) dissent, disposition of imperial treasures, and—very significantly—crafting an advantageous foreign policy. This article suggests, first, that there was no single, uniform early Soviet religious policy. Like the revolutions of 1917, religious policies ran on two tracks, central (elite) and local (popular), sometimes running in parallel, sometimes not. Second, it argues that early Soviet religious policies did not imperil faith: they empowered the faithful. Communities of faith not only survived, they became the repository for many of the popular aspirations of 1917—in the most unlikely of circumstances. Indeed, persecuted believers planted the seeds of a culture of dissent that flourished far beyond the parishes themselves in imaginative visions of economy, state, and society that became the blueprint for post-communist societies.

By January 1917, even Tsar Nicholas II recognized the end was near. In the course of a conversation with the capable chairman of the Fourth Duma, Mikhail Rodzianko, the tsar hung his head, pressed his temples and said, "Is it possible that for twenty-two years I have tried to do some good and that for twenty-two years I have failed?" Rodzianko recounted that the silence was long and trying before he replied, "Yes, your majesty, for twenty-two years you have followed the wrong trail."[1] Soon Nicholas's burden would be lifted, but the work of rebuilding had just begun. Conditions were desperate. The war devastated Russia more than any other wartime power. With all able-bodied men at the front, women and children were called upon to staff factories and shops, and generally hold up the system in deteriorating conditions. Stores of food and fuel dried up and hungry consumers were hit with a series of blows: bakeries closed for lack of fuel, and the price of salt and meat tripled between 1914 and 1916. By late 1916 only one-third of the normal food supply was reaching major cities. Then the value of ruble plunged to a quarter of its prewar value. The stresses of World War I, unrelenting pressure from opponents of the regime, and strikes and demonstrations of 300,000 strong in Petrograd sparked revolution—two of them. The tsar's abdication signaled the first, while the failure of the Provisional Government, Bolshevik control of the soviet movement, and a *coup d'état* in November resulted in a better-known second.

The soviet movement was an expression of the broad sweep of opposition to the imperial regime, and growing socialist opposition can be gauged by the composition of the three coalitions that ran the Provisional Government. The first, led by former Duma deputies keen to keep Russia in the war, collapsed in May. A second, set up with Alexander Kerensky as war minister, saw five of fifteen seats go to socialists. In the third and final coalition, in July, Kerensky was made prime minister over a government with a majority eight of fifteen seats held by socialists. But the Bolsheviks never enjoyed the support of more than 25 percent of the population. Election results from the long-promised Constituent Assembly held a fortnight after the Bolsheviks took power are revealing. Forty-one million votes were cast in Russia's first free elections. Seven hundred and fifteen deputies were elected, 87–88 percent of whom were socialist. The peasant-backed Socialist Revolutionaries (SRs) were the big winners with 410 delegates, the Bolsheviks tallying 175. The SR victory handed the Bolsheviks their first dilemma: nullifying the election results risked making a mockery of a legal, legitimate election, but then certifying them meant giving up power to a rival party. The Constituent Assembly met in January 1918—briefly. It was dissolved at gunpoint within hours by Bolshevik sympathizers, whose numbers had grown in November and December as the Bolsheviks took control of Moscow, Kaluga, Smolensk, Voronezh, Saratov, and Kazan.

What these epic events mask are very simple popular demands. Soldiers wanted an end to the war, workers wanted better labor conditions, and peasants more land. But then weary soldiers, workers, and peasants were also parishioners from a variety of Christian confessions. Was the popular movement in 1917 reflected in local parishes? It was indeed. Sources now published or accessible since the collapse of the Soviet Union demonstrate a broad religious revival in 1917, in many ways a natural part of the powerful popular uprising after the collapse of the Romanov dynasty. It was in this context that the Bolsheviks attempted to consolidate power, including the imperative to address the role of the Russian Orthodox Church and religion writ large.

"Give Absolutely No Offense to Religion"

It would be a mistake to assume that the religious renewal began in 1917. A moribund imperial church, emasculated by the reforms of Peter the Great, limping along into the Soviet era with ranks decimated by martyrdom and beset by moral compromise of the upper clergy—this traditional picture of Russian Orthodoxy has given way to a more complete, textured one. The last decades of the Russian Empire witnessed, among other things, growth in popular piety, pastoral initiatives, clerical social activism, a renaissance in biblical and theological studies, a conciliar movement, marked religious diversity, dialogues between clergy and intelligentsia, and broader interest in religious themes among the philosophers, novelists, poets, and artists of Russia's Silver Age. It turns out that 1917 was a high-water mark for renewal that had been underway for many years.[2]

But 1917 *was* different. What had gone before—the frustrated attempts at reform, voluminous writing, intense dialogue and debate—all this was now reenergized. Organizational efforts and practical initiatives multiplied. And something less tangible, too: a fresh sense of imminent possibility. That year witnessed scores of resolutions and petitions from assemblies all across Russia to the powers that be—the Holy Synod, the Provisional Government, or local soviets—calling for church and parish reform. One such petition serves as a succinct introduction to the movement. It comes from the Boris and Gleb Orthodox Church on what was Kalashnikova Quay (later Sinopskaia Embankment) in Petrograd. The petition was issued on May 4, 1917, by Archpriest Nikolai Rudinskii, and addressed to the chairman of the Council of Ministers of the Provisional Government. Days before, the Holy Synod of the Russian Orthodox Church, the body established by Peter the Great in 1721 to serve as the state's arm controlling religious affairs, issued a call to its vast network of parishes granting them (or, more accurately, acknowledging) greater latitude.

This particular petition expresses the will of a parish assembly, made up of elected representatives, one for every hundred parishioners, "out of many thousands." Called by the parish council or "soviet" (which possessed a revolutionary reverberation lost in English), the assembly affirmed "an unshakable faith that the sun of the church's freedom and happiness will itself soon rise over Russia." It also expressed "sincere confidence" in the Provisional Government, which was "the embodiment of the popular will of the whole Russian state." The assembly agreed that the Government was burdened with the prospect of a major "leap [*podvig*]" toward a revamped state, and that merited the ardent prayers of the faithful. That prayer was to restore "order and legality" to the state, to destroy "all instigators of sedition," and to "overcome the internal and external enemies of the state."

Two fundamental assumptions stand out. First, that state recovery is only possible "when the soul is enlightened by the light of Christ's evangelical [or Gospel] truth." Second, that "the state cannot be truly constructed without the regenerative activity of the Church," whose task is to "morally transform people's souls." In the view of this assembly in the capital, the local parish now spoke for the Church and its public activity to reconstruct a new order, perhaps even as the vanguard of liberation. But, critically, this assembly also believed that to fulfill its mission, changes were necessary: the Government "grant freedom of self-determination to the Russian Church" and the "rights of a legal person to every parish." Notions of legality (*zakonnost'*), self-determination, and legal personhood had obviously entered the working vocabulary of Orthodox parishioners in Petrograd. All told, the Boris and Gleb petition reflects ongoing innovation in restructuring higher Church administration, redefining the clergy's social role, empowering the parish with fresh responsibility, and spiritual renewal, and parishes across the former empire employed these opportunities in many imaginative ways in 1917 and 1918. No wonder the early part of 1917 was known as the "Ecclesiastical Revolution" and "Red Easter."[3]

As the parish revival swept across vast stretches of revolutionary Russia, assemblies in traditional hubs like Kiev and Nizhnii Novgorod created a new template for a moment that seemed to promise a free church in a free state. Like that of Boris and Gleb above, most of the new diocesan assemblies were called to prepare for the All-Russian Church Council of 1917–1918, but like other moments in modern revolutionary history (for instance, the cahiers of the French Revolution), their records offer close-up views of a host of issues. Kiev's huge assembly numbered eight hundred delegates. Its majority was politically progressive, and demanded that parish councils be chosen by the four-tail suffrage of direct, equal, universal, and secret ballot. Orenburg's resolutions went further. They addressed labor, educational, defense, and judicial issues such as an eight-hour workday; religious education on a voluntary basis; the abolition of armies, navies, and munitions factories; and the creation of an international criminal court. Other assemblies, like distant Tobolsk, seemed mainly to revel in the spirit of their gatherings, marking for them "renewed *sobornost'* (spiritual harmony) in the Russian Orthodox Church." They also concluded that their interests would be best served by new commissions empowered to remove the sitting bishop. They were not alone. Fourteen other dioceses decided that financial independence and removing their bishop would offer a fresh start as well. Often the organizational provenance pointed to the influence of the zemstvo, one of the creations of the Great Reforms of the 1860s and 1870s meant to address local problems like agriculture, education, and public health. Applied ecclesiastically, commission representatives (both lay and clerical) served three-year terms, would make decisions by majority, were subject to periodic oversight, and had fixed budgets, with a provision that the bishop had the right of appeal if left out in the cold. Thus parishes used local, "secular" associations from their past for inspiration and renovation in 1917.

None of the assemblies offers us a better picture of the parish revival in the Russian Orthodox Church in 1917 than that of Nizhnii Novgorod. The nearby working-class settlement of Sormova, dedicated to the empire's shipbuilding industry, ensured that the proceedings would have a distinctly political flavor to them. Nizhnii Novgorod held two diocesan congresses, in May and August, both well-attended and contentious. Factions struggled over electoral procedure, political priorities, diocesan resources and publications, and church land. The congresses became a window onto the discourse and major issues of the church over the next decade. Some circles called for the participation of women, limits on the powers of diocesan administrators, and joint meetings with members of the intelligentsia. The latter efforts may have reminded contemporaries of the attempts of Sergei Bulgakov, Marxist-turned-Orthodox priest, to foster this kind of exchange in religious-philosophical societies a little over a decade before. The forty agenda items of the progressive Committee of the United Clergy (KODM in Russian) in Nizhnii Novgorod are telling. Electoral proposals included the need for elected lay representatives to all assemblies, equal representation between lay and clerical delegates, and elected chairs for diocesan commissions. Major agenda items included a review of canon law for leadership qualifications, a terse action point that bishops "are to come from the white [married] clergy," ensuring cleric's civil rights and political participation, confirming legal personhood for the parish, decentralizing church bodies, review of the liturgy and ecclesiastical courts, and ending censorship of sermons. Agenda items 3 and 9 indicate the range of the discussions:

> Because the Provisional Government is well-behaved, there is no need to separate from it; but the church must be free in its inner life and restore the ancient right of petitioning to the secular power in matters of governance and society. The restoration among bishops, hierarchs, and priests to the way they were in the ancient apostolic church, and destruction of the spirit of despotism and secular domination prevalent beginning in the fourth century.[4]

Despotism and secular domination there would be but, under the Bolsheviks, of a distinctly twentieth-century variety. Yet not before the historic Church Council of 1917–1918 restored the Russian Orthodox patriarchate after a lapse of nearly two centuries. Vasilii Ivanovich Bellavin was elected and named Patriarch Tikhon, the eleventh patriarch of Moscow and All Russia, just days after the Bolshevik Revolution. Two other chief matters at the Council were elections and lay participation. Both of these were hallmarks of the parish revolution. Indeed, given the desperate economic and material conditions in the former empire, and the groundswell of popular support for revolutionary solutions, both the Church Council and early Soviet decrees on religion that followed were, in context, responses to (and catching up with) developments already underway.

"Imperial" decrees crossed the threshold of 1917 without missing a beat, and while they alone do not tell the whole story of aggressive Soviet attempts to secularize state and society, they are indicative of aims and priorities. For its part, the Provisional Government issued two decrees on freedom of conscience: On the Abolition of Confessional and National Restrictions (March 20, 1917) and On Freedom of Conscience (July 14, 1917). Both of these were tentative steps in the direction of a non-confessional state (beyond that promulgated by the imperial government in 1905), though the Orthodox were assured that they would serve as the "premier confession." Decrees on religion began to appear soon after the Bolshevik Revolution, and they continued in a steady stream into the 1920s. In fact, there were at least 163 decrees and other legal measures on religion issued between 1918 and 1925 (not including those dealing with Islam). A breakdown by year is worth a look: six in 1918, eight in 1919, six in 1920, eight in 1921, eighteen in 1922, thirty in 1923, fifty-one in 1924, and thirty-six in 1925—clearly more legislation as the years rolled into the era of the New Economic Policy (NEP).[5] These measures touched on every conceivable subject from separation of church and state to registration of births, marriages, and deaths; that alone should cause us to doubt if there was a single Soviet policy on religion. Another curious consequence was that proliferating regulations meant constant interference by the local soviets into church affairs: it meant that the relationship between church and state was anything but separate.

The watershed measure in the early Soviet period was also the Bolsheviks' first decree on religion: January 23, 1918's Decree on Separation of Church from State, and of School from Church. It had thirteen provisions that disestablished and dispossessed churches. The decree was signed by Lenin, eight commissars, and Director of Commissar Affairs Vladimir Bonch-Bruevich. Articles 12 and 13 are significant.

> Article 12:
> No church or religious associations have the right to own property. They do not possess the rights of juridical persons.
>
> Article 13:
> The property of all church and religious associations existing in Russia is pronounced the property of the People. Buildings and objects especially used for the purposes of worship shall be let, free of charge, to the respective religious associations, by resolution of the local or Central State authorities.[6]

Less than a week later, on January 29, 1918, another measure addressed chaplains (just weeks before the Treaty of Brest-Litovsk ended Russian involvement in World War I). The Decree on Abolishment of Military Chaplain Service contained six articles, signed by the four-member Commissariat of War.

Article 5:
Without exception, all property and all church funds of churches of military units (are) to be handed over the committees of the various units and in the case of reshaping of the latter—to the committees of the higher grades.

Article 6:
For the purposes of receipt and delivery of funds and property now at the disposal of the clerical department, special commissions will be appointed.[7]

Earlier in January, Patriarch Tikhon had pronounced a bitter anathema against the nascent Soviet regime, threatening them with the "fires of Gehenna" for their persecution of the church (and he should be taken at his word that the terror had already begun). At the end of February, he issued a thirty-three-article "Instruction to the Orthodox Church against Government Acts." Among its provisions:

Article 5:
In extreme cases, these societies [parishioners' organizations, not to be called a church or religious society] can declare themselves the owners of church property, in order to save them from seizure at the hands of the non-Orthodox or even those of another faith. Let the Church and church property remain in the hands of the Orthodox.

Article 13:
In case of attempted seizure of church vessels, appurtenances of the church service, church registers and other church property, the same should not be surrendered voluntarily, inasmuch as (a) church vessels and other appurtenances of church service as blessed for church use and the congregation should not even touch them; (b) church registers are indispensable for church uses, and the secular authorities, if in need of same, should see to the preparation of them themselves; church property belongs to the Holy Church, and the clergy and all Orthodox people are merely their guardians.

Article 15:
Should seizure nevertheless take place, it is absolutely necessary to make a report thereof to the diocese, signed by witnesses, with an accurate description of the articles seized, and indicating by name those guilty of the seizure.[8]

A number of issues are addressed here, not the least of which is that, by law, churches, as religious organizations *per se*, were nationalized into the hands of parish committees, the ecclesiastical equivalent of a local soviet. Churches were also removed from schools, with more exacting restrictions on private religious instruction, clarified in a later stipulation. In addition to the measures above, the Soviet Constitution of July 1918 disenfranchised clergy: they could not vote or be elected to any organs of Soviet government. Neither could they own land, unless neighboring citizens' needs were satisfied. It was, at least in print, still legal "to conduct religious and antireligious propaganda." Needless to say, Patriarch Tikhon's concerns about church valuables were becoming acute. At the same time, his Instruction indicates that he recognized that the decree had an unintended consequence: it could be used by parishioners to protect churches since they alone were empowered with rights of disposition, even to the point of resisting soviet officials' attempts to confiscate or destroy church property (which is exactly what happened four years later). To clarify the January Decree, the Commissariat of Justice issued "Concerning Execution of the Decree on Separation of Church from State, and of School from Church" on August 24, 1918. Its thirty-five articles, an appendix, and notations, leave little doubt about the new status of churches.[9] Further decrees of December 27, 1921; August 10, 1922; and April 27, 1923, dealt with, among other things, church property, registration, and permits for holding meetings and congresses. As late as July 1, 1923, the commissars were still issuing "Additional Instructions" to fully implement the landmark church-state decree of January 23, 1918. These later decrees restated and, in some cases, expanded on the original provisions but in less legalistic prose, with reworded party assertions about religion sprinkled in for good measure.

Initial aspects of this Soviet antichurch campaign had European precedents. Even a cursory consideration of the French law separating church and state in 1905 suggests that the Bolsheviks looked to their leftist counterparts there for a solution to the thorny problem of extricating themselves from a long-powerful state church. Some diplomats of the time, including US State Department officials cabling from their legation redoubt in Riga, recognized its provenance. Rear-Admiral Mark L. Bristol, writing the secretary of state in the fall of 1922, commented that "my informant stated that the Bolsheviks had adopted many features of the Combes legislation in France and that the title of Church property was vested in the State, but the use for purposes of worship was and is granted to the ecclesiastical authorities."[10] He is referring to Emile Justin Louis Combes, prime minister of France during the Third Republic, whose ministry was characterized by progressive labor and welfare reforms, as well as sustained efforts toward state secularism. Trained for the clergy, Combes became a Freemason later in life. With the support of the *bloc republicain* (a center-left coalition), he enacted three measures (1901,

1904, and 1905) designed to restructure the relationship between church and state. With input from Aristide Briand, Jean Jaures, and Francis de Pressensé, the French law of 1905 disestablished the Catholic Church and stressed the neutrality of the state. The Republic would no longer recognize, salary, or subsidize any religion. In concert with the law, thousands of religious schools were closed and religious orders were expelled; many priests and nuns emigrated for fear of a wider crackdown. Like the Bolshevik decree of 1918, the French law transferred fiduciary control to lay parish associations termed *associations cultuelles*, which took more coherent legal form after 1922. And like the Bolshevik decree, the application of the law mattered as much as the measure itself (the subsequent Briand government was relatively lax in its enforcement). Thus, in context, the Soviet decree of January 1918 was really nothing new.

Of course it did not stop there, and the campaign fed on a culture of violence that preceded the Bolsheviks. Then during the Civil War, in the unforgiving climate of endless conflict and utter chaos, Red, White, and Green forces ransacked and robbed churches, unleashed a battery of morbid antics on innocents, and murdered priests and other church figures at random and with impunity. Within this first year of Bolshevik rule, the Russian Orthodox Church lost nearly twenty bishops, over one hundred priests, over one hundred fifty deacons, and nearly a hundred monks and nuns, not to mention the hundreds of those imprisoned, the church confiscations and closures, and dozens of brazen, violent interruptions of processions and services. The first bishop to be killed was Metropolitan Vladimir of Kiev who, while being tortured, prayed that his persecutors be forgiven. In February of 1918, Red forces went on a rampage in the Don region and killed priests indiscriminately. Elsewhere priests were taken for ransom, humiliated, scalped, beheaded, mutilated, or crucified. Some were forced to watch as wives and children were molested and executed. A reliable tally of sacrificed souls in the first years of Soviet rule is hard to come by. One recent revised estimate puts the number executed (shot) at 1,434, considerably lower than previous estimates.[11]

At this point, in the midst of the Russian Civil War, the implications of Soviet decrees may have been clear, but their application was not. Local conditions—economic and political circumstances, the attitude of local Soviet officials, and their relationship with local confessional communities—mattered a great deal. Soviets in Baikal and Nerchinsk, for example, far from the reach of the party's eminent commissars, took earnest steps to implement the January 1918 decree. The Baikal regional party committee issued a twelve-article affirmation of the decree that included removing religious instruction from "all educational institutions," firing teachers of religion (except those in seminaries, interestingly), and ensuring that clergy do not teach in public schools. A later memorandum of April 8, 1918, sternly addressed a refusal by representatives from a local "seminary, the missionary college, and the Baikal diocesan women's college" to fulfill a demand to inventory "files, staff and funds, and movable and immovable property." In Nerchinsk, one Father Znamenskii was imprisoned "for the entire period of the revolution" for statements made during a Palm Sunday sermon, condemning the Bolsheviks for persecuting the church, for iconoclasm, and for sacrilege.[12]

Local responses were sometimes confused because there was shifting responsibility at the top of the Soviet bureaucracy. Religious policies emanated from a number of commissariats, including (in roughly chronological order) the Commissariat of Justice; the Commissariat of Internal Affairs; the Commissariat of Enlightenment (temporarily linked to the Department for Agitation and Propaganda under the aegis of the Central Committee); ad hoc commissions such as the one established to confiscate church treasures; standing commissions like Emelian Iaroslavksii's Antireligious Commission established at the Central Committee level; and in 1925 the League of Atheists (under the Agitation and Propaganda Department of the Central Committee), which in 1929 became the League of Militant Godless (with yet another incarnation after World War II). With organizational flowchart lines crossing in every direction, and with several commissars holding temporary portfolios, it is no surprise that there were real quandaries in carrying out Soviet religious policies. Those who were subject to them faced a maze of detailed laws, decrees, regulations, and instructions, some of them unwritten, and the world of the secret police. Those who attempted to carry them out were faced with another kind of quandary. One party official spoke of the dilemma this way:

> On the one hand [the clergy's] numbers should be reduced due to their religious influence, [but] on the other hand, the numbers of believers do not decline and there is a growing need for them; on the one hand, they ought to be compromised, on the other hand they are loyal, conduct their activities within law, know a lot and can influence many things, and, therefore, we are interested in carrying out with them certain work.[13]

Many party functionaries, like this one, ran out of hands and ideas. Ultimately, the dilemma came to this: Did the legal, constitutional provisions speak with one voice? Did the agencies and institutions charged with executing these provisions keep to a consistent line? In short, did the provisions and policies square? No: for the simple reason that the Soviets did not agree either, in the center or in the provinces. As a matter of fact, even before the revolutions of 1917, Russian Social Democrats were divided into hardcore, doctrinaire "fundamentalists" and phlegmatic, bureaucratic "pragmatists." Whatever their preferences, loyal party members consented to statements like Article 13 of the Eighth Party Congress, held March 18–23, 1919:

> With reference to religion, the All-Russian Communist Party does not content itself with the already decreed separation of church from state [of January 23, 1918]—i.e., with measures which are a part of the program of bourgeois democracies. [...] The aim of the Party is finally to destroy the ties between the exploiting class and the organization of religious propaganda, at the same time helping the toiling masses actually to liberate their minds from religious superstitions, and organizing on a wide scale scientific-educational and anti-religious propaganda. It is, however, necessary carefully to avoid offending the religious susceptibilities of believers, which leads only to the strengthening of religious fanaticism.[14]

Lenin was still of this opinion two years later, at the time of the critical Tenth Party Congress. He wrote to Viacheslav Molotov, "we must give absolutely no offense to religion."[15] Or to private traders, retail shops, or chartered banks, he could have added. The New Economic Policy (NEP) had just been adopted to promote economic recovery, and it offered a breather to a land reeling from at least four years of relentless upheaval. By 1926, the recovery was well underway, with impressive growth in retail trade and in industries that boosted the commanding heights of the economy. It would be tempting to conclude that religious communities shared in this recovery, but it was not that simple. Within a year of his temperate exchange with Molotov, Lenin called for priests to be shot, as many as possible, so that the "lesson" would stick. Time and again, party practice vacillated between wanting to go beyond mere disestablishment on one hand, and unleashing terror on the other, which of course risked "strengthening fanaticism." That practice also depended on whether the target was the Russian Orthodox Church, the most freighted of communities for the Bolsheviks; Catholics, whose regional history and loyalty to the Vatican gave them little chance of reprieve; or the various Protestant sects, some of whom saw the 1920s as a golden decade. Indeed, the confessional and international dimensions of Soviet policy began to overlap as Lenin's health declined, as the party-state's gold reserves dwindled, as foreign relations became ever more important, and as the leadership succession crisis of the mid-1920s intensified.

Benedicat Vos Omnipotens Deus

At the end of June 1922, the Soviet press began reporting on a dire famine in the Volga region. As many as 25 million people faced starvation. Patriarch Tikhon took the initiative to organize a church relief program. He approached Soviet authorities with the offer of the church's support but was rebuffed. Within months, party discussions focused on a plan to confiscate church treasures or "valuables." Tikhon suggested that the church would consider handing over a fixed sum equal to the value of assets targeted. Again, his suggestion was repulsed. On January 2, 1922, a decision was made to move forward with a plan to inventory and seize church treasures. Leon Trotsky, who had taken over church affairs the previous October, formalized an action plan by January 26. Part of laying the groundwork for this campaign was to use basic disagreements within the Russian Orthodox Church to foment a schism. For years, progressive elements in the Russian Orthodox clergy had chafed under the policies of the Holy Synod and then the patriarchate after November 1917. Differences ripened under the Soviets, who saw in this left-leaning faction an opportunity to divide and conquer.

On cue, Fr. Aleksandr Vvedenskii (who soon adopted the title metropolitan for himself) criticized Tikhon for his callous disregard of millions of desperate famine victims. By May, Vvedenskii had gathered around him a coterie of Renovationists, many of whom organized themselves as the Living Church. By that point, nasty clashes had taken place between parishioners and party operatives, and over the next year a ruthless confiscation program collected precious jewels, icons, and other items deemed ripe for harvest by party gangs. In many cases, the faithful refused to hand over their valuables; after all, Tikhon had warned in early 1918 that this might happen, and strongboxes were installed where possible to protect church property. In some places, like Ivanovo-Voznesensk and Iaroslavl, crowds were restive but the confiscations went ahead. Others resisted, like in Rostov-on-Don. The cavalry was called to Tverskaia Street in Moscow to maintain order; they did so by firing shots into the air to disperse a gathering crowd. Angry letters demanding the Central Committee stop the confiscations and rescind the decree complained that this would lead to an outburst of "religious fanaticism," in much the same language as warnings from earlier congresses. The campaign continued. A few of the confrontations, like those in Smolensk, Vologda, and Viatka, descended into pogroms, as Jews were accused of being the instigators of the Soviet confiscation campaign. Petrograd Jews endured racial slurs and beatings in the streets. On March 12, 1922, Shuya erupted into a wave of violence. Lives were lost on both sides, partly because of Lenin's missive (on record, if ever needed) that executions would make the church think twice before resisting again.

Trotsky, disappointed with the results of the campaign, called for a more intense antichurch campaign. This was tabled, but he persuaded the Politburo to forward the first installment of one million rubles' worth of hunger relief to the appropriate government agencies—then requested that 10 million be set aside for related expenses. All told, the confiscation plan brought in a little over 6 million rubles.[16] Still, despite this dubious campaign, and the valiant efforts of Red Army soldiers and of at least nine foreign aid organizations, perhaps as many as 10 million people starved. Millions worth of food stores sat undelivered in Russian ports between February 24 and March 4, 1922, on the eve of the confiscation clashes, because of a rail transportation breakdown. When word reached the American Relief Administration, Herbert Hoover curtailed and then ended the shipments.

Where did the money go? Where did the valuables go? Did the Soviet government need (or use) the money for something other than famine relief? Following the money opens up a whole panorama on state and church in the early Soviet era, with 1922 to 1925 being pivotal. When the Bolsheviks assumed power, they seized the assets of the imperial Russian state, refused to pay foreign debt obligations, nationalized property (domestic and foreign, especially French), and held nearly 11.4 million rubles confiscated in August 1917 by the Provisional Government from the Roman Catholic Church. Indeed, for the next decade, the Catholic Church in Russia suffered most consistently. By 1921, there were some 1.6 million Catholics in five dioceses, the largest of which was the Mogilev Archdiocese; two seminaries; and apostolic vicarages (mission outposts) in parts of Siberia and as far east as Vladivostok. Catholics in Russia, the vast majority of whom were Polish, were, like Orthodox believers, subjected to a police-supported schism and arrests of leading clerics. Those arrests began in the spring of 1919, when the Soviets tried Archbishop Eduard von der Ropp of Mogilev, who was assumed to be part of a Polish conspiracy during the Polish-Soviet War. His capital sentence was commuted. In early April 1923, Monsignor Konstantin Budkiewicz, the uncompromising dean of the Petrograd Catholic clergy, was executed, and the international reaction to his execution had a significant ripple effect.

By this time, Patriarch Tikhon had been arrested, along with Ropp's successor Jan Cieplak, and their trials were held simultaneously. Trotsky pressed to have them executed. Georgii Chicherin, the leading Soviet diplomat of the time, wrote Stalin on April 10, 1923, to warn against this. "The facts have shown how much damage we brought on ourselves by the execution of Budkiewicz." As evidence, Chicherin notes that politicians in the United States and Great Britain pushing for diplomatic recognition of Soviet Russia have decided "to delay this work for a time." There were also reports that the execution had cooled France's desire to include Soviet Russia in an international finance conference at Lausanne. "Anyone who knows even a little of what is happening beyond the border posts," Chicherin needled Stalin, "will confirm that our position in all our relations has grown much worse as a result of this [Budkiewicz] case."[17] A year before, at the height of the church confiscation campaign, Russian diplomats had to artfully maneuver around domestic affairs as they tried to position the new regime for international recognition and desperately needed trade agreements at the Genoa debt conference. There, Chicherin managed to conclude the Treaty of Rapallo with Germany. Thus, placed in international context, the church confiscation campaign became one factor in an intricate foreign policy calculation. Soviet religious and foreign policies were enmeshed.

And yet the Soviets needed more money, or so their back-channel deals suggest. In October 1922, Russian treasures were exhibited in Berlin. They came from the Gokhran collection, established by the Soviets not long after taking power, and have since been valued at between 70 and 140 million dollars. The next month, Olof Aschberg, a Swedish financier of Russian descent, under the more lenient terms of NEP, established a private charter for Ruskombank (Russian Bank of Commerce), capitalized at 5 million dollars. He later stated that between 1921 and 1924, he sold nearly $50 million in Russian treasures, including a cache of 277 icons. Markets in Stockholm, Berlin, and Vienna then attracted those in London, others in Italy and France. Perhaps the single most valuable confiscated church holding was a fourth-century codex Bible purchased by the British Museum in 1933 for 100,000 pounds sterling. One estimate is that the total "laundered" in this period is nearly $20 billion in current value, "comparable to the combined output of all the bankers of Switzerland in processing Nazi gold during the Second World War." The money, at least the portion that can be accounted for, went to capitalize purchases of German weaponry. A significant share, "at least a million pounds sterling," also went to foreign comrades to finance revolution and establish the Comintern, although evidently some of the latter was invested by budding communists in British War Stock and Liberty Loan Bonds.[18]

Thus early opportunities taken by the Soviets to weaken the church may have been ideologically motivated but, when taken in context, those motives are very much mixed with other considerations of hard-nosed international politics. Meanwhile, the parish revival was sustained in extreme circumstances. Even compared to other modern revolutions that carried out concerted attacks on clergy and the church—such as those in France or

Mexico—the Soviet campaign, for all its tactical flexibility, stands apart. However measured, it was a desperate time, and yet one that evinced a quiet, if bittersweet, revolution in grassroots faith that survived the first Soviet onslaught. In fact, the parish revival continued into the 1920s despite Soviet policies—perhaps even *because* of them. The revolutions of 1917 and early Soviet antireligious policies dismantled the traditional church apparatus, but far from imperiling faith, this empowered the faithful, the laity, to set in motion a parish revival that continued right through belligerent Soviet efforts to make religion disappear.

As in 1917, parishes in the 1920s continued to refashion church administration, the character of the clergy, the parish purview, and popular spirituality. At least one mistaken Soviet assumption (wrapped up in some complicated ecclesiology) contributed to the parish revival: that the institutional church is synonymous with Christianity, thus a successful antichurch campaign would equate to progress in the antireligious campaign. As practical matter, local soviets saw destroying a church building as destroying a community of believers. The parish, a living entity, had been elevated and enshrined in law by militant atheists. "All Power to the Parish" was the Soviet notion, with the unmistakable ring of 1917, and with all the unintended consequences that followed. One specialist puts it this way, "from 1917 to 1929—in law and everyday reality—the "church" *was* the "Church."[19] The regime's plan was to secularize by de-churching, and by de-churching to de-Christianize. The consequence, however, was not to de-Christianize at all. It was to laicize, "to free popular Orthodoxy from clerical control." Similar attempts—by the church—in prerevolutionary Russia were to protect against the influence of sectarians—Old Believers or Protestants. Not this time. The effect was to set the laity free to create, build, and minister in new ways, which had an impact on the entire structure of the Russian Orthodox Church.

First, links in the church's organizational apparatus and diocesan communication network began to snap. Public statements appeared in party-state news organs. Hierarchs and laity both called it chaos, but they took a different view of the anarchy. There is no doubt that as a territorial and diocesan institution, the Russian Orthodox Church was transformed. Some have concluded that it even ceased to exist in its traditional form.[20] Second, clergy whose callings were inspired by revolutionary events or otherwise were ordained without regard to social identity (or estate). There were fewer priests now, and over time they became less educated, and they were financially dependent on those they served. But for all the disadvantages, they were elected and more closely identified with their parishioners than before 1917. Third, as noted above, parishes took the 1918 law to heart and defended themselves against confiscations and incursions by the Renovationists—in many cases as much or more than their priests. One commission reported that they failed to seize inventoried valuables because "from all sides the public rushed toward us. They began to scream and curse, declaring that we are robbing not to help the starving, but for the communists (who are sending it all abroad)."[21] Renovationists discovered that their brand of progressivism—which included married bishops, vernacular liturgy, doing away with holy relics and monasteries, and adoption of the Gregorian calendar—was not welcome. It was the last reform that really raised the hackles of the faithful, interfering as it did with time-tested rhythms of village piety. At the peak of their influence in 1923, the Renovationists appeared to have succeeded in deposing Tikhon and in subsuming well over 50 percent of all Orthodox parishes under their control (with police and party support). By 1926, their fortunes had fallen considerably. Taken together, the upshot was that "the party—like the episcopate—capitulated before the wrath of the parishioners." Finally, a spate of miracles rattled Soviet authorities. They took to their desks to document nearly 590 reports of miracles in a single year—1924. This phenomenon, along with other signs of continuing life in faith communities, offered proof enough to party officials by 1925 that they had inadvertently helped to revitalize popular Orthodoxy: "religious fanaticism has ... not only failed to cease and die out ... it has reinforced the authority of the church and religion."[22] It seemed that the Soviets had run out of options, which had included anticlerical rhetoric, antireligious propaganda, schism, and sporadic terror. The turning point came in April 1929 with a decisive turn to systematic, coercive de-Christianization, many of whose victims were swept up in the Great Terror of 1936–1938. In the long run, however, there was a broad legacy of the parish revival, despite being eclipsed in the 1930s and 1960s. One of the most important was to prepare the ground for renewal in the 1980s and a churched and "de-churched" (or un-churched) religious revival in post-Soviet Russia, something observers now characterize as "believing without belonging."[23]

Believing *and* belonging characterized many Protestants in the 1920s, especially Evangelicals whose organizing efforts were critical to their growth. Their treatment and experience in the early Soviet period was, on the face of it, less precarious than the Russian Orthodox Church. Incorporated into the Russian Empire in the late eighteenth century (at the invitation of Catherine the Great to help settle the Volga region), Lutherans and Mennonites lost ground in the 1920s, partly due to immigration. Lutherans numbered 1.35 million in 1923 (a million of whom were Germans), which was down to 900,000 just three years later (540,000 being German). Evangelicals drew on pietistic roots and hailed from three separate regions of the former empire. Because of long-standing restrictions on their activity in the Russian Empire, churches in this tradition possessed little and were, relatively speaking, less affected by asset inventories and seizures. They lost few converts after the Bolshevik Revolution, and the decade of the 1920s has been called the "golden decade" of the evangelical movement in Russia. There are at least three reasons for the disparity in treatment between Russian Orthodox believers and Evangelicals. First, they were anything but collaborators with the imperial regime; revolutionaries had sometimes shared bunk space with persecuted believers in Siberian exile. Second, Evangelicals held tightly to the necessity for separation of church and state. Neither of these things made them friends of the Bolsheviks, but neither did they represent an immediate threat to them. Third, as a keen observer of the movement concludes, their experience may reflect not so much official neutrality as the fact that "Bolsheviks could not yet manage to have it any other way."[24] Even so, some of the 3 million Evangelicals (split into Baptists and Evangelical Christians) set up "Christian collectives" during the 1920s. Did Evangelicals share socialist goals? It is unclear. Vladimir Bonch-Bruevich, sometime secretary to Lenin, was their Bolshevik patron and his studies of them offer a rare cache of sources on religious life in the early Soviet period. At the Thirteenth Party Congress in 1924, Mikhail Kalinin noted that the sectarians "were cruelly persecuted by the tsarist regime and among them now there is much activity.... The sectarians are numerous." His recommendation was that through "a skillful approach" the Soviet regime could use the "considerable economic and cultural potentialities of the sectarians" and direct them into "channels of Soviet work."[25] The recommendation passed. But then so did the climate of the mid-1920s. And Protestant sects were not immune to Soviet meddling in their unity congresses, for example, in 1923, over the issue of pacifism. A January 1919 decree offered a waiver from military service, but that had changed by 1923 as tests of loyalty became more crucial.

Evangelicals were not simply another Russian Christian confession to note and annotate. They represent another type of genuine Russian identity in the revolutionary era, indeed another experience with Russian modernization. They have long defined themselves by cultural features: their local communities, their individual spirituality, and their stress on biblicism and conversion—which, among other things, has generated a wealth of source material. As members of international bodies, they expanded the definition of Russian Christianity at home and abroad and, in the context of the 1920s, they were in good company. By 1922, the "Russian Church" denotes two spheres of faith communities—one internal to the Soviet Union, and the other in the Russia Abroad. Soviet religious policies impacted both, but conceptions of Russian Christianity should not be limited to communities located within contemporary Soviet borders. Exiled church figures across the confessions, thinkers, politicians, and artists—many of whom took passage on the "philosophers' ship" at the end of 1922—all tried to piece together a new life in exile, some able to start afresh, many still hampered by suspended allegiances. Russian Christianity became "ecumenical," if for no other reason than international organizations, like the YMCA and its prescient leaders, worked tirelessly to maintain and sustain abroad what was sometimes needed, or under attack, at home.[26] Nothing captures the spirit of those at home or abroad facing fearful odds better than the benediction pronounced by Archbishop Jan Cieplak at his sentencing in March 1923: "*benedicat vos omnipotens deus*"—"May Almighty God bless you."

A Religious Psychology Turned Inside Out

Soviet legal measures may have European precedents, and it could be argued that totalitarian states of the twentieth century certainly had things in common: rejection of the pre–World War I liberal order, intolerance of dissent, and the use of fear and terror as instruments of government. But there was something unprecedented about the Soviet antichurch and antireligious campaign: its vengeful character. This was essential Bolshevism. Nikolai Berdiaev, one of the most intuitive exiles in the Russia Abroad, asserted in the early 1930s that revenge was the "soul" of Bolshevism. Revenge certainly was the most distinctive aspect of the Soviet antichurch and antireligious campaign. This was no accident. The campaign that apparently pitted the most aggressively secular of all modern regimes against Russian Christianity was actually a religious war. This was no spectacular match of secular versus sacred because both Russian communism and Russian Orthodoxy shared common roots. Berdiaev wrote that communism is formidable "precisely as a religion. It is as a religion that it opposes Christianity and aims at ousting it; it gives in to the temptations Christ refused, the changing of stones into bread and the kingdom of this world."[27] The militantly atheistic roots of Bolshevism lay in Christianity, in Russian Orthodoxy in particular, though in skewed prism, with the template of creation-fall-redemption-restoration eschatology unmistakably intact. Bolshevism was infused with worldly asceticism, but of a graceless variety, and the heroic avenger sought to right wrongs with the methods of the modern state and a new anthropology to create a "New Soviet Man." The best example of systematic and coercive state secularization in modern history had religious roots and a religious character.

In this light, early Soviet religious policies provide not only the best case of a modern antichurch experiment, but a stark example of a creedal (not simply ideological) response to the pressures of modern industrial society. The traditional garb, doctrines, and institutions of one creed (Christian Orthodoxy) were thrown aside with a vengeance in the name of another—communism. "The anti-religious psychology of communism is a religious psychology turned inside-out," Berdiaev wrote.[28] Berdiaev was not alone, and others in the Russia Abroad went beyond diagnosis to prescription. At least one other Russian thinker came to the same conclusion long before the collapse of the Russian Empire. Sergei Bulgakov, from whom Berdiaev drew inspiration, spilled considerable ink exploring the religious roots of Feuerbach and Marx, as well as leading Russian thinkers like Aleksandr Herzen. Bulgakov's prolific written and ecumenical work continued in exile. His legacy was to construct a profound, erudite anthropology for modern persons in stark contrast to that of the New Soviet Man.[29]

This Russian story fits into a much broader context. A leading critic of conventional secularization narratives, Charles Taylor, argued that secularization emanates from, rather than in opposition to, Christianity. More recent work suggests that the religious roots of modernity lay in those most often viewed as the principal players in the secularization drama—Baruch Spinoza, Voltaire, Feuerbach, and even Marx. Perhaps, they were, after all, "men of intense but bruised" religious convictions, attempting to construct a purer vision of justice than the one they saw around them. In this way, communism "was a millenarian revolt against a heavenly yet all-too-earthly theology of gain."[30] As Berdiaev concluded, it was a religious psychology from first to last. There can be no surprise that it faltered in the task of secularization. Shortly after the Russian Civil War, Trotsky sent a note to the Politburo: "There is a church outside my window. Out of ten passersby ... at least seven, if not eight, cross themselves when they walk past. And many of those who walk past are Red Army soldiers."[31]

2

COMBATING GOD AND GRANDMA

The Soviet Antireligious Campaigns
and the Battle for Childhood

Julie deGraffenried[1]

About one month after seizing power, on December 11, 1917, the Bolshevik government produced its first significant piece of antireligious legislation. This act removed all control over education from the church, placing it into the hands of the government's Commissariat of Education. A week later, civil authorities succeeded the church as regulators of marriage, family, and children. In 1918, Lenin's Decree on Separation of Church from State prohibited religious education in any school, public or private, allowing only for private spiritual instruction. The next major antireligious legislation, in the late 1920s, excluded children from the practice of organized religion altogether. Beginning in the late 1950s, atheist education became a standard feature of general education for children. At the same time, authorities cautioned parents to protect their young ones from the dangerous spiritual influences of ... grandmothers.

This essay asks the reader to think about the antireligious campaigns in the Soviet Union in a new way—as a battle for childhood—and lays out the possibilities inherent in such an approach. Historians have long viewed Soviet education and cultural policies as an attempt to mold children into "New Soviet Men and Women" by instilling certain values and political sensibilities into impressionable, young children. Rarely, however, do they regard the antireligious campaigns as part of this same effort to modernize childhood. The attempt to pull children away from ideologically harmful influences of faith and push them toward secularism and, ultimately, atheism, set up a conflict between public and private worlds, between state institutions and family. For the Soviet authorities, religion was incompatible with a modern Soviet childhood; for Soviet children and families, however, the issue appears to have been far more complicated.

One of the unique aspects of the Soviet Union, as it existed from 1917 to 1991, was its approach to religion. Marx famously called religion the "sigh of the oppressed" and "the opium of the peoples," while Vladimir Lenin called it a "sort of spiritual booze in which the slaves of capital drown their human image."[2] Despite Lenin's prerevolutionary assurances that socialist governance guaranteed freedom to practice or not practice any religion, the Bolshevik agenda included combating God (in any form) in a variety of ways in the days, months, and years following their ascension to power in October 1917. Many scholars have written about the methods, propaganda, consequences, legacies, dissidents, and heroes of the faith related to antireligious campaigns in the former Soviet Union, as reflected in this volume. A topic that has received less systematic exploration, however, is the emphasis placed on children, childhood, and religion by the Bolshevik/Communist Party throughout the twentieth century.

The potential in this project is immensely exciting and compelling, especially within the context of the history of Russia and the history of children and childhood. Historians of childhood look at how conceptions of childhood, definitions of "child" and "youth," and approaches to child-rearing have shifted profoundly over time and place. Many of the ideals of childhood taken for granted today developed over the last century and are quite specific to American culture. The history of childhood, which focuses on ideas about children and practices toward children, is often combined with children's history, which uses age as a primary category of analysis for understanding the past. Historians of children and childhood ask questions about the effects of events or ideas on children of the past, about children's understanding of and reactions to certain events or ideas, about children's effect on and participation in creating events or ideas, and how societies' ideas about children and childhood reflect a certain view of children's roles consistent with particular value systems or ideologies. It is a relatively new and dynamic interdisciplinary field, engendering studies by scholars of history, law, literature, film, philosophy, sociology, anthropology, and religion, among others, as well as generating significant works by historians of Russia.[3] This project proposes uniting several lines of scholarship—Soviet history, history of children and childhood, and history of religion—that have only occasionally intersected.

Such an approach will enrich the story of the Soviet antireligious campaigns told thus far, giving voice to children, who, despite comprising about one-third of modern-era populations, rarely have the power of voice in society. The campaigns also give us an additional means of understanding how Soviet authorities conceived of an ideal childhood and the complications they faced in its creation. A number of questions come to mind immediately: Is it fair to say that those in charge of the antireligious campaigns aimed at forging or reshaping Soviet childhood in specific ways? Could it be that children experienced these campaigns in unique ways because of their age, position in the family, and position in society? Is it useful to look at the Soviet campaigns through this particular lens? What seems clear, even upon preliminary investigation, is that the drive to eradicate religion in children's lives was by no means a simple or uncontested project. Instead, the antireligious campaigns appear to have transgressed boundaries of public and private life in children's lives in significant ways, setting up a complex competition to redefine Soviet childhood.

What follows is both an overview of this argument and a case for future inquiry, rather than a completed study. The primary source analysis of Soviet law and antireligious propaganda engaged in here is heavily supplemented with anecdotal evidence drawn from other historians' work with primary source materials. A few notes on scope: First, the term "children" refers to those aged sixteen and under, using Soviet-era law and practice as a guide. Second, the focus will be primarily on Russia and Christianity—more specifically, the Russian Orthodox Church and the small "sects" (or denominations) of Christianity that authorities considered so dangerous—occasionally throwing in examples relating to Islam and Judaism, with the acknowledgment that the Soviet Union eventually contained fourteen other republics and dozens of confessional communities. Geography and faith community mattered intensely, yet focusing on Christianity makes sense as it would have been the religious background of the majority of children in Soviet Russia, the largest of the socialist republics.[4] Third, the project will not address questions of religion, such as whether or not Soviet authorities or faith communities created a specific theology of childhood or how Soviet campaigns affected roles of children or perspectives on childhood in Christian, Jewish, or Muslim traditions. Clearly, there remains much rich work here for scholars of religion.[5] Fourth, in this essay, the words "public," "private" "state," and "family," are used, acknowledging the highly mutable nature of these categories and ongoing debate over the existence of privacy in the Soviet context, but recognizing as useful the distinctions between them made both by Soviet authorities and individuals.[6]

Soviet Authorities, Religion, and Children

In beautifully understated fashion, Felix Corley writes that "religion *mattered* to the Communist state."[7] Religion, like other trappings of prerevolutionary, capitalist society, was supposed to "wither away," unneeded in a communist new world. Separation of the church from the state and of the school from the church was a plank in the platform of Russian socialists long before 1917.[8] To accelerate the "withering" process, the newly formed and self-proclaimed Bolshevik government immediately began formulating plans that would continue to evolve over the next seventy years.

The first antireligious formal legislation appeared in January 1918, with the Decree on Separation of Church from State and of School from Church, sometimes referred to as the Decree on Freedom of Conscience, Church, and Religious Organizations. An act of "radical secularization against the church hierarchy and apparatus" that removed the privilege, funding, and property of the Russian Orthodox Church, this decree also announced that "the school shall be separate from the Church" and forbade the teaching of religion in any public or private general education schools, though individuals could continue to receive or provide private religious instruction.[9] Simultaneously, the Bolsheviks sanctioned violence against targeted groups, such as priests, "easily identified" by villagers and outsiders alike. Some had their homes confiscated while others were publicly executed.[10] This persecution continued during the Civil War (1918–1921), culminating in the seizure of church valuables taken ostensibly to feed the starving during the terrible famine of the early 1920s and a series of show trials in 1922 in which dozens of "princes of the church" or clergy were charged with counterrevolutionary activities.[11] More will be said about this later, but keep in mind that Orthodox priests, for the most part, were married and had children—*lots* of them.[12]

The 1918 decree affected not only the 42,000 schools run by the Russian Orthodox Church but all schools, whether run by the state, city council, or private individuals, launching a radical change in curriculum for children across the country. Emphasizing piety as much as loyalty to the tsarist regime by devoting twelve of twenty-seven hours of weekly instructional time to religion, prerevolutionary primary and secondary schools included compulsory church attendance and comportment grading, classes on religious knowledge, prayer, and moral education.[13] Reactions to the decree were mixed. For non-Orthodox children, the 1918 law promised unprecedented protection from discriminatory grading, unjust retention, and exclusion from higher education.[14] Parents and children of the intelligentsia lauded the triumph of a "rational" or secular education and the privatization of religion, while some

Orthodox became furious by the thought that the *Zakon Bozhii* (law of God) would no longer be taught in school.[15] For many children, religious decorations in schools came down and lessons in "religious knowledge" ended. For all, the law foreshadowed unprecedented state intervention in education, culture, and family.

Susan Reid points out that "in Soviet terms there was nothing shameful about attempting to intervene in the terms of everyday life" because such intervention was "a legitimate part of the effort to build communism."[16] Children, in particular, were considered an integral part of the "political legitimacy and viability of the Soviet state" from its inception.[17] The Marxist emphasis on change-the-environment, change-the-person meant that of all age groups, the Bolsheviks' best shot at creating the New Soviet Man began with its youngest inhabitants: children. A tutelary state could fill the blank slates (or empty beehives, as writer Maxim Gorky put it), molding from birth these future builders of communism through proper institutions and upbringing (*vospitanie*). Children became both object and symbol of a super–parent state that delegated but did not hand over the right to parent to biological mothers and fathers.[18] The exploitative, patriarchal family, like institutional religion, was part of the bourgeois past to be superseded by state care and guidance.[19]

The state's creation of a Soviet childhood was quite an ambitious project considering the vast majority of its citizenry were peasants, with conceptions of childhood common to agricultural societies—in other words, children were labor (highly gendered labor at that), and family and religious practices emphasized obedience in order to protect property; further, rural hygiene, medical resources, and practices meant high infant and child mortality rates. The party sought to modernize that childhood, to bring it more in line with ideas about childhood emerging in the West in the late nineteenth and early twentieth centuries: children should be safe and protected both from physical harm such as disease or superstition, and from the "adult" world by being in school. The communist variation of modernity involved massive state intervention in making this happen and an expectation, from the beginning, that children were "not just ... recipients of nurture, but ... an audience for political ideas."[20] Children should be *activists*, models for the adults around them.[21]

The party issued nearly one hundred decrees related to social services, many of them affecting children, in their first five years of power.[22] State-run publishing houses disseminated vast quantities of material on prenatal and infant care, discipline of children, and childcare.[23] Old bourgeois authorities, including priests, teachers, and parents, were to be challenged. As quickly as possible, children were to be in centralized, state schools designed to discipline the body and instill the sense of time so key to "modern living."[24] Overall,

Catriona Kelly describes the governing image of Soviet childhood in the first decade of Soviet power as rationalistic, anti-bourgeois, pro-child/anti-adult, and steeped in class struggle and politics.[25]

To come full circle: the 1918 legislation demonstrates how the Bolsheviks connected secular education and the attack on the Church with a modern Soviet childhood. Free education for all children—and an education free of religious influence but packed with correct socialist morality, established by a 1919 act creating the United School of Labor[26]—was an integral part of a larger program to modernize Soviet life. Secularization, in this case, was not simply compartmentalization (that is, check your faith at the door) but a secularization meant to go home and extend to family and private life.[27] In fact, Leon Trotsky called the social education of children one of the three major elements in the "complete transformation of morals" in the Soviet Union.[28] Good communists were not born, but *made*. So, for that matter, were good believers or non-believers.[29]

To enforce the 1918 decree, Soviet authorities created and empowered a number of institutions, most notably the Commission to Establish Separation of Church and State in 1922.[30] Headed by Emelian Iaroslavskii, the Commission brought in special representatives to "consult" on specific points with the committee; one of these was Nadezhda Krupskaia. Aside from being Lenin's wife, Krupskaia was also the foremost voice on children in the first decade of the Soviet Union. Her consistent involvement as consultant suggests that policies and practices related to children occurred with some regularity. It should be noted that, at this point, secular education did not mean atheist instruction or an end to the private religious education of children.[31] Krupskaia and Anatolii Lunacharskii, head of the Commissariat of Enlightenment, believed that a nonreligious, scientific content in school was sufficient and that the "special implanting of antireligious views into each child" was unnecessary to achieve their goal of a rational education, though they cautioned teachers to carefully observe children's free play to monitor progress.[32] In fact, their attitude here seems almost tame in comparison to the intensive campaign launched by the *Evsektsiia* (the Jewish Section of the Communist Party) against Jewish religious education. Lamenting the arrest of teachers and school closures, Rabbi Moshe Eisenstadt wrote to an American Jewish aid association in 1926 that "our younger generation is being torn from us by force."[33] While synagogues and public houses of prayer remained open, the *heder* (primary school) and *yeshiva* (upper school) were publicly liquidated, essentially disappearing by the late 1920s. The patient approach might be acceptable for adults ensconced in their faith, but not for young, impressionable students.[34] The aggressive tone of the Jewish Section echoed the message of the V. I. Lenin All-Union Young Pioneer Organization, or the Young Pioneers, the party's organization for children aged ten to fourteen founded in 1922. The Pioneers encouraged state-sanctioned child activism in the 1920s, asking children to participate in all sorts of campaigns intended to build Soviet socialism, including the struggle against backward religion or mysticism and for the promotion of atheism.

State authorities, however, faced a critical problem in making their ideal Soviet childhood a reality in the 1920s: lack of resources. Schools, nurseries, and childcare facilities promised to the countryside did not materialize—even when requested.[35] While the conversion of church buildings into schools addressed the problem in some places, in others, local party officials foiled such actions by selling dismantled churches for scrap.[36] The decree against religious instruction made tsarist-era textbooks and curricula unusable, but there was neither money nor paper available to replace an entire country's books in the 1920s. Further, about half the teachers in primary schools were children of clergy who tended to ignore the directives; yet the state had no personnel with which to replace them.[37] Students' poverty thwarted state plans as well: nearly half of the school-aged children in Russia did not attend school, either because they could not afford school fees or because they lacked proper clothing and shoes.[38]

Such overwhelming needs could not be subsidized by Soviet authorities, so "traditionalist"-dominated village councils or clergy took advantage, providing notebooks, textbooks, and hot meals to attract students to the schools they still controlled.[39] This coincided with an active effort by rural Orthodox clergy to appeal to youngsters, organizing discussion circles, children's choirs, nighttime parties for older children, sports teams, dances, craft circles, zoo trips or other excursions, and children's libraries, often well-supplied with cookies and candy. Circles of the Baby Jesus and Baby Mary competed with the Young Pioneers for the attention of children.[40] Participation in these events, no doubt, marks children's contribution to the religious revival of the 1920s.

This was too much. In 1928, the Commission to Establish Separation of Church and State took its first steps to address the problem, prohibiting religious organizations from setting up field trips or playgrounds and forbidding children to participate in religious choirs.[41] The big blow fell in April 1929 with the Law on Religious Associations, which introduced sweeping limitations on faith communities in the Soviet Union. Religious associations were prohibited from teaching religion to children, prohibited from holding special events for children, prohibited from doing charity work, and prohibited from organizing libraries.[42] The Law on Religious Associations coincided with a massive drive to collectivize agriculture, an event accompanied by a class struggle against kulaks and a fresh round of attacks on religion. Once again, priests and their families were targeted, disenfranchised, and deported.[43]

By 1933, the excesses of the class struggle, sometimes referred to as the Cultural Revolution, were rather abruptly halted. Joseph Stalin announced the "accomplishment" of socialism because of successful industrialization and collectivization, thus diminishing the need for activist children. In the 1930s, children could finally enjoy the bountiful, ideal "happy childhood" provided by the state and Papa Stalin. Authority figures and the family were restored as critical elements in the lives of Soviet children, an order that reflected both the paternal state and the fact that the state could not provide all the institutions needed to replace the family. Childhood remained politicized, through directed activism and, especially, children's role as visible symbol of Soviet success.

But beneath the surface of realized socialism lay the threat of "enemies of the people" and with it, Stalin's Terror. For a third time, a wave of repression struck clergy and their families. By 1941, for example, only one in forty Old Believer bishops remained free from imprisonment.[44] In 1937, an NKVD operational order mandated the arrest of wives and children of enemies of the people, with babies and toddlers going to prison nurseries, four-to-fifteen-year-olds to state orphanages, and children over fifteen to be assessed individually and sentenced according to "socially dangerous" qualities.[45] While children of the repressed experienced the effects of terror within their homes, many more children were to feel the terror through spatial change. Nathaniel Davis observes that the greatest wave of church closing occurred in the late 1930s; by 1939, only two to three hundred churches remained, down from 50,000 in the prerevolutionary era.[46]

War brought a liberalization of state treatment of religion in the 1940s, though the relaxation of policy did not show up meaningfully in state-produced children's culture. Priests were once again allowed, however, to proselytize and instruct groups of children, and a few Islamic regions felt emboldened enough to request approval to open *mektebs* (primary schools) and to teach the Muslim faith and Qur'an in school.[47] The period 1945–1954 saw the regimentation and control of religion, rather than brutality, as state-approved bodies representing the Russian Orthodox Church and other Christian sects appeared.[48] In the wake of three decades of repression, however, the Orthodox Church's postwar revival amongst laypeople was largely a rural and female phenomenon.[49]

The year 1954 marked the beginning of a new, vigorous campaign against religion under Nikita Khrushchev, a drive that fits with his efforts to modernize rural areas but contrasts with his relative liberalization of culture and political repression.⁵⁰ At the Twenty-Second Party Congress in 1960 and in years following, Khrushchev himself emphasized the importance of scientific-atheist education, calling for special attention to be given to children and adolescents.⁵¹ At the same time, authorities prohibited children from participating in or attending services altogether, a directive so contentious that it caused division among various Christian groups.⁵²

The post-Stalin Soviet view of children embraced a fully modern communist childhood, with the vast majority of children in school and in youth organizations by the late 1950s, infant/child mortality rates dropping rapidly, and a plethora of social services and child-centered institutions provided by the state. In part a revival of the "happy childhood" trope of the 1930s, minus the father-figure of Stalin, Soviet society, authorities, and culture essentially idealized children and childhood for the remainder of the Soviet era as a time of innocence and privilege. Children's happiness demonstrated Soviet power and commitment to world peace.

Official concerns about children and religion reflect this view. The Communist Youth League (or Komsomol) stoutly declared that "no parent should be allowed to cripple a child spiritually" as "freedom of conscience does not apply to children."⁵³ Khrushchev asserted the need to "protect children and adolescents from the influence of clergymen" while the Council of Religious Cults pledged to "guard against the influence of church people and sect members on youth and children."⁵⁴ Amended throughout the 1960s, Article 227 of the Russian Criminal Code made it a crime to run a group "whose activity, carried on under the guise of preaching religious beliefs and performing religious ceremonies, is connected with causing harm to citizens' health, or with any other infringement of the person or right of citizens, or with inducing citizens to refuse social activity or the performance of civic duties, or with drawing minors into such a group."⁵⁵ Thus, the law criminalized infant or child baptism (which was faulted for sickening or killing babies), prohibiting one's child from joining the Young Pioneers, or inviting a child to a church. The Fundamentals of Legislation of the USSR and Union Republics of Marriage and Family (or "Fundamentals") in 1968 allowed the state to remove children from unfit parents—those who were abusive, neglectful, immoral, antisocial, alcoholic, drug-addicted, in dissident religious sects, or who taught religion to their children.⁵⁶

A final wave of antireligious measures began in the late 1970s in response to factors including the end of détente, criticism from Pope John Paul II, and the Islamic Revolution in Iran. As in earlier years, children of believing families once again experienced persecution or loss of parents. Gorbachev ushered in a relaxation of antireligious policies, particularly in the years surrounding the millennial anniversary of Christianity in Russia, celebrated in 1988, which lasted until the fall of the Soviet Union.

Over the course of the Soviet era, authorities adhered to and generally achieved the establishment of a modern model of communist childhood, while overcoming many obstacles, some self-inflicted. For the most part, their views, policies, and practices on children and religion between 1917 and 1991 fit into their larger project: the creation of a Soviet childhood. Even a brief survey of children, childhood, and religion, such as is presented here, appears to indicate plenty of evidence of debate, policies, and actions in the antireligious campaigns specifically targeting and affecting children to warrant further investigation.

Gods and Grandmas

State authorities identified the family as a particular stumbling block to their efforts to create and mold New Soviet Children. While official policies and laws often identified ignorant parents and predatory priests as problematic, antireligious propagandists consistently pointed out the dangers of home and family. More specifically, propagandists targeted believing grandmothers.

A survey of antireligious propaganda posters, for example, reveals the regular use of images of *babushkas* in conjunction with images of children. Dmitri Moor's "Protect your children from the tenacious clutches of the Evangelical Baptist scoundrels" (1928) features two small Pioneers, a boy and a girl, all in red save for their black shoes and the boy's black hair in the center foreground. Surrounding them are seven ghostly old ladies in white, their skeletal hands reaching out in an attempt to clasp the children.[57]

In one of the most famous, N. B. Terpsikhorov's "Religion is Poison; Protect the Children" (1930), a black-clad elderly woman pulls the braid of a clearly distressed blond girl; while her gnarled finger points toward a dilapidated church in the back left, the child's open hands stretch out in opposition, toward a modern school building, complete with horn-blowing Pioneer and flying airplane to represent technological progress.[58]

Posters in the post-Stalin era depicted grandmas taking children to church, secretly teaching children the Gospel, baptizing babies under the nose of unobservant or indifferent parents, and preventing children from joining the Young Pioneers.[59] Trunev's "Sect" (1975) shows anthropomorphized fish being lured by the promise of a ticket to heaven on a giant fishhook. While one of the fish is an elderly man that wears vest and cap, three others are elderly, black-kerchiefed women; one of them clutches a tiny fish by the fin.[60]

Dmitri Moor, "Protect the children from the tenacious clutches of the Baptist and Evangelical scoundrels," *Bezbozhnik u stanka*, nos. 5–6 (1928). Image courtesy of Rubenstein Library, Duke University.

N. B. Terpsikhorov, "Religion is poison; save the children" (1930). Image courtesy of Poster Collection, Hoover Institution Archives, Stanford University.

I. V. Trunev, "Sect" (1975). Image courtesy of Keston Center for Religion, Politics, and Society, Baylor University.

While that grandmother acts out of gullibility, the elder in Travin's "You Cannot See God's Light" (1975) is less ignorant. She angrily pulls her grandson's arm, gesturing toward the icon with her other hand; her grandson leans away from her toward a well-lit window, gazing longingly at the Young Pioneer parade in the street.[61]

V. A. Travin, "You cannot see God's light" (1975). Image courtesy of Keston Center for Religion, Politics, and Society, Baylor University.

Clearly, propagandists were alarmed by what they viewed as grandma's negative influence on children. They were probably correct to be concerned. Plenty of anecdotal evidence and oral history supports the role of grandmothers in transmitting religious values to grandchildren, particularly in the postwar period.[62] They baptized grandchildren, sometimes without parents' knowledge or consent, told children stories based on religious tradition, or taught children prayers to say. And because many children recall having a special affection for their protective, good-hearted, forgiving grandmothers, any association with religion was all the more positive.[63]

Ironically, grandma's presence at home reflected realities about family structures, Soviet housing, and migration patterns. Extended families, especially couples with a young child living with one or two parents, were extremely common in the Soviet Union.[64] A survey of Muscovites born in the 1960s shows that one-third lived with a grandparent in early childhood and three-fourths had at least weekly contact with a grandparent.[65] This was the case in Central Asia, amongst Islamic households, as well.[66] This was due to a variety of factors, including housing shortages, a perennial problem in the

Soviet era.⁶⁷ During waves of migration from rural to urban areas, *babushka* came from the village to live with her children in the city, bringing her faith with her. Often this was because parents requested it. Despite Soviet authorities' intent to provide child care for all children, there simply were not enough spaces for them in state-run nurseries or preschools.⁶⁸ For a large percentage of working parents, bringing a grandmother in from the village to cook, shop, clean, and babysit was a good solution.⁶⁹

Thus, the state was in the unenviable position of having to vilify *babushka*, a useful, if not always beloved, member of the household and in the postwar era, most likely a war widow. Occasionally this resulted in sensational, headline-grabbing stories about child sacrifice and penitential murder, such as the woman accused of beating her grandson to death while in a fanatical religious state.⁷⁰ More frequently, however, propaganda depicted the grandmother figure as simply misguided and backward. Was this an effective tactic and why was it thought to be so? What was the effect on children of the well-documented feminization of Orthodoxy?⁷¹ To be sure, generational conflict long played a role in Soviet propaganda; sons educated in communist mores were expected to replace their fathers. Anecdotally, however, there seems to have been an exchange of sorts occurring between grandmothers and grandchildren in the home: children got to take care of their often illiterate elders, showing them how to navigate urban transportation, shopping, and entertainment, while grandmothers provided care and distraction at home.⁷² This reciprocity complicated the propagandistic message: perhaps grandma's lack of modernity confirmed what the state proclaimed about the backwardness of religion, but the generally positive affective association generated by grandparent-child relationships blunted the "danger" portrayed in antireligious propaganda. This relationship, and the meanings of female transmission of faith, both deserve further attention by scholars.

Antireligious propaganda exposes home and family as problematic for Soviet authorities. While the Soviet family was supposed to play a crucial role in socializing the socialist child, the campaigns against religion show that the family was not always a reliable partner in this task.⁷³ The state recognized this difficulty and blamed churches for exploiting the family for religious purposes.⁷⁴ In the mid-1960s, a Council for the Affairs of Religious Cults official in Turkmenistan went so far as to report that atheist school instruction mattered not at all in the face of family influence among Muslims.⁷⁵

Memoirs and oral histories are more mixed than this official's description. Some informants report of their families that "we were all atheists" while others remember the "everyday reality" of faith being played out at home rather than in public.⁷⁶ Many memories fall somewhere in between: "My upbringing wasn't atheist, it was just ordinary: no one in my friends' families celebrated religious holidays or went to church. If anything like that had gone on, it would have been laughed at."[77] The antireligious campaigns and reactions to them blurred the borders between public and private, the personal and the political—and children were in a pivotal position in the borderlands. Further exploration may help us better understand the limits and capabilities of Soviet policy and culture to affect children and childhood.

According to antireligious propaganda, religion and education stood in opposition to one another. Even more so than the family, the state envisioned the school as playing a key role in socializing children. This held true for antireligious/pro-atheist education as well. Lack of resources and personnel strained these efforts in the 1920s, but by the Khrushchev era, schools and their faculty became the faces of antireligious efforts for many children.

The Soviet Union never intended to eradicate values; instead, it meant to replace them. Khrushchev even arranged socialist values such as collectivism, discipline, sacrifice, honesty, and modesty into a moral code.[78] At various times in the Soviet era, teachers were asked not just to encourage socialist values and denigrate religion, but to teach atheism. Authorities expected these lessons to affect home life via children and faculty; in fact, teachers were sometimes dispatched to question or correct parents suspected of practicing religion. For children of believing families, this created a tension between home and school that could affect not only their school performance, but relationships at home as well. As Mikhail Men, son of Fr. Aleksandr Men, recalls of his early adolescent years, "It was very difficult both for my sister and me to study at school because there they taught one interpretation, and in our family we heard another."[79]

The methods by which teachers instructed children in these topics deserve to be studied further. A systematic review of children's literature, textbooks, science experiments, field trips, and toys used to teach atheism would help illuminate this subject.[80] Might the emphasis in school present an opportunity for children to confront a question of belief they may not have otherwise? Did teachers' encouragement to correct ignorant elders channel an inherent rebelliousness or hostility toward authority in appropriate ways? Or was it just confusing to children? After all, the same regime that asked children to question religious beliefs in the home prioritized an "orderly, tranquil private life [as] a fundamental requirement for the ideal citizen" in most other respects.[81] Discord at home, according to Khrushchev, only distracted from state-building goals.

Such instruction sometimes evolved into active persecution of believing students, though it is unclear why, how, and how often. Anecdotal evidence tells us that some students experienced ridicule from peers, shaming in wall newspapers, in-class humiliation by teachers, undeservedly poor grades, in-school interrogations from police—even teacher-sanctioned beatings by other students—while others escaped such cruelty.[82] The long-term effects of such persecution, on the accused child, on peers and other observers, and on instructors, are largely unknown. The relationship to the longstanding practice of self-criticism and a larger Soviet culture of denunciation merits exploration.[83]

Even the physical spaces of childhood were affected by the antireligious campaigns. Occasionally authorities converted churches into schools or Young Pioneer clubhouses. Moscow's historic Danilov Monastery was transformed into an NKVD reception center for children accused of crimes or removed from their parents.[84] How might children have interpreted this? Did state institutions or families acknowledge or ignore the shift? This aspect of landscape Sovietization deserves more attention.

Some of the most striking antireligious images, such as the Terpsikhorov and Travin posters, used light and dark as well as figure positioning to suggest faith and Soviet-ness as a dichotomous either/or choice.[85] In both images, the poster is visually divided in half, as grandma leans toward the dimly-lit past and child to the bright future. Undoubtedly, some people accepted the Soviet line that faith and modernity were incompatible.[86] For others, however, "either/or" images obscured lived experiences.

While sects such as Jehovah's Witnesses or Pentecostals could be portrayed as foreign, Orthodoxy could not. For many, then, to be Soviet and Orthodox was not necessarily contradictory, despite messages from the state.[87] Even the village church and village club could coexist without competing, with young people attending a church festival then a movie at the club.[88] As another example, families dealt with membership in the Young Pioneers in varying ways. While it is certain that some religious families prohibited their children from joining, evidence demonstrates that some believing children chose to join, with or without parental approval.[89] Interviewing Evangelical Christians in Siberia, April French encountered a mother who eventually recalled that oh yes, one of her daughters *had* been a Pioneer. "I paid no attention to it," she commented.[90] The ways in which children invested their associations with meaning and negotiated potential conflict at home and at school is worth further study. Adept at adaptation, many children learned to "speak Bolshevik" when needed and move smoothly between various worlds. Their unique position, at the crux of the state-family relationships, both necessitated and honed these skills.

Flexibility and adaptation could not always prevent suffering. Though antireligious propaganda suggested religion endangered children, being a part of a believing family placed children at risk of state persecution. Yet we know little about the children of clergy in the broader context of Soviet "enemies of the people." When clergy were disenfranchised, it meant they had no right to work, no state insurance, no pension, no medical care, no housing, no rations, and their children had no right to an education. They were portrayed in the press as vermin, reptiles, and dogs.[91] Vera Vorontsova, born in 1909 into an Orthodox clergy family, noted that in the early years of Soviet power, "I already sensed that people didn't treat us the way they treated other children. And the older I got, the more strongly I sensed this … That's the way it was."[92] In a 1932 letter to the Russian Red Cross from twelve siblings: "Maybe our father is being punished for being a priest, but what have we done? Why should children endure emotional pain and physical hardship? Use your authority to provide a little bit of joy on the 15th Anniversary of the Revolution. Show us that everything that's being written and said to refute the bourgeois lies is more than pretty words."[93]

The ways in which these children understood and coped with their experiences has been little explored. For example, did the longtime tradition of intermarriage among ROC clergy help or hurt these children? How did the "politics of forgetfulness" or a faith community's emphasis on holy suffering play a role in helping children survive? From the state's perspective, one might question the usefulness of this particular deviant childhood and the ways in which it was used to acknowledge differences in children's lives and legitimize the state's conceptions of childhood.

Lev Kopelev was born into a Jewish family in 1911 in Ukraine. Kopelev's Orthodox nanny secretly took little Lyova to church and taught him that his parents "belonged to the bad faith of the Yids." By 1923, at the age of twelve, he recalls having "lost God" altogether: he had never really believed in the Jewish God of his grandparents, but in the Orthodox God and then the Lutheran God of his successive nannies. As Kopelev approached the age of thirteen, his grandfather upped the ante, promising Lyova a bicycle if he would say one prayer at his upcoming bar mitzvah. Kopelev went back to his Young Pioneer troop, deeply conflicted about what to do, knowing that his instructions were to espouse atheism. The whole troop debated Lyova's predicament. Some of his friends urged him to say the prayer, take the bicycle, and use it for the revolution. Others advised him to be a hero and withstand cultic pressure. Sensing her son's distress, Kopelev's mother finally proposed that he be "sick" on his thirteenth birthday, and he complied. Having avoided the bar mitzvah and forfeited the bike, Kopelev reflected on his disappointment: he didn't feel much like a "valorous champion of atheism."[94]

One of the most important things that focusing on children and ideas of childhood can do is to remind us of the *many* possible responses to and perspectives on official policies and actions. The Soviet antireligious campaigns, meant to act upon children and shape their childhoods according to specific plans, also unleashed powerful opportunities for children to exert agency and created a distinctive space for family-state interaction in both public and private spheres. Further, they reveal the limits of state power to predict or fully control individual actions. Though debates about childhood are ongoing in the former Soviet Union, in this particular case, it seems that the Soviet state may have won several battles over seventy years, but God and Grandma won the war.

3

PERSECUTION, COLLUSION, AND LIBERATION

The Russian Orthodox Church,
from Stalin to Gorbachev

Michael Bourdeaux

Standing on the Nevskii Prospect in St. Petersburg today, you see immense changes in clear perspective. For the church in Russia, all has changed. If you stand with your back to the cathedral of Our Lady of Kazan you see why this great thoroughfare was once called the "Street of Tolerance." In view to the left is the restored Lutheran church—a swimming pool in communist days; to the right is the Roman Catholic Church of St. Catherine, also restored, but having been almost destroyed by fire in the early 1980s. Immediately ahead, your eye follows the straight line of a canal. Dominating it, in the middle distance, is the spectacular and multicolored "Church on the Blood," erected on the site where Tsar Alexander the Second was murdered in 1881.

When I first looked from this viewpoint in 1959 the churches were in ruins internally, even if their shapes stood bold against the fading grandeur of Leningrad's classical architecture. Despite the cataclysm of the overthrow of communism in 1991, however, religious tolerance is today by no means in universal supply. This essay takes us back into the communist period to look at the persecution of the 1950s and '60s, the rise of popular opposition to the policies of Nikita Khrushchev and the freeing of the church from its shackles under Mikhail Gorbachev.

Persecution, Propaganda, and the Beginnings of Dissent

If the outside of these churches was dilapidated fifty years ago, the insides had lost all appearance of a place of worship. The cathedral of Our Lady of Kazan, named after the icon which it once housed, had become a museum of the history of atheism and proclaimed itself to be the leading establishment of its kind in the whole of the Soviet Union. On my first visit, during the year that I spent in the Soviet Union as an exchange student (1959–1960), the choice illustrations of biblical errors printed large on the walls—and replacing the frescoes which had once adorned them—set out the ideology of the time. I noted down such statements as these:

> The ark Noah built could not have accommodated all the animals which then populated the earth, which disproves the legend of the flood. The biblical story about it served as a weapon against agitators and implanted an attitude of patience and submissiveness in the downtrodden masses.

> A whale's mouth is so constructed that it could not have let Jonah in, even if he could had lived three days inside the creature.

The culminating section, reached by descending a dark flight of stairs, was a chamber of horrors depicting the tortures of the Spanish Inquisition. It looked suspiciously as if the instruments were borrowed straight out of some local prison where they could have been in recent use. The whole exhibition was so near to farce that it looked almost like a parody of the anti-God movement.[1]

Some forty-four years later the BBC commissioned me to make a broadcast to mark the 300th anniversary of the founding of St. Petersburg (2003), which took me back inside the Cathedral of Our Lady of Kazan. This time, the clergy welcomed the Rev. Stephen Shipley, my BBC producer, and me with warmth and hospitality. In late April the cathedral was far from ready for the imminent arrival of world leaders, invited by President Putin to celebrate the anniversary. Carpenters still carved oak beams to hold the icons that would make up the iconostasis, replacing one that had been destroyed some seventy years earlier. Painters were still replacing frescoes on the walls and new icons were receiving their finishing touches.

The choir, however, was fully prepared and was put at our disposal for as long as we wished. The sound soon filled the vast spaces of this immense building. The deepest basses made the pillars reverberate, and the sound of spectacular sopranos flooded the domes. As we recorded them late at night to eliminate the sound of the passing traffic, my thoughts went back to the cathedral clergy who, in the early 1920s, were taken out on to the frozen River Neva and shot.

At the time of my first visit I knew little of this. The Iron Curtain erected by Stalin at the end of World War II had been effective in severing contacts between East and West. The Russia I first knew in 1959 was unvisited by tourists, except for a straggle of fellow travellers sponsored by Intourist. The few Western journalists in Moscow were mostly communists writing for such papers as the *Daily Worker* or *L'Humanite*. The BBC had no office in those days. The Soviet authorities prevented diplomats in the Western embassies from having any normal or regular contact with its own citizens.

I had learned Russian during my military service at the Joint Services School for Linguists' course at Cambridge, followed by five years at Oxford studying Russian, then theology. At the time of my arrival in Russia in September 1959 I was in almost total ignorance of the religious situation. It was common knowledge that Stalin had virtually eliminated the Orthodox Church in the 1930s, but that there had been a reversal of policy in the war years. It was assumed, on the basis of remarkably little evidence, that the improvement had continued during the postwar years. It had not. The Church's declaration of loyalty to the state remained the framework within which any religious activity must take place. Metropolitan Sergii had proclaimed on June 29, 1927: "Let us publicly express our gratitude to the Soviet Government for the interest it is showing in all the religious needs of the Orthodox.... We want to be Orthodox and at the same time to recognize the Soviet Union as our fatherland, whose joys and successes are our joys and successes and whose setbacks are our setbacks. Every attack directed again the USSR ... is resented as being directed against ourselves."[2]

Sergii's capitulation, bitterly contested by a group of bishops immured in the monastery-prison of Solovki in the Arctic Ocean as an act of "servility" and "hypocrisy," established the framework for a relationship of forced consent. Stalin's reaction was to treat the Orthodox Church as though Sergii's declaration had never been made and the letter from the Solovki bishops received no reply. The Law on Religious Associations of April 1929 claimed to guarantee separation of church and state while exercising complete control. Stalin was to make concessions during World War II and many of these contradicted the restrictions of the 1929 law.[3] It was here, for example, that the hated imposition of state registration of congregations was promulgated—but the legal title to all church property had been usurped by the state since Lenin's decree of January 1918. Any group of believers wishing to register must supply to the state a list of members—a virtual guarantee that there would be no applications.

Individual members can be removed from the executive body of the parish,[4] the state thus ignoring the constitutional principle of the separation of church and state. Religious education for children was banned (except in the family circle) and the churches were prevented from undertaking any charitable work whatsoever. *De facto* many religions and Christian denominations were outlawed—not only Jehovah's witnesses, but Roman Catholics (except for a single church in Moscow), and Lutherans and Methodists on Russian soil. This was never explicitly stated.

Stalin—a former theological student in his native Georgia—continued the physical destruction of the Russian Orthodoxy that Lenin had initiated. A particularly notorious example—but one among tens of thousands—was the reduction to rubble of the Cathedral of Christ the Savior in Moscow, an act recorded on film. After an abortive attempt to build the tallest skyscraper in Moscow, with a statue of Lenin on top, the site was transformed into a swimming pool, in response to Moscow's babushkas, who had declared that the desecrated ground was now accursed. By the start of the Second World War there were perhaps 100 churches open in the whole of the Soviet Union, no functioning dioceses or monasteries, no patriarch, no printed literature, no training for clergy. Nearly all clergy and key lay people were in prison or had suffered summary execution. A communist-sponsored attempt to establish a church sympathetic to the regime—the "Living Church" (*Obnovlentsy*) had failed, pleasing neither party ideologists nor the faithful.

Metropolitan Sergii had called for people to support the war effort as soon as disaster of June 1941 happened. Stalin summoned the four bishops remaining at liberty to the Kremlin in September 1943 and promised concessions. The Church could elect a patriarch. Nineteen bishops were found, some being freed from prison camps, to form a *sobor* (council) and they elected Sergii, who became the first to hold this office since the death—possibly murder—of Patriarch Tikhon on April 7, 1925. He survived only eight months, being replaced by Alexii I. A new administrative body emerged, the Moscow Patriarchate, which was under thumb of the Council for the Affairs of the Russian Orthodox Church. Clergy were released from the *Gulag* if they took an oath of loyalty. Clerical training was resumed, with the opening of two academies and eventually eight seminaries. The large number of parishes recorded for this period (perhaps 20,000) included large numbers in Western Ukraine and Belarus, which had not been within the boundaries of the Soviet Union prewar. There were also many in the Pskov region, where hundreds of churches had reopened under Nazi occupation. By 1947 there were seventy-four active bishops. A new publication began—the first Christian journal since 1917, but the *Journal of the Moscow Patriarchate* was little better than a propaganda tool.

A few hundred Bibles were printed, but these were mainly for presentation to foreign delegations. *The Russian Orthodox Church, Organization, Situation, Activity*, a substantial volume published in Moscow in 1958—in English, French, and other foreign languages—was pure propaganda, for distribution to visiting foreign delegations.

Indeed, far from enjoying independence from the state, the Church became an instrument of Soviet diplomacy. In the development of the Kremlin's foreign relations in vastly changed postwar Europe, clergy were invaluable as emissaries to Bulgaria, Romania, and—not least—to Estonia (where there was already an Orthodox Church). They could be used to pacify the local population and bring them around to a pro-Kremlin way of thinking. This was most important of all in the Western Ukraine, where the Greek-Catholic Church had been liquidated in 1946 and its properties taken over by the new Moscow Patriarchate. Russian clergy here could help stamp out the vestiges of Ukrainian nationalism in areas now part of the Soviet Union for the first time.

Most of this was unknown in the West. That the situation for Christians may have been worsening after Stalin's death was never contemplated. Soviet propaganda had done its work. Insofar as I was expecting anything when I first set foot in the Soviet Union, it was to see a church flourishing within limitations. Church delegations had gone back and forth after the death of Stalin and they were reported in Western media. There were several from the UK, including separate delegations of clergy and monks invited to Russia in 1956–1958. The propaganda purpose they served is clear, but this contact was also a huge breakthrough for a beleaguered church. By a strange coincidence, my arrival as a member of the first group of British exchange students in September 1959 was also during the precise month that religious persecution was renewed. There had been Communist Party resolutions calling for a resumption of the antireligious struggle, but this was virtually unknown even to the Soviet public at the time. Now the monthly *Nauka i religiia* (Science and religion) became the flagship of the new campaign—and I bought the first copy off a newsstand.

The Soviet papers soon became full of information on persecution, dressed up as an "ideological struggle" against religion. That the Soviets had unleashed a new campaign against religion was there in black and white for anyone to see, but this did not get through to the West, either to church leaders or to politicians, who continued to believe that all was improving. Was Khrushchev personally responsible for renewed persecution? L. F. Ilichov, his principal ideologist, wrote: "We cannot be complacent and expect that religion, as an anti-scientific ideology, will die by itself, without any effort or struggle. It is imperative to oppose religion *with militant, progressive scientific-atheistic propaganda.*"5

The papers were full of the confessions of priests with such titles as "Why I Broke with Religion." I heard former priest Aleksandr Osipov lecture in Leningrad in May 1960. Here was a man who had formerly enjoyed the highest regard among his students at the Leningrad Theological Academy as an Old Testament and Hebrew scholar, but who had betrayed them. At end of his lecture someone shouted from the back: "Judas received thirty pieces of silver: how much did you get?" Perhaps the Church under a new wave of persecution was beginning to find its voice. This would be the story of the next thirty years.

If one had to pick out a single event that both divided the Orthodox Church and energized the first generation of "dissidents," it would be the Synod of Bishops that convened on July 18, 1961. The essence of these proceedings was the removal of the parish priest from the executive body of the parish. This weakened the local structure to an unimaginable degree and left it open to the direct control of church affairs by the state. The Council for the Affairs of the Russian Orthodox Church appointed people to executive positions in the life of the parish. Sometimes these were atheists who did not even maintain the pretense of supporting Church. The result was the closure of perhaps all but two thousand (90 percent) of all churches, the vast majority of which had been reopened only some fifteen years previously, at the end of the war. All except three monasteries and three (of eight) theological seminaries suffered the same fate. Nikita Khrushchev was seen in the West as a liberalizer, a breath of fresh air after the closed postwar years. But his attitude to faith was uncompromising. He boasted that his grandchildren would see the last believing *babushka* visiting the Soviet Union's last open church.

This was particularly ironical, because the Kremlin was preparing its complaisant church leaders for a signal act: applying for membership of the World Council of Churches (WCC) in November 1961 at its General Assembly in New Delhi. During the height of the Cold War of the Stalin period, the leaders of the Russian Orthodox Church condemned the WCC along with all institutions in which America played any part. Yet in the slightly easier years after the death of Stalin in 1953, the Church put out tentative feelers toward believers in the rest of the world. The first official meeting with representatives of the WCC took place in 1958 in Utrecht. The leader of the Russian delegation was Metropolitan Nikolai (who had risen to the position of "foreign minister," being responsible for all external contacts of the Russian Church). Following this, Archpriest Vitalii Borovoi and his "interpreter" (or KGB minder) spent a month in Geneva at the WCC headquarters in the summer of 1959 and attended the meeting of the Central Committee on the island of Rhodes in August that year. Metropolitan Nikolai joined them and made a rousing speech supporting the cause of Christian unity. From here on, an application for membership was but a logical progression.

At this point I ventured briefly on the ecumenical scene—for the first and only time in the context of direct relations. A small WCC delegation visited Moscow in the autumn of 1959. I was invited to meet its leader, an English priest, Fr. Francis House. We developed a relationship which was to last, but whatever report he sent back to Geneva was not well received. Although I was better placed than most to know the situation on the ground in the Soviet Union, my verbal report to Fr. House on the menace of developing persecution was ignored in Geneva. I was never again consulted on any of these issues.[6]

Events moved rapidly toward the Third General Assembly of the WCC in New Delhi—but when the meeting took place, Metropolitan Nikolai was not there to head the Russian Orthodox delegation. Business was concluded and Russian membership agreed by the end of the congress on December 6. But Nikolai died just a week later, in circumstances that have never been explained. No documents have emerged in the new Russia to illuminate whether the KGB had a hand in his death. What is certain, though, is that at his funeral some voices were heard to cry out, "Murderers!"

Now Metropolitan Nikodim entered abruptly on the scene and was to dominate international church relations for the best part of the next two decades. One of his first acts was to state at a press conference in New Delhi: "The church is completely free from State interference, and it is necessary to say that we are quite independent in our inner life. Therefore it is not possible to speak of State approval or disapproval of our church's action in joining the WCC." So the Soviet Union carried off one of its greatest propaganda coups. The indisputable fact is that, at this very time, the iron hand of persecution was tightening its grip. The New Delhi initiative had blinded the world to a new reality—and anyone who proclaimed the truth (inside the Soviet Union or in the world at large) was to be branded a traitor to the cause of support for the Russian Orthodox Church.

Opposition was limited but significant. In the Soviet press, during the Thaw period of 1956–1958 and very occasionally afterwards, there appeared an article criticizing the destruction of "cultural monuments" (Soviet-speak for churches). For example, the widely read *Literaturnaia gazeta* (Literary newspaper) printed an article entitled "In Defense of Cultural Monuments." The text was astonishing—and unique, in that no similar voice was to be raised for the rest of the decade: "On 2 June this year the sound of an explosion was heard at Ufa. The dumbfounded inhabitants gazed and saw how the Smolensk Cathedral, a most valuable historical and architectural monument, tottered, collapsed and turned into a pile of stones. It had been destroyed despite the protest of the Academy of Sciences and the Ministry of Culture of the USSR."[7]

This voice could be raised because the destruction had gone against official policy. It would be several years before any murmur of independent dissent was heard. For the average Russian, with no access to any (what later came to be known as) dissident circles, the first indication that some breath of opposition was stirring on the religious front came with the publication of Alexander Solzhenitsyn's *One Day in the Life of Ivan Denisovich* in November 1962. In truth, though, the impact of the book was so stunning that few picked out the positive passages about religion as extraordinary. The prisoner, Ivan Denisovich, found himself in a bunk adjacent to a Baptist, Alyosha, imprisoned for his faith. Alyosha said to Ivan Denisovich: "If you suffer, it must not be for murder, theft or sorcery, nor for infringing the rights of others. But if anyone suffers as a Christian, he should feel it no disgrace, but confess that name to the honor of God."[8] Never before had anything so positive about religion been published in the Soviet Union.

Before further publication of his work was banned, Solzhenitsyn produced a short book of essays, which he called *Prose Poems* (1963). One of these, "Along the Oka," was an impassioned plea against the destruction of Russia's religious heritage:

> When you travel the by-roads of Central Russia you begin to understand the secret of the pacifying Russian countryside. It is in the churches ... Our forefathers put all that was finest in themselves, all their understanding of life into these stones, into these bell-towers.[9] Creeping up to the door of the desecrated church, the author prizes open the door: "Ram it in, Vitka, give it a bash, don't be afraid! Film-show at six, dancing at eight o'clock."

The persecution was growing in intensity after the bishops had caved in at the 1961 Synod of Bishops. The leading voice in opposition was that of Archbishop Ermogen of Kaluga, who had an impressive record in Tashkent, to which diocese he had originally been consecrated. His stance, though, was virtually unknown at the time. The *Journal of the Moscow Patriarchate* announced his "retirement" in November 1965, but stated that he had been "released from administration of the Kaluga diocese in accordance with his request."[10]

Behind this, of course, loomed the sinister hand of the state. As Archbishop Ermogen later made plain his letter to the patriarch: "The real reason for placing me on the 'retired list', as is well known to Your Holiness and the Synod, was a demand by V.A. Kuroyedov, Chairman of the Council on Religious Affairs [CRA]."[11] Archbishop Ermogen had, apparently, been promised another diocese after a short time out of the limelight, but this had not happened. The "crime" of which he had been accused was his opposition both to the resolutions of the 1961 Synod of Bishops and to the manner in which it had been convened. Now, too, he was protesting in the strongest possible way the intervention of the state in church affairs: "As for the chairman of the CRA, by virtue of the very same principle of separation of church and state, he cannot, without running the risk of discrediting this very principle, have the right to any active intervention in episcopal appointments."[12] Archbishop Ermogen would never emerge from his enforced retirement and he died without being reinstated.

To this day, more than twenty years after the collapse of communism, the Moscow Patriarchate has not publicly investigated any of the grave injustices that it endured in silence during the years of oppression. When it does investigate the reasons for its silence—if ever it does—Archbishop Ermogen, who built a cathedral in Tashkent in the face of opposition, will be seen to have raised an even greater monument: the moral one of organized opposition to communist persecution. He led the way for the emergence of the two who are often perceived as the founding fathers of opposition in the Russian Orthodox Church, Fathers Nikolai Eshliman and Gleb Iakunin.

Stagnation and Resistance: Twenty Years under Leonid Brezhnev and His Successors (1965-1985)

I went to Moscow in August 1964 to try to verify information about the increasing pressure on the faithful that Professor Nicolas Zernov of Oxford University had supplied to me. This was a series of documents written by a group of lay Orthodox believers from Pochaev, the site of a great and still-open monastery. The resident monks were being brutally oppressed. On my first evening I asked some friends whether this type of persecution had affected Moscow. Their reply was to send me to the Church of St. Peter and St. Paul. There was nothing visible in the middle of the square except a pile of rubble surrounded by a hastily erected wooden fence. Two old women were peering through a gap between the slats. I asked them what they could tell me about this catastrophe. They asked me to follow them and when we could finally talk in private they told me who they were: the very people who had written the documents Professor Zernov had sent me. On a previous visit to Moscow they had found a foreign lady, a French schoolteacher, who had smuggled them out. This was the first confirmation they had had that the documents had reached the West. Now they had new texts about the imminent threat of closure of the monastery, which they entrusted to me.

The resulting publicity may have been a factor in preventing the closure of the Pochaev Monastery.[13] Khrushchev's fall November in 1964 also seemed to inhibit the persecution—the new Brezhnev regime not wishing to take any untoward action before it was confident that its seizure of power would be permanent. In fact, persecution was to continue against individuals, although the closure of churches discontinued, except in individual instances.

Orthodox believers began to express outrage at the new persecution of the Church but no one was prepared for the open letters of December 1965 from Frs. Nikolai Eshliman and Gleb Iakunin. There were two—the first to Patriarch Alexii I, dated November 21, the second to Nikolai Podgornyi (chairman of the Presidium),[14] dated December 15; Naturally, they differed in presentation, but the substance was similar. These two letters are probably the most important texts on church-state relations ever to come out of the Soviet Union.

The introduction to the earlier text, addressed by faithful young clergy to the head of their church, contains the following words: "It is clear that the Russian Church is seriously and dangerously ill, and that her sickness has come about entirely because the ecclesiastical authorities have shirked from fulfilling their duties."[15] In the West some accused the young clerics of writing to the "wrong address," but these critics could not have been more mistaken, because a second and fuller letter followed less than a month later, addressed to no less than Podgornyi himself: "We, as citizens of the Soviet Union, address you with a protest against illegal actions of the leaders and representatives of the Council for Russian Orthodox Church Affairs.... These actions have flagrantly violated the principle of socialist law."[16] Under Khrushchev, the text continued, this Council (CROCA) "radically changed its function"—from being an instrument of arbitration it became one of illegal control over the actions of the Moscow Patriarchate.

Both documents adopt a legal framework, proclaiming Lenin's theoretical principle of the separation of church and state and the illegitimacy of state control of church affairs. They back up their assertions with a wealth of concrete detail gathered from their experience as clergy in two different Moscow churches. It has been claimed that this legal approach was an innovation, but that is not strictly true. Most specifically, the leadership of what has been called the "Reform Group" of Russian Baptists (*Initsiativniki*) sent a letter to Leonid Brezhnev, in his capacity as president of the Committee on the Soviet

Constitution, dated April 14, 1965.[17] The approach—concentrating on the illegality of the persecution—was almost identical to that of Frs. Eshliman and Iakunin. In retrospect, these two initiatives of 1965 form a key moment in the emergence of a civic consciousness, one of the roots of what would eventually become the democratic movement and be a factor in the destabilizing of the Soviet Union itself.

In the letter to Podgornyi the two priests raise such issues as CROCA's new practice of removing not only lay people from church councils, but also clergy from their parishes—always done without the presentation of any legal document. This weakening of the local structure had led to the mass closure of churches and monasteries. During Khrushchev's time in office, they continue: "No less than ten thousand churches and dozens of monasteries were closed, among which, most prominently, was the Monastery of the Caves at Kiev, the most ancient sacred place of the Russian people."[18]

Many other complaints follow, under eight headings in all. The document concludes with a basic challenge. The very existence of CROCA, the authors say, is illegal: "In 1959 and 1965 two collections of party and state documents on religion were published. In neither one is any mention made of CROCA."[19] Nor is there any teaching about current legislation in the theological seminaries. The appeal concludes with a plea that all these illegalities should be reversed.

The letter to the patriarch had covered more or less the same ground, but focusing on more detailed facts about the church's pastoral work. For example, baptisms had to be registered with the state—but there is no legal justification for this. The church authorities have simply caved in to these demands:

> The illegal registration of church ceremonies is undermining the trust of the people in the Mother Church and is a serious stumbling block for those who wish baptism for themselves or for their children. By actively permitting this illegal practice, the Moscow Patriarchate is taking upon itself a most serious sin, by giving rise to spiritual temptation and by turning human souls away from salutary grace.[20]

The next section gives far more details of the illegal closure of churches and theological seminaries than later appeared in the letter to the government. The shepherds had failed to lay down their lives for the sheep:

> A flood of complaints and protests, signed by thousands of Orthodox, swamped the diocesan bishops and the administration of the Moscow Patriarchate. Hundreds of plaintiffs filled the chancelleries of the ruling bishops during those days. Messengers from suffering parishes and monasteries came thousands of

kilometers to Moscow, in search of protection and support from the Holy Patriarch. Alas, these hopes were in vain![21]

The key conclusion is a call for a meeting of a new Synod of Bishops to rescind the uncanonical decisions of 1961, where all these woes began.

The outcome of the priests' initiative was predictable, though the tactics were especially nefarious. The authorities pressed the Moscow Patriarchate to discipline the two. After several exchanges of correspondence, Metropolitan Pimen of Krutitsy and Kolomna (later to be patriarch) removed both from their parishes in a letter dated May 13, 1966, and imposed silence upon them.[22] This led to a ban that lasted ten years. Fr. Nikolai Eshliman never resumed active ministry or human rights work after this, but Fr. Gleb Iakunin was to reemerge, breaking his silence precisely upon the expiry of his ban. That he had kept it to the letter is an extraordinary testimony to his seriousness of purpose and loyalty to his ecclesiastical superiors. We shall hear more of him.

The voice of the two priests may have been silenced for a decade, but they had opened the floodgates to an extraordinary twenty years during which the persecuted Orthodox Church found its feet. Furthermore, these letters opened the sleepy eyes of millions of well-wishers in the world outside—from New Zealand to New York—who could never quite believe again with such unquestioning naivety the assertions of the Orthodox leaders at international gatherings that there was no persecution of the Russian Church.

The Moscow Patriarch has never, despite freedom to do so over the past twenty years, permitted any open discussion of the issues raised by the two priests. The decisions of the Holy Synod of 1961, though no longer relevant, were never debated; no fault was admitted, except by implication when Metropolitan (now Patriarch) Kirill introduced the proposal for new *ustav* (regulations) in 1988; nor was there ever a word of reconciliation or understanding for Fr. Gleb Iakunin. His name continues to attract bitter criticism, his reward for an initiative of unprecedented bravery and integrity. Unheeded though it was by officialdom and unheard by millions of the faithful, the church had found its voice.

It is possible that the concerted defense of the church by Frs. Eshliman and Iakunin (as well as Archbishop Ermogen) was instrumental in restraining the state from continuing these attacks against the very fabric of the church. The fact is that they did stop soon after the fall of Khrushchev and the Brezhnev era was marked by a stasis in church-state relations. A new *status quo* emerged, during which the church, guided by the young Metropolitan Nikodim, made swathes of new contacts in the ecumenical field, not least in the Vatican.

Mikhail Gorbachev was later to dub the Brezhnev period as one of *zastoi* (stagnation) in many aspects of life, though of course he did not mention church-state relations. This was the time when a "dissident" movement clearly emerged, the beginning of which was marked by the trial of Andrei Siniavskii and Iulii Daniel in 1966 for sending their novels abroad for publication (not in fact a crime under Soviet law). It was a remarkable period in the life of the Russian Orthodox Church. Dozens of figures broke their silence. Religious *samizdat* became a subject of endless fascination, both to those whom it reached inside the Soviet Union and to the outside commentator. The authors were mainly, but not exclusively, lay people. The names of Anatolii Levitin, Vladimir Poresh, Aleksandr Ogorodnikov, Zoia Krakhmalnikova, Boris Talantov, and Vadim Shavrov are just a few. They were joined by priests such as Frs. Dmitrii Dudko, Pavel Adelheim, and Vsevolod Shpiller. Other clergy kept their heads down, concentrating on a teaching and preaching ministry, rather than on writing *samizdat* on church-state relations. The prime example was Fr. Aleksandr Men. It is impossible either to summarize their achievements or to describe their work in chronological order, so rich was the flood of their inspiration.

One of the earliest was Anatolii Levitin, born in 1915, who had been a deacon in the "Living Church."[23] Like others (Frs. Pavel Adelheim and Aleksandr Men, for example) he was of Jewish stock, but became a Christian in the family of his converted parents. During World War II he was in Ulianovsk, where Metropolitan Vvedenskii secretly ordained him as a deacon. He joined the mainstream as a layman in 1949 and was sentenced to ten years in 1949 for bringing Christianity into the classroom. He served only seven years before being rehabilitated by the decree of the Twentieth Congress of the Communist Party of the Soviet Union (CPSU) in 1956. He returned to teaching, but concentrated on writing, using the pseudonym A. Krasnov to publish no fewer than forty articles in the *Journal of the Moscow Patriarchate*. He wrote a short unpublished autobiography in 1966 and became a polemicist, writing a long defense of the faith ("Degeneration of Atheist Thought") against the various charges printed in *Nauka i religiia*.[24] In October 1966 this journal published a long indictment of his activities, but for the time being he remained at liberty..[25]

Central to Levitin's ministry was his work with young people. In an important article of 1979, he suggested that a revival was underway among them:

> Young people today in the USSR are being drawn to religion. Why is this? General disillusionment with Marxism-Leninism is one important factor. The infallibility of Soviet ideology received a fatal blow in 1956 when Stalin was

> dethroned. Now young people no longer take it seriously, so there is an ideological vacuum. How is this usually filled? Mostly, sad to say, with alcohol.... Young intellectuals in the towns find their way to religion through conscious and prolonged searching, whereas workers and peasants in the provinces are drawn to faith because of an elemental impulse, which comes from the subconscious and is inspired. The urban intellectual youth usually join the Orthodox Church, but in the provinces young people usually turn to one of the many different religious sects which exist outside the Orthodox Church.[26]

Levitin emigrated, under KGB pressure, to Switzerland, where he died, run over by a car. But his role within a minor Christian renaissance of the late twentieth century should not be forgotten.

To illustrate what Levitin said about the Christian revival among young urban intellectuals, the best example is that of Vladimir Poresh, Aleksandr Ogorodnikov and the Christian Seminar they founded. Tatiana Shchipkova, Poresh's French teacher in 1966, describes him at the age of seventeen—a young man searching for something he could not find.[27] His conversion was still seven years away. In 1973 Poresh came to find Shchipkova in Smolensk. He said: "I've found a new phase in my life. I've got to know someone called Sasha Ogorodnikov. We've decided to create a culture within a culture."[28] By this he meant a philosophical discussion group within the framework of the Orthodox faith. His baptism followed in October 1974. He was then twenty-five and he and Ogorodnikov began working on the *samizdat* journal *Obshchina* (Community), soon to be suppressed by the KGB. Ogorodnikov was working as a janitor in a Moscow tuberculosis clinic. The shed outside it—not designed to be lived in—became Sasha's home and also the meeting place for this small, innocuous "seminar": "The door of that house was open to all and anyone could take part and speak. Newcomers were struck by the variety there: they might meet old men or sixteen-year-old hippies, scholars or speculators."[29]

Innocuous as it may have seemed, Vladimir Poresh was arrested on August 1, 1979. His sentence was five years of strict-regime prison camp, followed by three years of exile. Ogorodnikov was also arrested and sentenced. This enterprise was doomed from the moment of its inception, but these young men had illustrated the bankruptcy of Marxism-Leninism for many of their generation. Both are still active laymen, Poresh in St. Petersburg and Ogorodnikov in Moscow.

Fr. Dmitrii Dudko was a very different figure, a "dissident" priest who had immense influence, suffered imprisonment, and then recanted on television. Incarcerated in January 1980 as one of Russia's bravest dissidents, who upheld the honor of the Russian Orthodox Church, he appeared on Soviet television on June 20 to renounce his activities. The twenty-minute interview was subsequently reported *verbatim* in nearly every Soviet newspaper. The KGB had clearly prepared this event as a decisive measure, not only against the "anti-Soviet" activities of Moscow proto-democrats, but also against any residual independence within the Russian Orthodox Church itself.

Fr. Dmitrii Dudko had had an immense influence on literally thousands of would-be neophytes who flocked to his sermons. These had latterly taken on the form of "conversations" in which he answered questions put to him by his Moscow congregation, first in writing, but later in direct dialogue. Often it was impossible even to find space inside the church and people crowded outside the open doors, hoping to hear even the merest snatch of his spoken words. These sermons, reconstructed from notes, circulated in *samizdat*, appeared in French in 1975, in English as *Our Hope* two years later, and in eight other languages. No priest living in Russia in modern times—except Fr. Aleksandr Men, who was murdered in 1990—had more influence inside or outside the country. It was Fr. Dmitrii who baptized Aleksandr Ogorodnikov, who brought some of the priest's ideas into the Christian Seminar. The ringleaders of this group were themselves all in prison by the time of his arrest in 1980. The KGB thrust copies of Fr. Dmitrii's recantation under their noses.

Dudko was born into a poor peasant family in the village of Zarbuda, Briansk region, in 1922. He embraced the Christian faith through finding a copy of the Bible when all the churches in his region were closed. He lived under Nazi occupation from 1941–1943, when a few churches reopened. After liberation he served in the Soviet army, being arrested in 1948 for writing a poem criticizing the destruction of Russia's holy places and serving eight and a half years before release under the post-Stalin amnesty. As an ex-political prisoner, he was accepted only with difficulty as a theological student at the Moscow seminary (Zagorsk) that had opened after World War II. The KGB kept a careful watch on him from this time on. Perhaps they even allowed his sermons of 1973 to continue only as a provocation to draw out his latent attitudes toward the regime. He was also the victim of pressure from the church. The weak Patriarch Pimen, the successor of Alexii I, bowing to the KGB, demanded to know why Fr. Dmitrii was acting so unconventionally and ordered him to stop. Always dutiful and respectful toward church authority, he conducted further sessions in the public "privacy" of his home.

In 1975 he was visiting his mother in his home village. It was a day of perfect visibility and he was being driven on a clear road, when a truck, appearing out of the blue, hit his car. The accident was almost certainly the work of the KGB, but he recovered from two broken legs to resume his work as an assistant priest at Grebnevo, twenty miles from Moscow. Even though he had deliberately sought to lower his own profile, a new press campaign against him began in 1977. Fr. Dmitrii once stated that no week of his life had ever gone by without some interference or pressure by the Soviet authorities. It seems that this was already grinding him down before his arrest and the KGB, monitoring him closely, chose its moment carefully. After his recantation, in the Gorbachev era his influence was virtually nil. He still wrote voluminously, not least as the "spiritual adviser" to the hard-line nationalist newspaper *Zavtra* (Tomorrow), but the great fire that had burned in him seemed to have been extinguished. He died in 2004.

By the time that Fr. Gleb was released from the imposition of silence in 1975, much had changed. The Helsinki Accords had been signed that year, committing the Soviet Union, along with other signatory states, to the monitoring of each others' human rights record. And in November 1975 the Fifth General Assembly of the World Council of Churches took place in Nairobi, Kenya—another hugely significant event for persecuted Christians in the USSR. Although religious liberty and human rights in the Soviet Union found no place on the official agenda, the issue was forced when a Kenyan newspaper published an "Appeal to the Delegates of the Fifth Assembly of the World Council of Churches." It had been written by Fr. Gleb Iakunin and a layman, Lev Regelson, a respected physicist. It was a long and passionate statement, begging for ecumenical help for persecuted believers and presenting a practical plan of action.[30]

The response from the delegates of the Moscow Patriarchate was swift and sure-footed in the misinformation it presented.[31] After questioning the credentials of the authors, the metropolitan made no attempt to respond to the substance of the letter, but emphasized "the ever-increasing development of democratic principles" in the USSR, which gave "great hope" for the future. Whether or not there would be any formal discussion of these issues, which everyone was discussing behind the scenes, remained an open question until two days before the end of the Assembly, when there would be a debate on the Helsinki Accords that had been signed earlier in the year and that included provision for the monitoring of human rights within the confines of the nations that had assented to them.

A Swiss delegate, Dr. Jacques Rossel, proposed an addition to the proposal for that debate: "The WCC is concerned about restrictions to religious liberty, particularly in the USSR."[32] The Rev. (subsequently bishop) Richard Holloway of the Episcopal Church of Scotland seconded the motion, and, in an atmosphere of great tension the Soviet delegation opposed it. The proposal was put to the vote and carried on a show of hands by a huge majority—the only time in the history of the WCC that there has ever been such a resolution. The chairman of the session was the British Baptist leader, Dr. Ernest Payne, who then adjourned the session for a "tea interval." He came back to claim to the Assembly that the motion had been out of order and that it should be referred back to the Resolutions Committee. Out of this came a substitute motion, which now referred to "alleged infringements of religious liberty," but which excluded any reference to the Soviet Union. It was a frail compromise but the issue had been raised in a vital forum.[33]

Fr. Gleb's follow-up was to gather massive documentation on persecution of all religious groups under the banner of the Christian Committee for the Defense of Believers' Rights (CCDBR). His prodigious energy led him to collect, over the next three years, no fewer than 423 documents, totaling 1302 pages from all denominations.[34] Fr. Gleb managed to send most of these documents abroad and many of them opened up new perspectives on persecution of religion during the period of Brezhnev's so-called "stagnation." There was *samizdat* supporting Baptists, Pentecostals, Adventists, and Catholics, as well as Jews. The enterprise may be considered one of the outstanding ecumenical activities of the twentieth century. A businessman from San Francisco, Henry Dakin, later financed the publication of some of these documents in translation, others in summary, a significant contribution to the growing worldwide awareness of religious persecution in the Soviet Union. The Moscow Patriarchate was now under pressure to demonstrate conformity with the Helsinki obligations, and the WCC was finally apprised of the difference between what was said about religious freedom in the Soviet Union and what was actually happening.

For the first time I was summoned to Geneva for a consultation in March 1976. So secret was the meeting that we convened, not at the headquarters of the WCC, but at the railway station (whence, admittedly, we crossed the road to the nearest hotel). Also present was Pastor Eugen Voss, of Glaube in der 2 Welt Institute (Zurich) and Professor Hans Hebly, of the Inter-Academic Institute for Missiological and Ecumenical Research (Utrecht). The substance of the consultation would soon go on record, because the WCC was secretly asking for documentation, but it would be attributed to the "trinity" of institutes and not to the WCC. There was little time to compile this, because the consultation at which the documentation must be presented was scheduled for July 24–28 in Montreux, Switzerland. But we managed to fulfill our task and the resulting documentation was one of Keston's most influential publications.[35] Its hundred pages could hardly be comprehensive, given the time constraint, but it did present a panorama, while focusing on the last decade. An essay by Hans Hebly illustrated how great was the WCC's concern for religious liberty in earlier days and how that ideal had faded. Also available for the Montreux meeting was the much more comprehensive record, *Discretion and Valour*, which covered all the relevant countries of Europe, and which the British Council of Churches had sponsored in reaction to these momentous events.

However, the meeting suffered grievously from not calling directly on the expertise of the authors. The WCC sidestepped the issues. The Central Committee of the WCC did set up a Human Rights Advisory Group and resolved to strengthen the work of the Churches Commission on International Affairs (CCIA), a body formally independent of the WCC, but with premises in the same Geneva building. The Advisory Group's recommendations led to the recruiting of a Swiss pastor, Dr. Theo Tschuy, whose main working experience had been in South America. But instead of an honest or realistic examination of the situation, an astonishing document appeared, *Human Rights on the Ecumenical Agenda*, by Erich Weingärtner, an employee of the CCIA. The publication could have been penned, not in the Moscow Patriarchate, but in the offices of the Soviet Council for Religious Affairs.

In no less than six separate passages Weingärtner implied that there was something dishonorable in the motivation of those in the West who defended religious liberty and human rights in Eastern Europe. Their accusations boiled down to politics. "Communism," he asserted, "has guaranteed employment, food, shelter, education, medical care and social security. ... Soviet society is evolving in the direction of an extension of democratic principles."[36] Such was the voice of a pro-Soviet advocate speaking from within the structure of the ecumenical movement at a time fraught with tension. It is not surprising that the Sixth General Assembly of the World Council of Churches closed off further discussion of human rights and religious liberty. The next assembly at Vancouver (1981) was a door closed. Meanwhile Fr. Gleb Iakunin, arrested in 1979, was to languish in prison for eight years. All the visible signs were that the Christian dissident movement had been broken by the power of the KGB. It had not.

Liberation: Mikhail Gorbachev (1985–1991)

Rome had its "year of the three popes" (1978) and the Kremlin was to experience something similar with the deaths closely following one another of Yuri Andropov and Konstantin Chernenko, followed by the immediate accession of Mikhail Gorbachev as chairman of the Central Committee of the CPSU in 1985. Gorbachev did not make immediate changes, but there was one sign that something might change in the field of human rights. Anatolii Shcharanskii, the Jewish activist, was the highest-profile political prisoner in Russia for more than a decade from 1975. On February 11, 1986, he walked free after eleven years of incarceration. Communist Party officials continued to talk about the "resolute struggle" against religion, but Gorbachev himself kept silence on the subject for almost a year, until at the Twenty-Seventh Party Congress on February 25, 1986, he made a pronouncement that was far from being sharp-edged or clear: "It is inadmissible to depict in idyllic terms reactionary, national and religious survivals contrary to our ideology".[37] It was a weak utterance of a jaded orthodoxy—and the last time he would speak in such terms.

My theory, which Gorbachev himself has never refuted, is that the Chernobyl disaster of April 1986 profoundly shook him and persuaded him to reconsider his relationship to humanity. This occurred in early April. A week of shock and silence followed, but then a new man emerged. Any discussion of the environment had been virtually treasonable in Soviet times, being taken as a criticism of the political system itself. This was now to change. Gorbachev would soon recall the nuclear physicist, Andrei Sakharov, to Moscow from his enforced exile in Gorky. For many years he had campaigned for a moratorium on the development of atomic weapons. Now the use of nuclear energy could be openly debated and it was no longer to be considered a panacea for the human race.

Later that year there was to be the next in a series of summits between Gorbachev and President Reagan. The Reykjavik meeting was designated for October 10, 1986. On such occasions there was always a hiatus while the two chief participants were on their way to the meeting. On this occasion Gorbachev chose that morning as the time the news would come out on the release of Irina Ratushinskaia, a Christian poet who had become the highest-profile imprisoned dissident following the release of Anatolii Shcharanskii. She had committed no crime, but was apparently condemned for writing Christian poetry. In prison she had suffered terribly and there were fears for her life. Therefore the news of her release was greeted with joy around the world, but it was also a clever propaganda coup by Gorbachev, indicating that human rights were now on his agenda. The release of most other religious and political prisoners followed in a steady stream in 1987. This included Fr. Gleb Iakunin, but, significantly, not the leaders of the Lithuanian Catholic Church. This indicates that the age of *glasnost* (openness) and *perestroika* was not yet ready to encompass a new deal for the republics of the Soviet Union. The Baltic States and Ukraine would have to take their own initiatives on the path toward greater autonomy and eventual independence.

There was already a feeling in the air, though, that a new era for the Church was becoming a reality. The demand for change was significantly passing from dissidents to the official church—and soon to Gorbachev himself. Nineteen eighty-eight was a year of cataclysmic developments. This was the thousand-year anniversary of the baptism of Rus' and the first year there could have been a celebration on anything like the scale that was soon to be envisaged. On April 29, 1988 (fifty-nine years to the day after Stalin's devastating legislation of 1929), Gorbachev received Patriarch Pimen and the senior bishops in the Kremlin, the first and only such meeting since September 4, 1943. In a long, statesman-like speech, he said: "Mistakes were made in relations with the church and believers in the 1930s and subsequently: these are being rectified. ... Believers are Soviet people, workers, patriots, and they have the full right to express their convictions with dignity. *Perestroika, demokratizatsiia [democratization]* and *glasnost* concern them as well—in full measure and without restrictions. This is especially true of ethics and morals, a domain where universal norms and customs are so helpful for our common cause."[38]

Our common cause? No communist leader in power had ever before used such words, but they would become the basis of official policy over the next three years, though Gorbachev fell from power before their full outworking could be implemented. At the same time he promised new legislation on religion and he kept his word. This was promulgated in September 1990, overturning Stalin's legislation, still theoretically operative, and replacing it by a set of laws that guaranteed complete freedom of religion, including the right to teach it in schools.

Patriarch Pimen's reply, according to observers, put more emphasis on *perestroika* than on God. Monasteries and churches were already reopening in many parts of the Soviet Union, but, curiously, Pimen thanked the Council for Religious Affairs for this, even though it was this body that had sanctioned the most recent destruction and desecration of church property.

It was not long before the great change could be seen by the world. President Reagan visited Moscow in May 1988 for another summit. The world's cameras dogged his footsteps and showed him meeting Christian and Jewish activists, many of whom had been in prison until recently. Then he visited the Danilov Monastery, scene of a weird and checkered history. Formerly it had been a boys' prison, the defensive monastic walls providing a ready barrier against escape. Strangely, it had been returned to the Church under Andropov, a favor that seems out of place at that time and that has never been explained. Now it was being prepared for the millennium celebrations and a magnificent restoration was well underway.

For the Church internally the key event of these celebrations was the holding of a *sobor* that preceded the international celebrations, unusual in that it was not convened to elect a new patriarch. The key item of business was the acceptance of Metropolitan Kirill's *ustav*, the draft new internal regulations over which he had toiled for so many years in Smolensk. This was the first time since the *sobor* of 1917, which met as the guns of the Revolution were firing, that the church had been able to hold a free discussion about anything. It was a momentous event. Every diocese—abroad and in Russia—sent three representatives: the diocesan bishop, a priest, and a layman. Metropolitan Antony Bloom, head of the diocese of "Sourozh" (Western Europe and the United Kingdom) was a key delegate, enjoying as he did a huge reputation inside Russia as a spiritual authority. This he had gained through his frequent broadcasts on the airwaves of the BBC Russian Service. Accompanying him were Archpriest Sergei Hackel and Professor Dmitri Obolensky, the respected historian from Oxford. When asked about his most surprising experience, Obolensky replied that it was the moment when the hall shook with laughter, something which had never before happened in the Soviet period.

While the *sobor* did not take up the issue of the "modern martyrs," the victims of communism, the press was now full of accounts of Stalin's crimes, so the subject was not far from anyone's mind. Metropolitan Iuvenalii of Krutitsy and Kolomna (the bishop of Moscow) said in another context that the time was "not yet ripe" for this. It soon would be. Metropolitan Vladimir of Rostov and Novocherkassk stated that more than sixty new parishes had begun to function in the past year and the plan was that this would soon increase. In fact, 2,815 new parishes opened in 1989. The years 1988–1991 were a time of massive reconstruction of church life, both repairing its administration and rebuilding its churches, cathedrals, and monasteries. All over the Soviet Union negotiations were taking place, often complicated and confronting those with vested interests, over the return of church property that had been confiscated by the Communist Party and put to all manner of secular usage.

At the *sobor* there was open criticism, too, of some individuals. Metropolitan Pitirim of Volokolamsk met particular opprobrium for a poor performance as head of the church publishing house. Since its establishment at the time when Stalin was making concessions to the Church at the end of the Second World War, this had been little more than a mouthpiece for communist propaganda, though *the Journal of the Moscow Patriarchate* did publish some theological articles that contained no political references.[39]

The events of the public celebrations marking the millennium of the baptism of Rus', as it was called, were truly stunning. Every day they were reported at length by television, radio, and in the press. People processed around the streets carrying icons and banners and the old communist slogans, which had been universally on display, disappeared overnight. It was as though the Revolution had never happened. At the end of this astonishing week the Bolshoi Theatre became the focus of the public events. The "Solemn Act," as it was called, opened at 10 a.m. on Friday June 10 and continued with a succession of speeches that lasted many hours, including congratulations to the Russian Orthodox Church from seventeen world church leaders. Metropolitan Iuvenalii gave the address, which contained evidence of a new openness about the past. Formerly any mention of Stalin's persecution had been taboo. Now he addressed the assembly in these words:

> After the Revolution, at various times which were so difficult for the people ... the church fully shared the fate of all other citizens. Now it is openly stated that many thousands of communists and non-Party members, agricultural and military brigades, scientists and representatives of the arts were subjected to mass repressions. Among their number there were both priests and laity.[40]

The day ended with a jubilee concert in the presence of dignitaries representing the state as well as the Church. Mr. Gorbachev's wife Raisa was present, as was the titular head of state, President Andrei Gromyko. No fewer than six orchestras and several stars of Soviet screen and concert stage took part in the program. There were seven choirs, with church and secular groups alternating. The great actor Sergei Bondarchuk read, in a deeply resonant voice, the account of the conversion of Rus' a thousand years ago, as set out in the monastic *Chronicle* of Russia's earliest history by the monk Nestor. When, according to the account, Prince Vladimir of Kiev's emissaries returned from Byzantium, they said that when they experienced the worship of the Greek Orthodox Church, "We did not know whether we were in heaven or on earth."[41] Doubtless there were many present, including Communist Party officials, who could have said the same.

The deepest symbolism was reserved for the very end of the celebration. The Bolshoi Chorus and Orchestra first combined to sing the traditional Russian paean of praise, *Mnogoe leto* (long life), to the Church. Live television conveyed this event throughout the Soviet Union. Even this was not the climax. The heavens—literally—were about to open to reveal a new future. The final scene of Glinka's opera, *A Life for the Tsar*, makes just such a promise. As it was being performed to the cries of *slava* (praise), the blue sky above the stage set opened to reveal a carillon of real church bells that engulfed the Bolshoi Theatre in a peal more stunning than a crack of thunder. Anywhere else this would have been a *coup de théâtre*. In a country where the ringing of church bells had been outlawed for decades this was more than symbolism: it was a visible and audible sign that a new era had begun, reinforcing the tone of optimism that Metropolitan Iuvenalii had expressed earlier in the day.

The culminating event took place in the Danilov Monastery: an open-air celebration of the liturgy. Although access was restricted, a greater number of the faithful were able to attend than had been possible at any previous event during the past week. Six Orthodox patriarchs and an archbishop representing seven different nationalities concelebrated. At the conclusion Cardinal Glemp of Warsaw spoke, representing the pope and all the Catholics present. He gave thanks for the renewal of the faith of the Russian people, a remarkable statement when one considers the traditional hostility between Russian Orthodox and Polish Catholics.

The debate surrounding the new law on religion, promised by Gorbachev earlier in 1988 and passed in September 1990, was long and passionate. It took place partly in public, with much informed comment published in the press. In the end, it guaranteed complete religious liberty, including teaching of religion in state schools.

The old atheist guard seemed to have disappeared, yet all was not so simple. Of the clergy who took best advantage of the new spirit of the times, Fr. Aleksandr Men stood out. His extraordinary ability to communicate the Gospel to believer and atheist alike led to a round of constant lectures, radio, and television appearances. He was also an author of enormous achievement. He quoted an amazing range of writers: François Mauriac, G. K. Chesterton, C. S. Lewis, T. S. Eliot, Graham Greene, Thomas Mann, Alexander Solzhenitsyn. He wrote a six-volume history of world religions, in which he paid tribute to the beautiful and positive elements he found in Buddhist, Hindu, and Muslim scriptures. This was one of the reasons why his works were never approved by the official church in Russia.[42] During the last year of his life Fr. Aleksandr Men is reported to have given over two hundred lectures and talks in the Moscow region, as well as continuing his work as a parish priest without interruption. But this unique ministry was to come to a sudden and brutal end. He was struck down with an axe by an unknown assailant just outside his house in the outer suburbs of Moscow, while on his way to celebrate a morning liturgy. The murder has never been properly investigated. The manner and timing of Father Men's death presaged deeper challenges for the Russian Orthodox Church in the years ahead. Father Men was a potent symbol of an unwanted renaissance, a twentieth-century revival of the Christian faith, and his work continues.

4
"I AM A FIGHTER BY NATURE"

Fr. Gleb Iakunin and the Defense of Religious Liberty

Wallace Daniel

The death of Father Gleb Iakunin on December 25, 2014, marked the end of an era. A key member of a group of intellectual young priests who emerged in the early 1960s, he was the last of the group to survive. Living from the Stalin period through the ascendency of Vladimir Putin, Iakunin witnessed at first hand the most difficult, tumultuous times in the history of the Soviet Union. As a priest in the Russian Orthodox Church, he gained a worldwide reputation as a defender of freedom of conscience who challenged both the Soviet state and the Russian Orthodox Church. A fierce and determined fighter for the dignity of the human being and for religious liberty, he stands alongside the physicist Andrei Sakharov as a major champion of the human rights movement in the Soviet Union. But while Sakharov and others came out of scientific and literary circles, Iakunin's origins lay in the Orthodox Church, and his emphasis on religious liberty relates to his theological understanding. As a priest and activist, his career disputes the common view of the Russian Orthodox Church as otherworldly, removed from the social and political concerns of the temporal world. His trial by the state in 1980 for anti-Soviet behavior, the events that led up to it, and the immediate aftermath provide the main framework of this study.

To Unmask Delusions

Gleb Iakunin is rarely viewed as a poet. Yet in the 1980s, while serving in a labor camp and then in exile in a remote region of Siberia, he wrote poetry, both to reflect on Russia's past and to project a vision for Russia's future. The result was a long, narrative poem, a personal, probing account of the ideals for which he had fought with such passion and determination. In the poem, he said repeatedly, are his theology, his hopes, and his perspectives on humanity.[1]

Iakunin titled his poem "Eulogy of a Simple-Minded Fool of God: In Honor of God, the Universe, and the Homeland" (*Khvalebnyi primitiv iurodivyi v chest' Boga, mirozdan'ia, rodiny*).[2] In the first lines, he pays homage to Fr. Aleksandr Men for the large personal influence Men had on him. By the 1980s, Fr. Aleksandr had attracted a significant number of young members of the intelligentsia to his small parish in Novaia Derevnia, to the northwest of Moscow. His vast knowledge of literature and history, perceptive understanding of the Gospels, and openness to the world, as well as his uncommon ability to communicate across educational and generational lines commanded a large following, even during the difficult years of Leonid Brezhnev's administration. Iakunin, who had known Fr. Aleksandr since both were young, records Men's imprint on the poem's theology:

> This very menu
> For the poor in spirit,
> Came into being from the penetrating thought
> Of Aleksandr Men.[3]

Iakunin wrote about what he saw as Russia's twentieth-century "catastrophe," the events that had befallen his country since 1917. He particularly focused on how this cataclysm had affected the Russian Orthodox Church.[4] The tragedy, in his view, had only deepened into the present.[5] He thus felt a sense of obligation to tell the story, not only to review certain events, but also to emphasize how the Church might recover its purpose and its identity. In the labor camp and in exile, Iakunin did not have the essential scholarly resources to write a narrative poem. He would work on it for many years afterwards. In the making of the poem, he went through periods of depression and anxiety, thinking that he would not be able to complete the writing.[6] Ultimately, however, the long poem was finished, most likely in the 1990s. But the original conception and the main ideas belong to that earlier period, his years of imprisonment and exile.

"Eulogy of a Simple-Minded Fool of God" treats a wide range of topics. The poem discusses the conditions of the labor camp, the cold, hunger, and isolation the author had to endure; he mentions the extreme cold and fog of the Siberian town in which he was exiled. But the poem is also Iakunin's spiritual testimony, including long, lyrical verses about nature, the skies, the seas, and the earth, with reference to the Book of Genesis and the creation of the world; the wisdom of the Creator and his compassion for human beings; the tree of creativity that extends from heaven to earth; the sanctity of labor and how God did not make man to be a slave, but a creative being; and the relationship between faith and creativity. Iakunin's verses speak to the immorality of lies and the importance of truthfulness; he explores the existence of evil and its opposing elements, and the biological evolution of the physical and natural world. He underscores his love for Russia, its people, and traditions. Most important, Iakunin's poem emphasizes the importance of freedom of conscience, which it maintains is a central component of human dignity.

In the course of its introduction and development in a pagan land, which Iakunin carefully traces, Orthodoxy has become entwined with paganism. A magical worldview had dominated the long pagan prehistory of humanity, a lengthy period in which shamans and witch doctors held sway over local populations, casting magical spells and claiming sanguine powers.[7] In the Church, the magical vision still held sway, and Iakunin's poem points out the specific manifestations of its influence, its antithesis to Christianity. It may be seen in the desire for power, in deceptions and lies, the cult of the emperor, the creation of the Russian Empire, the Church's willing subordination to the state (or Caesaropapism), its excessive commitment to rituals, and, most insidiously, its collaboration with the KGB.[8]

The Russian literary scholar Elena Volkova, who has written a fine introduction to Iakunin's work, describes the poem as written in the genre of "prophetic primitivism," a form of writing popular in the seventeenth century.[9] As Volkova points out, Iakunin's work is filled throughout with popular speech and images, the language of the street, and a play on words, "characteristic of the 'dark' unchained language of idiots, who like children, loved to play with shapes and gestures."[10] The purpose of these so-called "idiots" was to "unmask delusions" and to forecast what the future held. It was Iakunin's attempt to "unmask delusions" that had led to his arrest earlier and his sentencing to the labor camp and exile. He broke no Soviet law; contrary to what government officials charged, he did not seek to undermine the Soviet state. He did aim to expose hypocrisy and to champion freedom of conscience and human dignity, goals that, in the words of two well-known supporters on the day following his arrest, have "always represented the living tradition of the highest form of Christian compassion."[11] The pursuit of such goals proved deeply threatening to the ideological underpinnings of the Soviet state.

A Carefully Orchestrated Event

On August 28, 1980, a small crowd outside the Moscow city courthouse stood by helplessly. As a green van pulled slowly away, the prisoner's weeping aunt threw pink gladioli against its darkened back window.[12] Several in the crowd tried to comfort the prisoner's disconsolate wife, the mother of his three small children. Inside the police van, Fr. Gleb Iakunin took a final look at his loved ones gathered nearby on the street. He did not know whether he would see them again.

Iakunin's trial had lasted four days, from August 25 to August 28, 1980. Accused of "parasitism" and "slandering the Soviet state," under Article 70, section 1 of the Russian Soviet Federative Socialist Republic (RSFSR) Criminal Code, his trial garnered worldwide attention. He was one of the Soviet Union's best known priests, whose activities on behalf of religious believers had challenged the practices of Soviet authorities. A creator of the Christian Committee for the Defense of Believers' Rights in 1976, and an early champion of human rights, he had courageously fought for people who lacked a voice in the struggle to express their deepest convictions. His trial represented a milestone in the judicial history of the Soviet Union: it was the first trial of a Russian Orthodox priest since the signing of the Helsinki Accords and its Declaration on Human Rights in 1975.[13]

Soviet authorities had declared the trial to be an "open event," although except for Iakunin's wife, Iraida Georgievna, his supporters were refused admittance to the courtroom.[14] A British Foreign Office representative, Lord Carrington, and Western journalists were also turned away, told that the courtroom was full, and they could not enter. At least four KGB officers were shown to their seats.[15] Workers and students, sympathetic to the state's cause and critical of Iakunin, packed the visitors' gallery.[16]

The trial took place in the Moscow City Court building. The judge, Valentina Lubentsova, had previously presided over three other cases concerning Soviet activists.[17] The public prosecutor called all the witnesses, and used the opportunity to summon representatives of the Moscow Patriarchate. Repeatedly, they denounced Iakunin's contacts with foreigners and his false claims about the state's violations of freedom of conscience. By his collusion with "subversive centers abroad," they said, Iakunin had one aim in mind: to undermine the established order.[18] The state prosecutor charged him with engaging in deliberate actions to destroy the Soviet system.

From the outset, the prosecutor carefully orchestrated Iakunin's trial. Witnesses were thoroughly prepared; officials from the Church who testified against him for demeaning the Orthodox Church were given precise instructions on what to say. The prosecutor accused him of defaming the state by publishing materials falsely claiming violations of the laws, a charge to which Iakunin pled not guilty. Only witnesses for the prosecution were allowed to testify. Near the end of the trial, Iakunin asked the judge for permission to "talk about his motives that led him to engage in his defense activity." The judge interrupted him and "said that the court was not interested."[19] The court proceedings moved quickly to the predictable conclusion.

Not everything, however, went according to the prearranged script. A churchwarden who was called to defame Iakunin and who had done so in her pretrial testimony, changed her mind on the witness stand. She said that she had not agreed with him on every matter, but she had always found Fr. Gleb to be a dedicated Christian and a person of unquestionable integrity. She expressed appreciation for having known him.[20] Despite her support for him, the court sentenced Iakunin to punishment of five years in strict-regime camps and a subsequent five years of internal exile.[21]

The charge Iakunin faced in his trial concerned the activities of his Christian Committee for the Defense of Believers' Rights in the USSR. He and two Orthodox Christian colleagues, Hierodeacon Varsonofii Khaibulin and Viktor Kapitanchuk, founded the committee in Moscow in 1976. The committee's work will be discussed later in this study, but it should be noted here that state authorities had regarded the committee with suspicion from the moment Iakunin announced its formation at a press conference in Moscow in late December 1976. The KGB had warned Iakunin about the committee's activities.[22] KGB officials had also told him to cease his protests against government attempts to suppress the informal Christian seminars of young people that had emerged in 1974 to discuss religious and philosophical topics.

Insisting that he had broken no state laws, he continued to engage in all these activities. The KGB was equally recalcitrant, and in 1979, they moved against him, three times arriving unannounced to search his home. On one of these occasions, they confiscated his archives.[23] In September, two months before his arrest, while searching his home, they seized documents relating to the Christian Committee, as well as materials supporting young people involved in the so-called Christian Seminar.[24]

Iakunin's arrest on November 1, 1979, represented part of an assault by the government against religious dissidents. In an effort to curtail an emerging network of intellectuals who were searching for views of life's purposes different from Soviet ideology, the police moved aggressively against such individuals. But the government also broadened the framework to an attack on individuals who, in the name of human rights, sought to defend them. Despite the harsh terms he received from the court in the summer of 1980, Iakunin vowed to continue his fight and not to be cowed by the suffering that lay ahead. Such a vow is implied in his final words to the court after his sentencing to a labor camp and to exile: "I thank God for the fate he has given me."[25]

The Rebel as Outsider

He bounded out of the metro station on that May morning in 2007, a short, well-built, gray-haired man, carrying a well-worn leather briefcase. I recognized him immediately from the photographs I had seen multiple times in books on famous Russian dissidents. Sent by our hostess to greet him, I walked with him and a fellow priest through back alleys to the high-rise apartment building where, after lunch, I spent most of the afternoon talking with him about his life and, more generally, about the Russian Orthodox Church and its relationship with the Russian state.

I went to see Iakunin specifically to ask about his friendship with Fr. Aleksandr Men. The two men met when they were in their late teenage years. In the early 1950s, both were students in a zoological institute in the southern suburbs of Moscow. Both had a passionate interest in the sciences and a similar interest in books, particularly books in philosophy and theology, subjects that lay outside the mainstream of thought in the late Stalinist era. The two teenagers were introduced to each other by a mutual friend, Viktor Alekseev, a fellow student on a train transporting them, on a Sunday afternoon, from Moscow to their institute.[26] On the train, Iakunin was reading M. V. Lodyzhenskii's *Higher Consciousness and the Paths to its Achievement* (*Sverkhoznaniia i puti ego dostizheniiu*), the controversial work by a prerevolutionary theosophist, whose books were banned by Soviet authorities.[27] At the time, Iakunin was not a believer, but he had a deeply curious mind, and he read widely on a variety of topics. While the young men were much different in personality, temperament, and personal goals, they began a friendship that lasted for many years, with major consequences for each of them.

Gleb Iakunin was born on March 4, 1934, in Moscow, into a musical family: his father, educated as a scientist and a musician played clarinet in a Moscow orchestra. What began as a fairly comfortable childhood, however, quickly became treacherous. During the Great War, the family evacuated Moscow, moving to a small settlement on the Volga River, where his father unexpectedly died, leaving the mother and son in dire straits. His mother had to accept hard, physical work in order for her and her child to survive. These were extremely difficult years, and they continued after the two of them returned to Moscow at the war's end, and Gleb began his schooling.[28]

Gleb's mother, Klavdiia Iosifovna Iakunina, a devout Orthodox Christian, had always taken him with her to the services in an effort to inculcate in him her beliefs. In what might be considered his first act of rebellion, he resisted his mother's attempts to make him an Orthodox Christian. By the age of ten or eleven, he had lost his faith in God and had become, he told me, a "diehard atheist": "My mother was a devout believer, a traditionalist who held fast to church rituals, a simple person, who could not answer the questions that were emerging in my mind."[29] These questions concerned the Church's doctrinaire teachings, its closed-mindedness to the world, and its seeming indifference to social problems.

In 1955, the zoological institute in which Iakunin and Men were students moved from the southern suburbs of Moscow to Irkutsk, to become part of large agricultural institute in that Siberian city. The move led to a deepening of the friendship between these two students. Iakunin told me that they had a "circle of friends, both in the institute and in Moscow with whom they could talk freely about philosophical and religious, as well as political, questions."[30] But it was Men, most of all, who brought him back to Christianity and to the Church.[31] Men's knowledge of literature and the Bible, his seriousness and his work ethic, and his commitment to service to the Church and to the people helped Iakunin formulate ideals that would stay with him all his life.

In his development as a student in Irkutsk and, then, as a young priest, several formative events had a large influence on Iakunin's worldview. First, in Irkutsk in 1955 and for two years, Aleksandr Men and Gleb Iakunin did not live with the other students. They found a room on the outskirts of Irkutsk with a local family. There, each morning from the window in their room, they observed inmates of a nearby labor camp being marched into the fields, most of them serving sentences for political crimes. These experiences fostered in both young men a deepening sense of injustice, of the large dichotomy between ideals and the practical realities of daily life.

Second, Men and Iakunin became acquainted with a Fr. Vladimir, priest of a small church parish in Irkutsk. "We had long conversations with him," Fr. Gleb said. This priest "had spent some time in the labor camps, before being pardoned, we learned, and he knew the history of the Church very well. I learned that the true church was not the official church connected with the Moscow Patriarchate, but the one underground that had rejected the Moscow Patriarchate."[32] Iakunin spoke of the "catacomb church" that had thrived in the 1930s and 1940s. This revelation, he said, set him on the path to thinking about how the Orthodox Church might be reformed, how it might be more responsive to the needs of the people, and how it might become a defender of religious liberty.[33]

It is unclear precisely when Gleb Iakunin decided to take the difficult road to becoming a priest, but his association with Aleksandr Men likely moved him in that direction. A year after finishing his studies in Irkutsk and working the compulsory term as a forest ranger, Iakunin entered the Moscow Theological Seminary. He spent only one year there. Discouraged by the doctrinaire teaching and having become involved in a scandal over a library book, he left the seminary. He served as a psalm reader in a church near the Moscow-Riga railway station. By now married, he and his wife Iraida, their baby, and his mother lived together in one room. On August 9, 1962, he was ordained as a deacon and the following day, in the Novodevichii Monastery, his sponsor, Archpriest Leonid Plykov, also a surgeon, ordained Gleb Iakunin as a priest. He served for a brief time as the second priest in a church in Zaraisk. Later that same year, he was appointed priest in a church in the historic town of Dmitrov, forty miles to the north of Moscow.[34]

The third event is closely connected with the second. In 1962, shortly after becoming a priest, Iakunin joined a small circle of like-minded individuals organized by Fr. Aleksandr Men. At the time, Fr. Aleksandr served a small church parish in Tarasovka, a town located about thirty miles to the north of Moscow. Nearly all the members of the group were young; in addition to Men and Iakunin, the members of the group included Frs. Dmitrii Dudko, Nikolai Eshliman, and six other young priests from nearby dioceses. Explaining his thinking in joining, Iakunin said, "We came together, because in those times many young priests who had entered the priesthood understood that Church meant more than celebrating the liturgy, and were looking for ways to bring about a renaissance in the Church, so that it could compete and be viable in our society. This was the main reason behind our gatherings and discussions."[35]

Iakunin's prominence beyond Russia began in December 1965, shortly after Nikita Khrushchev's fall from power the preceding year. He and Nikolai Eshliman wrote two incendiary letters, one addressed to the patriarch of the Russian Orthodox Church, Aleksii I, and the second to the head of the government, Nikolai Podgornyi.[36] The two letters have been analyzed many times in the historical literature, and they do not warrant repetition here.[37] But one major theme in the letters is relevant to the main subject of this essay. Government policies and the failure of the patriarchate to stand up to abuses of power, they emphasized, undermined the internal unity of the Russian Orthodox Church. Addressing the government, the two priests maintained that the government had made a mockery of religious freedom, which they claimed to be a fundamental right. Multiple times Eshliman and Iakunin used the words "flagrant violation" of socialist justice and what they called "radical distortion" of the laws, which had transformed the socialist system into something beyond the laws.[38] They spoke of the state's "intrusion into the realm of the sacred," and they urged the patriarch to take action against this abuse of power.[39] They claimed that the failure to speak and to act had "perverted the spirit of Orthodoxy," and had made it into something it was never intended to be.[40] The Russian Orthodox Church, Eshliman and Iakunin maintained, had become a submissive tool of the Soviet government. Its compliance and lack of courage had fostered within the Church a deadly disease—the "spirit of indifference, servility, and pharisaism."[41]

Eshliman's and Iakunin's letters set out emphatically the opposing principles that were at issue: the dignity of the believer against the power of the state; the aspiration for a renaissance within the Church versus the political need to keep the Church submissive and weak; the letter of the law versus the arbitrariness of state policies; the respect for canon law versus its political manipulation; and the need for a fresh vision versus the Church's predominating silence. Using medical terminology, Eshliman and Iakunin likened the silence of the Church to a "sickness of the whole body."[42] They prescribed the path to healing, and, in this process, they connected the need to speak out to Russia's religious heritage. It was not for this silence, they wrote, that

> the glorious army of Russian saints stand in the church, "invisibly praying to God for us"; not for this [silence] did St. Sergius—the great servant of God—shine forth in the heart of Russia; not for this did the holy blood of Russian martyrs flow abundantly; not for this have the Easter bells rung out over Russia for a thousand years with such triumph as has never been heard elsewhere in the world. Are all those riches, this sacred treasury, this beauty and glory to be terminated by a pitiful bureaucracy, by a submissive agent of powers which are against the Church?[43]

Thinking they had the proper authority, Eshliman and Iakunin circulated their letter to Patriarch Aleksii I among the bishops of the Russian Church. Aleksii I's reaction might have been anticipated. He had little sympathy for their recommendations, and characterized the actions of the two priests as "evil."[44] Accusing them of behavior "prejudicial to the Church" and of destruction of the Church's internal peace, the patriarch demanded that they recant their words.[45] When Eshliman and Iakunin refused, he suspended them from the priesthood.

The reactions of the two men, psychologically, could hardly have been more different. Nikolai Eshliman was crushed by the patriarch's dismissal of the letters and his personal criticisms of the authors. In response, Eshliman resigned from all dissident activities, and disassociated himself from the Church. During the next few years, he withdrew into himself, later suffered from depression and ill health, and died in 1985, at the age of fifty-seven.[46] Unlike his compatriot, Iakunin did not retreat. "I am a fighter by nature," he said.[47] Rather than back down, he became determined to persevere against what he viewed as cowardice, falsehood, and injustice. The threat of prosecution, he said, "did not frighten, but rather incited me further, with the result that I entered the dissident movement and eventually the human rights movement."[48] Despite extremely difficult circumstances, having lost his position as a priest, he pressed on, determined to make the state and the Church more accountable for their actions and to contribute to the ideal he and others had held as young priests: a renaissance in the Orthodox Church.

Iakunin's persistence on behalf of his ideal would exact a heavy price not only on himself but also on his family. He might not have gone forward with such conviction without the support of his wife, Iraida. They lived in meager circumstances. After his suspension, with little income, he and his family existed on the edge of poverty. They survived largely through the help of friends, who provided them with material support. Barred from office, unable to officiate in church services, his appeals for reinstatement ignored, he held several low-paying jobs as a watchman, janitor, and a reader of psalms in several Moscow churches, sometimes suffering dismissal from these positions.[49]

Freedom of Conscience

In the eight years following his suspension from the priesthood, little was heard publicly from Fr. Gleb Iakunin. It would, however, be a mistake to think that these years were spent in idle endeavors, in intellectual stagnation and personal inactivity. Given the events that soon transpired and the thought that lay behind his later actions, one might logically surmise that he read a great deal, especially in the works of Nikolai Berdiaev, Sergei Bulgakov, Semen Frank, and other prominent members of Russia's nineteenth- and twentieth-century philosopher-theologians, whose writings he greatly prized. He also closely followed the political events in this era of Leonid Brezhnev and the severe, often violent, suppression of dissent.[50] About several of these events, he would soon speak out.

As a student and as a young priest, Gleb Iakunin was greatly influenced by a book written by the Russian philosopher-theologian Nikolai Berdiaev, *The Philosophy of Freedom*.[51] Aleksandr Men had recommended Berdiaev's book when they were students in Irkutsk, and he had read it then.[52] He repeatedly went back to it for guidance and for ideas. Berdiaev (1874–1948), a leading member of the philosophical-theological school of Russians in the early twentieth century, whom Lenin exiled in 1922, wrote some of the most important works in Russian philosophy in the twentieth century.[53] His view of freedom derived from his own experience:

> I never had the experience of living under authority. I did not know it in my family or at school; neither did I know it in my philosophical studies or in religion. In my childhood, I decided that I will never enter any service and will never subject myself to any authority. The struggle for freedom which I have continued all my life has been its most positive and valuable element.[54]

Berdiaev describes himself as a free religious philosopher. His *Philosophy of Freedom* is a complex work, which deserves lengthy discussion, but within the limits of this essay, only several major themes bear emphasis. Freedom, he maintains, is a choice a person makes; it is not predetermined; it is mystical, and it forms the very essence of creativity.[55] Freedom means spiritual freedom, the capacity and the openness to hear one's calling and the willingness to respond to that calling, despite the forces that attempt to pull one in a different direction.[56] A human life is enshrined in mystery, which infuses all of life and is the way God communicates with the universe. Berdiaev defended "personalism," the fundamental importance and sacredness of the individual against the impersonal forces brought on by recent scientific discoveries, by technology, and by all attempts to reduce human beings to automatons. People willingly give up their freedom, the most important possession a person has, for security, delusion, and material gain.[57] When the Church allies itself with the government in the pursuit of power and gain, rather than in the quest for social justice, the Church's mission is corrupted.[58] Reading and re-reading Berdiaev's book showed Iakunin the direction he had to follow.

If Iakunin's public actions had gone no further than the two letters he and Eshliman wrote to the patriarch and the president of the Soviet Union in 1965, he would be known only for the brief, but courageous, stand he took against the political and religious powers. These circumstances would not have led to his trial in 1980. He had accused the patriarch and other members of the church hierarchy of unacceptable "silence," when the government interfered in what were clearly "sacred matters." When the Church continued to follow the same course, he could not silence his own voice any longer.

The specific occasion was an article, written by Metropolitan Serafim of Krutitsy and Kolomna, published in *Pravda* in February 1974. The metropolitan had written in support of Aleksandr Solzhenitsyn's expulsion from the Soviet Union, a day after Solzhenitsyn was charged with treason on February 14, 1974. Accusing Solzhenitsyn of spreading lies in his recently published *Gulag Archipelago*, Serafim denounced the writer for slandering the Soviet Union; he claimed that Solzhenitsyn deserved to be banished for his disloyalty to the country of his birth. On February 18, 1974, Gleb Iakunin wrote an "Open Letter to Serafim," in which he responded to the metropolitan's article. Iakunin reminded Serafim of his responsibility to stand up for those who had died in the Gulag. In accusatory and straightforward language, Iakunin chastised the church leader for his willful blindness to the facts about suffering and persecution. "Are you not afraid, Your Holiness, dreadfully afraid?" Iakunin wrote. "And did you not feel a twinge of conscience? Our martyrs have perished in the Gulag camps. Don't you know about this?"[59]

Iakunin's letter to the metropolitan would not have aroused the attention of the KGB, but his two subsequent letters most certainly provoked their ire. The first was co-authored with the layman Lev L'vovich Regelson, a physicist and friend, who, like Iakunin, had found in the writings of Nikolai Berdiaev guidance for his actions. Regelson and Iakunin addressed an appeal to fellow Christians in Portugal.[60] Surveying the political situation in Portugal, Iakunin and Regelson maintained that it currently stood at a crossroads; Portugal faced a situation similar to the one Russia had confronted on the eve of the Revolution of 1917, when Russia had broken with its traditional cultural model and "begun a process of spiritual, national, and political decay."[61] Their appeal is remarkable for its treatment of political freedom, which they saw as a prerequisite for spiritual freedom and the Church's own freedom. They urged the Church not to succumb to the temptations of totalitarianism, but to preserve its freedom, which, they claimed, was much easier to preserve than to regain.[62] They forecast the future calamities that would befall the country should it succumb to the same forces as Russia had, and they implored Portuguese Christians to become actively involved in politics.[63] This last appeal could not have been agreeable to the KGB and its fervent belief that the Church must never become an oppositional force.

The second letter was written by Iakunin and Regelson to the delegates of the Fifth Assembly of the World Council of Churches, meeting in Nairobi, in October 1975.[64] It attracted universal attention. Their "Appeal," according to historian Jane Ellis, "was probably the single most effective religious samizdat document to come out of the Soviet Union."⁶⁵ Iakunin and Regelson's "Appeal" called attention to the "lies" spread by Soviet propaganda about the true situation of religious believers in their country. They spoke of the illegal incarcerations, the use of terror to threaten believers, and the plight of innocent believers who had been arrested for practicing their faith. They especially called for an international inspection of psychiatric hospitals, where psychiatrists tried to "cure" religious believers of their "irrational" proclivities: "there we encounter a threat to mankind no less dangerous than nuclear bombs and bacteriological warfare."⁶⁶

Iakunin's and Regelson's letter to the World Council of Churches (WCC) represents a significant step in the effort to expose the dichotomy between pretension and reality. They challenged the government's claim that religious freedom existed in the Soviet Union. They asked members of the WCC to help the large number of prisoners who were incarcerated because of their religious beliefs, and they prescribed eight steps the delegates could take to alleviate such suffering. They referred to religious believers in psychiatric hospitals in the Soviet Union as feeling "abandoned and deserted."⁶⁷ In words that might have been taken directly from Berdiaev's *Philosophy of Freedom* they called for "support to confessors of other religions as well as for all fighters for freedom, human dignity, and for preservation of God's image in man."⁶⁸

In their discussion of Iakunin's letters and appeals, scholars have treated them as separate documents, as though they existed independently of each other.⁶⁹ But a further look at these materials suggests another perspective. Rather than a series of disconnected protests, the appeals show the development of Iakunin's thought, as he moved from instances of what he perceived as social injustices to a broader set of social and religious concerns. From protest about specific Orthodox Church issues, his appeals became larger, more historical, more national, and even more international in scope. The dignity of each human being and freedom of conscience, which were mentioned in his and Eshliman's 1965 letters, became central themes in his 1975 letter to delegates of the WCC. He and Regelson emphasized the "spirit of tolerance," the need for compassion, the freedom of the human mind, and abhorrence of the "suppression of truth."⁷⁰ They addressed the needs not only of Orthodox, but also of Jewish and Muslim believers.⁷¹ Most importantly, they spoke in defense of human rights. In so doing, they entered risky and dangerous terrain that led to direct confrontation with the Soviet government.

Dangerous Journey

On August 1, 1975, the representatives of thirty-five nations, including the United States and the USSR, meeting in Helsinki, signed the Final Act of the Conference on Security and Cooperation in Europe. A signature diplomatic accomplishment, the Final Act promised East-West mutual cooperation on a wide range of important issues. Chief among them was the agreement to respect the inviolability "of one another's frontiers as well as the frontiers of all States in Europe and therefore they will refrain now and in the future from assaulting those frontiers."[72] The Helsinki agreement thus guaranteed the legitimacy of the Soviet Union's control of the states of Eastern Europe, an accord widely heralded in the Soviet Union as a major diplomatic victory. The Politburo trumpeted this achievement, calling it a progressive movement from Cold War confrontation to an "era of détente" and peaceful coexistence.[73]

Contrary to the authorities, however, a small group of Russian dissidents in Moscow also recognized the diplomatic accord as a signal achievement. In Point 7 of what is known as the Concluding Act, all signers of the diplomatic accord committed to "respect human rights and fundamental freedoms, including freedom of thought, conscience, religion or belief, for all without distinction as to race, sex, language, or religion."[74] Some political leaders both in the United States and the Soviet Union did not take this seriously; they believed it to be a meaningless statement that had little bearing either on reality or on the future of diplomatic relations.[75] But the group of Russian dissidents thought otherwise; they saw the statement on human rights as an opportunity to hold the Soviet government accountable.[76]

On May 12, 1976, in the apartment of Andrei Sakharov, physicist Iurii Orlov and his fellow human rights activists held a press conference to announce the formation of the Moscow Helsinki Monitoring Group.[77] Although few in number, the group strongly believed in their mission "to monitor Soviet compliance with the human rights provisions of the Helsinki Final Act"; the group's goal, which Orlov proclaimed at the press conference, was "to inform the heads of the signatory states as well as the world public 'about direct violations' of the Helsinki Accords."[78] Members of the Moscow Group were prepared to hear directly from Soviet citizens about abuses that interfered with their "fundamental freedoms," as stated in the Helsinki Final Act.

Iakunin and Orlov were friends, and Orlov invited him to join the Moscow group. But Iakunin preferred to create a parallel organization that focused more on matters of belief.[79] On December 27, 1976, he and two colleagues, Hierodeacon Varsonofii Khaibulin and a layman, Viktor Kapitanchuk, formed, in Moscow, the parallel organization Iakunin had in mind, the Christian Committee for the Defense of Believers' Rights in the USSR (CCDBR). Like Orlov's group, Iakunin's committee aimed to hold the authorities to their word; having organized the committee, its leaders began, in earnest, to broadcast as widely as possible abuses of the rights of religious believers.

In announcing the Committee's creation, Iakunin and his colleagues defined its primary goals as follows:

> to collect and disseminate information about religious conditions in the country and advise religious believers when their rights were violated;
> to provide assistance in the writing of legislation on religious rights;
> to conduct research and appeal to relevant government bodies when local authorities infringed upon the rights of religious believers;
> to work to improve the laws on religion;
> to represent not only Russian Orthodox people but people of all denominations and confessions and to provide them assistance.[80]

Iakunin and other leaders of the Committee emphasized that they did not intend to accept the philosophical principles on which the Soviet Union was founded. They pledged their loyalty to the state; they declared their allegiance to its laws and their aim of carrying out the laws, but they expressed their fundamental opposition to Marxism-Leninism.[81] They justified their dissent by pointing to what they saw as the contradiction between the Constitution and the goals of the Communist Party. The former proclaimed the freedom of religion; yet the party repeatedly stated its intention of making war on religious belief and its ultimate aim of obliterating it. The committee's charter stressed the contradiction: "The documents of the Communist Party leave no doubt that communism and religion are incompatible. All members of the Party are pledged to lead the struggle against religion, and an integral part of Communist Party policy is not only atheist propaganda but antireligious activity."[82]

The dichotomy between the laws and the policies of the party becomes even more pronounced with the passage of time. In 1977, the government issued a long-awaited updated Soviet Constitution. This document, also called the "Brezhnev Constitution," codified the social and economic changes that had taken place in the last forty years. In it, lawmakers described the Soviet Union differently than before. No longer did they identify the Soviet Union as a country in economic transition. Rather, they defined it as a nation of "developed socialism," clearly referencing the progress it had made toward achieving its desired goals. Yet the contradiction that Iakunin and his colleagues targeted also could be found. The new constitution emphasized the role of the Communist Party as leading and directing society, thus again supporting the party's opposition to religion. But Article 6 of the 1977 Constitution expressed the commitment to fundamental human rights, including freedom of conscience.

It was such contradictions between promise and practice that Iakunin and his colleagues protested. The 1977 Constitution, they wrote to the hierarchs of the church, "describes a Communist society as being one in which the best strivings of man are allowed to exist, but religious ideals, and ideals of spiritual and moral union of man with God and man with man through God are excluded."[83] Most important, Iakunin, Khaibulin, and Kapitanchuk demanded that the requirement that each party member had the obligation to "lead a decisive struggle vs. religion," be removed from the Constitution.[84] Freedom of conscience was incompatible, they maintained, with the Constitution's failure to give believers equal freedom of religious propaganda. It was also incompatible with teaching in Soviet schools, where only lessons with antireligious content were permitted. Such contradictions, they pointed out, placed Soviet citizens in a conundrum: if they respected the Constitution's guarantee of freedom of conscience, Soviet citizens were forced to disobey other laws.[85]

A cardinal feature of Soviet ideology maintained that Western countries used their own versions of "freedom of conscience" as political instruments to undermine the Soviet Union. Since the time of Lenin, according to this interpretation, the Soviet Union understood "freedom of conscience" differently than did "bourgeois propagandists" in Western Europe and the United States. They, according to a leading Soviet spokesperson, used the term to protect class interests.[86] He denied religious persecution in the Soviet Union, since the Constitution clearly protected freedom of belief. Western apologists, asserting "freedom of conscience" and human rights, used these terms as part of their political assault on the Soviet Union. Moreover, their accusations represented hypocritical claims. In Western countries, the laws guaranteed protection of religious groups, but "in not one of the bourgeois governments are there laws protecting atheistic points of view. In not one of the bourgeois countries are there words that underscore the right of citizens to be atheists and to conduct atheistic propaganda. The interests of millions of people who do not believe in God are completely ignored."[87]

In various international gatherings, representatives of the Moscow Patriarchate heralded the Constitution's guaranteed freedom of conscience. But the large number of reports collected by Iakunin's committee tells a different story. The many letters from the bottom of Soviet society present concrete accounts of abuses. They challenge the Moscow Patriarchate's claims about the unity of Soviet citizens within the Russian Orthodox Church and outside in society. The picture these documents presents is a society deeply divided at the bottom, a society in which sizable numbers of people did not adhere to the government's policies and looked for ways around them, despite threats of imprisonment and even death. The materials gathered by the Committee suggest that levels of non-conformity within the population existed much beyond what either the government or the patriarchate contended.

Human rights abuses are found repeatedly in these reports. Iakunin cited Andrei Sakharov's recent address at the International Sakharov Hearings, in which the academician spoke about the common "falsification of criminal acts for the purpose of political repression."[88] The CCDBR worked closely with Sakharov, Iakunin said; "we supplied him with materials on which he built his cases about religious persecution in our country."[89] Iakunin provided ample evidence of police harassment and arrests of groups engaged in discussion of religion, and searches of private residences in which savings passbooks were confiscated, depriving families of their life's savings.[90] On December 23, 1977, for example, the police arrested M. M. Iurkiv, a Pentecostal, who, for religious reasons, had sought permission for his family to emigrate. The police searched his home, "hounded his wife and small, sick children out onto the street," and confiscated their money, "thus depriving his family of the means of support."[91]

In another case, in May 1978, the Committee took up an appeal dealing with the case of a Jewish teacher, one Iosif Begun, a specialist in the field of mathematical statistics. Begun's university dismissed him from his teaching position after he applied for permission to emigrate to Israel. After his discharge, Begun began offering informal classes in Modern Hebrew. In 1977, he was arrested and sentenced to two years of exile "for parasitism." According to the Committee's appeal, "he is being prosecuted because he has devoted all his strength to the revival of the religion and culture of Soviet Jews."[92] Arrested again in June 1978, Begun was charged under Article 198 of the Criminal Code of the RSFSR for violating the passport system, and sentenced him to three years' exile.

Social justice demands free and equal treatment under the laws and support for the most disadvantaged members of society. Whether an action is just or unjust depends on whether it offers the opportunity to lead a fulfilling life. In the many cases collected by the Committee, religious believers were among the most disadvantaged members of their society. Viewed as mentally deranged, in many cases, they were sent by the police to psychiatric hospitals. In the cases collected by the Committee, religious believers were among the most disadvantaged members of their society. The CCDBR's files contain multiple examples of such treatment.

The following case concerns a young member of the intelligentsia, Aleksandr Argentev, a member of the Christian Seminar that flourished in Moscow in the early and mid-1970s. On July 14, 1976, the police arrested him and sent him to a Moscow psychiatric clinic. In desperation, he appealed to

Patriarch Pimen for help. His letter to the patriarch bears quoting, in part, for its details about abuses of Orthodox religious believers:

> On July 14 this year, I was forcibly sent to a clinic for the mentally ill, though I have never previously been registered in a psychiatric institute. As the doctors openly told me, the sole reason for my detention was my faith in God and my membership in the Orthodox Church. I am healthy and I sleep well, but here they persistently give me sleeping pills; I am a balanced, placid person by nature, but here I was forced to take a psychotropic (mind-influencing drug) aminazin, allegedly to calm me down, with the threat that if I did not take it I would be subjected to forcible treatment by injections. I am kept with seriously ill people, who are tied to their beds because of their violent behavior. I have to listen to their wild howling, and these surroundings, and also the effect of the medicines, are oppressing me. The attitude of the doctors has an even more oppressive effect on me. Completely ignorant of everything concerning religion, they insistently try to convince me that my religious feelings are a mental illness. The doctors assert that our Christian religion forbids believers to defend their homeland, that the progress of aviation and space travels testifies to the fact that there is no God, that priests officiate only for the sake of money, and that young believers are basically pathological idiots.[93]

Argentev stated that his parents, both militant atheists, considered him to be a healthy person and had demanded his release from the hospital. The clinic psychiatrists rejected the demand; he wrote that his doctors told him they intended to "'beat all of this nonsense' out of me, by 'nonsense' meaning faith in God."[94] Their words "horrified me by their inhumanity, and what is now being done to me here proves that these words were not empty threats." Argentev asked the patriarch for his intervention and help; the patriarch did not respond.[95]

The KGB warned Iakunin and his colleagues to cease the activities of the committee, but they refused to back down.[96] A derogatory article, published in the mass circulation newspaper *Literaturnaia gazeta* on April 13 and 20, 1977, likely written by a KGB official, also served as a warning. The article, composed under the byline of one Boris Roshchin, had an ominous heading, "Svoboda religii i klepki" (Freedom of religion and the slanderers).[97] In it, the author discounted the truth of the abuses of human rights, and maintained that those who publicize these alleged persecutions acted on behalf of reactionary circles in the West.[98]

In 1977 and '78, the KGB's arrest of human rights activists took place in rapid succession, beginning with members of the Helsinki Monitoring Group.

Then, on March 12, 1979, the KGB arrested Viktor Kapitanchuk, and charged him with "anti-Soviet slander." The arrest of Gleb Iakunin soon followed on November 1, 1979, Lev Regelson on December 1, and Fr. Dmitrii Dudko on January 15, 1980.[99] These events took place nearly concurrently with the Soviet Union's invasion of Afghanistan in December 1979, world condemnation of this action, and the upcoming Olympic Games scheduled for the summer of 1980 in Moscow. The Soviet government moved quickly and assertively to silence its most outspoken internal critics.

Determined to build public cases against each of these activists, the KGB sought to get confessions from each of them. In June 1980, in a stunning development, disheartening his many followers, Fr. Dmitrii Dudko admitted to his personal guilt for anti-Soviet behavior and, in a television appearance, renounced everything he had previously done to "slander" the Soviet Union and its people.[100] At Iakunin's trial, Regelson and Kapitanchuk, both held in Lefortovo Prison in Moscow, pled guilty to collaborating with Iakunin in preparing several of the documents they had circulated. Regelson especially emphasized that "Fr. Gleb had always pointed out the importance of the Christian and legal defense aspects of their compositions and had opposed inserting political statements."[101]

That Gleb Iakunin held up under the near constant pressure, the repeated interrogations and threats of severe punishment, is testimony to extraordinary fortitude and conviction. Supported by his wife Iraida, who well knew the hardships that she and her children would face in the future, Iakunin refused to follow the same road as Dudko. In a nighttime visit to his cell, a move engineered by the KGB in an effort to persuade Iakunin to change his mind, Iraida told her husband that he must not let his people down.[102] He had to follow the dictates of his conscience; he had to adhere to the principles for which he had long struggled. Both in the pretrial preparation and his trial, Iakunin did not confess, but chose instead to receive the severe punishment dictated by the court.

Poetry "Is a Golden Treasury"

As emphasized throughout this essay, Iakunin had always cultivated a kind of inner freedom, the freedom of mind and spirit emphasized in the writings of Nikolai Berdiaev. Berdiaev had drawn a connection between freedom and creativity. Yet the external conditions he confronted in incarceration mitigated against such freedom. The labor camp, the infamous Perm 37, to which Iakunin was sentenced, did not readily lend itself to either pursuit.

Iakunin, however, in important ways, did not give in fully to his captors. Upon entering the labor camp, he was required to relinquish his books and other reading material he had brought with him. Failing to have these returned, he engaged in the only form of protest open to him. On September 16, 1980, he began a hunger strike.[103] (Other sympathetic prisoners joined him in his protest.) As his hunger strike went on for weeks and his physical condition deteriorated, camp officials transferred him to Perm Camp No. 35, which had hospital facilities. There, he was fed intravenously.[104] Eventually, his protest succeeded, as the authorities relented and allowed Iakunin his books. They gave him a spiritual and intellectual pipeline to a world that extended beyond the labor camp.

Despite the harsh physical conditions he faced in the camp, Iakunin began to write poetry. It became for him a means of connecting to the imagination, of bringing to the surface memories that lay buried in his consciousness. Poetry has a "very special place in this country," writes Nadezhda Mandel'shtam, the wife of one of Russia's greatest twentieth-century poets. That is because, she says, poetry "is a golden treasury, in which our values are preserved; it brings people back to life, awakens their conscience and stirs them to thought."[105] This awakening of conscience and stirring of thought, of which Mandel'shtam writes, characterized the poetry Iakunin wrote from the depths of Perm 37. He returned to his aspirations as a younger man and to his hopes of being part of a renaissance within the Church. The desire for such a renaissance and its attendant practices of redemption and healing are key elements in his poetry. They were, he believed, more important than ever in Russia's present condition. As mentioned at the beginning of this study, the long narrative poem he wrote, he began in the labor camp and continued during his exile.

After completing his five-year term in Perm 37, Iakunin was sent to the distant Siberian village of Solnechnyi, in the southeastern corner of Iakutiia. In this remote location, far from the nearest railway line and in one of the coldest regions of the world, he lived on the fringes of Russian civilization. He was assigned to work as a carpenter in a small village shop.[106] There, whenever time permitted, he continued to write his narrative poem. It is difficult to establish precisely the parts of the poem that belong to this period of his life. But he tells the reader that human history is neither static nor regressive. It moves forward. Despite the extremely difficult circumstances in which he found himself, Iakunin neither lost his vision of hope nor his commitment to reforming the Russian Orthodox Church.

In the wide range of subjects that his poem addresses, one theme is threaded throughout, and it applies to every part of his life and theology. He emphasizes the need for human beings to be open to the world—to the beauty of nature and to creative activity. Since the world's creation is an ongoing process, the person is a participant in its creation.¹⁰⁷ Too often, Iakunin says, the Church has closed itself off from the world. He is especially critical of the Church's closed-mindedness to science. It had shut the door to scientific discovery, and had done so to its own impoverishment. Similarly, he had strong criticism for the atheistic teachings that predominated in Russian schools and the media and their rejection of religion on the grounds that its superstitious beliefs impede scientific advancement:

> And in celebrating victory
> atheism summons everyone to a dinner
> but its poverty is revealed by its one-course meal.¹⁰⁸

Despite the suffering he had endured throughout this period of his life, Iakunin never lost hope in his homeland. His poem issued a call for the Church to cleanse itself, to purify itself of the non-Christian elements that had entered its body.¹⁰⁹ In his mind, Russia had already experienced the beginnings of such a renaissance. They lay in the late nineteenth- and early twentieth-century philosopher/theologians, writers to whom his poem pays homage: Vladimir Solov'ev, Sergei Bulgakov, Nikolai Berdiaev, and Viacheslav Ivanov.¹¹⁰ But Iakunin claimed this early Russian renaissance had been too narrow in scope and too limited by time.¹¹¹ Through the pathway set by these writers, he aspired to recover the revelatory traditions they embodied. It is this clarion call to reconnect to these traditions that reverberated strongly in his poetry and in his actions:

> The Renaissance burst in—like a great knight,
> ordered the darkness to stand aside:
> rehabilitated the humanistic beginning,
> from liberty the human being began to stir.¹¹²

More Than a Religious Dissident

Fr. Gleb Iakunin is commonly depicted as a religious dissident. This essay has argued that the designation only partially describes him. In the evolution of his thought and activities, Iakunin became a defender of religious liberty, an advocate of social justice, and a champion of human rights. His long quest to promote a renaissance in the Russian Orthodox Church was predicated on the belief that it would lead to healing the gap between the Russian Orthodox

Church and the Russian people. In his poem, "Eulogy of a Simple-Minded Fool of God," he cited the French scientist and theologian Teilhard de Chardin that human society was evolving towards a higher form of consciousness.[113] Like Teilhard, Iakunin believed that in the future both the rationality of the sciences and the mystery of Christianity would play important roles. A renaissance within the Church was essential, Iakunin maintained, for it to fulfill its promise.

In his view, the reawakening of the Church and of Russian society required recovering and rebuilding connections with the treasures of Russia's past. Iakunin's poetry and his petitions to the government identified who and what he considered those gems to be. He included the twelfth-century saints, Boris and Gleb, whose passive suffering in their confrontation with violence stood as models of behavior; Saint Sergii of Radonezh, the spiritual leader of medieval Russia and the country's patron saint; the early twentieth-century patriarch Tikhon, who refused to compromise with the Bolshevik government; the great nineteenth-century elder Saint Serafim of Sarov, whose moral teachings and acts of charity were renowned; and Russia's religious-philosophical writers in the nineteenth and early twentieth centuries.[114]

The rediscovery of these venerable individuals extended far beyond the simple recognition of their achievements; their moral examples and teachings offered a new understanding of the world. In place of civil strife and fratricide, the models he held up stood for non-violence, charity, human dignity, and freedom. At his trial, Iakunin's opposition charged him with political subversion, primarily motivated by Western governments. In reality, however, both his actions and thoughts derived from his beliefs in Russian Orthodox Christianity and his readings in Russian sources.

The suffering Iakunin endured in prison and exile neither dampened his spirit nor lessened his resolve. "As long as you have the strength left, you have to push forward to see the realization of your ideals. When you believe in something, you have to fight for it," he said, reflecting on his experiences.[115] Granted amnesty by Mikhail Gorbachev in 1987, he returned to Moscow and immediately reentered the cause to which he had committed himself, a renaissance in the life of the Church. From 1987 to 1992, he again served as a parish priest; he won elections to the state legislature, where he worked from 1990 to 1995. As deputy chairman of the Parliamentary Committee for Freedom of Conscience, he coauthored the law Freedom For All Denominations. He gained access to KGB archives and, in March 1992, published documents revealing the earlier complicity of top church hierarchs, including Patriarch Aleksii II, with the KGB. In 1997, he was excommunicated, after defying the Church's recent ban prohibiting clergy from holding political office. Throughout the eras of Boris Yeltsin and Vladimir Putin, he continued to struggle for freedom of conscience and the protection of human rights. He joined a schismatic movement, modeled after the catacomb church of the 1930s. In 2012, he defended the young women of Pussy Riot, whose protest against the close relationship between the church and the state in Moscow's main cathedral led to a prison sentence for two of them. To the end of his life, he held fast to the ideals for which he so deeply and courageously stood: a free and democratic Church that spoke to the spiritual needs of the Russian people.

Gleb Iakunin played a significant role in Russia's national revival that connected nationalism and democratization in the last decades of the Soviet Union. In his letters, appeals to the government and the patriarch, his leadership of the Christian Committee, and his poetry, he fearlessly confronted the power structure and its ideology. In his 1977 letter to the Soviet Politburo, he already saw that the ideological train, "built only on an uphill track," had "run out of fuel."[116] His committee to defend religious believers emerged spontaneously from the grassroots of Russian society; its struggles for "freedom of conscience," one of the most basic of human rights, became a major focus of an emergent democratic culture in the Soviet Union. In Iakunin's case, the impetus behind his thoughts and actions derived from his religious consciousness, his developing sense of injustice, and, as he wrote in 1977, the patriarch's "present blindness and deafness to the needs of the suffering spiritual offspring of the Church." His devotion to the Church, to a revitalized Church, led him, as others among his contemporaries, to an interest in social and political problems. As the offshoots of his committee to defend religious believers spread into the Russian provinces, service to the Church also came to mean service to society. Therein lay, in the words of a perceptive Russian observer, the "processes of democratization and spiritual rebirth."[117] How deeply these processes took hold would have then, and continues to have, a large bearing on Russia's political direction.

5

"AN INWARD MUSIC"

Revolution and Resurrection in *Doctor Zhivago*

Dominic Erdozain

"He came, light and clothed in an aura, emphatically human, deliberately provincial, Galilean, and at that moment gods and nations ceased to be and man came into being..."

—Nikolai Nikolaievich ("Uncle Kolia"), *Doctor Zhivago*

"History," mused Yurii Zhivago, as he committed his deeper thoughts to paper, "cannot be seen." Its "organic agents" are as silent as the growing of grass or the gentle action of yeast. "No single man makes history," wrote the thoughtful doctor. And ideas, too, were overrated. Human cultures simply do not march to the beat of great men or grand theories. Reality abhors a dogma. Only in the Soviet Union, a regime built upon a drama of ideas, could such statements qualify as dissent. *Doctor Zhivago*—a "novel in prose"—was less a grenade hurled from a bunker than a series of awkward questions, expressed in an idiom of ordinary life. It was a work of demystification: a great unmasking of the Soviet Utopia performed under the modest rubric of love, decency, and human survival. Pasternak's ailing, all-feeling protagonist was a good man, but not a hero, and the genius of the novel was to fight the grandiloquence of revolutionary violence with tools that gained power from their fragility and weakness. *Doctor Zhivago* was a political event of some magnitude. It is also a work of deep and unconventional spirituality. Pasternak's novel, and the ferment of literary protest that it helped to ignite, may be considered part of the Russian religious renaissance of the twentieth century.

"Words Are Also Deeds": Poetry as Politics

Russian literature contained a long and distinguished current of prophetic resistance—a tradition that was political above all because it was ethical. A great writer, wrote Alexander Solzhenitsyn, was like "a second government." It was without exaggeration that the poet Evgenii Evtushenko could locate the origins of perestroika in the poetry readings of the 1950s. "The poetry of our generation was the cradle of glasnost," he claimed in the 1980s. A "hidden glasnost" had always existed in the nation's poetry and prose, he suggested, for Russian literature is the "literature of conscience."[1] The writer and dissident Andrei Amalrik agreed, suggesting that it had been a mistake for the regime not to ban the works of Tolstoy and Dostoevsky, for here was a body of writing "passionate in its defense of the individual against the system."[2] Russian literature, Amalrik argued, was a vital factor in the rise of dissidence in the 1960s and '70s, enabling what another writer termed an "internal emigration" from the scorched landscape of a totalitarian regime. As Philip Boobbyer has written, "The importance of literature was partly due to the fact that people were often isolated from one another" in the Soviet Union.[3] Literature was a refuge of resistance and a repository of values proscribed elsewhere. "Words," acknowledged a rueful party figure in 1968, "are also deeds."[4] In an "ideocratic" system, feverish in its pursuit of intellectual purity, the artist and phrasemaker was an active adversary.[5] Like the "holy fool" of Orthodox Christianity, the writer could go where others feared to tread.

There was a story that, after reading Mikhail Sholokhov's novel *And Quiet Flows the Don*, Stalin praised the work but advised the author to "convince" the main character, Melekhov, to stop loafing about and start serving in the Red Army. At their next meeting, Sholokhov pleaded the prerogatives of a writer: "I tried to do that, but Melekhov does not want it."[6] Not everyone enjoyed a dictator's favor, and Pasternak, for one, saw colleague after colleague succumb to the silent terror of the purges. How he survived to write and publish *Doctor Zhivago* is a mystery in keeping with the rambling serendipity of the novel—where lives are spared through no wisdom of their own; where life is an attitude, not a strategy. Like his candid and almost fatalistic creation, Zhivago, Pasternak scribbled his heresies in plain sight of the Soviet authorities, and he may only have escaped the fate of a friend such as Osip Mandel'shtam (who perished in the Gulag for his reckless "Stalin Epigram") because he did not insult the party leadership directly. Whatever the reasons for his survival, Pasternak's writing typifies the ambiguity of the artist who can be political only by burying politics within a story. Pasternak's tale of love and survival under the menacing "skies of war and turmoil" held a candle to the scarred surface of an all-knowing ideology without seeming to touch it. *Doctor Zhivago* was not the counter-thrust of dialectic—an "answer" clothed in a story—but a rising humanism that would one day justify Evtushenko's claims as to the literary origins of perestroika.

Pasternak was the son of a leading Russian painter, Leonid Pasternak, who introduced him as a child to Leo Tolstoy, Sergei Rachmaninov, and the poet Rainer Maria Rilke, among other luminaries. Tolstoy was a close friend of the family, and Pasternak recalled being swept off to see him on his deathbed, as his father hurried to sketch the novelist's final moments of consciousness. Having failed in his first love of music, Pasternak studied philosophy at the University of Marburg before establishing himself as one of Russia's leading poets. As one of a body of intellectuals that beheld the Revolution in mingled sentiments of awe, horror, and disgust, Pasternak could not bring himself to desert his country when the opportunity arose in the 1920s. He continued to admire Lenin, whom he saw in person at the Ninth Congress of Soviets in 1921, and he gradually cultivated that most potent dissent of all: disappointed hope. When two of his friends, Vladimir Maiakovskii and Nikolai Aseev, advocated the subordination of the arts to the needs of the Communist Party, in 1927, Pasternak "broke off relations" with them, writing darkly of the pressures exerted by politics on "conscience and feeling." The need of the hour was not usable art, he protested, but "great, courageous purity."

Pasternak showed plenty of it during the purges of the 1930s, when his refusal to sign a statement supporting the death penalty for the defendants in a show trial brought him under Stalin's radar. The statement had been drafted by the Union of Soviet Writers, and it is a telling comment on the latent power of the artist in Russian life that the party coveted its approval, as late as 1937. Pasternak bravely invoked this tradition of artistic immunity, urging his family's long-standing Tolstoyan convictions, and protesting that he could not stand as a judge between life and death. Briefly moved by "this pure poetic offshoot of Old Russia," as one scholar has put it, and sensing perhaps "a certain occult power in the one who defined the poet as 'brother to a dervish,'" Stalin spared him.[7] It is said that Stalin crossed his name off an execution list with the words, "Do not touch this cloud dweller." Or in another version of the story: "Leave that holy fool alone." Pasternak survived.

It remains a sobering commentary on the cruelties of Stalinism that the Second World War—"The Great Patriotic War"—came to many Russians as something like salvation—"a breath of fresh air, a purifying storm, a breath of deliverance," as Pasternak wrote in the epilogue to *Doctor Zhivago*. Pasternak served with enthusiasm (in a non-combatant role), before watching, with horror, as the Stalinist machine resumed service after the war. Families, awaiting the return of prisoners of war, saw them instead swept through their homeland in sealed carriages to the greater misery of the Gulag. In the scrambled reasoning of a maniacal dictator, a captured soldier was a traitor to the revolution, an enemy of the people. Damaged people, starving and broken, would now be worked to death in the concentration camps of the north. Everybody could see that there was something unique to Stalin in the frenzied cruelty of these years, the monstrous energy of a cult of terror. But the dangerous idea was to identify Lenin among the executioners, to trace the purges to the clearest and best of Soviet thinking. Still more shocking was to implicate Marx. This is where a love story would enter politics.

The first signal of a major work of dissent came in April 1954, during the "thaw" after Stalin's death, when Pasternak published ten "poems from the novel in prose, Dr. Zhivago." Three years later, a book that blurred the boundaries between poetry and prose, art and defiance, emerged from the press of an Italian publisher to international acclaim and the panicked indignation of the Communist Party. One year later, in 1958, *Il Dottor Zhivago* earned for its creator the Nobel Prize for Literature, an honor Pasternak was forced to decline in a statement that only highlighted the subversive pedigree of the project. Rarely, it seems, has the CIA worked so hard to promote a work of fiction, steering copies into the hands of Soviet visitors to Europe, and ghosting a lightweight, paperback edition back into the USSR. Demand for the novel was intense, and the emergence of a work Pasternak considered inferior to his poetry came to be regarded, for an American writer, as an "historic utterance," "an act of testimony as crucial to our moral and intellectual life as the Hungarian revolution [of 1956] to our political life."[8]

"It Was Then That Untruth Came Down on Our Land of Russia": Demystifying The Revolution

> Peter drew sword and thrust the cutthroats back
> And struck a man and smote off his ear.
> Whereupon he heard, 'No metal can resolve dissension.
> Put up thy sword again into his place.'
>
> —"Garden of Gethsemane," The Poems of Yurii Zhivago

Doctor Zhivago is the story of a Russian intellectual—a physician and a poet—living through the turbulence of the 1905 Revolution, the First World War and the numbing carnage of the Civil War. It is a story of loss and survival, in which the ordinary pleasures of human existence and the beauty and power of nature are magnified into instruments of salvation. Losing both parents in early childhood, and separated from his family by the War and the Revolution, Yurii Zhivago clings to the sanctity of life through the kindness of a stranger on a train, the rumbling energy of a waterfall, the calming rhythm of writing, and the unconventional providence of an affair. If Zhivago represents humanity—decent, hopeful, flawed—Larisa Feodorovna Guishar (Lara) graces the text as an awesome presence: a symbol of the beauty savaged, though not destroyed, by the Revolution. The central drama of the novel takes place around the town of Yuriatin, in the Ural Mountains, where Zhivago had taken his family to escape the revolutionary violence in Moscow. There he was reacquainted with his childhood friend, Lara, whose intense, bookish husband, Pasha, was now a commanding officer in the Red Army and the "terror of the region"—known to friend and foe alike as "Strelnikov": "the Shooter." Forced to serve as a military doctor to a unit of crazed and committed partisans, Zhivago gained privileged access to the disintegrating heart of the revolution: a fanaticism consuming itself.

It is to Pasternak's credit that he never loses sight of the grandeur and nobility of the original cause. But the bold rendering of the revolutionary mind as a mania, a "psychic illness," and an ever-widening license to kill is devastating in detail and historical judgment. While never attempting to justify the morality of an extra-marital affair, Pasternak sets the authenticity of his all-too-human protagonists against the violent delusions of a revolutionary consciousness. The purity of human intimacy judges the sundered, sundering career of a dogma. Like a twentieth-century Martin Luther, Pasternak seemed to be saying that truth is revealed in imperfection.

The trouble with the revolution was that it thought in concepts, not souls. Heir to the Russian Enlightenment of the nineteenth century, the Russian Revolution was criticism with ammunition. It was a glistening vision of the future with the means to make it happen. It was an intellectual experiment in which the youngest and weakest of the nation supplied the materials. As Yurii's friend Gordon explained the difference between Enlightenment and Revolution: "Now the metaphorical has become literal, children are children and the terrors are terrible, there you have the difference." Central to Pasternak's critique was an acknowledgment that the revolution had started well, with noble and virtuous ideals. But all relationship between method and cause had been lost. The revolution was an aching protest against "dirt, hunger, overcrowding, the degradation of the worker as a human being, the degradation of women." It was, in Strelnikov's phrase, a war on "the world of impunity, of brazen, insolent vice; of rich men laughing or shrugging off the tears of the poor, the robbed, the insulted, the seduced; the reign of parasites, whose only distinction was that they never troubled themselves about anything, never gave anything to the world, and left nothing behind them." "For us," explained the professional revolutionary, "life was a campaign. We moved mountains for those we loved, and if we brought them nothing but sorrow, they did not hold it against us because in the end we suffered more than they did." Socialism, Strelnikov continued, was the idea that "gave unity to the nineteenth century." It was a necessary rebellion, "absorbed and expressed in Lenin, who fell upon the old world as the personified retribution for its misdeeds."[9]

Courage and sacrifice were the marks of a "truly revolutionary temperament" and neither Pasternak nor his fictional self ever doubted that they were real. The revolutionary mind was an awesome phenomenon, registering in a man's appearance, speech, and movement. Zhivago is stunned when he first meets Strelnikov, in a military carriage in the Urals. He had never "come across anything so definite as this man's personality. . . . He took [everything] in his stride; he was disturbed by nothing. . . . In some inexplicable way it was clear at once that this man was entirely a manifestation of the will." There was something genuine here. Something historically exceptional. Yet the weakness of a revolutionary mindset, and the key to its descent into lazy brutality, was "mimicry." People copied one another. Killing became a habit. But Pasternak wanted to show the purity that preceded the barbarism. Not every revolutionary was a monster. "It is," he writes, "only in mediocre books that people are divided into two camps and have nothing to do with each other." Indeed one of the silent heroes of the book, the generous, mysterious Samdeviatov, is an enigma of torn duty: "a genuine supporter of the revolution" who nevertheless risks punishment by shielding and protecting a family who are escaping it. "He is," we are told, "just as familiar with Dostoievsky's *Possessed* as with the Communist Manifesto, and he talks about them equally well."[10]

Though Pasternak's sympathies were with the measured apocalypse of 1905, his rendering of the October Revolution is a marvel of anguished esteem. The revolution was a mystical event, redolent of the early days of Christianity: "Mother Russia is on the move, she can't stand still, she's restless and she can't find rest, she's talking and she can't stop. And it isn't as if only people were talking. Stars and trees meet and converse, flowers talk philosophy at night, stone houses hold meetings. It makes you think of the Gospel, doesn't it? The days of the apostles." The revolution, continued a breathless Zhivago, was "like a sigh suppressed too long. Everyone was revived, reborn, changed, transformed." "It seems to me that socialism is the sea, and all these separate streams, these private, individual revolutions, are flowing into it—the sea of life, the sea of spontaneity." The world of the nineteenth-century intellectual, "of writers racking their brains" in Parisian garrets, was taking physical form, and the experience was intoxicating. "Only now," enthuses Zhivago, "people have decided to experience it not in books and pictures but in themselves, not as an abstraction but in practice."[11]

Abstraction and alienation was not long in coming, however, and Pasternak did not pull his punches. Yet even as he contemplated the gleeful vengeance of the Bolsheviks, Zhivago's sarcasm was laced with awe: "What splendid surgery! You take a knife and with one masterful stroke you cut out all the old stinking ulcers. Quite simply, without any nonsense, you take the old monster of injustice, which has been accustomed for centuries to being bowed and scraped and curtsied to, and you sentence it to death." But "injustice," he quickly counters, means people. The stinking ulcers of the past were human beings. The crime of the Bolsheviks was to create "a new era" without concern for the old. "This new thing," reflects Zhivago, "this marvel of history, this revelation, is exploded right into the very thick of daily life without the slightest consideration for its course." The Bolsheviks were idealists and intellectuals, he never denied. They were also professional killers, and Zhivago moved that the two realities were linked. The cause swallowed the costs. "It has often happened in history that a lofty ideal has degenerated into crude materialism," reflected Gordon in Pasternak's mournful epilogue.[12] Rarely so completely as in Soviet Russia.

Against the steady, reliable rhythms of nature, Pasternak set the breathless progress of the revolution and its "merciless" emissaries. For a critical force does not know how to stop. Liberation became incarceration. The "death penalty, which had recently been abolished, was restored." Terror was the chosen instrument of redemption, and the Russian people "exchanged the oppression of the former state for the new, much harsher yoke of the revolutionary superstate." "Where is reality in Russia today?," complained Zhivago to a defender of the Bolsheviks' agricultural policy. "As I see it, reality has been so terrorized that it is hiding. I want to believe that the peasants are better off and flourishing. It is an illusion." As he later reflected to Lara, "Revolutionaries who take the law into their own hands are horrifying not because they are criminals, but because they are like machines that have got out of control, like runaway trains." Motives may have been originally pure, but consequences were ugly, "and now the blood of the defenseless flows in rivers." "The sea of blood will rise until it reaches every one of us," Zhivago had earlier prophesied. "The revolution is this flood."[13]

Clean-cut commissars, "aflame with the highest ideals," became hardened executioners, "invested with dictatorial powers." "They knew the slinking bourgeois breed, the ordinary holders of cheap government bonds, and they spoke to them without the slightest pity and with Mephistophelean smiles, as to petty thieves caught in the act." Class warfare became an orgy of vengeance: a flood of "pitiless remedies elaborated in the name of pity"; a torrent of cruelty unleashed in the name of freedom—"Such freedom as is not enjoyed by any other people in the world." It was a messianic consciousness evolving into something demonic.[14]

As a doctor, Yurii Zhivago was possessed of a singular gift: he was a brilliant and unerring "diagnostician." He could name an illness. And the gift transcended his profession. As a thinker and philosopher Zhivago's talent was for penetrating and unyielding judgment. To half-truths and comforting extenuations he was constitutionally immune. Zhivago's diagnosis of Russia's malady came in two parts, intellectual and spiritual, before blending into a final, summary judgment upon the Soviet experiment. The first was a withering analysis of the degree to which a pompous, posturing intellectualism had furnished the credentials of violence. Here, he and Lara were in perfect agreement. Pasha started to become Strelnikov when he began to study late into the night, started to suffer from insomnia, and slowly "turned into an arrogant, know-it-all misanthrope." The fierce clarity of an idea eclipsed the plodding mandates of love and filial duty. Intellectualism became an alibi for inhumanity. As Lara recalled, she and Pasha "began to be idiotically pompous with each other. Something showy, artificial, forced, crept into our conversation—you felt you had to be clever in a certain way about certain world-important themes. How could Pasha, who was so discriminating, so exacting with himself, who distinguished so unerringly between reality and appearance, how could he fail to notice the falsehood that had crept into our lives?," she wondered. Cocksure intellectualism, Lara lamented, crushed honest and authentic reasoning, until it became an offense to think beyond the scope of grand, dialectical arguments. The crisis of their marriage was the tragedy of Russia. For next came the descent of theory into maddening cliché:

> It was then that untruth came down on our land of Russia. The main misfortune, the root of all the evil to come, was the loss of confidence in the value of one's own opinion. People imagined that it was out of date to follow their own moral sense, that they must all sing in chorus, and live by other people's notions,

notions that were being crammed down everybody's throat. And then there arose the power of the glittering phrase, first the Tsarist, then the revolutionary.[15]

Both sides, in other words, were at it: substituting rhetoric for thought. The process, agreed Yurii, was insidious. The new thinking sounds so plausible, "Then you find in practice that what they mean by ideas is nothing but words—claptrap in praise of the revolution and the regime." The revolution was awash with phrases like "the dawn of the future," "the building of a new world," "the torch-bearers of mankind." "The first time you hear such talk," Yurii admitted, "you think 'What breadth of imagination, what richness!' But in fact it's so pompous just because it is so unimaginative and second-rate. Only the familiar transformed by genius is truly great." "How one wishes sometimes to escape from the meaningless dullness of human eloquence," Zhivago protests, "from all those sublime phrases, to take refuge in nature, apparently so inarticulate, or in the wordlessness of long, grinding labor, of sound sleep, of true music, or of a human understanding rendered speechless by emotion!"[16]

Eloquence was a tarnished commodity because it tempted its possessor with hubris. It was a kind of pharisaism of the mind: the sin of taking control with no living knowledge of the subject matter; it was power without sympathy. As Zhivago erupted as he endured the pieties of his partisan commander, "Liberius":

> Reshaping life! People who can say that have never understood a thing about life—they have never felt its breath, its heartbeat—however much they have seen or done. They look on it as a lump of raw material that needs to be processed by them, to be ennobled by their touch. But life is never a material, a substance to be molded.... The people you worship go in for proverbs, but they've forgotten one proverb—"You can lead a horse to water but you can't make it drink"—and they've got into the habit of liberating and of showering benefits on just those people who haven't asked for them.

Revolutionary principles were simply a "torrent of words . . . alien to life itself." Theory, dogma, and "textbook admirations" had paralyzed the senses. And among the casualties of a pontificating humanism was humanity itself. As Zhivago identified the great flaw in Strelnikov, after that ghostly first meeting, he determined that the otherwise brilliant individual "would not have made a scientist of the sort who break new ground." Strelnikov was a man at once energized and controlled by his principles. He was the walking embodiment of an ideology. "And if he were really to do good, he would have needed, in addition to his principles, a heart capable of violating them—a heart which knows only of particular, not of general cases, and which achieves greatness in little actions."[17] Such was Doctor Zhivago's protest.

To expose Strelnikov was to confront Lenin: a savage brilliance. It was also to encounter Marx and the whole "science" of human emancipation. Marxism was, Pasternak affirmed, a shimmering protest against "the brute insolence of money" and the systematic exploitation "of the poor." It ran a good race in the discipline of critique. The problems came when it started to build—mistaking its own, essentially destructive cosmology for historical fact. "Marxism a science?," Zhivago challenged a still-believing Samdeviatov. "Marxism is too uncertain of its ground to be a science. Sciences are more balanced, more objective. I don't know a movement more self-centered and further removed from the facts than Marxism." The difficulty was that it was still treated as a science, a science of human affairs, and "the men in power" were addicted to the "myth." For the myth of scientific socialism was "the myth of their infallibility." Theory and politics were inseparable. The revolution was built upon something approaching a lie. "Samdeviatov took the doctor's words for the fooling of a witty eccentric."[18]

A more subtle line of attack was an audacious mimicry of the Communist Manifesto itself: the robust accusation that communism had failed humanity precisely where it accused capitalism of failing. Where Marx and Engels complained of a reckless bourgeoisie tearing "asunder" the ancient ties of human society, "drown[ing]" conscience, ethics and "the most heavenly ecstasies of religious fervour … in the icy water of egotistical calculation," "stripp[ing] of its halo every occupation hitherto honoured and looked up to with reverent awe," and "reducing the family relation to a mere money relation," Pasternak simply returned the charges.[19] "Nothing was sacred any more,"[20] he complained of the socialist antidote—echoing Marx's summary indictment of capital in the Manifesto: "all that is holy is profaned." Marx and Engels protested a factory system that brutalized workers, divided families, and transformed children "into simple articles of commerce and instruments of labour."[21] Pasternak submitted the same complaint to an omnivorous revolutionary cause. As Zhivago finally snapped, under the weight of another sermon from Liberius: "I suppose I have to bless you for keeping me a prisoner and thank you for liberating me from my wife, my son, my home, my work, from everything I hold dear and that makes life worth living for me!" Lara's complaint was kindred: "They are made of stone, these people, they aren't human, with all their discipline and principles." "The workers of the world, the remaking of the universe—that's something! But a wife, just an individual biped, is of no more importance than a flea or a louse!"[22] She was talking about her husband.

The sin of the bourgeoisie, urged Marx and Engels in the Communist Manifesto, was a kind of idolatry: a cringing deference to "that single, unconscionable freedom—Free Trade." The market reduced life to pecuniary calculation. It created a world in its own, mangled "image." Pasternak would have agreed, but in the destruction of conscience and truth, the cure had eclipsed the disease. The revolution taught people to lie—a phenomenon augured by the vogue for nicknames, assumed identities, and an adolescent contempt for the past. As Yurii's father-in-law spoke of the new breed of posturing revolutionary: "Your Potpourris and Miroshkas are people without a conscience. They say one thing and do another."[23] Strelnikov was again the chilling exemplar. As Pasternak described his condition, as he and Zhivago met for a second and final time: "It was the disease, the revolutionary madness of the age, that at heart everyone was different from his outward appearance. No one had a clear conscience." Even as Strelnikov was "swayed by the impulse to unmask himself," to repent of his sins, his desiccated conscience was "monstrously distorting everything," rewriting the story and rationalizing his crimes.[24]

The effect of such delusions was a kind of moral and intellectual entropy, averred Zhivago, and the consequences were physical. In the failed utopia of the Soviet millennium, lying was literally a sickness:

> Microscopic forms of cardiac hemorrhages have become very frequent in recent years. They are not always fatal. Some people get over them. It's a typical modern disease. I think its causes are of a moral order. The great majority of us are required to live a life of constant, systematic duplicity. Your health is bound to be affected if, day after day, you say the opposite of what you feel, if you grovel before what you dislike and rejoice at what brings you nothing but misfortune. Our nervous system isn't just a fiction, it's a part of our physical body, and our soul exists in space and is inside us, like the teeth in our mouth. It can't be forever violated with impunity.[25]

This was powerful dissent. It asserted a link between the butchered idealism of Lenin and Strelnikov and the unbridled criminality of Stalinism. Under the exacting eye of revolutionary socialism, mistakes could not be acknowledged. To conceal the failures of collectivization, reflected one of Zhivago's surviving friends, "people had to be cured, by every means of terrorism, of the habit of thinking and judging for themselves, and forced to see what didn't exist, to assert the very opposite of what their eyes told them. This accounts for the unexampled cruelty of the Yezhov period." The reference was to the Great Purge. The Bolsheviks had achieved something perhaps unique in history: the annihilation of conscience. And it was in this context that war came as deliverance in 1941, "its real horrors, its real dangers, its menace of real death a blessing compared with the inhuman reign of the lie." "[T]hey brought relief because they broke the spell of the dead letter."[26] Behind the crimes of Stalinism lay more than a cult of personality. Violence was hard-wired into the revolutionary creed. Pasternak's final contention was that it would consume itself.

Strelnikov was nicknamed "Razstrelnikov"—"the Executioner"—by the soldiers. He was a "wild beast when it comes to counterrevolutionaries," guilty of crimes that made Lara's "blood run cold." He had, Lara feared, "handed himself over to a superior force, but a force that is deadening and pitiless and will not spare him in the end."[27] A cruder example, perhaps more typical of the revolution as a whole, was the appalling figure of Pamphil Palykh, a champion of the revolutionary cause who descended into brutalized insanity. Zhivago was asked to treat him, during his time with the partisans, and he was repelled by the task. Palykh was a zealot, who had always been "for extreme measures, harshness, execution." Such men, Zhivago soberly reflected, "needed no encouragement to hate intellectuals, officers, and gentry with a savage hatred." They "were regarded by enthusiastic left-wing intellectuals as a rare find and greatly valued. Their inhumanity seemed a marvel of class-consciousness, their barbarism a model of proletarian firmness and revolutionary instinct."[28] But it was important to call criminality by its name.

"I've done away with a lot of your kind," Palykh flatly informed the doctor, "there's a lot of officers' blood on my hands. Officers, bourgeois. And it's never worried me. Spilled it like water. Names and numbers all gone out of my head." Except one. Now he was experiencing hallucinations, reliving the moment he killed one "little fellow" just for fun, because the boy had made him laugh. The murdered youth was now appearing in his dreams, dancing upon his sanity. He also now feared for his family, his children, and the possibility of retribution for his many crimes. These children would wander into the camp, where Palykh would shower them with affection, carving out toys from freshly felled birch trees. And then he cracked. Tormented with anxiety for their future, "he killed them himself, felling his wife and three children with that same, razor-sharp ax that he had used to carve toys for the small girls and the boy, who had been his favorite."[29]

Strelnikov's fate was no happier. Three times, in that final interview with Zhivago, he uttered the words, "Forgive me"—a conversational courtesy that hinted at a dawning repentance. Zhivago probably would have forgiven him. But his crisp, dexterous suicide, which left blood in the snow "like rowan-berries," is Pasternak's judgment upon a worldview.[30] You cannot "expect variety from a gun," thought Zhivago, as he mused upon the madness of revolutionary violence.³¹ Strelnikov's death, so mundane and unromanticized, made the point: an extraordinary man made ordinary in violence.

"A New Interpretation of Christianity": The Art of Living

> "There will be no death, says St. John."
>
> —Yurii Zhivago

The tragedy of Pasha Antipov (Strelnikov) was a loss of personality and a loss of soul. Wounded and embittered by his own sufferings, he became an agent of vengeance, taking at last his own life. The glory of Lara Antipova was that suffering did not destroy her: it armed her with sympathy, and a rare sensitivity to the promise and wonder of life. "Lara was not religious. She did not believe in ritual. But sometimes, to be able to bear life, she needed the accompaniment of an inner music." "That music," Pasternak continues, "was God's word of life, and it was to weep over it that she went to church." As a priest "rattled off" the Beatitudes, at a pace that suggested a certain closure to the mysteries upon his lips, Lara "started and stood still," translating them into her own language: "This was about her. He was saying: Happy are the downtrodden. They have something to tell about themselves. They have everything before them. That was what He thought. That was Christ's judgment."³²

Salvation in *Doctor Zhivago* is often humdrum: the "strong refreshment" of sleep; the stolid ecstasy of physical labor; the glory of "a big bowl of cabbage soup." Some have detected philistinism in Pasternak's gentle odes to domesticity. But the task of the poet was to transfigure the ordinary, said Zhivago, and there were unknown riches within the world that is mistakenly termed mundane. As Yurii expressed one of the book's celebrated aphorisms: "Man is born to live, not to prepare for life." Yurii and Lara shared a moral and intellectual protest against messianic violence, but the stronger protest was existential: a lived dissent against cleansing utopias and calculating futures. Zhivago "realized that he was a pygmy before the monstrous machine of the future. . . . Ordeals were ahead, perhaps death." But he did not attempt to rationalize his circumstances: "the doctor saw life as it was." He resisted the vertigo of analysis by focusing on what was before him: "His wife, his child, the necessity to earn money, the humble daily ritual of his practice—these were his salvation."³³

That separation from his family, and later Lara, did not drive Zhivago to despair was, however, testimony to a resilience that ran deeper than honest toil and cabbage soup. The difference between resignation and survival was for Yurii, as for Lara, an "inner music": a doctrine of eternal life. "All great, genuine art, resembles and continues the Revelation of St. John," reflected a young Zhivago. Genuine art had "two constant, two unending concerns: it always meditates on death and thus always creates life."[34] Like the poems that emerged after Zhivago's death, and Lara's conversion from violated teenager to godlike savior, *Doctor Zhivago* is a story of survival against impossible odds: a study in resurrection. In the words of Zhivago's poem, "Holy Week":

> And when the midnight comes
> All creatures and all flesh will fall silent
> On hearing spring put forth its rumor
> That just as soon as there is better weather
> Death itself can be overcome
> Through the power of the Resurrection.[35]

One of the sites of Pasternak's theology of resurrection is nature: a reality personified into a force that refuses to cooperate with the folly surrounding it. Throughout *Doctor Zhivago*, nature carries hopes rudely denied elsewhere. A "moonlit night" was, for the poet-physician, "like merciful love." The arrival of spring was a mystical event, when "everything was fermenting, growing, rising with the magic yeast of life. The joy of living, like a gentle wind, swept in a broad surge indiscriminately through fields and towns, through walls and fences, through wood and flesh." The melting of snow "all over Russia" presaged deeper awakenings: "At first the snow thawed quietly and secretly from within. But by the time half the gigantic labor was done it could not be hidden any longer and the miracle became visible. Waters came rushing out from below with a roar. The forest stirred in its impenetrable depth, and everything in it awoke." Nature was more than a metaphor for Zhivago: "Ever since his childhood, Yurii Andreievich had been fond of woods seen at evening against the setting sun. At such moments he felt as if he too were being pierced by shafts of light. It was as though the gift of the living spirit were streaming into his breast, piercing his being and coming out at his shoulders like a pair of wings."[36]

Nature was a "refuge" from the failed grandeur of "human eloquence." It was an escape from human artifice, both silly and cruel. Yet it was secondary, in the novel, to a profoundly spiritual doctrine of human personality. That nature bore the scars of human folly was crime enough, but a single human life counted for more. When Zhivago was forced into combat by his partisan captors, he could not bring himself to train fire on the enemy. Instead, he aimed his rifle at a tree—always a symbol of life for Pasternak—watching as its noble fabric rippled with the impact of the bullets. But as one shot flew toward the adopted target it was intercepted by a moving body, which crumpled with a hideous elegance. As the enemy command retreated, Zhivago "went out into the field to the young White Guardsman whom he had killed. The boy's handsome face bore the marks of innocence and of all-forgiving suffering. 'Why did I kill him?' thought the doctor." He carefully unbuttoned the boy's coat, discovered his name, and unfolded a piece of paper he had been carrying inside a gold case: it bore the words of the Ninety-first Psalm. But as Zhivago mournfully scanned the flawless Slavonic text, the boy "groaned and stirred." Standard procedure would have been to kill him there and then. It was the time "when savagery was at its height. Prisoners did not reach headquarters alive and enemy wounded were knifed in the field." But Zhivago skillfully replaced the boy's outer clothing with the uniform of a fallen comrade and secretly nursed him "back to health." He finally released the young soldier in the full knowledge that he would go back to his commander and "continue fighting the Reds."[37] It was an act of folly, but so was war. Zhivago was moved by the soldier's trust in the promises of "the Most High" and he anchored his own humanism to a similarly religious grasp of the sanctity of life.

The central figure in Zhivago's spiritual education was Nikolai Nikolaievich, "Uncle Kolia," a priest-turned-writer who took care of Yurii after the death of his parents. Uncle Kolia had been defrocked at his own request, turning his literary talents and subterranean theology to a career in progressive journalism before achieving fame as an author. Emigrating to Switzerland after the revolution, Uncle Kolia developed a mystical theory of "history as another universe, made by man with the help of time and memory in answer to the challenge of death." Such works "were inspired by a new interpretation of Christianity, and led directly to a new conception of art." It was from Kolia that Yurii gleaned his exalted view of creativity as creation, and a bracingly theological account of human relationship as divine intercourse. "Yura realized the great part his uncle had played in molding his character," and his friend, Gordon, was similarly indebted, admitting that "we both got our ideas from your uncle" as he expatiated on the true meaning of "the Gospel." For the Gospel "does not make assertions" or issue commands. It simply asks: "Do you want to live in a completely new way?"[38] This was the new Christianity.

Yurii's first lesson in this bravely realized eschatology came as he listened to Uncle Kolia expounding his philosophy of history to Ivan Ivanovich, a teacher and popular author, as they worked on some proofs. Yurii and Ivan listened politely as Kolia raged against the intellectual fashions of the day: the insufferable habit of swearing by "names"—whether "Soloviev or Kant or Marx"—rather than cultivating knowledge at first hand. "Only individuals seek the truth," he insisted. What was learned from others was never really learned. This was the message and example of Christ, the supreme contrarian. At this point, Ivan Ivanovich looked confused. Hadn't Kolia been "unfrocked"? Who was he to talk about Christ? Uncle Kolia continued:

> As I was saying, one must be true to Christ. I'll explain. What you don't understand is that it is possible to be an atheist, it is possible not to know whether God exists, or why, and yet believe that man does not live in a state of nature but in history, and that history as we know it now began with Christ, and that Christ's Gospel is its foundation. Now what is history? It is the centuries of systematic explorations of the riddle of death, with a view to overcoming death. That's why people discover mathematical infinity and electromagnetic waves, that's why they write symphonies. Now, you can't advance in this direction without a certain faith. You can't make such discoveries without spiritual equipment. And the basic elements of this equipment are in the Gospels.

What were they?

> To begin with, love of one's neighbor, which is the supreme form of vital energy. Once it fills the heart of man it has to overflow and spend itself. And then the two basic ideals of modern man—without them he is unthinkable—the idea of free personality and the idea of life as sacrifice. Mind you, all this is still extraordinarily new. There was no history in this sense among the ancients. They had blood and beastliness and cruelty and pockmarked Caligulas who had no idea of how inferior the system of slavery is. They had the boastful dead eternity of bronze monuments and marble columns. It was not until after the coming of Christ that time and man could breathe freely. It was not until after Him that men began to live toward the future.[39]

Ivan Ivanovich protested that such ideas were not good for his stomach. His doctors had forbidden metaphysics. But Yurii was listening. He suddenly perceived that the truth of Christianity was that "all human lives were interrelated." Everything was sacred. Human events took place "not only on the earth, in which the dead are buried, but also in some other region which some called the Kingdom of God, others history, and still others by some other name." Christianity was not duty but wonder. It was a way of seeing. After Christ, nothing could be considered ordinary. Uncle Kolia again elaborated:

> But don't you see, this is just the point—what has for centuries raised man above the beast is not the cudgel but an inward music: the irresistible power

of unarmed truth, the powerful attraction of its example. It has always been assumed that the most important things in the Gospels are the ethical maxims and commandments. But for me the most important thing is that Christ speaks in parables taken from life, that He explains the truth in terms of everyday reality. The idea that underlies this is that communion between mortals is immortal, and that the whole of life is symbolic because it is meaningful.[40]

This was the meaning of the Incarnation: a reappraisal of the mundane; an inversion of the stale arithmetic of social prestige. Rome had been "a flea market of borrowed gods and conquered peoples," a sick and bloated civilization. "And then, into this tasteless heap of gold and marble, He came, light and clothed in an aura, emphatically human, deliberately provincial, Galilean, and at that moment gods and nations ceased to be and man came into being—man the carpenter, man the plowman, man the shepherd with his flock of sheep at sunset, man who does not sound in the least proud."[41]

Kolia's sermons serve as the manifesto of Pasternak's humanism. Time and again, he links the inward music of individuality to Christian sources, indeed Christ himself. This was what a messianic revolution had left behind. "Greek philosophers, the Roman moralists, and the Hebrew prophets" had each spoken of equality before God. But none could speak as Christianity had of "the mystery of the individual." "When the Gospel says that in the Kingdom of God there are neither Jews nor Gentiles," urged Gordon, what it meant was: "In that new way of living and new form of society, which is born of the heart, and which is called the Kingdom of Heaven, there are no nations, there are only individuals." This was why Christianity came, to those who understood it, as a "glorious holiday"; a "liberation from the curse of mediocrity." Pasternak drew the ire of Jewish readers by adding that the Jewish people, still committed to the idea of being "a nation and nothing but a nation," missed the historic moment: "they actually saw and heard it and let it go!" They clung to the nationalistic miracle of the Exodus above the greater miracle of a child who would end all nationality. They allowed the "power and beauty to leave them."[42] It was an uncomfortable assertion, but the larger point was that Christianity was now speaking to the new Rome of Soviet ideology: the empire that destroys in order to save. Against this addiction to collective identity Pasternak set the incomparable individual: the sacred person who cannot be coached into conformity.

Later in the story, Yurii listened intently as Lara's friend, Sima, expounded the meaning of Christianity in history. She lamented the tendency of Christians to miss the significance of the Gospel by blending the Old and New Testaments into one. Christianity was not continuity but rupture. Christ's birth, of "an everyday figure who would have gone unnoticed in the ancient world," was an event "equal in significance to the migration of a whole people." A gentle and powerless savior was an idea of political genius, and more than an idea. "Something in the world had changed. Rome was at an end. The reign of numbers was at an end. The duty, imposed by armed force, to live unanimously as a people, as a whole nation, was abolished. Leaders and nations were relegated to the past." "They were replaced," she continued, "by the doctrine of individuality and freedom. Individual human life became the life story of God, and its contents filled the vast expanses of the universe. As it says in a liturgy for the Feast of the Annunciation, Adam tried to be like God and failed, but now God was made man so that Adam should be made God."[43]

This was a new Christianity, Sima urged, because it "repudiates all compulsion." The story of Christ's treatment of Mary Magdalene, she continued, was a revolution still waiting to happen: "What familiarity, what equality between God and life, God and the individual, God and a woman!" Zhivago listened to Sima through a "mist of oncoming drowsiness" and "her reflections delighted him. 'Of course, she's taken it all from Uncle Nikolai,' he thought. 'But how intelligent she is, how talented.'" Lara, meanwhile, said nothing. Hers was to live the sermon, and it was her poised, humble, unbroken individuality that made her "a living indictment of the age." Without formal religiosity, Lara breathed a Christianity of kindness, purpose, and compulsive goodness. Her love for Yurii was "like a breath of eternity."[44]

Some have considered this "Pasternakian Christ" simply "a conceptual moment," a rhetorical device. Others have perceived "rationalism" in Uncle Kolia's left-field "homilies about immortality."[45] Pasternak's Christianity, it has been said, was of a kind that even an agnostic might applaud. This was perhaps the point. In Uncle Kolia, Gordon, Lara, Sima, or Zhivago himself, Pasternak is very far from preaching a return to orthodoxy. He is venturing ideas lost to the churches. Christianity had too often served as a vehicle of repression and an unworthy escape from the mundane, but it was in the world that true religion entered its stride. Being "true to Christ" meant honoring the now. That such a Christianity parted company with conventional piety does not reduce the theological force of the novel. One scholar has detected "a constructive Christian economy" in *Doctor Zhivago*, "a truly and essentially Christian attitude," while Thomas Merton found "a deep and uncompromising spirituality" in the novel, describing it as "deeply religious and even definitely Christian."[46]

Pasternak was explicit if not open about his religious inspiration. Baptized by Akulina Gavrilova, the nanny who introduced him to Christianity and took him to Russian Orthodox services, Pasternak attributed his creativity to his half-secret faith. As he explained in a letter to Jacqueline de Proyart in 1959, "the fact of my baptism was accompanied by various complications and remained semi-secret and private." But, he insisted, it provided him "with rare and exceptional inspiration rather than calm habit." "I believe this to be the source of my originality," he wrote. "During the years 1910–1912, when the main roots and foundation of that originality—together with my vision of things, of the world, of life—were taking shape, I lived most of my life in Christian thought." "I very nearly became Orthodox," he added, "marrying an Orthodox woman would have done it."[47] In his terse and eccentric autobiography, *Safe Conduct*, Pasternak describes the Bible as "the notebook of humanity."[48]

Part of the dynamism of this new Christianity was that it did not sit comfortably with institutions, ecclesiastical or otherwise. Pasternak was in conflict with flesh-hating religion as well as life-crushing communism, though the weight of his protest clearly fell on the latter. Zhivago dies in genteel poverty, a symbol of a ragged and decimated intelligentsia, while Lara—the novel's purest entity—falls grimly to Stalin's reign of numbers: "One day Larisa Feodorovna went out and did not come back. She must have been arrested in the street at that time. She vanished without a trace and probably died somewhere, forgotten as a nameless number on a list that afterwards got mislaid, in one of the innumerable mixed or women's concentration camps in the north."[49]

Doctor Zhivago—whose name means "living"—gave dignity to the victims of Soviet terror and hope to survivors. Literary scholars may have assigned the book a rather cool "B+ to A– rating,"[50] but the Kremlin delivered its own approbation. "No figure within the USSR," wrote one scholar, "was treated to a more shrill and vulgar chorus of official denunciation during 'de-Stalinization' than this mild poet." Pasternak's last years were spent in forced isolation, "surrounded by petty harassments and veiled threats." Pasternak had challenged the whole conception of the "writer-as-cheerleader" and he had skewered the technocratic bombast of the Soviet order by "creating an essentially passive sufferer" with a credible and appealing "inner life." In one scholar's perceptive summary: *Doctor Zhivago* was "not a contrary revolution, but the contrary of a revolution."[51] The medium was very much the message. As a still-youthful Zhivago explained his disenchantment: "I used to be quite revolutionary-minded, but now I think that nothing can be gained by violence. People must be drawn to good by goodness."[52] It was for such sentiments that Pasternak was pursued with more venom than "an avowed capitalist." He had named the illness of the communist utopia.[53]

Pasternak exerted an enormous influence on a generation of dissidents that began to emerge after the trial of the poet Iosif Brodskii in 1964. Andrei Siniavskii and Iulii Daniel, whose trial for "anti-Soviet agitation and propaganda" brought the Soviet legal system to international attention in 1966, had both been pallbearers at Pasternak's funeral in May 1960. This was, writes Philip Boobbyer, "in itself a gesture of defiance of the regime." Indeed Siniavskii, who worked at the Gorky Institute of World Literature and taught courses at Moscow University, was a specialist on Pasternak.[54] Meanwhile, *Doctor Zhivago* continued to enrich that wider stream of "Christian personalism" of which it was both product and exemplar. One of the most important religious dissidents of the late Soviet period was Aleksandr Ogorodnikov, whose conversion to Christianity in 1973 was stimulated by access to the works of Dostoevsky, Solov'ev and "a copy of Boris Pasternak's novel *Doctor Zhivago*" supplied through a "contact person at the US embassy in Moscow." Such works led him to the New Testament and, from there, a "sensation of the presence of God in his life."[55] *Doctor Zhivago* was not a religious work but it was part of a religious renaissance: a vital link between the muzzled giants of Dostoevsky and Tolstoy and the gathering ferment of Solzhenitsyn and Sakharov. It proclaimed "freedom of the soul" to a world that had forgotten the meaning of either. Pasternak concluded his masterpiece with two of Zhivago's friends, leafing through one of the doctor's surviving works, breathing the new air of Moscow after the War:

> To the two old friends, as they sat by the window, it seemed that this freedom of the soul was already there.... Thinking of this holy city and of the entire earth, of the still-living protagonists of this story, and their children, they were filled with tenderness and peace, and they were enveloped by the unheard music of happiness that flowed all about them and into the distance. And the book they held seemed to confirm and encourage their feeling.[56]

6
"THE PEARL OF AN UNREASONABLE THOUGHT"
Religion and the Poetic Imagination

Josephine von Zitzewitz

This essay explores the revival of religious, and specifically biblical, imagery in late Soviet "unofficial" poetry, that is, poetry that only circulated in samizdat. Religious imagery was central to the work of a literary current that dominated the underground in the 1970s and early 1980s. The epicenter of this current was in Leningrad, the home of poets such as Viktor Krivulin, Sergei Stratanovskii, Elena Shvarts, Oleg Okhapkin, Vasilii Filippov, and others. A similar orientation can be found in the work of certain Moscow-based writers, notably Olga Sedakova and Ivan Zhdanov, who will also be discussed in this essay.

For most, but not all of these poets, the turn toward Christian motifs in their work went hand in hand with a discovery of Orthodox Christianity in their personal lives. "Religiousness" was embraced widely by underground intellectuals in the 1970s.[1] In most cases however, it is unproductive to read their poems as confessional literature. Elena Shvarts, one of the protagonists of this study, once said: "Poetry began as holy madness [...] how gorgeous poetry was when it dived into the sea of madness and came back up to the light of reason, in its predators' teeth the pearl of an unreasonable thought."[2] Shvarts hints at a tremendous power inherent in poetry, a power that opposes and challenges the materialism and positivism of Soviet ideology. Soviet ideology negated the existence of a metaphysical dimension, suppressing both the irrational and the religious. Shvarts claims boldly that poetry touches upon both these spheres. This essay will explore how Christian imagery is harnessed in order to convey something of the irrational power and metaphysical dimension of art—a dimension that is expressed aesthetically rather than discursively and as such is irreducible to content.

Nowhere is Russian literature's belonging to the European tradition more evident than in the use of biblical imagery, where Russian writers have used and adapted the archetypical stories and images of the Judeo-Christian heritage in order to interpret historical change and bring into sharp relief the universal qualities of current events. Arguably, the early twentieth century was a special period in this respect. Russian religious philosophy was flourishing and fertilizing literature, and vice versa.[3] To give a few select examples, biblical motifs helped the Symbolist Aleksandr Blok explore the "music of the revolution" that was in the air in the 1910s ("Na pole Kulikovom" [On Kulikovo Field]) and erupted in 1917 ("Dvenadtsat'" [The twelve]); the Bible supplied the imagery for the technocratic fantasies of the proletarian poets (for example, Vladimir Kirillov's "Zheleznyi messia" [The iron messiah], the anti-bourgeois visions of the Futurist Vladimir Maiakovskii ("Oblako v shtanakh" [A cloud in trousers]) and the highly individual adaptations of Marina Tsvetaeva (for example, "Magdalina" [Mary Magdalene], "Blagaia vest" [The good news], "Doch Iaira" [The daughter of Jairus]).[4]

This heritage, suppressed by the Bolsheviks over several decades, resurfaced in the 1960s when the nascent cultural underground rediscovered the modernists. The poetic current under study here that sought to reestablish the connection with this tradition has been dubbed "metaphysical poetry,"[5] "spiritual lyrics,"[6] and "Leningrad religious poetry."[7] Other researchers call it "metarealism," acknowledging the fact that these poets portray a multilayered reality.[8] Vladislav Kulakov summarizes the motivation of the underground as follows: "People really wanted something 'meta-,' a different dimension in poetry that had been forgotten during the Soviet years. Soviet poetry was utilitarian, pure physics, and what people wanted was metaphysics."[9] Religious imagery was one of several poetic devices used to invoke the metaphysical dimension.

Among the first writers in the 1960s to use Christian imagery in this way were Iosif Brodskii and Leonid Aronzon. Olga Sedakova, a pertinent observer, hones in on inspiration as the most metaphysical aspect of Brodskii's 1962 poem "*Rozhdestvenskii romans*" (A Christmas ballad): "The phenomenon of inspiration moves my contemporaries more profoundly than most other things. After all it means that our world is open and permeable to a different kind of power; it brings festive news of a different kind of depth inherent in all events."[10] The poem in question contains few palpable Christian motifs beyond the title. Rather, it chimed with the zeitgeist, giving expression to the "inexplicable longing" of Brodskii's generation and those who came after him.

Yet the mere mention of Christmas is sufficient to allude to the dimension beyond that which is visible.[11] The still considerable allusive power of the Christian mysteries invokes the inalienable inner life and affirms the power of art. Understanding literature in this way invested poetry with subversive force and posed a challenge to official Soviet culture with its compulsive rationality and insistence that literature be accessible and transparent. Sedakova has rightly identified this kind of poetry as "aesthetic and spiritual resistance" to the Soviet project.[12]

Religious imagery thus had cultural rather than strictly religious functions. It served the poets as a token of belonging to a cultural sphere that had nothing in common with Soviet culture, a culture that included the metaphysical dimension and the segment of literary heritage that had always acknowledged this dimension. Moreover, religious imagery also served purely aesthetic purposes. The exploration of the spiritual dimension went hand in hand with the longing for a language that acknowledged the transcendence of reality, as well as a rejection of both the materialism of Soviet ideology and the prescriptive official aesthetics.

Once poetry becomes a bridge to the metaphysical dimension, the association with madness made by Elena Shvarts seems less far-fetched. Madness and metaphysics are both located outside the rational sphere and as such easy to reconcile. Moreover, poetic inspiration as mad frenzy is an accepted cultural stereotype. The inspired poet is granted a sudden, fleeting glimpse at "something"; he or she can temporarily access a knowledge normally hidden in the unconscious. Insight is a profoundly personal experience not accessible to reason; it can thus be neither straightforwardly described nor explained. Yet the poet's rare literary gift communicates his or her vision to the reader without rationalizing it. Olga Sedakova calls inspiration a "miracle": "And since this principle, usually called inspiration, is wonderful [...] the special power of poetry, its non-discursive idea and practical contemplation lie in its ability to draw the reader into this experience."[13] According to this definition, the poet is a contemplative, a mystic. And yet poetry has an inherently practical side. In the words of Sedakova, this kind of poetry activates "a liberating force, of the same nature as poetry, a force that opens other areas of meaning and feeling, a force that establishes a *connection*, [that] appeared like a lightning strike. That was the phenomenon of the free soul. The soul's speech."[14] There is thus a consonance between poetry and "the soul," a word that was taboo in official Soviet poetry. Poetry liberates that part of the soul that seeks connection. This longing for connection with something larger than ourselves, yet essentially *of the same nature* is arguably the original religious impulse.[15] In this sense poetry expresses the religious impulse in its purest form.

A Role Model? Boris Pasternak and the Centered World

Boris Pasternak (1890-1960) came of age as a poet during the 1910s. One of the few great modernists who neither emigrated nor perished under Stalin, he was a living link to the prerevolutionary tradition. Pasternak was of Jewish origin, baptized in childhood and thoroughly familiar with the Christian tradition. Yet the seminal work in which the archetypical images and stories of the Bible provide the basis for understanding the human condition and interpreting present historical circumstances came late in his life.[16] *Doctor Zhivago* (1957), as Erdozain notes above, won Pasternak a Nobel Prize that he was forced to return, and the novel was available in the Soviet Union only in samizdat or foreign ("tamizdat") editions until 1988. What follows is a brief discussion of some motifs from the "biblical" poems of *Doctor Zhivago* as they will help us to compare and contrast the approach taken by later poets who looked back on the modernist tradition.

The worldview that defines the novel, and the appended cycle of poems, is synthetic and professes the interconnectedness of all things in the world, visible and invisible, through a common center. This is Pasternak's key principle of *stseplenie*, linkage.[17] The function of biblical stories is not to explain life discursively, but to show it. They are important not for their discursive content, but rather their symbolic power:

> We still think that the most important aspect of the Gospels are the moral pronouncements and rules inherent in the commandments, but for me the most important thing is that Christ speaks in parables taken from everyday life, explaining the truth through the light of the ordinary. This is based on the idea that any exchange between mortals is immortal and that life is symbolic because it is important.[18]

In a life that is symbolic, the poet has an important role as the interpreter of the metaphors life throws up. In this sense poems are equivalent to biblical texts because they both explain and interpret life.[19]

Nine of the twenty-five poems from the cycle at the end of *Doctor Zhivago* feature biblical subject matter.[20] Most of them are nature poems, in which animated nature proclaims the indissoluble link between human beings and their surroundings. Trees in particular function as a universal symbol of life and fruitfulness. Their symbolic power is acknowledged in many religions. In the Bible there is the tree of the knowledge of good and evil (Genesis 2-3); the burning bush in which Moses encounters God (Exodus 3); the barren fig tree cursed by Christ (Matthew 21); the thorny bush whose twigs are wrought into the crown of thorns that adorns Christ's head (Mark 15, John 19); the vine and branches that come to symbolize the relationship between Christ and his church (John 15); and finally the ultimate "tree," the cross from which new hope grew. Pasternak was fond of trees, and all the late Soviet poets discussed below used trees as multifaceted symbols, too. Thus the focus of this analysis is on "tree" poems, without claiming to offer direct comparisons.[21]

The "earliness of the world" in "Na strastnoi" (During Holy Week) describes the dark of an early spring morning. Yet the same stanza mentions Easter, making it clear that the "sleep" also refers to the state of the world before the resurrection:

> Еще кругом ночная мгла.
> Еще так рано в мире,
> Что звездам в небе нет числа,
> И каждая, как день, светла,
> И если бы земля могла,
> Она бы Пасху проспала
> Под чтение Псалтыри.

> [Night is still dark all around
> It is still so early in the world
> That it's impossible to count the stars
> Each one burns as bright as the day
> And if earth could
> She would sleep through Easter
> Listening to the Psalms]

Toward the end of the poem, the trees seem to participate in the Easter liturgy, almost anthropomorphic in their "nakedness," yet always recognizable for what they are:

> А в городе, на небольшом
> Пространстве, как на сходке,
> Деревья смотрят нагишом
> В церковные решетки.[22]

> [And in the town, in a small space
> Trees seem to gather
> and in their nakedness
> They look through the church's lattice.]

"Na strastnoi" bears witness to an experience of connection and unity between things and between heaven and earth. The Easter liturgy turns the archetypical motif of spring as the return of life into a symbol of a new beginning that is spiritual as well as physical. Christian imagery thus serves to express a mystical cosmic experience. For Pasternak, this experience lies at the heart of poetic inspiration.

It seems that "resurrection," for the poet, implies a return to creativity. In "Chudo" (The miracle), the poet imagines Christ's encounter with the barren fig tree. Jesus is journeying through an inhospitable desert landscape on to Jerusalem, tormented by the premonition of the suffering he will have to endure. On this path he encounters the barren fig tree and curses it. In the Gospel version (Matthew 21) the tree merely withers upon being cursed. Pasternak's imagination goes further, and Christ's condemnation burns the tree to the core:

> По дереву дрожь осужденья прошла,
> Как молнии искра по громоотводу.
> Смоковницу испепелило до тла.

> [A shiver of condemnation went through the tree
> Like a spark of lightning through a lightning conductor
> The fig tree was burned to the core.]

In the final stanza, the voice changes from third person observer to first person plural:

> Но чудо есть чудо, и чудо есть Бог.
> Когда мы в смятеньи, тогда средь разброда
> Оно настигает мгновенно, врасплох.[23]

> [But the miracle's a miracle, and the miracle is God.
> When we are in turmoil
> It strikes in an instant
> Amidst the confusion, by surprise.]

It is thus not just the tree that is affected by the "miracle that is God" but all of humanity. Jesus condemns the tree because it of its refusal to bear fruit. This is a failure to participate in life when necessary; and this topic was picked up by Olga Sedakova, an admirer and scholar of Pasternak, in the 1980s (see below). Seen in the context of the entire Zhivago cycle, the "miracle that is

God" also refers to the poet's own creativity, which strikes from above and during moments of utter vulnerability. Poetry requires sacrifice on the part of the poet.[24] This notion is encountered, in various forms, in the work of the 1970s writers.

The late Soviet underground poets were formed in a fundamentally different world. Russian Orthodoxy, the omnipresent state religion of the Russian Empire, had been factually banished from official life for fifty years. Although never outlawed, the official church was crippled by the closure of seminaries, a shortage of priests, and the prohibition of proselytism.[25] The religion the young poets recovered was fragmented. The five poets briefly discussed below all bring their very own perspective to their engagement with the biblical world. What they have in common is that their "free soul" still regards the remnants of the Christian universe as the best way to establish a connection with that which is greater than them. It is perhaps evidence of the fundamental connectedness of the (European) world that a crucial feature of late twentieth-century Christianity among the educated is the rejection of the traditional anthropomorphic "Father" God in favor of a mystical (and therefore individual) experience of God.[26]

Olga Sedakova—Vulnerability and Harmony

Olga Sedakova, born in 1949 and based in Moscow, is not only a poet, but also a historian of the Russian language, university lecturer, accomplished translator, literary critic, and essayist. She has written on many of the great poets of Russia and Western Europe, as well as on her contemporaries, late Soviet unofficial literature, and contemporary culture.[27] Unlike most of the underground writers who became interested in Christianity in the 1970s, Sedakova had been familiar with the Russian Orthodox tradition since childhood, through the example of her much-loved grandmother, a practicing believer.

Sedakova's central tenet is that poetry is not *about* something, and as such not about religion either.[28] For Sedakova, poetry is "participation" in the world and its ongoing creation. The poet's particular path of participation is the search for beauty, which in poetry is synonymous with harmonious form. Of all the poets discussed, Sedakova's work constitutes the clearest continuation of a literary tradition that is grounded in the belief in a harmonious, centered universe in which all things are connected through a common essence. In some of her early poems, this center, where all things collapse into one, is invoked in literal terms:

Туда, где росли мы, [...]
туда, где услышать мы были должны
одну тишину от струны до струны,
[...]
мне однажды случится вернуться.²⁹

[To the place where we grew ...
where all we needed to hear
was silence from one string to the other
...
I will once have the chance to return.]

In 1982 Sedakova, pondering Pasternak's idea of linkage, remarked: "Something whole is clearly in charge of all separate things, each one of which constitutes merely a momentary service, and the cramming of him who is omnipresent and moves all things into the burning bush of the cloud of one thing or the other."³⁰ It is intriguing that she should invoke the burning bush in this place. Trees and gardens in an explicitly biblical context are a staple of her work.³¹ Two seminal examples are "Elegiia smokovnitsy" (Elegy to the fig tree), dedicated to Ivan Zhdanov, discussed below, and "Dikii shipovnik" (The wild rose), the title poem of her first collection.

"Elegiia smokovnitsy" interweaves some of the best-known New Testament parables and stories, including the barren fig tree (Luke 13), the cursing of the fig tree (Matthew 21), the ten virgins (Matthew 25), and Mary Magdalene anointing Jesus's feet with oil (John 12) into a hymn to the quality most needed in a Christian—faithfulness and the willingness to serve:

без факела выйдешь—позор!—
к Тому, кто не извещал ни о дне, ни о часе,
но о том, что небо нуждается в верности,
светильник—в масле,
жажда—в плодах.

[You leave without a torch—the shame of it—
to meet Him who gave neither the day not the hour
but said that heaven needs faithfulness,
a lamp needs oil
and thirst needs fruit.]

Through the association with the virgins who forgot to bring oil for their lamps and thus missed out on the wedding banquet, the barren tree becomes the symbol of all those who failed to prepare for the coming of Christ. The poem ends with an enigmatic, contradictory vision of impossible hope in future unity:

> Кто просит—однажды получит.
> Кто просит прощенья—
> однажды будет прощен. [...]
> Сердце ему обнимает лишенье,
> как после долгой разлуки жениха обнимают или отца.³²

> [He who asks will receive some day.
> He who asks for forgiveness
> will be forgiven one day....
> Deprivation will hug his heart
> As one embraces, after a long separation, one's groom or father.]

The dog rose in "Dikii shipovnik" grows in a garden while also standing for the garden as a whole. This garden carries echoes of the Garden of Eden, the paradise from which humanity was driven out as a punishment for their rebellion against God. It is thus an image of both perfection and irrecoverable loss. Yet the most salient features of this garden are its universality—it encompasses the universe in its entirety—and the inevitability of injury:

> Ты развернешься в расширенном сердце страданья,
> дикий шиповник,
> о, ранящий сад мирозданья.

> [You unfurl in the wide-open heart of suffering
> wild rose,
> oh wounding garden of the world.]

At the same time this garden is very "earthly"; it needs to be tended to in order to flower:

> Дикий шиповник
> идет, как садовник суровый,
> не знающий страха,
> с розой пунцовой,
> со спрятанной раной участья под дикой рубахой.³³

> [The wild rose
> walks, like a stern gardener

who knows no fear,
with the crimson rose
the wound of participation hidden under his wild shirt.]

The beautiful crimson rose can only be brought forth for the price of participation, which inevitably results in wounding. The "hidden wound of participation" and the "stern gardener"[34] invoke Jesus Christ, who according to Christian teaching was wounded to death for his loving participation in the fate of humankind while wearing a crown of thorns. Through the allusion to Christ the bush comes to represent the path of self-sacrifice that perhaps leads to salvation.[35]

In poetry, it is the poet herself who does the tending and pruning; it is she who has to become involved in order to bring forth beauty. "Dikii shipovnik," a highly melodious poem, affirms life and simultaneously highlights the necessity of sacrifice for the sake of beauty; poetic language can create the beauty that allows us a glimpse of that which lies beyond.[36]

Ivan Zhdanov: Nature and Point of View

Ivan Zhdanov was born in the Altai region in 1948 and educated at the Literary Institute of Moscow State University. Zhdanov was active in the literary underground, but he was also an "official" poet—his first collection, "Portret," was published by a Soviet publishing house in 1982. He is active to the present day. Zhdanov is regularly discussed alongside his friend Sedakova as a typical representative of "metarealism."[37] Zhdanov uses Christian imagery more sparingly.[38] He is a nature poet, and it is in his nature poetry that the interconnectedness of different planes of reality, of the physical and metaphysical, are most evident. Sometimes, he animates the natural environment, to the point that the poem's point of view becomes that of a plant or field. An example of this is found in "Melkii dozhd' idet na net" (A drizzle running dry). The initial image likens the branch of a maple tree to a house in which the light has been turned off:

Вот и выключили свет
в красной ветке клена.
И внутри ее темно
и, наверно, сыро

[And now they turned off the lights
in the maple tree's red branch

And inside it is dark
And probably damp]

Almost unnoticeably the perspective of the narration changes to that of the tree itself. Suddenly it is the branch that is looking in on a brightly lit house:

и глядит она в окно,
словно в полость мира.
И глядит она туда,
век не поднимая,-
в отблеск Страшного суда,
в отголосок рая.
В доме шумно и тепло,
жизнь течет простая.³⁹

[And it looks into the window
as if into the cave of the world.
And it looks in that direction
not lifting its eyelids
into the reflection of the Last Judgement
into the echo of paradise.
Inside the house there is warmth and noise
Simple life is going on.]

The tree and the house are absolutely equal in their spaciousness, their ability to host life inside themselves; they are equal at the end of the poem too, when the lights in the house are turned off and both tree and house sink into the darkness of night.[40] Yet unlike the house, the tree is animate, conscious, and capable of assuming the role of observer. Zhdanov states this so casually that the reader accepts it. And the metaphysical, eternal dimension is introduced just as casually: the "simple life" the tree harbors inside itself and looks in on contains "both the Last Judgment and Paradise," the ultimate categories, beginning and end, in a sense that transcends the individual life. The affinity with Pasternak is evident and has been noted.[41]

A plant that plays a special role in Zhdanov's work is the poppy, traditionally associated with sleep and death.[42] In the double poem "Proroki" (The prophets), the red poppy becomes a symbol of life itself, defined by injury: there is a thorn, or splinter of wood, stuck to the poppy's side (an odd image if understood literally). Its own bravery, never clearly defined, means that the poppy/life is bleeding: "Можно вынуть занозу из мака живого, / чтобы он перестал кровениться в отваге" (One could take the splinter out of the living poppy / so that it stops bleeding in its bravery). The splinter of wood and the blood link the poppy to another tree—the cross,[43] that instrument of torture and "tree of death" on which Jesus Christ was crucified and which is transformed into the tree of life by Christ's resurrection.[44]

"More, shto zazhato v kliuvakh ptits" (The sea clutched in the beak of birds) is an enigmatic poem. It features a long list of constituent elements of our world, such as "water," "night," and "light," redefined in unusual, almost mythological terms, for example: "небо, помещенное в звезду—ночь" (The sky, placed into a star, is night).[45] There are only two "elements" that appear repeatedly, and they are arguably not everyday categories: "srez" ("cut" or "section," repeated three times) and the almost-rhyme "krest" ("cross," four times). The cross thus permeates the poem as a kind of refrain. And the cross is emphatically a tree—a tree that has been cut down in order to build a cross:

И копится железо для иглы,
и проволоку тянут для гвоздя,
спиливают дерево на крест.[46]

[And iron for the needle is accumulating
And they pull a wire for the nail
cut down a tree to make a cross.]

This very cross resolves the poem's tension in the final line, syntactically as well as semantically. This line, which features the only personal pronoun in the entire poem, reads "небо, разрывающее нас—крест" (the sky, tearing us apart, is the cross). The cross thus implies pain and destruction, but also an essential opening to that which is above. To any reader even superficially familiar with Christian teaching it is clear that the end implied by this cross is also a beginning.

The inner, unseen relation between tree and cross is something Zhdanov is keen to stress. It seems that the tree carries within it the premonition of the cross while the cross retains the memory of being tree. And the poet is the one who can see both aspects—the metaphysical in nature and material life at the core of that which is metaphysical. The cross in "Kamen plyvet v zemle" (A stone is swimming in the earth) is spacious inside, it can look out on life, just like the tree in "Melkii dozhd'" discussed above: "То, что снаружи крест, то изнутри окно" (That which from the outside is a cross, is a window from the inside). That which looks like a burden is an opening onto something new when seen from the inside. Zhdanov uses the image of the cross in a perfectly Christian, even conservative manner, namely as a symbol of hope.

Viktor Krivulin—Unity through Language

Viktor Krivulin (1944–2001) was a prolific poet, whose large and varied output exemplifies some of the most pertinent features of the "cultural renaissance" in poetry. He was also one of the key figures of the Leningrad underground. Among other things he was co-convenor and host of the Religious-Philosophical Seminar (1974–1980), cofounder and editor of the samizdat journal "37" (1976–1980) and later of *Severnaia pochta* (Northern mail) (1979–1981). Like many of his contemporaries, he began to take an interest in religious questions around 1970 and converted to Orthodox Christianity.[47] For Krivulin, poetic insight was not so much an encounter with beauty, but the discovery of a connection with the tradition to which he felt he belonged—the classical tradition of Russian poetry and the Silver Age. The focus on literary heritage and his and his peers' own place within literary tradition was at the center of his work.[48]

The epigraph to his essay "Dvadtsat' let noveishei russkoi poezii" reads: "Поэзия—как приобщение к святости. / Прошел год—и человека не узнать" (Poetry is like initiation to holiness. / A year has passed and the person is unrecognizable). Poetry—reading and writing—is thus construed as a quasi-religious experience, a special path that provides a way out of the cultural and spiritual stagnation of his time. Rather than change an unbearable environment, poetry makes it possible to exist in a space "above," which Krivulin dubbed "счастливо обретенная вертикаль жизни" (a happily acquired vertical of life).[49] Living in this "vertical" enables the poet to overcome the limitations of the here and now (cultural isolation, the dictates of Soviet official aesthetics, the repression of the metaphysical dimension, and so on) and choose his environment according to affinity. The bridge into Krivulin's (literary) environment of choice was poetic language. Reading and writing poetry enabled him to enter into a "dialogue" with the classics and modernists he admired, a dialogue that became as real as any conversation in the here and now. The concept of vertical time was not Krivulin's own: Joseph Brodskii remembered a moment of literary epiphany that seems very similar to Krivulin's own.[50] More important perhaps was the influence of Osip Mandel'shtam, the Silver Age's great poet of culture, whose work is steeped in both classical and Judeo-Christian heritage.

And yet it was very difficult for a poet of the late Soviet underground to put himself on equal footing with the modernists. The relationship was primarily one of apprenticeship and desire. The longing to connect to cultural tradition through language, as well as doubt in the possibility of this connection, is the theme of "P'iu vino arkhaizmov" (I drink the wine of archaisms). "P'iu vino arkhaizmov" is heavily indebted to Mandel'shtam's 1925 poem "V Peterburge soidemsia snova" (We'll meet again in Petersburg), in which Mandel'shtam was exploring his fear that the new age would destroy culture as he knew it.[51] Krivulin picks up on the older poet's image of a literary culture burned to ashes, but to him it is uncertain that his generation has inherited even these ashes: "Я верую! Нет. Я хотел бы уверовать / в пепел хотя бы" (I believe! No. I would like to believe / in ashes at least).[52]

Understanding this inherent insecurity helps us engage with Krivulin's self-irony and his fleeting, ambiguous religious images, for example in "Neopalimaia kupina" (The burning bush).[53] Ostensibly, this is Krivulin's version of the encounter between Moses and God described in Exodus 3. However, the bush features only fleetingly. The poem itself consists of several loosely interwoven strands, separated by layout and line length, that combine images from the Old and New Testament with pronunciations about the nature of art and blurred (or drunken?) visions of a ruined church building. A blind artist engages in a forty-day fast reminiscent of the forty days Christ spent in the wilderness before beginning his mission of teaching and healing that would lead him to the cross (Matthew 4, Luke 4). It is during this fast that the artist "turns his gaze to a past millennium" and has a vision of a burning bush that seems to oscillate and merge with the image of a ruined church building:

> Художник слеп. Сорокадневный пост
> сплетён как тень висячего моста
> из чёрных водорослей и шершавых звёзд . . .
> Он сорок дней не разомкнёт уста,
> пока пустой реки не перейдёт
> по досточке колеблемой, пока
> босой подошвой не оставит след
> на зыбкой памяти прибрежного песка—
> тогда и в нём прозреет память. Лет
> на тысячу назад он обращает взор,
> и перед ним—неопалимый куст,
> и образ храма светел, как костёр
> средь бела дня. Но храм пока что пуст.[54]

> [The artist is blind. A forty-day fast
> is woven like the shadow of a hanging bridge
> of black seaweed and shaggy stars
> For forty days he will not part his lips,
> until he's crossed the empty river

via the shaky little plank, until
his naked sole has left a trace
on the unsteady memory of the sand on the bank–
that's when he'll recover his memory. He
turns his gaze to a past millennium,
and before him there is a burning bush
and the image of a church shone like a fire
in bright daylight. But the church is still empty.]

The fact that the ruined church is "still empty" implies hope for the future, and indeed the artist, who stands for the poet, intends to "fill the empty spaces with himself." His fast implies not that he is rejecting food, but rather that he will not speak (that is, write) until he has managed to make a contribution to culture—"left his mark on the sand of his time."[55] Just as in "P'iu vino arkhaizmov," then, poetry is interpreted as nourishment in a time of scarcity. Both poems focus on the role of literary tradition as a reservoir of memory that is both cultural and spiritual, simultaneously a source of hope and ever-elusive.

"Neopalimaia kupina" is one of many poems where it is unclear whether they are meant to be read as "real" visions—the allusions to drunkenness are too prominent, the overall tone is too playful. And yet their ambiguity fails to negate the central insight they afford, namely the recognition of art as a spiritual practice and the distinct possibility that the practicing artist, or poet, is indeed stepping on sacred ground, the site of the encounter between Moses and God in the wilderness. Krivulin is a poet in whose work the identification of creative with religious practice is particularly evident.

Elena Shvarts—A Dark Visionary

Elena Shvarts (1948–2010) published her poetry in all the "mainstream" samizdat journals. After the fall of the Soviet Union, she became widely known beyond the borders of her native country. Unlike some others, she seems to not have been tempted to experiment with institutional religion and the Orthodox Church, yet the religious quest in her writing is even more pronounced than in the case of her peers. Shvarts stands in the tradition of poets of Jewish origin who were fascinated with the Christian heritage, such as Mandel'shtam, Pasternak, and Brodskii. She was baptized in the Orthodox faith only in the 1990s.[56]

Shvarts shared neither Sedakova's faith in the salvific properties of harmonious poetic form nor Krivulin's optimism about language's ability to establish connections. And yet she placed her poetry explicitly in the service of what she calls "spirit": "I am an instrument, yes, but not of language [...] but rather of the spirit."[57] In fact, many of her poems have a devotional focus, and this seems a very conscious choice on the part of Shvarts, who describes her writing as the attempt at "sing[ing] Him that which he had never heard before."[58]

Shvarts is the author of the title statement about poetry yielding the "pearl of holy madness." In her poetic practice Shvarts explicitly invoked the cultural stereotype of the poet as holy fool,[59] someone who renounces ordinary life, including sanity and rationality, in order to serve God by challenging societal norms. Their appearance, lifestyle, and focus of attention questions established notions of what is beautiful.[60] The holy fool is a truth-teller, but the truth they proclaim is often, literally, "ugly."[61] It is no exaggeration to say that the holy fool is a staple figure in Shvarts's work. Not only is it possible to read many of her poems as the utterings of a holy fool, she also makes holy fools the protagonists of some of her most famous works. A salient example is the nun Laviniia, one of Shvarts's poetic alter egos, at once heroine and purported author of the cycle "Trudy i dni Lavinii, monakhini iz ordena obrezaniia serdtsa. Ot Rozhdestva do Paskhi" (The works and days of Lavinia, nun in the Order of the Circumcision of the Heart. From Christmas to Easter) (1984).

Another detail of Shvarts's poetry that supports reading her as a mystic and holy fool is the almost scandalous intimacy of the lyrical heroine's interactions with God: In "Igra v priatki" (A game of hide-and-seek) God plays hide-and-seek with the poet.[62] Even more astonishing is the God-figure in "Moisei is kust, v kotorom iavilsia Bog" (Moses and the bush in which God appeared), ostensibly referring to the familiar scene in Exodus 3. But the poem reflects little of the mystery inherent in the Old Testament story. The lyrical voice, who is someone other than Moses, but no omniscient narrator either, addresses God in the second person. This God is anthropomorphic, therefore his ability to enter the bush makes him quite literally small:

> Как скромен Ты!
> Каким усильем воли
> Ты помещаешься
> В одном кусте—не боле.
>
> [How modest you are!
> How much strength of will
> To fit yourself
> into a single bush, not more.]

Moreover, he seems hapless, a threat to his own creation who requires the support of his angels in order to control himself and avert calamity: И ангелов Тебя поддерживают крылья— / Чтобы нечаянным усильем / Всего творенья не спалить (And the wings of angels support you / So that you don't burn down / All of creation by some unintentional effort). In this poem, the bush, God's "receptacle," is the most enduring presence. Surviving the departure of God from its "flesh," its bare branches point to the future and a more seminal encounter with divinity: "Расти, расти, цвети, терновник, / Еще ты нужен для Христа" (Grow, grow and flower, blackthorn bush / You are still needed for Christ).[63]

Shvarts thus uses the image of the bush to explicitly link the Old and New Testament. Yet while the bush in "Moisei i kust" at least pointed to the future appearance of Christ, in the short cycle "Chernaia Paskha" (Black Easter) it turns into a symbol of utter hopelessness:

> Мы ведь—где мы?—в России,
> Где от боли чернеют кусты,
> Где глаза у святых лучезарно пусты,
> Где лупцуют по праздникам баб ...
>
> [Where are we after all? In Russia
> where the bushes blacken with pain
> Where the eyes of the saints are radiantly empty
> Where they flog women on feast days ...]

"Chernaia Paskha" transforms the great Christian celebration of hope in resurrection and eternal life into a glimpse into hell rather than heaven. The reader is swept from the gruesome scene of a man smashing his fist into his wife's face to a vision of Petersburg—symbolizing "Europe" and "culture"— being submerged by "dark, drunken" Russia:

> Но рухнула духовная стена—
> Россия хлынула—дурна, темна, пьяна.
> Где ж родина? И поняла я вдруг:
> Давно Россиею затоплен Петербург.[64]
>
> [But the spiritual wall has collapsed
> And Russia gushed in, evil, dark, and drunk.
> Where is my motherland? And then I got it:
> Russia had flooded Petersburg long ago.]

But Russia is more than the site of a particular scene of violence, and more than the specific city of St. Petersburg doomed. The bush blackened by pain is one of the manifestations of Black Easter, an Easter that is powerless to transcend the pain of Good Friday. The poem ends on a vision of death when the poet fails to tell a personified death from life. "Chernaia Paskha" is a vision of resurrection made impossible. Shvarts exhibits no faith in the power of this God to redeem either the poet or the world—he is not an omnipotent, redeeming divinity. Yet poetry is her vehicle for seeking closeness to God, her greatest desire. When she is writing, she enters a state of creative madness that grants her the license to be intimate with God, to "play hide-and-seek" ("Igra v priatki") or "soothe his pain" ("Tantsuiushchii David"). Yet this ecstasy demands an exceedingly high price, literally destroying the poet's physical self;[65] for Shvarts, it seems that poetic inspiration is primarily a physical process, in fact, she identifies her poetry as "poisoned with pain."[66]

A poem featuring all these elements, as well as demonstrating just how inextricably entwined poetic inspiration and religious ecstasy are, is "Tantsuiushchii David" (Dancing David), part of a longer cycle. The heroine emulating the Old Testament prophet and psalmist[67] is dancing herself into a frenzy that reduces her body to her constituent elements; she becomes "щекочущая кровь, хохочущие кости" (tickling blood, giggling bones). However, this mystic's desire for unity with the divine is never attained; the heroine's desire to be "thrown up to God's throne" remains a wish: "трещите, волосы, звените, кости! / Меня в костер для Бога щепкой бросьте" (Crackle, my hair and clatter, my bones! / Throw me, a chip, in the fire for God).[68] Poetic inspiration and religious ecstasy fulfill the same function. Both reveal a dangerously unstable, but multilayered world in which even the fragments speak. The poet-mystic is the one who pays the price of suffering to access this world.

Vasilii Filippov—Chronicler of the Underground

Born in 1955, Vasilii Filippov (1955–2013) was a decade younger than his peers. He made friends with Krivulin, Shvarts, and others in the 1970s, attended the Religious-Philosophical Seminar that Krivulin cohosted, and published theological ideas in the journal "*37*."[69] His own path as a poet began only in 1984, after the first of his many spells in a psychiatric hospital. Reading his poems offers unique insight into the worldview and life of the late underground from the perspective of someone who was simultaneously one of the initiated and a bystander. In some sense, Filippov became a chronicler of the movement he was almost part of.

Filippov is an intensely metaphorical poet. He has a special gift for transitioning seamlessly between recognizable everyday scenes populated by his friends and intense flights of the imagination. The reader of his poems will benefit from being familiar with the underground setting, because Filippov's protagonists are frequently real people, referred to affectionately.[70] In Filippov's imagination, the Leningrad underground and its protagonists mingle effortlessly with biblical protagonists and scenes. To give an example, in an untitled poem from 1984, Filippov wakes late in the morning, having attended a poetry reading by Elena Shvarts the previous evening. Lying in bed nursing his hangover, he suddenly has a vision of Shvarts telling him, and all her listeners, to rise, using the words Jesus Christ pronounced when resurrecting a young girl (Mark 5:41): "И руками обнимая грязь / Публики, восклицала Лена: "Тавифа, встань!" (And, hugging the dirt of the public / with her arms, Lena cried out: "Talitha, rise!")[71]

Filippov is definitely a poet of the city rather than of nature. Whenever nature is mentioned, it is infused with references to civilization. Religious categories become part of the natural landscape of Leningrad and the environs, and historical and mythical time collapse into one: За болотом рай-лес, / Где Илия воскрес (Beyond the bog is the paradise-forest, / Where Ilia rose from the dead). This poem and others are evidence of both the fascination of discovery and the familiarity with which the underground poets treated the religious heritage. Reading the church fathers, Filippov observes: "Вспоминаю церковных писателей, / Терновый куст расцвел в их творениях ("I remember the writers of the church / In their work, the thorn bush flowered").[72] Familiarizing himself with the key theological texts, Filippov experiences the key Christian mystery—Christ crucified—coming to life.

Another poem starts with a girl lying naked in bed, enticing her lover. The explicit erotic scene—something that would be unacceptable in a Soviet publication—is "elevated" by the presence of a Bible next to the bed, open to the Song of Songs, the Old Testament's great erotic love poem. Filippov then proceeds to evoke a landscape that is unmistakably Leningrad and at the same time literary. The protagonists are Filippov's friends, and the setting is the well-known Café Saigon, meeting place of Leningrad's poets and bohemians: "В Старом Сайгоне новое поколение сайгонщиков / [...] Тут же и старые сайгонщики. / Впереди их идет небритый Петр Чейгин" ("There is a new generation of Saigonists in the Old Saigon / [...] And here come the old Saigonists / The unshaven Petr Cheigin walks ahead of them"). The phrasing faintly echoes one of the most contentious and enigmatic lines in twentieth-century Russian poetry, that is, the final line of his cycle "Dvenadtsat'" (The twelve), in which Christ marches ahead of a column of revolutionaries.

And indeed, a few lines further down the poem leaps into the Silver Age: Filippov wishes to encounter Akhmatova, Tsvetaeva, and Mandel'shtam in present-day Leningrad. Their absence is just as keenly felt as that of Christ, whose time is promptly conflated with the Silver Age when Filippov conjures up Maksimilian Voloshin's well-known literary summer idyll at Koktebel in the 1910s:

> Но в центре все поросло полынью.
> Мандельштам, Ахматова, Цветаева,–
> Где они?
> В полыни Коктебеля?
> Где жизнь Христова?
> Я старею.
> Где буколические, коктебельские романы?
> Где Волошин, в тоге и пьяный?[73]

> [But in the center everything is overgrown with wormwood.
> Mandel'shtam, Akhmatova, Tsvetaeva—
> where are they? In the wormwood of Koktebel?
> Where is the life of Christ?
> I'm getting old.
> Where are the bucolic romances of Koktebel?
> Where is Voloshin, drunk in his toga?]

Filippov's poetry is a summary of all the aspects of the bohemian underground in Leningrad. The omnipresence of a culture construed as "eternal" because of its long tradition and seemingly unbreakable link with religion elevates and sanctifies the underground poet's everyday doings, including sex and drunken excess. And it seems that Filippov even recapitulates the words of his friend Elena Shvarts about poetry yielding "holy madness": "Листая листы стихов, исписанных жемчужными зубами, / Я нахожу тайное пламя" (Leafing through leaves of poetry, written by teeth of pearl / I find a secret flame).[74]

Poetry is ecstasy, poetry requires initiation and sacrifice, poetry affords suffering and insight. Religious imagery, in this context, is a giver of meaning, it shows how the poets of the underground understood and explained their own life with the help of the remnants of the Christian universe.

It is thus evident that religious imagery in late Soviet poetry had primarily literary and cultural functions. Moreover, the poets' religious vision was highly individual. Some writers realized this for themselves and, having found a contradiction between their callings as poets and as Christians, gave up poetry.

Boris Kuprianov became a priest.[75] Those who remained in their previous surroundings did not use their writing to preach. Poetry's function was to make the metaphysical present to the senses, without giving it discursive representation.[76] Poetry was the bridge that provided access to that which is transcendent, ungraspable, and eternal. This is the religious property of poetry. In some cases this means that poets came to regard writing as a quasi-religious activity. It is easy to see how that happened: in a flat, unidimensional world the insistence that art might actually belong to the invisible, irrational dimension rather than the rational naturally brought aesthetic experience close to religious experience.[77] This is what Viktor Krivulin was referring to when he wrote: "The atmosphere of spiritual adventure permeated the destitute daily existence in Leningrad."[78] Even so, the poetry neatly chronicles the existence of a fragmented, non-ecclesiastical spirituality that was uncomfortable with the "grand narrative" of humanity's path from creation to salvation, a feature that is symptomatic of the postmodern world. Yet Christianity was part of a cultural heritage that served as a reservoir of images and associations and the Christian archetypes helped the underground poet understand their own persona as part of history.

7

"I HASTEN TO ESTABLISH A COMMON LANGUAGE WITH YOU"

Orthodox Christian Dissidents and the Human Rights Movement

Lauren Tapley

"I am surprised that our Church and believers are considered persecuted. No one is persecuted for religious convictions in the Soviet Union," stated Metropolitan Filaret of Kiev and Galicia in 1976.[1] This was a proclamation that had been rendered again and again by Russian Orthodox hierarchs by the early 1960s. The Russian Orthodox Church had reconciled itself to its new role in the post–World War II era. After World War II, Stalin employed the Church in a number of diplomatic campaigns designed to slow the onset of the Cold War, which was quickly escalating due to his aggressive expansionist policies.[2] Increasingly, Orthodox sermons assumed a political nature, offering prayers and praise for Soviet leaders. In order to keep the *Journal of the Moscow Patriarchate* open, the Church leadership virtually ceased reporting on church openings and ecclesiastical activities, and although Stalin kept the eight seminaries and two academies open, the shortage of priests remained so dire that the training of new priests was hurried, sporadic, and of poor quality. In turn for the Church hierarchy's cooperation, Stalin slowed the level of persecution against the Orthodox Church. Khrushchev's ascent to power in the mid-1950s brought about changes for religious communities in Soviet Russia, but the role of the Russian Orthodox Church remained one of collaboration with the Soviet government. Khrushchev wanted the Russian

Orthodox Church to join the World Council of Churches and participate in the World Christian Peace Congress of 1961 in an attempt to demonstrate that believers enjoyed religious freedom in the Soviet Union. Indeed, one of the responsibilities the Church leadership was forced to accept was the continuous testimony that the Soviet authorities protected freedom of conscience amid claims of religious persecution. In 1977, the future patriarch of Moscow Aleksii II claimed that "every citizen has the right to profess any religion or none at all. The fact that he is a member of this or that faith never affects his employment, promotion and things like that.... The laws of this country forbid persecution of citizens for their religious beliefs."[3] Almost none of this was true. The Orthodox hierarchy's subservience to the Soviet state in providing false information concerning the situation of religious believers propelled a number of Orthodox intellectuals into active dissent beginning in the 1950s.

The Orthodox dissident movement in the Soviet Union sprang to life alongside the Soviet human rights movement, both beginning slowly in the mid-1950s and gaining strength and momentum through the 1960s and 1970s. Russian Orthodoxy remained the dominant religion of Russian believers, including intellectuals, and many of the activists taking part in the early human rights movement were Orthodox believers themselves. This chapter explores the relationship between the Soviet human rights movement and Orthodox dissidents, showing how each exchanged ideas, support, and a rhetoric of revolt against the "common danger" of the Soviet state. It challenges conventional distinctions between secular and religious resistance by demonstrating deep affinities and affections between the two traditions, the human rights movement becoming a church of first resort for many embattled Christians.

Khrushchev and the Foundations of Soviet Dissent

Khrushchev's rise to power after Stalin's death in 1953 generated new opportunities and new challenges for Soviet citizens. In the last years of his life, Stalin discontinued much of the religious persecution that marked so much of his early leadership. The Soviet Union was still struggling to rebuild after the devastating losses suffered during World War II, and Khrushchev initiated a number of reforms to aid in revitalizing the country, including agricultural, educational, and scientific reforms. As a means of separating his new administration from Stalin's, Khrushchev delivered his "Secret Speech" in 1956, which attacked Stalin as a criminal, guilty of "grave abuse[s] of power" and of generating an elaborate system of "insecurity, fear, and even desperation."[4]

The Secret Speech coupled with de-Stalinization and the "Thaw"[5] that subsequently followed allowed for an exhalation of breath among citizens, and many of them seized the momentary relaxation in censorship and greater freedom to speak openly and honestly to others about their opinions. Reflecting on her initial reaction to the Secret Speech, Soviet dissident Liudmila Alexeeva wrote, "Nikita Khrushchev shocked the delegates ... and the entire nation—with the revelation that the deceased Great Leader was actually a criminal. The congress put an end to our lonely questioning of the Soviet system."[6] Intellectuals throughout the Soviet Union slowly established small gatherings around kitchen tables to discuss poetry and politics.[7] These fledgling meetings eventually formed the core of resistance known as the Soviet human rights movement.[8]

The Soviet human rights movement is best defined as a loose conglomeration of individuals publicly campaigning for change in an attempt to secure "civil and political rights for the future of mankind."[9] While Soviet human rights activists did not always agree politically or philosophically, they were all committed to change through non-violence and supported basic human rights, including the freedom of movement, religious liberty, press, and assembly, for all groups. Indeed, the strength of the movement was its own refusal to manifest a specific political agenda. Physicist and human rights activist Sergei Kovalev described the movement as:

> act[ing] according to your conscience. That was the basis of the human rights movement of the 1960s–1980s. It was not a political platform—there was no such thing then. Only naïve people thought that we were engaged in politics. Political platforms were not the basis of our behavior, but rather moral incompatibility.[10]

Similarly, Larisa Bogoraz wrote in 1991 that the emphasis on elementary human rights "predetermined the non-political nature of the human rights movement."[11]

Human rights activists emphasized unity through a commitment to moral principles, such as justice, freedom, and conscience. They sought change through public activism, the promotion of *glasnost* (openness), and a call for the Soviet authorities to uphold the Soviet constitution. Liudmila Alexeeva claims that the principles of the movement emerged from concern and empathy for "the little man on which the Russian classics are based."[12] It was perhaps natural therefore that the movement's first efforts in finding its voice were in the realm of literature. The temporary relaxation in censorship and Khrushchev's encouragement of the arts assisted in this effort, and soon poetry, stories, and novels were published by writers attempting to "confront the reality of Soviet life."[13] One of the earliest and most important was Vladimir Dudintsev's *Not By Bread Alone* (1956), followed by Boris Pasternak's *Doctor Zhivago* (1957), both of which sparked enormous debate.[14] However, it was Alexander Solzhenitsyn's *One Day in the Life of Ivan Denisovich* (1962) that had the greatest impact in the post-Stalin period. Thousands of Soviet citizens rushed to obtain a copy and Soviet publishing houses were flooded with stories detailing personal accounts of experiences in the prisons and camps during the Stalin period.[15] Additionally, intellectuals soon to step into human rights activism launched underground publications such as Aleksandr Ginzburg's *Syntax*, which is believed to be the first *samizdat* (literally "self-published") publication in the post-Stalin era.[16] Other examples of early *samizdat* literature included poems read at the Maiakovskii Square meetings in 1958 before such gatherings were prohibited. Other early *samizdat* journals included *Phoenix, Boomerang,* and *Cocktail*. The Maiakovskii Square readings were particularly critical in contributing to the blossoming of literary freedom and the formation of the Soviet human rights movement.[17]

While *samizdat* began with poetry, it quickly evolved to include memoirs, political essays, letters, and petitions. Emerging at a time when censorship of self-expression was lessened as a result of de-Stalinization, essays discussing domestic problems and the Soviet leadership were only natural. Vladimir Bukovskii writes that early *samizdat* was about the "concrete freedom to create" and that it was *samizdat* writings and the subsequent meetings set to discuss the works that prompted many to join the rising human rights movement.[18] Iurii Galanskov's *Manifesto of Man* was one of the early *samizdat* works that influenced the thought of future Soviet activists. It was frequently read at the Maiakovskii Square meetings because it "expressed exactly what [the dissidents] felt and... lived by."[19] The poem captures several themes later embodied by the Soviet human rights movement, including an unyielding commitment to freedom, individuality, and openness and honesty.

"The Mission of Christianity Consists of More Than Going to Church": Human Rights and Religious Freedom

Khrushchev's Secret Speech and de-Stalinization threw the legitimacy of the Soviet system into question and left many disillusioned, which subsequently created a desire to seek truth in other areas. For a significant number of members of the intelligentsia, the discovery of the truth entailed a harkening back to Russia's past and a fresh embrace of their historical roots, leading them to the Russian Orthodox Church.[20] Others did not enter the Church but read the works of Solzhenitsyn and Pasternak, both of whom advocated a return to Christianity.[21] Even after decades of atheist propaganda, human rights activist and Orthodox writer Anatolii Levitin estimated in 1974 that the Soviet Union contained over 40 million Orthodox believers.[22]

Some of the earliest human rights advocates in the Soviet Union were also Orthodox Christians. The intellectual connection between many such Christians and the human rights movement provided an innate support system for Orthodox dissidents who did not possess an organization or unified movement of their own. In addition, the human rights movement publicized information and drew attention to Orthodox dissent and the persecution of Orthodox believers early on in the movement's activities. Unlike the Russian Baptist tradition, Russian Orthodox dissidents lacked a tradition of active dissent. They found one in the human rights movement and its stirring literature of revolt. Anatolii Marchenko's *My Testimony*, for example, heavily influenced Russian Orthodox priest Sergei Zheludkov. After reading Marchenko's book, an autobiographical account of his time in Soviet labor camps and prisons, Zheludkov wrote to a number of world religious leaders in order to publicize the persecution of political prisoners in the USSR and asked for all Christians to speak up in their defense.[23] Zheludkov became involved in other human rights activities when he voiced appreciation to individuals who protested on behalf of Iurii Galanskov and Aleksandr Ginzburg, both Russian writers and poets, during their trial in 1968. Known as the "trial of the four," Galanskov and Ginzburg were charged with writing and distributing *samizdat* literature along with Aleksandr Dobrovolskii and Vera Lashkov, who were charged with assisting Galanskov and Ginzburg in creating *samizdat*. In a letter to Pavel Litvinov, a physicist and active dissident in the human rights movement, concerning the Ginzburg/Galanskov trial, Zheludkov remarked that "in defense of your friends, I have not heard the name of a single servant of the church. Allow me to associate myself in sincerest sympathy with your sorrow."[24] This was a powerful statement of solidarity.

Although many in the human rights movement were professed atheists, the "good deeds" they performed in defending freedom for all, including religious believers, garnered trust and admiration among Orthodox dissidents and led Orthodox intellectuals such as Anatolii Levitin, Dmitrii Dudko, and Sergei Zheludkov to equate the activities of the human rights movement with the work of Christians. As Sergei Zheludkov wrote to Pavel Litvinov:

> I have heard that you are an atheist. That in no way qualifies my admiration.... I am extremely glad to write to you that you yourself are a living

proof of the truth of Christianity. Every Christian who hears about what you have said will ... experience the presence and action of the Spirit of Christ among mankind. I hasten to establish a common language with you: if everywhere that I pronounce the name of *Christ* ... you put the principle of spiritual *Beauty* ... this will be sufficient for our practical unity. For Love, Freedom, Truth, Fearlessness, Loyalty are all names of our Lord, whom you honor without knowing it, and whom you have so marvelously proclaimed in your noble and brave declarations.[25]

Writing on behalf of Anatolii Marchenko and other political dissidents, Sergei Zheludkov equated the overall struggle for human rights with Christian conscience and Christian duty:

They [political dissidents] have merely sought to give effect to some of the human rights proclaimed back in 1948 by the United Nations. And these are human rights, which at the same time constitute a man's religious duty. A Christian is bound before God to be a whole man, a free man—free to think not to be untruthful.... To persecute a person for exercising this freedom of personal peaceful beliefs, the freedom to express the truth, is Caesar attempting to take something that is God's. It is essentially a crime against humanity, against the free and sacred humanity bestowed upon him by God in Christ.... The above-named Marchenko and other unknown representatives of the Russian intelligentsia are today suffering in the "severe regime" conditions on behalf of that Christian principle.[26]

Anatolii Levitin, meanwhile, spoke up in defense of General Petro Grigorenko, a former Soviet army commander, writer, and human rights activist, and wrote in that he saw a greater Christian spirit, not in the representatives of the Orthodox Church, but in what he termed "good Samaritans": *"liudiakh, prishedshikh so storony"* (people from the outside).[27] In his essay "A Light in the Little Window," Levitin asks, "Are Petr Iakir, Pavel Litvinov, Larisa Bogoraz, Vladimir Bukovskii, Viktor Krasin, Aleksandr Ginzburg, Viktor Khaustov, Iurii Galanskov, Irina Belogorodskaia not good Samaritans?—people who have given their whole lives to others, for they have given everything to the people."[28] It was human rights activists such as Grigorenko that "led Levitin [and others] to the wider problems of the struggle for democracy and humanity" in the Soviet Union and caused Orthodox dissidents to understand the necessity of the support system that the human rights movement offered. The "good deeds" of human rights activists produced for Orthodox dissidents the idea of solidarity, in which they found the support they needed to confront religious persecution and other human rights violations. Anatolii Levitin came to view his work with the human rights movement as his Christian duty.

Indeed, Orthodox intellectuals and dissidents equated their struggle increasingly with the overall struggle for human rights. In a letter to Philip Potter of the World Council of Churches in 1976, Lev Regelson, an Orthodox believer and physicist, and Gleb Iakunin, a priest, wrote about the developing connection among Christians on the question of the "defense of human rights and the struggle against religious discrimination."[29] Responding to an article by Soviet writer Boris Roschin that attacked four well-known Orthodox dissidents, including himself, Iakunin described the article as symptomatic of the "current crack-down by the Soviet authorities on those fighting for human rights in the USSR."[30] Iakunin equated Orthodox dissidents with human rights activists in the Soviet Union when he asked, "Would it not be simpler to carry out the arrests immediately, as was done with Ginzburg, Orlov, and Shcharansky?"[31] Similarly, Orthodox dissident, human rights activist, and mathematician Igor Shafarevich likened the struggle for freedom with the concept of God. In his essay, "Does Russia Have a Future?" Shafarevich argued that the success of the struggle for freedom depended on the resurrection of religion in Russia:

> Nietzsche's literary phrase "God is dead!" has become a reality in our country and by now the third generation is living in a terrifying world without God. Here, I would say, is the key to the whole question: it is the efforts applied in this sphere that will determine the life, death or resurrection of Russia. This most vital of all the fields of activity for our people will require hundreds of thousands of hands and heads (let us recall that there were three hundred thousand priests in Russia before the revolution).... Thus we may take the first and perhaps most precious steps toward freedom.... If more than just a few individuals can rise to the pitch where they are ready to sacrifice themselves, souls will be cleansed and the soil prepared for religion to grow in.[32]

Religious freedom and the struggle for human rights were causes that were linked if not united. Andrei Sakharov, the most celebrated of human rights activists, epitomized the spirit of collaboration and unity. Speaking about freedom of conscience in 1972, he stated, "it is essential to encourage freedom of conscience.... There should be a guarantee of the real separation of Church and State, and legal, material, and administrative guarantees of freedom of conscience."[33] In 1971, during Anatolii Levitin's trial, Sakharov sent an appeal to Podgornyi, president of the USSR Supreme Soviet, stating, "I was present in court and am convinced that there has been no violation of the law in anything Levitin has done."³⁴ Other human rights activists in the Initiative Group for the Defense of Human Rights in the USSR appealed to the United Nations, Pope Paul VI, and the General Assembly of the Russian Orthodox Church, describing Levitin as a "man of high morals" and his conviction as "another act of arbitrary tyranny by the authorities against dissenters, against believers, against fighters for Human Rights in our country."³⁵ In 1973, Sakharov sent a petition on behalf of Evgenii Barabanov, an Orthodox intellectual and dissident arrested for distributing the *Chronicle of Current Events* and other human rights literature to the West.³⁶

The support offered to Orthodox dissidents in turn encouraged dissidents like Levitin to work with human rights activists in defending other religious believers and political prisoners. In 1974, during an interview, Levitin spoke about how he advised and encouraged Sakharov to appeal on behalf of persecuted Baptist Georgii Vins.³⁷ Also in 1974, Levitin along with Sakharov and others sent an appeal to the United Nations pleading to allow the Crimean Tartars to return to their homeland.³⁸

Working within a larger movement influenced many Orthodox intellectuals to look beyond their own quest for religious liberty and to defend other basic human rights, as well. Orthodox priest Dmitrii Dudko expressed solidarity with the larger cause of human rights in the Soviet Union when on December 10, 1975—Human Rights Day—he signed a collective statement by human rights activists on the state of human rights in the USSR. One month later in 1976, he signed a letter defending Sergei Kovalev, a prominent Soviet human rights activist convicted of participating in the publishing of the *Chronicle of Current Events* and the *Chronicle of the Catholic Church in Lithuania*.³⁹ In 1968, Levitin made his first foray into the broader human rights movement when he came to the defense of Iurii Galanskov and Aleksandr Ginzburg in an appeal highlighting violations of freedom of speech and conscience in the Soviet Union. Aleksandr Ginzburg, also a devout Orthodox Christian, was well known in intellectual circles and produced some of the earliest and most important *samizdat* pieces in the 1950s and 1960s. Ginzburg's *The White Book* detailed the trial of the two dissident writers Andrei Siniavskii and Iulii Daniel.

In 1969, Levitin carried his activism further when he, along with other human rights activists including Tatiana Velikanova, Natalia Gorbanevskaia, Viktor Krasin, and Petr Iakir, formed the first official human rights organization in the Soviet Union: the Initiative Group for the Defense of Human Rights in the USSR. At his trial in 1971, when he was accused of slandering the Soviet system, Levitin explained that "the mission of Christianity consists of more than going to church. It consists of putting the behests of Christ into practice. Christ called upon us to defend all who are oppressed. That is why I defend people's rights, whether they be Pochayev monks, Baptists or Crimean Tartars, and if convinced opponents of religion should some day be subjected to oppression, I shall defend them too."[40]

Levitin was one of many Orthodox intellectuals who found support and solidarity in the human rights movement. Human rights activists Tatiana Velikanova and Natalia Gorbanevskaia, an Orthodox believer, worked on the *Chronicle of Current Events* at separate times and kept the publication going when the other was imprisoned. Velikanova assisted in compiling information from all branches of the human rights movement. Orthodox dissident Andrei Tverdokhlebov helped Sakharov found the Human Rights Committee in 1970. He became particularly concerned with prison and labor camp conditions for political prisoners, writing a report "On the Confinement Conditions of Prisoners" to raise awareness abroad and in the Soviet Union.[41] In 1971, he worked with other human rights activists including Roi Medvedev, Valerii Chalidze, and Aleksandr Esenin-Volpin to compile a collection of documents concerning psychiatric repression in the Soviet Union.

The human rights movement also offered a home to the iconic figure of Alexander Solzhenitsyn. Solzhenitsyn's importance to the human rights movement was evident from the thousands of letters and petitions sent to the Soviet authorities after his forced emigration in 1974. Orthodox intellectuals such as Anatolii Levitin, Gleb Iakunin, Evgenii Barabanov, and Igor Shafarevich as well as other human rights activists such as Andrei Sakharov and Pavel Litvinov spoke out in defense of Solzhenitsyn. In the "Moscow Appeal" for Solzhenitsyn, the authors wrote, "The solidarity of people cannot be limited to words. It must be effective. In this lies our hope."[42] Solzhenitsyn's work within the human rights movement revolved around his belief that free speech and free press was essential for Russia to progress. In 1967, he wrote to the Soviet Writers' Congress demanding an end to the "no longer tolerable oppression, in the form of censorship, which our literature has endured for decades."[43] Solzhenitsyn's work with the human rights movement in his homeland continued after his emigration when he chose fellow Orthodox intellectual and dissident Aleksandr Ginzburg to distribute the Solzhenitsyn Fund, set up to aid political prisoners in the Soviet Union.[44] Solzhenitsyn found overwhelming support in the human rights movement and once proclaimed that Sakharov and other human rights activists possessed the "indomitability of spirit which could protect mankind from destruction."[45]

"For Your Freedom and Ours!": Ecumenism and Collaboration

As Orthodox intellectuals and dissidents increased their involvement in the human rights movement, they understood the need for religious believers of all faiths to unite. Human rights activists acquired information from and defended the rights of virtually every group of dissidents, including believers of all faiths in the Soviet Union. From the beginning, the persecution of citizens for their religious beliefs and practices struck a chord with many in the human rights movement. Sakharov believed that freedom of conscience was essential in order to maintain a just society. In 1975, he spoke up in defense of Vladimir Osipov, an Orthodox dissident and publisher of the *samizdat* journal *Veche*. "I do not share most of Osipov's beliefs or the standpoint of the journal produced by him (which Osipov himself describes as nationalistic and Christian)," Sakharov declared, "but I am convinced that this kind of persecution for one's beliefs is absolutely intolerable."[46] In 1976, freedom of conscience was the first issue addressed by Sakharov in a letter to US President Jimmy Carter. Sakharov asked, "Do you know the truth about the situation of religion in the USSR—the humiliation of official churches and the merciless repression (arrests; fines; religious parents deprived of their children; even murder, as in the case of the Baptist Biblenko) of those sects—Baptists, Uniates, Pentecostals, the True Orthodox Church, and others—who seek independence of the government?"[47] One of the primary objectives of the Initiative Group for the Defense of Human Rights, the earliest human rights group in the Soviet Union, was the "restoration of religious freedom, including that of religious propaganda" for all believers.[48] On the first anniversary of the Initiative Group's formation, its organization issued an open letter, stating that its members included "believers and nonbelievers, optimists and skeptics, those with and those without Communist views."[49]

In a similar spirit, Tatiana Velikanova sought out religious believers of all faiths, especially Pentecostals and *Initsiativniki* Baptists as part of her cause against all human rights injustices.[50] On March 29, 1971, Vladimir Bukovskii was arrested and searched. Soviet authorities found numerous documents in his possession including Anatolii Levitin's "The Living Word" and material of the All-Russian Social Christian Union for the Liberation of the People.[51] Levitin's essay "The Living Word" argues from a Christian perspective that "the living word is the word of the struggle for liberty, equality, fraternity, and justice among people."[52] It was a universal language, with unlimited potential. In 1971, activists in the human rights movement started publishing information on the persecution of Catholic believers in Lithuania, and one year later, the Catholic Church in Lithuania established their own publication called the *Chronicle of the Lithuanian Catholic Church*, inspired by the human rights movement's own *Chronicle of Current Events*. Dissident and human rights activist Valerii Chalidze appealed to the Presidium of the Lithuanian Supreme Soviet after the arrest of Roman Catholic priest Juozas Zdebskis in 1971, claiming that the only infringement on the law was the priest's arrest.[53] After receiving a letter from Jewish religious prisoner Iosef Mendelevich, Chalidze appealed on behalf of all religious believers when he wrote the USSR minister of Internal Affairs, demanding that the constitutional guarantee of freedom to worship be upheld. In his appeal, he observed that "the ability to respect the beliefs and ethical standards of others is a fundamental mark of culture. It is doubtful whether convicts being educated will regard an administrator as a cultured man if he is incapable of recognizing the right (and religious obligation) of a Jew to wear a skull-cap [or] . . . of a Christian to wear a cross."[54]

Early in 1977, during a search of Aleksandr Ginzburg's home, personal correspondence and religious literature, particularly from the *Initsiativniki* Baptists, was discovered, including the *Bulletin of the Council of Prisoner's Relatives*, *Herald of Salvation*, and *Fraternal Leaflet*.[55] Ginzburg was one of the first human rights activists to communicate regularly with the *Initsiativniki* Baptists and to provide the *Chronicle* with information about their struggle, establishing a channel between the larger human rights movement and Baptist dissent. As a member of the Moscow Helsinki Group, which was established in 1976, he helped to compose documents protesting the removal of children from the families of Baptists and Pentecostals.[56] Orthodox dissident Andrei Tverdokhlebov was arrested in 1974. During a search of his flat authorities discovered issues of the *Chronicle of the Lithuanian Catholic Church*, the *Bulletin of the Council of Prisoner's Relatives of Evangelical-Christian Baptist Prisoners*, prisoner lists, and documents defending civil rights.[57] Soviet human rights activists seeking to help persecuted religious believers of all faiths facilitated communication and eroded feelings of animosity among religious groups.

Writer and reporter David Kowalewski found that cooperation between religious dissidents had developed in part through the growth of *samizdat* literature, "as well as solidarity felt by geographically separated believers."[58] Liudmila Alexeeva noted that contact between various dissident groups commenced through the dissemination of the *Chronicle of Current Events*, which subsequently allowed groups to establish better connections.[59] Orthodox intellectual and dissident Dmitrii Dudko, an Orthodox priest noted for holding a series of illegal discussions to answer religious and philosophical questions for Soviet youth, recognized the necessity of ecumenism in confronting the persecution that religious believers faced from the Soviet authorities. During one of his discussions, Dudko observed that "in the face of common danger, we must all unite.... When people flaunt their allegiance to a given confession too much and don't have love for their neighbor, they turn into 'publicans and Pharisees,' and even a non-believer is closer to God than such an 'Orthodox.'"[60] Dudko urged Christians to relate to other believers with "love," not hostility. Dudko believed that through respecting other faiths, the Orthodox believer could learn from them. He encouraged ecumenical activity between believers as a "universal phenomenon" not to be reduced to conferences and meetings.[61]

During an interview in 1974, Levitin applauded what he saw in Russia as "an authentic ecumenism in living religious practice. For decades Orthodox and sectarians (i.e., Protestants) suffered together in [Lavrentii] Beria's camps, slept side by side in prison bunks, gulped the same prison soup out of the same rusty bowls. The old mistrust and bitterness is gone; rather there is mutual respect and sympathy."[62] Speaking of the unity and growing ecumenism among participants in the human rights movement, Levitin confessed that he possessed,

> the misfortune never to be unmoved when I see people suffering. Whoever they may be—just people. Whether they are Soviet generals or elderly sectarians, whether they are Orthodox priests or convinced atheists and Communists, I find any kind of human suffering intolerable.... I believe that there are many such people in the world [who share my misfortune] and that, if they join hands together, they will help all those who are suffering for their convictions.[63]

The unity displayed by activists in the human rights movement served as an example to many Orthodox dissidents. And the fight for freedom of conscience by religious dissidents willing to die for their cause garnered admiration and respect among dissidents of every faith, regardless of their doctrinal differences. In 1974, Levitin defended *Initsiativniki* Baptist Georgii Vins, calling for his release and declaring that if "Vins suffers for his convictions then he must be helped. He is an exceptionally brave and persistent man. I cannot agree with his views, for he is a Baptist, but I appreciate his activities.... When I was in the prison camp with Baptists and Catholics, I took part in the arguments between denominations. They were passionate arguments—but afterwards we all broke bread together."[64] In 1978, Aleksandr Ogorodnikov, an Orthodox believer and dissident, included a report of the disruption of a Baptist meeting in Rostov by the KGB in his Orthodox journal *Obshchina (Community)*.[65] The spirit of ecumenism was growing.

Father Gleb Iakunin came to epitomize the method of ecumenism among religious believers through his work with the human rights movement. Iakunin, born March 4, 1934, in Moscow, was the child of an old noble family. While at a forestry institute in Irkutsk, Iakunin began reading philosophy and religious writers such as Rudolf Steiner, Nikolai Berdiaev, Helena Blavatsky, Vladimir Solov'ev, and Sergei Bulgakov, which stimulated his interest in religion. Shortly afterward, he converted to Russian Orthodoxy and decided to devote his life to the work of the Church. He was ordained a priest in 1962.[66] His work as a dissident began in 1965, when he and priest Nikolai Eshliman sent an open letter to Patriarch Aleksii of the Russian Orthodox Church. The letter delivered a scathing attack of the Church hierarchy for its subservience to the state and its continued compliance in allowing the state to interfere in Church life. They accused the patriarchate of allowing the "closing of churches, monasteries, and church schools," "forceful estrangement of children from the Church," and "interference of 'secular officials' in the ordaining of priests."[67] One month later, Iakunin and Eshliman sent a similar letter to Nikolai Podgornyi, the chairman of the Presidium, Aleksei Kosygin, the chairman of the Council of Ministers, and Roman Rudenko, the attorney general of the USSR, accusing the government of "illegal registration of clergy," "the illegal campaign of mass closing of churches and monasteries," "the unlawful registration of baptisms and other church rites," "the violation of the principle of separation of church and state," and "the illegal limitation of the number of members of a religious society to twenty."[68]

Iakunin equated the struggle for freedom of conscience with the larger Soviet human rights movement's struggle for freedom. His work in both led him to adopt a more ecumenical approach to achieve religious liberty. Iakunin's ideas and activities within the broader Soviet human rights movement and his thinking on ecumenism were shaped to a great extent by Anatolii Levitin and Orthodox priest Aleksandr Men.

Aleksandr Men, who was not directly involved in the human rights movement, also encouraged the Orthodox community to engage and work with other denominations. During his time at the institute in Irkutsk, Iakunin shared a room with Aleksandr Men, and in the late 1950s Iakunin, Men, Dudko, Eshliman, and Levitin met together to discuss religious issues in the Church, including the submission of the Church hierarchy to the state.[69] Men helped Iakunin and Eshliman craft the infamous 1965 letter to the Moscow patriarch, but at the last minute, he took the advice of Bishop Ermogen and decided against signing his name to it. Speaking of Iakunin, Men praised him, asserting, "He is our army, whereas I'm just a partisan detachment."[70] While Orthodox dissidents such as Levitin and Iakunin confirmed their advocacy of ecumenism in *samizdat* essays and signing petitions while working within the larger human rights movement, Aleksandr Men did not sign petitions or actively participate in the human rights movement. Rather his advocacy of ecumenism is evident in his writings and lectures. "Every religion," he once claimed, "is a path towards God, a conjecture about God, a human approach to God." "In the twentieth century," he continued, "for the first time a serious dialogue has started between the churches and between religions."[71] Men argued that it was essential for Christians to open their minds "to all that is valuable in all Christian denominations and non-Christian beliefs," citing the Gospel of John to illustrate his point.[72]

Men and Iakunin both read the work of Christian philosophers Solov'ev and Berdiaev. While Solov'ev emphasized the shared unity of man in search for God, Berdiaev stressed freedom directly derived from a personal relationship with God and the subsequent value given to each individual.[73] Such influences enabled Iakunin to become one of the strongest champions of ecumenism in the Soviet period. Though his early work centered on religious freedom and specifically the Orthodox Church, it expanded to include all basic human freedoms and all faiths. Aside from testifying on behalf of Levitin in 1971, Iakunin participated in several small committees consisting of other Soviet human rights activists. In 1976, Iakunin served on a public committee created to write and send letters to various public and state organizations abroad on behalf of Petr Starchik, a man forcibly committed to a psychiatric institution. Other members of the committee included Aleksandr Ginzburg, Sergei Zheludkov, Lev Regelson, and Tatiana Velikanova.[74] Iakunin signed numerous documents created by the Moscow Helsinki Group, including a document examining the struggle for human rights in the Soviet Union and Czechoslovakia ten years after the Soviet invasion in 1968.[75] The document called for human rights activists in Czechoslovakia to "withstand the test" (*vyderzhat' ispytaniia*) and celebrated the similarities between the two movements struggling for freedom. The document concluded with a call to solidarity: "For your freedom and ours!" (*Za vashu i nashu svobodu*).

Most significantly, Iakunin's work within the larger human rights movement influenced him to create the first truly ecumenical organization in the Soviet Union. After a suggestion from human rights activist Professor Iurii Orlov, Iakunin organized the Christian Committee for the Defense of Believers' Rights in 1976.[76] The initial group consisted of Gleb Iakunin, Varsonofii Khaibulin, and Viktor Kapitanchuk. Iakunin's decision to undertake Orlov's suggestion and make the organization ecumenical demonstrates the sense of solidarity and commitment to freedom for all epitomized by the Soviet human rights movement. The Christian Committee for the Defense of Believers' Rights was an example of the new type of watchdog group that sprung up in the aftermath of the Helsinki Accords in 1975. Its ideals and techniques were crafted from the Soviet human rights movement. But even before the creation of the Christian Committee, Iakunin's work with human rights was pushing him toward the defense of all faiths. In an appeal Iakunin and Lev Regelson sent to the delegates of the World Council of Churches at the Fifth Assembly in Nairobi, Kenya in 1975, they proclaimed, "We believe that it is proper to support confessors of other religions . . . we do not regard our suggestions as the only possible or as the only right ones. Pluralism in our modern life requires that each community apply its particular creative efforts in order to establish new forms of Christian life and new forms of ecumenical cooperation."[77]

In June 1976, as a precursor to the creation of the Christian Committee, Iakunin, along with Orthodox dissidents Dmitrii Dudko, Lev Regelson, Igor Shafarevich, and Evgenii Barabanov, as well as representatives from the *Initsiativniki* Baptists, Pentecostals, Adventists, and the Catholic Church of Lithuania collectively wrote an appeal to the Presidium of the Supreme Soviet and the World Council of Churches.[78] In March 1976, in a letter to Philip Potter, the general secretary of the World Council of Churches, Iakunin and Regelson addressed a number of issues plaguing religious believers in the Soviet Union, drawing particular attention to the plight of the *Initsiativniki* Baptists. When discussing the issue of registration, Iakunin and Regelson explained that "the main victims of the anti-religious law on registration were the *Initsiativniki* Baptists."[79]

Iakunin's Christian Committee for the Defense of Believers' Rights was not only aimed at gaining religious freedom for believers, but also sought to work on behalf of basic human rights.[80] Through various channels of communication and word of mouth, the Christian Committee began receiving hundreds of letters and appeals from believers and congregations throughout the Soviet Union. Catholics, Adventists, Pentecostals, *Initsiativniki* Baptists, as well as non-Christian groups contacted the Christian Committee to detail their persecution and seek help. One of the earliest appeals the Committee received was from the Khailo family. In November 1977, a member of the *Initsiativniki* Baptists, Vladimir Pavlovich Khailo, sent a letter to the Christian Committee asking for help in receiving permission to emigrate after three of his children were removed from the home and moved to various institutions and prisons. Khailo ended his letter, writing, "I appeal to all Christians, to all people to whom human rights are precious, to come to the defense of my family."[81] For some religious believers and churches, the Christian Committee functioned as an effective means in getting information published abroad and also of keeping fellow believers informed across the Soviet Union. The *Initsiativniki* Baptists utilized the Committee in this way, sending the Committee information gathered from their own organization, the Council of Prisoners' Relatives.[82] The All-Union Church of the True and Free Seventh Day Adventists also sent information about their plight to the Committee. On March 20, 1978, the Committee received a letter from Rostislav Galetskii detailing a decree handed down by the Commission on Juvenile Affairs by which the Mikhel family was ordered to pay a fine of thirty rubles for keeping the children in the home out of school on Saturdays because of their religious convictions. Perhaps knowing one of the Christian Committee's members through previous work, Galetskii asked that the Committee send copies of the appeal to the *Chronicle of Current Events*, the press, and radio broadcasting stations.[83] A few months after creating the Christian Committee, Iakunin wrote a letter to Pope Paul VI, not only asking for the Catholic Church to defend persecuted Catholic believers in the Soviet Union, but also requesting the blessing of the Vatican for the success of the Christian Committee.[84] Anyone familiar with the history of these Christian traditions will recognize that these were historic gestures.

The Committee produced an astounding 417 documents, amounting to 2,891 pages, in only the first three years of its existence.[85] The group publicized the case of Iosif Begun, a Jew sentenced to two years' imprisonment for teaching Hebrew, and sent information to the *Chronicle of Current Events* calling attention to the Soviet Central Committee's continued resolutions to increase atheist education among the population. The Christian Committee noted that their research showed that despite the state's efforts, there was a continued increase in the influence of religion on the young and a decline in antireligious sentiment among communists and Komsomol members.[86] The Committee also raised awareness of human rights issues not necessarily associated with religion, such as Lev Regelson's letter to the participants of the Belgrade Conference in 1977 concerning forced labor, not only in the Soviet Union, but in other communist countries as well.[87] Additionally, Gleb Iakunin published information in a press release about Zviad Gamsakhurdia, a Georgian human rights activist, dissident, and future president of post-Soviet Georgia, and asked "all those who cherish human rights ... not to be indifferent to his fate."[88]

The threat the Christian Committee posed to the Soviet state resulted in the eventual arrest of nearly all its members. In August 1979, Iakunin issued a radical statement suggesting that Orthodox believers establish unregistered, and therefore illegal parishes to function outside of state control. Iakunin argued that the unregistered parishes would create a parallel structure to the Moscow Patriarchate, which would result in less pressure on the Church.[89] The success of unregistered Catholics and Protestants, particularly the *Initsiativniki* Baptists, in the Soviet Union acted as an example to Iakunin. Following the publication of the statement, Iakunin was arrested on November 1, 1979, and after a four-day trial, he was sentenced on August 28, 1980, to ten years—five served in prison and five served in internal exile. After Iakunin's arrest, the Christian Committee's activities diminished, but the organization did succeed in doing some work through Vadim Ivanovich Shcheglov, the secretary of the Committee.[90]

Iakunin's arrest and sentence provoked a strong reaction from Soviet human rights activists, particularly Sakharov, and religious dissidents of all faiths, securing Iakunin's importance as a member of the human rights movement and an advocate of ecumenism. Particularly notable among the numerous statements and appeals written on Iakunin's behalf following his arrest was a statement published by a group of Pentecostals. They praised Iakunin as playing "an active part in the struggle against violations of the rights of religious minorities in the Soviet Union. We wish to express our sincere gratitude to Father Gleb Yakunin for his invaluable work in dissipating the hostility which the atheistic state sows between Orthodox and non-Orthodox Christians."[91] Persecution by the state, and a rising ecumenism that transcended both confession and creed, had fostered an unprecedented trust between hitherto hostile traditions.

Human Dignity and Freedom

A third area of exchange and mutual enrichment was language: a rhetoric of dissent, turning on three concepts: "human dignity," "humanity," and "freedom." In an appeal read in London at an Amnesty International gathering, Sakharov wrote, "I call on you to raise your voices in defense of prisoners of conscience. Their suffering, their courageous, nonviolent struggle for the noble principles of justice, openness, compassion, human and national dignity, and freedom of conscience, obligate us all not to forget them and to obtain their release from the cruel clutch of the punitive apparatus."[92] Sakharov's use of the word "apparatus" invokes an image of the Soviet state as a machine seeking to rob the citizen of her basic dignity and humanity. On what would have been dissident writer Iurii Galanskov's thirty-fifth birthday, several human rights activists released a statement commemorating Galanskov's work and "remind[ing] all who are alive to compassion that the present regime for political prisoners in the USSR is a well thought out system for the destruction of their health and for the mockery of human dignity."⁹³ This was language that Christians could work with.

The words "human dignity" and "humanity" appeared in the writings of many Orthodox dissidents. In his essay "A Light in the Little Window" (1969), Anatolii Levitin wrote, "Freedom of speech, freedom of press, freedom of conscience, freedom of civic action ... all these freedoms elevate human dignity. ... We are raising our standard in a fight for humanity. ... We are fighting for freedom, equality, and brotherhood between people. And if necessary we will die for this."⁹⁴ By 1969, Levitin was heavily involved in the Soviet human rights movement. His use of "we" denotes unity with those beyond his own circle of activists. Orthodox dissident Aleksandr Ogorodnikov also utilized the idea of "humanity" and "human dignity" in his writings. His primary concern was the Orthodox Church and Orthodox believers, but in the "Declaration" of his journal *Obshchina*, he writes that the Christian Seminar participants, "having turned aside the greedy hand of the state which has sought to grasp our souls. ... In defending the dignity of Mankind ... we see how the aims of the Church correspond to the most profound aims of human hearts."⁹⁵ Ogorodnikov equates the defense of all human dignity with the aims of the Church. The goals of the Soviet human rights movement and the "faithful children of the Orthodox Church," as Ogorodnikov referred to himself and others in his group, were the same. The "dignity" that Ogorodnikov and human rights activists were defending was just that—human and universal. And like other human rights activists, Ogorodnikov associates the state with a lifeless mechanism resolved to rob and corrupt the essence of a person's humanity.

Gleb Iakunin also absorbed the rhetoric of the Soviet human rights movement, particularly in his later writings. In the appeal sent to the delegates of the Fifth Assembly of the World Council of Churches, Iakunin wrote, "We believe that it is proper to support ... all fighters for freedom, human dignity, and the preservation of God's image in man."⁹⁶ In a letter to David Hathaway, a British pastor responsible for bringing thousands of Bibles into Eastern Europe during the Cold War, Iakunin discusses the plight of Orthodox dissident and human rights activist Andrei Tverdokhlebov. Tverdokhlebov, Iakunin writes, "has courageously and with great nobility of spirit raised his voice on the violations of the Universal Declaration of Human Rights in the USSR, when human dignity was grossly violated."⁹⁷ Often playing on various forms of "human," in the same letter, Iakunin praised the "confessors of humanism" and the "selfless fighters for human dignity."⁹⁸ Writing in 1977 to the directors of Voice of America, the BBC, and Deutsche Welle, Iakunin requested that the stations include Russian-language programs of a "general humanitarian nature and religious ones for children. . . . Such an innovation would fully correspond to the realization of Article 26 of the Universal Declaration of Human Rights."[99] Iakunin loved to describe human rights activists as "fighters," a term he also used to describe himself. The language of human dignity was at once universal and potent, secular and spiritual. It was generous, supple, and it led Christian activists to broader understandings of divine agency. In "A Light in the Little Window," Levitin said that he "learned humanity" through the example of Aleksandr Ginzburg's fiancée and her struggle to receive permission to visit him after his arrest.[100]

Another word taken up by Orthodox dissidents from human rights activists was "freedom." While human rights activists used "freedom" in the sense of legal rights, as in the freedom to worship, the freedom of expression, the freedom of press, and so on, "freedom" is often used suggest the simple liberty to exist and think without arbitrary repression and imprisonment. This aspect of the concept of "freedom" suggests a higher ideal than just basic concrete rights; it suggests the freedom of the mind, soul, and spirit. Human rights activists in the Soviet Union often spoke of the Soviet government attempting to imprison dissidents in order to "break" their spirit. Their willingness to endure arrest, exile, and imprisonment was for more than physical rights; the human rights movement was a struggle for man's right to exist freely.

On August 25, 1968, a handful of Soviet citizens, many of them important figures in the Soviet human rights movement, including Natalia Gorbanevskaia, Pavel Litvinov, and Larisa Daniel Bogoraz, the wife of Soviet writer Iulii Daniel, gathered in Red Square at noon to protest the Soviet army's invasion of Czechoslovakia. Gorbanevskaia—herself a Christian—wrote most of the slogans used in the protest: "Long live free and independent Czechoslovakia," and "For your freedom and ours."[101] "Freedom" emerged as the most commonly used word in chants and slogans. High school students in Lithuania chanted "Freedom" and "Freedom for Lithuania" in 1972 as they marched to the city garden in Kaunas out of respect for Romas Kalanta, a student who committed self-immolation in protest of the Soviets occupying Lithuania.[102] Dissidents and activists in the Soviet Union referred to Human Rights Day as "Freedom Day," and often used December 10 as an opportunity to write to the Soviet authorities listing violations of the Universal Declaration of Human Rights.[103] After the arrest of human rights activist and Orthodox dissident Andrei Tverdokhlebov in 1976, slogans defending him appeared across Leningrad. One of the slogans declared, "You Are Trying to Suffocate Freedom, but the Spirit of Man Knows No Chains!"[104] In this way, "freedom" was used to signify emotion, unity, and the simple right to exist. For activists in the human rights movement, "freedom" was more than a generic word employed in advocacy for physical freedoms. "Freedom" represented the natural right that every person innately possesses to think and exist without fear of oppression.

From initially pragmatic notions of religious liberty, Orthodox dissidents moved toward this fuller, existential concept of freedom. In a letter to the Belgrade Conference in 1977, Lev Regelson, writing on behalf of the Christian Committee, discusses violations of society's "moral foundations," including "freedom of thought and creativity."[105] Levitin often utilized the concept of "freedom" in his writings as mankind's liberty to think and exist. In an appeal to British citizens in 1976, he wrote that he had "devoted his life to the struggle for freedom in his country and its renewal on the foundations of Christianity, humanism, and freedom."[106] Later in the same statement, Levitin discusses concrete, individual rights, jointly referring to these rights as "freedoms"—in the plural. His use of "freedom" in the singular form suggests an intangible ideal—the liberty to exist and think. Similarly, in a plea appearing in the West, Orthodox dissident Evgenii Barabanov wrote, "the normative cure for dissent is a monstrous social distortion, a crime against the very nature of man, against the right to think, speak, believe, and be free."[107]

Such language testified to a deeper unity forged over many years of struggle. While they certainly advocated for concrete, physical freedoms such as the freedom to publish, the freedom to assemble, and the freedom to worship, Orthodox dissidents and human rights activists together struggled for a more fundamental freedom: the right to live and breathe uninhibited by the "chains" of a totalitarian regime.

8
THE ORTHODOX LITURGY AS POLITICAL RESISTANCE

John P. Burgess

During nearly seventy-five years of communist rule, the Orthodox Church in the Soviet Union was restricted to one major religious activity: the celebration of worship. For most of these years, the state prohibited the Church from operating Sunday schools and conducting social ministries. Until the end of the Gorbachev era, the Church was not allowed to canonize saints or publicly commemorate those believers who died for their faith in the Gulag. The KGB vetted candidates for the priesthood, and state authorities used the Church hierarchy as a tool of Soviet foreign policy and controlled appointment of bishops and priests. Despite these constraints, the divine liturgy and other services of prayer went on, although even here the state put up obstacles to people's participation.

To be sure, other forms of religiosity survived outside the institutional Church. Many people continued to baptize their children, keep icons in their homes, pray at the graves of loved ones in cemeteries, and make pilgrimage to holy springs. Moreover, small groups of believers gathered underground for spiritual fellowship and theological conversation. But it was especially the celebration of worship, both in the official, institutional Church and in the "catacombs," that enabled believers to endure spiritually under conditions of political repression and sometimes active persecution.

Central to Russian Orthodox thinking is the notion that worship draws one into a world beyond this world. Eternity breaks into time; the everyday world is transformed by the divine presence. According to legend, Vladimir, the tenth-century prince of Rus', sent envoys to neighboring lands to bring back reports of their religions. Those who returned from Constantinople exclaimed that when they worshiped in the Church of Hagia Sophia, they no longer knew whether they were on earth or in heaven. The Orthodox liturgy had swept them up into a different time and space. A millennium later, even a politically accommodated Church in the Soviet Union remained faithful to this spiritual inheritance.

The Liturgy as Alternative Worldview

A premier interpreter of Orthodox worship was Father Alexander Schmemann, the son of a Russian émigré family, who eventually became rector of St. Vladimir's Orthodox Theological Seminary in New York. While he never visited Russia, his sermons were broadcast into the Soviet Union for thirty years and won a wide intellectual following. Schmemann saw clearly how the Orthodox liturgy sets forth a vision of reality that challenges the ideologies of this world, including Marxism-Leninism.

Schmemann insisted that Christianity is an eschatological faith, that is, that Christianity witnesses to an ultimate, divine order of beauty, peace, and joy that is already breaking into history. While he sought to point to this dynamic in all that he wrote, his diaries, first published in the United States in 2000 and then in Russia in 2005, offer especially eloquent testimonies to it. At one point, reflecting on his childhood in Paris, Schmemann writes, "I remember ... when, walking to church in the golden morning light, there was a breakthrough, a touch with a mysterious bliss. And all my life, deep down, has been a search for this contact, this bliss. To feel it again!"[1] In other entries, he recounts how encountering natural beauty or experiencing human friendship moved him in a similar way. But, for Schmemann, it is especially in the Church's worship that this other world reveals itself among us here and now.

Schmemann writes, "This morning during Matins I had a 'jolt of happiness,' of fullness of life and at the same time the thought: I shall have to die! But in such a fleeting breath of happiness, time usually 'gathers' itself. In an instant, not only are all such breaths of happiness remembered but they are present and alive.... It seems to me that eternity might be not the stopping of time, but precisely its resurrection and gathering."[2] Or, again, "The Church is the home each of us leaves to go to work and to which one returns with joy in order to find life, happiness and joy, to which everyone brings back the fruits of his labor and where everything is transformed into a feast, into freedom and fulfillment, the presence, the experience of this 'home'—already out of time, unchanging, filled with eternity, revealing eternity."[3]

Within worship, this glimpse of what Christians call the kingdom of God comes into particular focus in the Eucharist. For Schmemann, Orthodoxy "is simply a vision of life, and what comes from that vision is the light, the transparency, the referral of everything to the 'Other,' the eschatological character of life itself and everything that is in it. The source of that eschatological light, the lifting up of all of life, is the sacrament of the Eucharist."[4] When the Church celebrates the Eucharist, "she always *becomes that which she is*: the Body of Christ, the Temple of the Holy Spirit, the gift of the new life, the manifestation of the Kingdom of God, the knowledge of God and communion with Him."[5]

In maintaining its worship, the Orthodox Church offered Russians and other Soviets a fundamental alternative to Marxist-Leninist ideology, which Schmemann regarded as one manifestation of the secularism so characteristic of the modern world. The secularist sees no world beyond this one; ultimate justice and peace depend on human efforts here and now. As Schmemann says, "A secularist views the world as containing within itself its meaning and the principles of knowledge and action.... [He rejects] 'epiphany': the primordial intuition that everything in this world and the world itself ... are *themselves* the manifestation and presence of that *elsewhere*."[6]

To be sure, communism did not lack religious-like symbols and rituals. As Russian historian Olga Kazmina has noted, "The religious cult transformed itself into a cult of great leaders. Elements of divinizing Lenin were apparent: whatever he said was regarded as indisputable truth, it was customary to venerate his body, and there was even a kind of sainthood accorded to his relatives and associates, of whom it was forbidden to speak negatively. Portraits of the great leaders were treated like icons, and the Ten Commandments were replaced by the Ten Principles of 'The Moral Codex of the Builder of Communism.'"[7] But communism used these religious elements not to reveal another world breaking into this one, but rather to sanctify its utopian vision of a classless society in this world. The Church was the only public organization in the Soviet Union that referred people to a divine order that transcended, yet revealed itself in, this world. And the state recognized that the Church therefore posed a danger to its aspirations to create the "New Soviet Man." As one historian has written, "Because Orthodox 'ideology' provided an alternative worldview to that of the Soviets, the Soviet authorities considered the very act of strengthening people's faith to be 'counterrevolutionary.'"[8]

Theologians more generally—not only Orthodox believers—have noted the political implications of Christianity's religious vision. In the 1940s, Protestant theologian Reinhold Niebuhr argued that while the Bible affirms government as a God-given principle for social order, it refuses to equate the state with divine power, with the result that "the 'rulers' and 'judges' of the nations are particularly subject to divine judgment."[9] More recently, Jewish biblical scholar Jon Levenson has observed how the Hebrew idea of a divine-human covenant has shaped Jewish and Christian political theology: "That no human ruler can claim the same degree of allegiance that God claims; that God's kingship or suzerainty relativizes all human regimes; that all human political arrangements fall short of the kingdom of God: these are ideas that have reverberated over the centuries and into our own time."[10]

The Liturgy as Political Threat

Alexander Schmemann called for a "liturgical theology" that attends to how belief is shaped and propagated by worship.[11] His approach, though developed in terms of Orthodox Christianity in the East, harks back to an ancient Latin formulation in the West: *lex orandi, lex credendi*, "the rule of prayer is the rule of belief." Worship of God is central to every Christian tradition but perhaps especially so to Orthodoxy, which over the centuries has developed a comprehensive set of services on daily, weekly, and annual cycles. Prayers and hymns to a saint on the day of his or her death (and, hence, liturgical veneration), icons and frescoes that surround worshipers on the walls and ceilings of the church building, and days and seasons of fasting and feasting are understood to shape the very foundations of the Church and the lives of the individuals who participate in it.

From the outset, the Bolsheviks did all that they could to suppress the alternative vision of reality that Orthodox worship set forth. In 1918, the state nationalized all church property, including church buildings and their contents, and eliminated the Church's juridical status.[12] In 1919, it issued guidelines for local authorities to expose and examine the relics of saints, typically located in reliquaries in the church nave, where they were objects of veneration before, after, and sometimes during worship.[13] The Bolsheviks wanted to prove that these "holy" remains, often reputed to be incorrupt, were merely dry, crumbling bones or even straw puppets. Some of the most famous relics belonged to monasteries. Once the state confiscated the relics, it typically closed the monastery and placed the relics at a later date in one of its museums of religion and atheism.[14]

In 1922, the government launched a campaign to seize other church treasures—including gold and silver implements needed for worship—in the name of raising money to feed millions of Soviet citizens who were starving in the wake of World War I and civil war and failed Soviet agricultural policies. In reality, the communists' goal was to make the Church's worship impossible and enrich their own pockets. As Lenin wrote in a secret memo, he saw the moment as one in which "we are given ninety-nine out of 100 chances to gain a full and crushing victory" over the Church.[15]

Another action that struck at the heart of Orthodox worship was confiscation of church icons, which state authorities then sold abroad, destroyed, or placed in national museums of art—as in 1928, when Andrei Rublev's famous Trinity icon was removed from the Holy Trinity-St. Sergius Monastery in Sergiev Posad and transferred to Moscow's Tretiakov Gallery.[16] In Orthodox thinking, icons are not merely pictures or illustrations of Christ, Mary, and saints, but—more importantly—are means of drawing worshippers into the heavenly world that all of worship evokes. Icons, like relics, are understood to make heavenly personages and their spiritual power available to their venerators. Moreover, some icons attain a reputation for miracle-working properties—believers may experience healing or relief of bad fortune after they pray before the icon, and the icon itself may, at least to the eyes of faith, exude fragrant oil or cleanse itself of the soot that burning candles have left upon it over the years.

In 1923, the Soviets abolished Christmas and other church observances as state holidays, and soon began requiring people to work or participate in state-sponsored activities on Sunday mornings, the time of the divine liturgy. By the late 1920s, the government had further undermined Orthodox worship by banning production of new Bibles, service books, and liturgical garments, vessels, and supplies. In 1929, the state ordered most church bells to be seized and smashed into scrap metal, and prohibited the ringing of the few that remained.[17] Traditionally, bells have called Orthodox believers to prayer, whether they have been in the church building itself or at work in the surrounding fields or towns. As Alexander Solzhenitsyn once wrote about the Russian past, "[When] the bells for evening prayer have rung ... [they have reminded people] to set aside trivial earthly matters and offer the moment to eternity."[18] By silencing church bells, the state eliminated one more pointer to a transcendent dimension of human existence within everyday life.

During these years, the government supplemented its actions against the Church's worship with antireligious propaganda that accused priests of corruption, immorality, and counterrevolutionary activities.[19] The state also encouraged schismatic movements within the Church that wished to alter the liturgy by replacing Church Slavonic, the language of worship for a millennium, with contemporary Russian or substituting the Gregorian (New Style) calendar for the Julian (Old Style).[20] The most direct assault on the Church, however, was the forcible removal of clergy and closure of churches. Within days of the October Revolution, the Bolsheviks were arresting, exiling, and killing Orthodox Christians: both priests, who celebrate the divine liturgy and Eucharist, and lay believers, who participate. Bishops, whose principal responsibility is to maintain the liturgy both by celebrating it themselves and by ordaining and assigning priests to serve it, also came under attack. In February 1918, Metropolitan Vladimir (Bogoiavlenskii) of Kiev became the first bishop martyr.

By August of that year, Church officials had documented 121 martyrdoms and were investigating reports of many others.[21] According to one historian's reckoning, "approximately 1000 clergymen and lay people were victims of the terror regime [in 1918 alone]. By 1920, the number of murdered bishops had risen to 28, and about 12,000 laypeople had become witnesses to the faith with their blood."[22] During Stalin's Great Terror, the persecution reached its climax, and by its conclusion in 1939, 85 percent of clergy and monastics—perhaps close to 150,000 persons—had been arrested, with the majority dying by execution or under the hardships of prison, exile, or the Gulag. Of 139 hierarchs prior to the October Revolution, only four remained active.[23]

Moreover, the Bolsheviks closed the buildings in which the priests had once served. The state now controlled all church property, and parishes could rarely raise enough money to rent back their facilities at the requested exorbitant rates.[24] Many churches were simply sealed shut, demolished, or converted to secular uses, such as gymnasiums, laboratories, cultural centers, or dormitories. In St. Petersburg, the Fedorovskii Cathedral was stripped of its icons and liturgical furniture and turned into a milk factory, while the Kazan Cathedral became a museum of religion and atheism. In 1931, Moscow's Christ the Savior Cathedral, Russian Orthodoxy's largest church edifice, was razed at Stalin's orders, eventually to be replaced with a huge, heated, outdoor swimming pool. By 1941, every monastery had been closed, and out of 50,000 parish churches in 1917, perhaps only 100 remained open—and not all of them had a priest available.[25]

Although the Bolsheviks came very close to eliminating the official Church, thousands of believers gathered in underground churches that observed as best they could the rhythms of Orthodox prayer and worship. Priests and believers, at the risk of arrest and punishment, would secretly come together for the divine liturgy in a clearing in a forest, a remote cemetery, or a believer's apartment, where the curtains would be drawn and liturgical garments and implements brought out of their hiding places.[26]

In one of history's great ironies, Hitler's invasion of the Soviet Union in 1941 helped save the institutional Church and public celebration of the liturgy. As the German armies moved eastward, their generals, in a move to win popular support, allowed churches to reopen. Stalin, feeling his hand forced, began allowing parishes to reestablish themselves in areas that he controlled. Although waves of church closures would occur again after the war, government authorities increasingly saw advantage in moving religious practice out of the underground into an official, institutional Church that they could control. In the 1950s and '60s, under Khrushchev, open persecution of the Church diminished, but promotion of a scientific, atheistic education intensified. A new kind of underground church emerged, attracting members of an intelligentsia who had become disenchanted with Marxist-Leninist ideology. Independently minded—and in some cases, openly dissident—priests of the official Church, such as Aleksandr Men, also attracted large followings. By the 1980s, approximately 7000 parishes and 18 monasteries were again officially in operation.[27]

The Liturgy as Solace and Strength

During these years, persecuted and pressured believers, both above and below ground, looked to the liturgy and Eucharist for comfort and courage.[28] In the last two years of his life (1923–1925), after several months of imprisonment, torture, and interrogation at the hands of the secret police, Patriarch Tikhon committed himself to celebrating the liturgy every day in Moscow-area churches, until he became physically too weak to continue. Even though he had declared in 1923 that he no longer regarded the Bolsheviks as the Church's enemies, state authorities regarded his continuing public celebration of worship as an act of political disloyalty. A secret police report of that year noted with grave concern that Tikhon had celebrated funeral prayers in a Moscow cemetery, with a huge, supportive crowd gathering around him. The report noted with further alarm that Tikhon intended to celebrate the divine liturgy in a Moscow church on the coming Sunday.[29]

Russian Orthodoxy has stressed the importance not only of the hierarchy—the patriarch and bishops—but also laypeople's personal spiritual fathers (and sometimes spiritual mothers) for sustaining the Church's faith. The years of Bolshevik persecution made the bonds between these spiritual fathers and their spiritual children all the deeper. A spiritual father would give his parishioners or monastic followers practical and spiritual counsel, pray with and for them, and if conditions allowed celebrate the liturgy with them. In turn, his spiritual children cared as best as they could for him, offering him a hiding place if the secret police were in pursuit, or travelling hundreds, sometimes even thousands, of miles to visit him if he were arrested and sent into exile.[30]

Father Sergei Mechev served the Church of St. Nikolai in Klennikakh, a historic neighborhood near the center of Moscow. His father, Aleksei, had begun preparing his parishioners for political repression and persecution soon after the Bolsheviks came to power. When Aleksei died in 1923, Sergei continued cultivating lay leadership that would be capable of sustaining prayer, worship, and fellowship if the church were closed or he were removed, as then happened in 1929, when he was sentenced to three years of exile in a small town three hundred miles to the northeast of Moscow. His spiritual children regularly travelled back and forth to him to deliver and receive letters.[31]

Sergei movingly testified to the centrality of worship for Christians: "Do not grieve about yourselves," he writes in one of his letters, "because you still have what is most important but has been denied to many others, including me: worship. Guard it. Indeed, this is my commandment to you, not only to my spiritual children but also to my friends. Guard worship, guard the clergy. ... Instruct one another, strengthen one another, comfort one another. 'Bear one another's burdens and in this way obey the law of Christ' (Gal. 6:2)."[32]

When authorities closed the Church of St. Nikolai in Klennikakh in 1932, parishioners valiantly fulfilled Sergei's spiritual testament. They regularly visited Aleksei Mechev's grave in a Moscow cemetery and prayed for him to grant them safety and strength. They also gathered clandestinely in small groups in parishioners' apartments, where a trusted lay leader, male or female, led prayer and Bible study. On Saturday evenings, the groups chanted vespers, matins, the hours, and Akathists (special hymns to a saint). On Sundays, a priest might secretly celebrate the liturgy.

The testimonies to the priestly service of Father Arsenii Strel'tsov, first collected as samizdat during the Soviet period and then published openly after the fall of communism, demonstrate the centrality of prayer and worship to believers in Stalin's prison camps. One account tells of how Father Arsenii survived severe cold and hunger by reciting the Church's matins service each evening; offering Akathists to the Theotokos (Mary, the Mother of God), St. Nikolai, and St. Arsenii; and commemorating in prayer his spiritual children, with whom authorities had forbidden him all contact.[33] According to another account, a prisoner once offered Father Arsenii a stolen Book of the Gospels and a Book of Services. On the inside of the binding of one of the books, Father Arsenii found what in Orthodoxy is required for celebrating the divine liturgy—an antimens, a small piece of silk cloth into which the relics of a saint have been sewn. With great joy, he began secretly hearing prisoners' confessions and offering them the Eucharist, even though he knew that if he were discovered, he faced severe consequences, even death.[34]

That celebration of the liturgy posed a political threat to the Bolshevik regime is also evident in the case of Archimandrite Serafim (Tiapochkin). When sentenced in 1941 to ten years of hard labor for secretly celebrating the liturgy at the factory to which authorities had assigned him after closing his church parish, he quietly and successfully continued his priestly service. But toward the end of his term, a confrontation with the authorities occurred. The prison commander asked him what he intended to do upon release, and Serafim replied, "I am a priest, I will serve [the liturgy]," with the result that the commander ordered him to be held for five more years.[35]

Even after the Gulag was dismantled by Khrushchev, the state continued to exert massive pressure on the Church. Parish councils were typically in the hands of a lay elder who represented government interests. Secret police informants reported on priests' sermons and activities. At state-sponsored conferences and ecumenical religious gatherings, Church leaders were expected to express gratitude for religious freedom in the Soviet Union and enthusiasm for the government's international peace policies. Antireligious agitation—as well as the fear that their career advancement could be threatened—discouraged many people from attending church services or even bringing their children to be baptized. Some of the Church's most talented priests felt deeply isolated and lonely—and, as earlier in the century, found solace and strength in the liturgy.

Vsevolod Shpiller headed Moscow's Church of St. Nikolai in Kuznetsakh from 1951 until his death in 1984. His letters from the 1960s and '70s document a profound inner struggle to sustain ministry under the repressive social and political conditions. A special source of consolation and inspiration became a relationship by correspondence with a holy elder who lived in an isolated rural area several hours outside of Moscow. Shpiller knew that this holy man secretly celebrated the liturgy—and included Shpiller's name in the prayers. Shpiller also sensed that the elder was somehow present to him when Shpiller himself celebrated the liturgy. Even at age 90, while growing increasingly weak, the elder could write, "I come to life again, when I am with you in Vishniakovskii Lane [where Shpiller's church was located]. I try to serve the liturgy often, then I lie down."[36] Worship and prayer created mystical bonds that held the two men together.

Muting the Liturgy

The Orthodox liturgy survived Lenin's and Stalin's efforts to eradicate religion. But the communists did succeed in driving the Church out of public view, such that many Soviet citizens were no longer aware of what was going on within its walls. In retrospect, it is not possible to say clearly why the state did not close all of the churches, or on what basis it allowed some to remain open, while shuttering others. But persecution and pressure took their toll. That the liturgy sets forth an alternative worldview, calling existing social-political arrangements into question, was not always evident. A Church that had accommodated itself to worldly realities in order to preserve its worship had come to celebrate it in ways that muted—although never completely eliminated—its capacity to inspire resistance.

Alexander Schmemann reflected deeply on the ways in which Christian worship and celebration of the Eucharist can become distorted. On the one side he saw the danger of a "spiritualism" that reduces religion to rituals and rules by which individuals try to escape into a holy realm beyond this world. That kind of Church may help people endure the troubles of everyday life, but it does not inspire them to challenge the status quo. On the other side is an "activism" that reduces religion to moral and political causes. According to Schmemann, advocates of this position constantly call us to repent "for having spent too much time in contemplation and adoration, in silence and liturgy, for having not dealt sufficiently with the social, political, economic, racial, and all other issues of real life."[37]

As Orthodox Christians sought to negotiate life in the Soviet Union, they succumbed to both of these failures, sometimes in response to state pressure and at other times due to a lack of courage. The capacity of the liturgy to point to another dimension of existence—to a God from whom all life comes and returns—was too often hollowed out by spiritualism or activism. Perhaps the communists believed that they did not need to shut every church building if they could persuade the Church to survive by reducing its worship to mere ritualism. A political passivity would result, something that deeply worried Alexander Solzhenitsyn when he wrote Patriarch Pimen in 1972 that "the Russian Church never has anything at all to say about things which are wrong here at home.... By what reasoning is it possible to convince oneself that the planned *destruction* of the spirit and body of the Church under the guidance of atheists is the best way of *preserving* it? Preserving it for whom? Certainly not for Christ. Preserving it by what means? By *falsehood*. But after the falsehood by whose hands are the holy mysteries to be celebrated?"[38]

Some of the Church's leading priests, including Vsevolod Shpiller, criticized Solzhenitsyn at the time for defining the Church primarily as an opposition political body. They remembered the politicization of the Church after the October Revolution, with groups such as the Renovationists endorsing the Bolshevik political program, while supporters of the monarchy sometimes asked the Church to support armed resistance to the new communist state. Shpiller and others believed that Patriarch Tikhon had saved the Church by calling it to rise above politics, to align itself with neither the Reds nor the Whites, and to serve as a loving presence to all Russians.

Schmemann saw clearly that ritualism and activism are actually not far apart from each other. Both are a response to—and an acceptance of—secularism, rather than a proclamation of how divinity has entered into history in order to restore humanity to its true self. Similarly, Solzhenitsyn rightly worried that a Church "above politics" merely becomes a tool of the state. Nevertheless, Schmemann believed that the liturgy, even when seemingly compromised, retains a critical potential. The Church's task is to free itself of both spiritualism and activism, so that its liturgy will clearly set forth the biblical vision of human life before an ultimate Creator and redeeming Judge.

After the October Revolution, one of the key struggles within the Orthodox Church was whether the prayers of the liturgy should include the new government. The Church traditionally prays not only for its hierarchs, priests, monastics, and the gathered people but also its "God-fearing rulers." What was the Church to do after the Bolsheviks murdered Nicholas II in July 1918? The question was further complicated by the relation of the Church hierarchy to the communist state. In 1927, Metropolitan Sergii (Stragorodskii), serving as head of the Church after Tikhon's death and the arrest of the patriarchal representative, Petr (Polianskii), issued a controversial declaration of political loyalty: "We wish to be Orthodox believers and at the same time recognize the Soviet Union as our earthly home, whose joys and successes are our joys and successes, and whose misfortunes are our misfortunes."[39] In protest, other prominent Church leaders, such as Metropolitan Kirill (Smirnov), refused to commemorate either the state or Sergii in their liturgical prayers. Their "non-commemoration" was for them a profound expression of political protest.[40]

Aleksii (Solov'ev), a holy elder in the famous Holy Trinity-St. Sergius Monastery, took a different tack. For him, commemoration was not only stabilizing but also destabilizing. He believed that Church unity demanded submission to Sergii, its head, so long as he did not violate its canons. Moreover, as one historian has noted, "Aleksii declared that it was a sin not to pray for [the Soviet authorities].... Indeed, from [his] viewpoint, it was necessary to pray for them because only the grace of prayer could 'break down the wall of enmity and hatred which stands between the Church and Soviet authorities.'" "Pray," declared Aleksii, "—perhaps the grace of prayer will break through the wall."[41]

Christian Freedom

Resistance, of course, can take many forms. The Christian tradition, including Orthodoxy, has generally discouraged armed rebellion, concerned that the result will be an anarchy that is even more destructive of social relationships than the previous unjust state. More recently, liberation theologies have reminded Christians that sometimes only violent resistance can overcome the systemic violence that oppressive regimes perpetrate against their citizens. The Orthodox liturgy does not suggest what may be necessary for Christians in one specific social context or another. It offers not a concrete political program, but rather a vision of freedom before God. In worship, people encounter a God who delivers them from every human ideology. The One who reveals himself in the cross of Christ offers them the possibility of knowing beauty, justice, and peace within themselves and with other human beings and indeed the creation as a whole.

In the Soviet era, the Christian freedom nourished by the liturgy found its most poignant expression in the lives of those who under secret police interrogation refused to compromise themselves or others. These believers discovered a remarkable capacity to tell the truth about the Bolsheviks' crimes, while nevertheless treating their persecutors as fellow children of God. As Russian Church leader Vladimir Vorob'ev has stated so eloquently, "[Under the circumstances of Bolshevik persecution] only one path remained ... to try to find in one's enemy, even an enemy of the Church, some dimension of humanity and to appeal to this humanity in the hope that he would suddenly be moved ... and ashamed ... and choose mercy. This strategy required meekness and humility."[42] It was Orthodox worship and Eucharist that gave thousands of Christian believers—nearly two thousand of whom have been canonized—the spiritual courage to speak this kind of truth in love. Today, they also offer this freedom to all who participate in the Church's liturgy, which daily commemorates them as "the new martyrs and confessors of Russia."[43]

9

"AND I WILL TELL OF THE BEST PEOPLE IN ALL THE EARTH"

Faith and Resilience in the Gulag

Xenia Dennen

Why do some people survive the horrific conditions of a Nazi concentration camp or a Soviet labor camp and others die quickly? Why does a person not commit suicide? These were questions that the psychotherapist and writer Dr. Viktor Frankl explored with his patients, and their answers formed the threads that he gradually wove together to create what he called Logotherapy, his version of existential analysis. In *Man's Search for Meaning* he explores this subject and comes to the conclusion that those who had a sense of "meaning" in their lives, who felt their existence was part of a metaphysical framework, were able to survive and even sometimes to demonstrate extraordinary inner strength and human goodness.[1] Simone Weil took an opposite view: in her essay "The Love of God and Affliction," she claims that extreme human suffering, which she calls "affliction," is always dehumanizing and destructive. It "deprives its victims of their personality and makes them into things. [...] it freezes all those it touches right to the depths of their souls. They will never find warmth again. They will never believe any more that they are anyone."[2]

These two diametrically opposed views are illustrated in the form of two figures from literature—the first view through Lukeria, a character in the short story "A Living Relic" by Ivan Turgenev,[3] and the second through Gregor in Franz Kafka's *Metamorphosis*. Gregor endures a terrifying life, imprisoned within the carapace of an unwanted and unloved insect who shrivels up, until in death he is no more than a flat piece of shell that is swept up like rubbish, and which his family do not even bother to bury. He is totally destroyed. Very different is the life-affirming Lukeria: although paralyzed as the result of a fall when she was young, she exudes joy and peace, she loves life, loves listening to the pigeons, watching the bees and chickens. Her head "looked exactly like an ancient icon," writes the agnostic Turgenev, who feels there is something holy about her. The Soviet Gulag is a rich source for examples of life-affirming individuals who could support Frankl's theory. Among them was the poet Irina Ratushinskaia.

Irina Ratushinskaia

Ratushinskaia was determined that the fortitude she witnessed in the Gulag should not be lost to posterity. "And I will tell of the best people in all the earth," she wrote in her poem "*I Will Live and Survive*"—"The most tender, but also the most invincible." The poem was written in November 1983 after seven months in prison where she was beaten and put in solitary confinement in freezing conditions, until many thought she would die from her injuries.[4] Her remarkable memoir, *Grey is the Colour of Hope*,[5] describes her years in the Small Zone, a special unit for women political prisoners within the Barashevo labor camp in Mordovia. Here, despite the near-starvation rations and the regular spells in the SHIZO[6] (the prison isolation cell) where prisoners had to wear just a thin smock in freezing temperatures, these women still put others first, supported one another, shared any extra food they received, and refused to compromise their principles. Frequently they even went on hunger strike if one of their number was put into the SHIZO or was refused the regulation annual family visit. Ratushinskaia writes: "Probably this is the best way to retain one's humanity in the camps: to care more about another's pain than about your own."[7] The women did not respond rudely to the insolence of the prison warders; they simply refused to speak. They were careful to avoid hating their persecutors and tried to laugh instead. Out of their bleak, inhuman environment, they created a garden, growing nettles and anything that would add some nutrition to their appalling diet.

Irina Ratushinskaia was born in 1954 and lived in Odessa, Ukraine. She graduated from Odessa University in 1976 with a degree in physics. As a student she discovered the poetry of Akhmatova, Mandel'shtam, Pasternak, and Tsvetaeva and became an active dissident. In November 1979 she married Igor Geraschenko and moved to Kiev. Accused of "manufacturing and disseminating" poetry, which was defined according to the Criminal Code as "anti-Soviet agitation and propaganda," she was arrested in 1982 aged twenty-eight and sentenced in March 1983 to seven years in strict regime labor camps with a subsequent five years of internal exile, the maximum punishment possible under Article 70 of the Criminal Code of the USSR.

Labor Camp Brutality

Soviet reality and the labor camp environment were based on a construct of lies in which the aim of the authorities was to turn people into slaves or even to drive a person mad. Isaiah Berlin during just a short visit to the USSR in 1956 felt the Soviet world was divorced from normality: "If one stays in the USSR more than two weeks one's perspective and values are fatally transformed: to leave it is like waking from a dream: there is no bridge with reality."[8] For someone like Ratushinskaia who faced years in prison, it could have been a real threat to her sanity, as she admitted: "it seemed to me that the normal human world no longer existed, and that I was living in a huge mental asylum."[9] In a BBC broadcast in 1987 she explained:

> When prisoners are held in a camp or punishment cell, one of the KGB's main aims is to reduce them to a state where they lose all human dignity. To achieve this, they place people in conditions which are inconceivable, incomprehensible to the rational mind. Sometimes the prisoner's psychological defence mechanism is to retreat into madness. People try to substitute an imaginary reality for the horror which their mind can no longer bear. This is more of a threat to creative people, and I knew that I faced that risk. But I always hoped that I had sufficient resilience to withstand the reality of the KGB's making and hold on to my sanity.[10]

Conditions in the Barashevo labor camp were inhuman. Orders came at one point for Natalia Lazareva (a former theater director from Leningrad), one of the woman prisoners in the Small Zone, to be moved to Saransk. She was running a high temperature so some of the other prisoners demanded that a doctor come and examine her. Instead she was grabbed by her hands and feet and hauled by two warders out of bed clad only in a blouse and briefs:

> She is towed through the snow which already lies on the ground, and thrown into a cart. The gate slams shut. Natasha [Natalia] screams for help. Major Shalin kicks her with a heavy boot once, twice, three times. Then they all fall on her, kicking her into unconsciousness.[11]

On a number of occasions Ratushinskaia went on hunger strike for which a prisoner would get fifteen days in the SHIZO; there was no heating in winter and you were allowed to wear only thin clothes. During one such spell she felt extremely ill and was saved only because Tatiana Velikanova (one of the leaders of the human rights movement in the USSR) was in the cell with her and shouted for a doctor: "I lay flush up against the heating pipes, but to no avail, because they were cold. I fell into a delirious fever: in that delirium, I kept feeling that I was being drawn into the shapeless stain on one of the walls, and clutched at the pipe to avoid being sucked into that dark patch."[12] On another occasion in the SHIZO Ratushinskaia again nearly died: totally exhausted she slept and allowed her mind to flee her cell going whither she knew not, but the memory of her husband, Igor, helped to pull her back to life:

> Then I would find myself in a dark tunnel, at the end of which someone was waiting for me. And I would fly towards it, yet every time, just as I neared the end, the realisation would come that I had to go back. And, oh, how I did not want to go back! But I had to because it was not yet my time. And, then what about Igor? So I would go back.[13]

Ratushinskaia's resilience was extraordinary, strengthened by her religious faith and, as she later acknowledged, by the prayers and support of many organizations and individuals who publicized her situation and campaigned for her release. As a young person, before her imprisonment, she had loved airplanes and dreamed of flying one.[14] She continued to fly in her imagination and was able to preserve a sense of inner freedom during her imprisonment. Indeed, she likened to flying a particular sort of strength that she experienced:

> The security which I felt in the labour camp—of knowing that they could only kill my body with torture, nothing more—was something which I'd understood theoretically before. But it was another thing to learn that this was actually true. [...] It produced a special kind of strength, like imagining yourself flying, then suddenly finding that you are.[15]

Faith and Compassion

Ratushinskaia's attitude to other human beings, even to the criminals who were imprisoned with her, was always positive, affirming that "there is something else to them as well—and that I will never forget. I shall try to appeal to that 'something else' which exists in even the most hardened criminals, and the guards."[16] She believed that hatred should be expunged from within yourself as "it will flourish and spread during your years in the camps, driving out everything else, and ultimately corrode and warp your soul."[17] Most of all among those in the Small Zone she admired Tatiana Velikanova, who established "the honourable practices of dignity and care for others in the Zone!"[18] The two women would have lengthy debates about what constitutes a human being to prevent themselves losing touch with "the normal human world" and treasured above all the warmth of the friendship that grew between them and the others in the Small Zone. On returning from a spell in the camp's "icy, filthy hospital," Ratushinskaia recorded: "I already feel much better within these walls, but even better than the walls of this our home is our friendship."[19]

This attitude to other human beings flowed from her Christian faith, which she had discovered early on in her life in Odessa. She wrote warmly about her fellow prisoner, a Lithuanian school teacher, Jadvyga Bieliauskiene, whose Catholicism was "the cornerstone of her existence": like her Ratushinskaia was not interested in denominational differences as "God is one, after all, and it is to Him that we shall all come in the end."[20] Another fellow prisoner, Galina Barats-Kokhan, after working as a Moscow University lecturer on Marxism, had become a Pentecostal: in her letters to her husband she called her hunger strike a fast and, commented Ratushinskaia, she would "depend only on water and prayer to sustain her. [...] What a mixed bunch we are: a Catholic, a Pentecostal, several Orthodox, an unbeliever ... later we were to be joined by a Baptist. Yet we were always deeply respectful of one another's convictions. And God did not turn His face away from our small patch of Mordovian soil."[21]

When Natalia Lazareva had two cardiac seizures in the SHIZO, Ratushinskaia prayed that she might live and although desperately weak from a hunger strike, when Natalia cried out with pain, Ratushinskaia mysteriously found within herself enough strength to reach her on the other side of the cell: "From what reserves? I don't know. Strange things happen when you have nothing to depend on except God's help."[22] During another spell in the SHIZO some of the women sang hymns and psalms, and one Christmas Eve when back in the Small Zone they gathered around a table, said the Lord's Prayer while Bieliauskiene divided up a Communion wafer from Lithuania that had been sent in an envelope by her relative: "And we, despite our various creeds, never doubted for a moment that God was looking down on us all at that moment."[23]

After her release from prison and her arrival in Britain in December 1986, Ratushinskaia was interviewed by Keston College staff: she explained that in a labor camp the authorities aimed to break you spiritually and she recounted a mysterious experience of warmth in the punishment cell:

while I was still in the camp, we all—my fellow prisoners and I—were frequently aware, actually physically aware, of the support of prayer. It is very hard to explain, it sounds very mystical, but we all at varying times, felt what could be described as an active flow of strength, a sort of warmth, and bearing in mind the icy conditions of punishment cells, this warmth could only have been the force of prayer, sustaining and protecting us.[24]

The Poet

Iosif Brodskii wrote a moving introduction to a 1986 edition of Ratushinskaia's poetry published in translation. He described her arrest and imprisonment "as a Neanderthal shriek; or rather, it testifies to the degree of bestialisation achieved by the first socialist state in the history of mankind." He considered her "a remarkably genuine poet, a poet with faultless pitch"[25] whose crown of thorns had turned into a laurel.

Her Christian faith often comes clearly through her poetry. In "*I Will Live and Survive*" she testifies to experiencing a "second birth" and describes an epiphany in her cell brought about by "a frost-covered window."[26] In the midst of what was meant to destroy her, she had acquired a level of perception that transfigured her surroundings and gave her the strength to survive. In January 1984 she wrote the poem "*I Talk to the Mice and the Stars*."[27] In this she becomes aware that her poetic gift is a divine calling. Echoing Pushkin's poem, "*The Prophet*," her mouth is touched by a six-winged seraphim. She proudly wears the marks of the rank awarded to her by a divine hand, and Christ-like is prepared to drink the cup that is presented to her. In the midst of death-dealing reality, she transforms the horror into something life-giving and beautiful.

While imprisoned Ratushinskaia sometimes managed to write down her poems on four-centimeter-wide strips of cigarette paper, which were then tightly rolled into a small tube "less than the thickness of your little finger"[28] that were sealed and made moisture-proof by a method of her own devising. These "capsules" were then secreted out of the prison when an opportunity presented itself. She would write poetry in her head while sewing gloves on sewing machines that made a racket like "machine-guns": "After arriving at the final version of five or six lines, I jot them down on a bit of paper which is concealed under a pile of unsewn gloves. When the poem is complete I commit it to memory and burn the paper."[29]

Her poetry was much in demand in the Small Zone and even by the non-politicals in the main part of the camp. A thief called Vasya who because of his TB had been sent to the prison hospital, jumped over a fence into the Small Zone one day and was fascinated by the uncompromising moral standards of Irina and the other women; he asked her to write down some of her poetry and there ensued a correspondence between the Small Zone and some of the thieves, who through their contacts and the use of bribes managed to get letters from Ratushinskaia out to her husband, until the warders carried out a detailed search and moved the women to different quarters. While in the SHIZO she would recite her poems to those in the neighboring cell, speaking into a mug by a pipe that, running along the wall, would help carry the sound. She described how prisoners demanded more and more poetry, how she began to flag but "was filled with new strength which came from some source I did not know I possessed."[30] This occurred on New Year's Eve, when she felt so much delight at "bringing at least a few minutes of pleasure to the driven and the suffering [...] in the midst of so much everyday sorrow."[31]

International Campaign

Thanks to an international campaign Ratushinskaia was eventually released in October 1986 and soon thereafter allowed to come to Britain. Keston College,[32] founded during the Cold War to study the religious situation in communist countries, played a key role in this campaign, as Alyona Kojevnikov, who was editor of the *Keston News Service* and translated *Grey Is the Colour of Hope*, testified.[33] Of the numerous prisoners of conscience brought to the attention of the global media by Keston, the case of Ratushinskaia had the most successful outcome. Kojevnikov stated:

> Public attention is notoriously fickle, but the case of this young woman roused the sympathy and concern of people from all walks of life around the world. Demonstrations were held, petitions were signed and the clamour refused to die down until four years later Gorbachev, descending from his plane for a summit meeting with US President Reagan in Reykjavik, announced immediately that he would not be answering any questions about Ratushinskaya "as she has already been released."[34]

In the words of Irina's husband, Igor Geraschenko, Keston College played "the most decisive role"[35] in the campaign because Keston kept the international media constantly up-to-date about her situation. Many organizations such as PEN International and Amnesty International joined the campaign in support of Ratushinskaia, but it was the work of Keston that attracted the most attention, Kojevnikov claimed:

> Our extensive contacts with families and friends of prisoners of conscience in the USSR earned us their trust. In as much as was possible, we maintained telephone contact with many of them despite KGB blocking the lines, so we were almost always the first to know what was really happening. As the demands calling for Irina's release escalated, the Soviet authorities could not continue to ignore them. It was probably the KGB's hope that after some initial fuss, interest would die down and no action would be required. Their hopes were dashed. We did not know it at the time, but this was when pressure was stepped up to bully Irina into signing appeals for clemency, which she resolutely refused to do.[36]

During the last four months before Ratushinskaia's release, Keston, through Alyona Kojevnikov, was lucky enough to establish telephone contact with her husband in Kiev. This regular contact enabled Keston to inform the world about exactly what was happening to her:

> This was not without its humorous moments. It was decided that I, as a native speaker, would phone Igor. He had no way of knowing who I was, nor was I certain that he was at the other end of the line, or some KGB functionary responding to that number. I started reciting one of Irina's poems, then broke off and said I could not remember the next line. Igor promptly continued. After we had played this game four or five times, we were both satisfied that we were who we claimed to be. We still laugh about it.[37]

In December 1986, two months after her release, Ratushinskaia rang Keston and told Kojevnikov the number of her flight to Heathrow. Then "on the morning of that December day I received a sudden phone call from Igor saying: 'We'll see you in five hours at Heathrow!'"[38] Keston College staff turned out in force to meet them, and although they were both very tired they agreed to a short appearance at the airport's press center, which was packed with journalists, photographers, and television cameras. A regular press conference was scheduled for the next day during which Ratushinskaia made a short appeal:

> Ladies and gentlemen! Soon we shall all be celebrating Christmas in the warmth of our homes. But at the same time, the best people of our country will spend their Christmas in camps, prisons and punishment cells. They are prisoners of conscience: let us not forget about them!

Shortly after Ratushinskaia's arrival in London she and her husband were received by Margaret Thatcher at Number 10 Downing Street and met numerous other prominent political and religious figures. In 1987 Ratushinskaia was invited to spend a year as "Poet in Residence" at Northwestern University in the United States, and afterward returned to England. Several years later, thanks to excellent medical care in the West after the appalling physical suffering of her time in the Gulag, Ratushinskaia gave birth to twin boys, Sergei and Oleg. She and her husband never intended to emigrate permanently, but as they had been stripped of Soviet citizenship they were not able to return to Russia until they eventually received Russian passports in 1998 during Yeltsin's period in power. When the twins were school age the family returned to Russia and now live in Moscow. Kojevnikov ended her account with the words:

> Fairy-tale endings are very rare in life, but after the sufferings endured by Irina and Igor all those years ago, it is truly wonderful to be able to say that they were reunited despite all the odds "and lived happily ever after."[39]

During an interview with Keston College staff in early 1987 Ratushinskaia expressed deep gratitude to all those who had taken part in the campaign for her release, and dedicated to them the following poem, which was published by Keston in its magazine *Frontier*:

> Believe me, it was often thus
> In solitary cells, on winter nights
> A sudden sense of joy and warmth
> And a resounding note of love
>
> And then, unsleeping, I would know
> A-huddled by an icy wall
> Someone is thinking of me now
> Petitioning the Lord for me
>
> My dear ones, thank you all
> Who did not falter, who believed in us!
> In the most fearful prison hour
> We probably would not have passed
>
> Through everything—from start to end—
> Our heads held high, unbowed,
> Without your valiant hearts
> To light our path.[40]

Forgotten Heroes of the Gulag

Irina Ratushinskaia was one of many cases highlighted by Keston College. In 1978 Keston translated and published a remarkable memoir by an anonymous author. This was *The Unknown Homeland,* about the life, arrest, exile to Siberia and death of a Russian Orthodox priest from Leningrad called Fr. Pavel.[41] The book includes a foreword by the Russian Orthodox writer and human rights activist Anatolii Levitin, who met Fr. Pavel and duly confirmed that this was indeed a real person. Fr. Pavel's arrest and subsequent journey to what turns out to be his final resting place become a parable of Christ on the way to the Cross, of everyman's journey to God or to the promised land, unknown until it is reached. After his arrest, Alya, Fr. Pavel's niece, goes in search of her uncle and eventually finds him in a Novosibirsk transit prison where these words are put into her mouth:

> But it was not his paleness, nor his human exhaustion that made her step back. The face she had known from early childhood rose before her in the full force of its suffering and anguish. The blue veins stood on his temples, trembling as they had a minute ago: the awful picture before her was not clear enough for reasoned thought, but obvious and vivid to her sorrowing heart. Behind the partition stood, not Uncle Pavel, but Another Man, younger than him. The centuries vanished, all was as it once had been. Had the rough rope really been tied round his pale hand? The sweat running down from his temples, the tears streaming from his eyes—were they not really trickles of blood? Were the lips of this Man not whispering to her of Love, of the Cross, of Heaven? This lasted for only a few seconds ... and once more it was Father Pavel coughing behind the partition, her dear Father, her uncle.[42]

The backdrop to Fr. Pavel's long and painful journey first down the Angara River and then through mountains and forest, sometimes on horseback, sometimes in a coffin-like box, to his place of exile at Ust-Vikhorevo, is the beauty of Siberia. As Fr. Pavel reaches this village a wonderful view, like the land of Canaan, opens out before the exhausted travellers and he is recorded as saying: "This is my rest for ever, here will I dwell."[43] He ended his days in a *kulak*'s house where he ministered to the village's inhabitants from his bed. He died on the eve of Candlemas whispering the words of the *Nunc Dimittis*. The book ends with the words:

> A light wind was whirling dust over the new grave-mound and flying up into the branches of the bird-cherry bush. [...] So the story of the exiled pastor came to an end ... But though the storm blows over the new and old grave mounds,

covering them with snow, though the snowstorm whirls over the distant cemetery, wrapping it in a mantel of white snow, though time goes by and the years disappear, though no-one comes there anymore and the small cross with its worn inscription falls off its base and collapses onto the ground ... still the bird-cherry tree will go on arraying itself anew in its wedding colours every spring, and the path of remembrance, prayer and veneration, which leads to such graves, will never be overgrown.[44]

Another memoir that relates a story of prison and exile is by Elena Chicherina, who, like Irina Ratushinskaia and Fr. Pavel, is another life-affirming individual from the world of the Gulag. It was published in 1996[45] (by this time the author had become a nun called Sister Ekaterina in the Convent of the Dormition in Vladimir) and is divided into two parts: the first is about Elena's spiritual father, Archimandrite Georgii Lavrov, whom she joined in exile. A monk in the Danilov Monastery, he was arrested in May 1928 and in June exiled to Kazakhstan for three years. Sent to a tiny village in the steppe called Kara Tiuba, east of Uralsk (about 1,300 km from Moscow) he found himself in a place in which the winter temperatures could drop to -60°C. Here Fr. Georgii lived in a small *fanza* (the local name for a house) and was sometimes buried alive under snow during the night. Elena was sent out to help him by what amounted to a community of Fr. Georgii's spiritual children. She describes her extraordinary journey, first from Moscow to Saratov, then across the Volga to Engels, then on to Uralsk in Kazakhstan, from where she travelled in a sledge pulled by a camel to Dzhambeity until she eventually reached Kara Tiuba. In the snow-covered steppe the moonlight caught the glint of wolves' eyes.

Despite the hardship, Elena's account of life in this god-forsaken place is full of wonder and joy. She tells how she rushed about cleaning the home, getting the stove going, preparing their meager meals each day. She describes lovingly their "savior," their one cow, Burenka, without whose milk they could not have survived. Fr. Georgii took care of her, would clean out her shed and feed her, and one day returned triumphantly from a walk in the steppe with Burenka and a newborn calf. The years of exile finally ended when Fr. Georgii was allowed to return to European Russia. By this time, however, he was suffering from advanced throat cancer, was unable to eat and hardly able to breathe. Somehow Elena helped him back to Nizhnii Novgorod where he died in 1932.

The second part of Elena's memoir describes her own imprisonment in 1933 after she and other members of her family had gathered in Moscow for a friend's name-day and were all arrested. After a spell in the Lubianka and then the Butyrskaia Prison, she was transported to the Altai in southern

Siberia. She was taken first to a labor camp that had been set up to help construct a railway line into Mongolia, and then to two others where the prisoners worked as lumberjacks. Against the background of near starvation, constant illness, and hard labor, Elena's account again is full of wonder, this time before the extraordinary beauty of the Altai, Russia's Switzerland:

> In the morning I went out to look at where we had been brought. And what did I see? The Kurai steppe—a high plateau, surrounded by mountains. On one side there were mountains covered in forest, and on the other, far in the distance a chain of snow-covered mountains glowing in the pink light of the rising sun. [...] Lower down the mountains were coniferous woods with mostly larches and cedar trees. Add to all this, the incredible clear air, the overwhelming space, the abundance of light, the sun. [...] The whole thing was miraculous, a fairy tale.[46]

Whenever possible she sang, managing to form tiny choirs, and one year celebrating Christmas, hidden in the bathhouse away from the prying eyes of the guards.

A thin, poorly printed pamphlet entitled *Tolmachi: Reminiscences about My Father* by Serafim Chetverukhin and edited by his brother Sergei contains a beautifully written memoir that describes parish life and the fate that befell the author's father Fr. Il'ia Chetverukhin, an intellectual from an aristocratic background who was a good pastor and preacher.[47] He was arrested in 1930 and sent to work in a labor camp at Krasnaia Vishera (Perm oblast) where he died in a fire in 1932. A sensitive person whose health was ruined and who sometimes felt abandoned by God, he still managed to preserve his kindly nature, his compassion, and his Christian faith. A short section of these reminiscences is written by Fr. Il'ia's wife, Evgenia (née Grandmaison) who had secured permission to visit her husband in Krasnaia Vishera in the spring of 1932. It was the last time she saw him. In her account he tells her not ever to expect him to return home:

> I am sure we will be together for all eternity, but not on earth. I shall probably be given another three years in prison. Here I am going through another Theological Academy without which I would never be permitted to enter the Heavenly Kingdom. Every day I await death and prepare to die."[48]

Fr. Il'ia's last recorded conversation was with Dr. Sergei Nikitin (later he became a Russian Orthodox bishop) who, when he returned from prison, recounted to Evgenia what Fr. Il'ia had said to him:

"St. Serafim said: Strive for peace of soul, and thousands around you will be saved. I have striven here after that peace of soul, and if I take back to Moscow even a tiny fraction of that peace, then I will be the happiest of men. I have lost much in life. Now I'm not afraid of loss, every day I'm ready to die. I love the Lord and am ready to be burnt alive for His sake." The next day his words were fulfilled. Batiushka [little father] died in a fire.[49]

Fr. Il'ia's inner peace did not disappear with him but continued to have an effect after his death. In 1936 his son Serafim Chetverukhin was also imprisoned, and after his eventual release in 1949 he found his way to his mother's home in Moscow. Serafim describes how alienated he felt from ordinary life, how he did not even feel at home when he sat down in his mother's flat. The only thing with which he could connect was a portrait of his father painted by Vladimir Kirsanov in 1932 in the labor camp:

The portrait showed a thin man with shaven face and short hair, dressed in a dark blue knitted jacket and a ridiculous yellow coat. The look in his short-sighted eyes was tense and concentrated as though he wanted to convey something important. [...] And so I am sitting in the room where I hadn't been for sixteen years. I look at all the intimate family possessions and the most intimate of all—the portrait of my father. I understand the important thing he is trying to say through the look in his eyes. He is saying: "Say, Glory be to God for everything, my son ... Forgive offenses committed against you so that you also are forgiven. [...] I was weak, I experienced pain, insults, and bewilderment—no one, after all, can understand everything, but I preserved the faith. My faith helped me not to be crippled when I was exiled. It turned the labor camp into a second Theological Academy. It gave me what is most precious—inner peace. And to my last breath I affirmed: Glory be to God." I wiped my eyes and looked round. My mother was tidying up. My wife was sleeping peacefully. My son was building something with great concentration. The green arms of the poplar were waving in welcome outside the window, the sparrows were singing joyfully. The faces in the icons were thoughtful and kindly before the glimmering icon lamp. Everything was so peaceful. I felt at home. And there were no prison bars. I said: "Glory be to God for everything."[50]

A memoir by Vera Bobrinskaia about her father, Fr. Sergii Sidorov, is a vivid record of the life of a parish priest in the 1920s and 1930s.[51] A highly educated man from an aristocratic background with intellectual tastes, he is caught up in the social ferment of early 1917 and then, after the October Revolution and his ordination in 1921, he serves as a priest in a parish near Kiev, Ukraine. In 1923 he moved with his wife to Sergiev Posad, north of Moscow, where many others of similar backgrounds and tastes had moved to escape as far as possible the watchful eye of the NKVD in the capital.

In October 1924 Fr. Sergii was arrested for the first time and spent two months in the Butyrskaia Prison where he suffered a nervous breakdown. He was then held in a prison hospital until March 1926. Here he suffered hallucinations and tried to commit suicide. His daughter includes some of his heartrending letters from prison. After his release in July 1926 he was able to work again, first in a parish near Vladimir and then, from 1928 until his next arrest in 1930, in a village nearer to Moscow. Following his release in 1933 from labor camp in the north of Russia, the family moved to a village near Murom, enduring abject poverty and only surviving thanks to food parcels and money sent by relations and friends in Moscow. Vera's account of their life now moves on to the terrible year of 1937:

> It was a dark and terrible year for Russia. Those remaining people from upper class intellectual backgrounds faced deadly danger. Those who survived that year will never lose the fear they felt before cruel, uncontrolled force, at the sound of footsteps approaching at night, the screech of brakes as cars stopped at the entrance downstairs. I then moved into the fifth class and remember our teacher filling in the routine questionnaires about the pupils' families: in a large class of forty, only seven had a father at home.[52]

Fr. Sergii was arrested in April 1937 on a warm sunny weekend when the snow had melted; Vera and the other children were running about happily in the courtyard outside until it was time to go in for lunch:

> Fr. Sergii went out to get some bread that was hanging in a bag in the entrance hall. There he met a policeman. Fr. Sergii came back: "They've come for me," he said in a kind of strange voice. His words contained fear and dismay, and a hint of guilt: what had been expected and feared had happened, he would be taken away and his family left alone. The children froze. The rather short stocky policeman in uniform stood in the doorway. [...] Tatiana Petrovna [Fr. Sergii's wife] did not cry. As always during terrible times, she summoned all her strength in order to do what was necessary. [...] She quickly opened the chest, threw to one side the children's clothes and torn sheets.... There it was, the bundle prepared since the winter. It contained an enamel mug, a clean shirt, a spoon, socks. Before he left, she needed to add a piece of bread and some salt, that was all.[53]

Vera ends her memoir with an account of how in 1991 she was given permission by the KGB to see her father's case file. He had been shot in September 1937.

The pieces of paper from the investigation into his case were silent about my father's inner state, and only his large eyes, the eyes of a man going to his death, stared at me with deep sadness from the prison photograph. From among some notes written by Fr. Sergii, I read: "Sometimes the fear of death opens the way to repentance for the most indifferent sinner. It is fear of what is inevitable and unknown, sadness about what is happening in the world like a cloud in the sky, the wake behind a ship, a withering spring flower. Such fear is part of every human being, and in vain humanity tries to suppress this sadness with grand words and alluring ideas. Instantly its depths open up in anyone at the moment he must part from life. Death is not only the end of earthly life; it is a power that since the Fall sanctifies the earth. Blood poured out cleanses sin, weakens its power over a person."[54]

A brief but moving text entitled "Dates and Milestones of My Life" by a Russian Orthodox bishop, Afanasii Sakharov (1887–1962), was included by Michael Bourdeaux in his book *Patriarch and Prophets*. Bishop Afanasii spent most of his life, between 1922 and 1954, after being made a suffragan bishop within the Vladimir Diocese in 1921, in prison or exile. This text reads:

I served 33 months in my diocese. I was free but not officiating for 32 months. In exile 76 months. In prison and doing forced labour 254 months. It is usual in life that the longer the separation, the weaker connections grow. Christian love reverses such a rule. Those dear people who cared for me [...] each year made their concern and solicitude more manifest. [...] Whereas in the first two years and four months I was sent 72 parcels (30 a year), in 1954, the last year, I received 200.[55]

Fr. Vasilii Arkhangelskii spent time with Bishop Afanasii doing forced labor and remembered him as "an example of Christian humility and endurance, he had a kind word for each person, he cheered everyone up with the bright hope of an early release."[56] He always shared his food parcels, strongly resisted the behavior of those who tried to steal from others and constantly gave thanks to God; he particularly loved the words from Psalm 119 (verse 94), "I am thine, O save me." He had the spiritual gifts of discernment and of healing. His laughter was memorable as was his love of jokes: "He never talked about the difficulties, the trials, even the suffering that had come his way, and if he did say something it was always accompanied by a cheerful joke."[57]

After his release from prison in 1954, he was eventually allowed to live in the village of Petushki, less than seventy kilometers from his home town of

Vladimir. In his final years Nina Fioletova looked after him and remembered how he would sometimes frown, and yet smile at the same time:

> The bishop had a habit of frowning, of putting on a stern expression but while smiling, and would say: "The bishop is cross." Just as he looked at me like that, I once asked him: "Dear Bishop, are you cross?" "I'm cross, cross. Well, one can always get cross with you." Then he smiled with the kindest of smiles: "Now go, my dear, quickly get some food for everyone."[58]

A brief four-page memoir by M. E. Gubonin dated 1958[59] evokes his presence eloquently during this final period of his life:

> A small wooden cottage. Behind a partition in a tiny box room with one window placed low in the wall, amid icons and shelves of books, sits an ancient *starets* in a cassock by the table. His face, the position of his body, all of him looks dreadfully broken and exhausted. [...] But the simple Russian face of an old man, rather puffy and covered in wrinkles going in all directions, is graced with the most remarkable eyes, filled with goodness, which through age have lost most of their color. Their expression is thoughtful and melancholy. [...] you only have to go into his room and start talking to him and he is instantly transfigured, he livens up, welcomes you with immense kindness and touching sweetness, and starts fussing over you. Whoever you are, he will sit you down, look after you as his guest, invite you to have something to eat; he will pile jam or bits of some pie onto your plate. And then he will ask you about yourself, talk to you, gesticulate and be lit up with such love and sincere warmth, ready to say something delightful and cheering, that even the hardest, coldest heart will feel warmed and at home in the light of this old man's intense concern and heartfelt welcome.[60]

Although Bishop Afanasii died at the height of Khrushchev's antireligious campaign in 1962, his funeral in Vladimir's Dormition Cathedral was a memorable event, attended by enormous numbers of clergy and laity who all revered him in both life and death.[61]

The USSR's Demise

As early as 1969 the historian Andrei Amalrik foretold the collapse of the USSR in his book *Will the Soviet Union Survive until 1984?*[62] Yet when it came it took most Kremlin-watchers by surprise. The start of perestroika with the advent of Gorbachev as Communist Party leader in March 1985 uncannily almost coincided with Amalrik's prophecy. Gorbachev realized that the Soviet Union was dying, its economy unproductive and its political system in need of reform. The Chernobyl disaster in 1986, which revealed the system's dishonesty and criminal incompetence, gave an additional impetus to the system's demise. In 1988 Communist Party policy toward religion dramatically changed after the Soviet press began portraying religion in a more positive light and following amnesties of political and religious prisoners. That year also marked the millennium of the Russian Orthodox Church, which was allowed in June to celebrate this important occasion far more elaborately than initially expected. Then, in late June 1988, followed the Nineteenth Conference of the Communist Party, when Gorbachev condemned both disrespect toward a spiritual worldview and discrimination against religious believers.

Keston College staff were delighted to see the many prisoners of conscience, whose cases they had been publicizing over the years, released from labor camps and prisons. But at the same time many of Keston's large number of supporters gradually melted away as most people in the West during the 1990s could not see that there were problems any longer for religious believers in the former communist bloc. Consequently, to many Keston no longer had a role to play. By the early twenty-first century the organization was faced with potential financial disaster, compelling its trustees to put the college through its own perestroika and to steer the charity into a new phase. Keston could no longer afford to employ anyone, so its research and publishing work was cut back, the trustees sold Keston's academic journal *Religion, State and Society* to its publisher, and discontinued the *Keston News Service* and the more popular magazine *Frontier*. Most important of all, the trustees found a new home for the, by now, very large Keston archive and library, which as of 2007 have been housed in the Keston Center for Religion, Politics, and Society, specially created by Baylor University to promote research in Keston's field.[63] Keston's work will continue, and the memory of "the best people in all the earth" will be preserved for future generations.

10

"THERE ARE THINGS IN HISTORY THAT SHOULD BE CALLED BY THEIR PROPER NAMES"

Evaluating Russian Orthodox Collaboration with the Soviet State

Geraldine Fagan

A century after the communist seizure of power in Russia, and more than a quarter century since that regime's demise, the issue of collaboration between the Russian Orthodox Church and the Soviet state might be expected to have lost relevance. As the political climate under President Vladimir Putin grows more authoritarian and defensive of the Soviet record, the opposite is the case. The issue is vital to any appraisal of Russia's direction. The Orthodox Church served as society's moral compass for centuries before 1917, and is the only prerevolutionary Russia-wide social institution to have survived Soviet rule. But not unscathed: the price was assimilation to an atheist agenda. Gauging the nature and extent of this fundamental compromise is essential if the Church is to amend its bearings and chart a future course in line with its Christian vocation.

This was proclaimed by Orthodox dissidents long before the Soviet collapse, and has been substantially addressed by Church historians since. Yet their observations are unfamiliar even to committed Orthodox Christians in Russia, and criticism of the Church's Soviet record remains contested, including by prominent clerics. Historical context is vital to understanding these sensitive debates.

1917–1927: From Opposition to Assimilation

There could be no mistake: eradication of religion was an explicit aim of the regime that seized power in Russia in October 1917. Vladimir Lenin was adamant that "every religious idea, every idea of god, even every flirtation with the idea of god is unutterable vileness [...] of the most dangerous kind."[1] Coopting the Russian Orthodox Church as a partner in its own destruction was also a Bolshevik tactic from the outset. In a 1921 report, the Cheka secret police urged the use of clergy—whether by playing on their ambitions, ensuring financial dependence, or threatening arrest—to render them its "eternal slaves."[2]

The Russian Orthodox Church's response was to reject collaboration outright. In 1918, its newly elected Patriarch Tikhon excommunicated all Bolsheviks who remained nominally Orthodox; the behavior of the new regime was not only brutal, he explained, but "truly the work of Satan."[3] Yet once placed under house arrest in 1922, Tikhon's position gradually softened until his death three years later. In 1923 the patriarch declared himself no longer an enemy of the Soviet government, and "a return to the previous order impossible." In a final testament published shortly after his death in April 1925, he urged Orthodox to be sincere to the Soviet authorities in civil affairs, albeit "without allowing any compromises or concessions in the sphere of faith."

It remains unclear what effected this change. In a 1923 interview with a British journalist, Patriarch Tikhon claimed he had been treated well while under arrest. Whether this was true—and indeed whether the patriarch's later statements were fully his own—tactical considerations had begun to influence his judgment. One was the hope that "pure, sincere relations will encourage our authorities to fully trust us, give us the opportunity to teach children, have theological schools, publish books and journals in defense of the Orthodox faith." Another was the fear that, for as long as he remained under arrest due to his refusal to cooperate, the Soviet authorities could supplant the Church's legitimate hierarchy with schismatic movements.[4]

Patriarch Tikhon thus reached a pragmatic acknowledgment of Soviet power. Yet he did not commit the Russian Orthodox Church to measures supporting its antireligious agenda. Metropolitan Sergii (Stragorodskii), Tikhon's *de facto* successor, also underwent a transformation during his period of leadership. This went so far down the path of collusion, however, that by his death in 1944 Church subservience to Soviet power utterly contradicted the stance adopted by Patriarch Tikhon in 1918.

The details of this rapprochement with the Soviet regime warrant special scrutiny here as they continue to resonate. The authoritative nature of opposition within the Church to Sergii's policies only became fully apparent in Russia in the mid-1990s. Yet Orthodox support for them is nevertheless gaining traction, particularly in the increasingly pro-Soviet atmosphere since Vladimir Putin's 2012 return to the presidency.

Metropolitan Sergii would never have led the Russian Orthodox Church were it not for Bolshevik manipulation. Patriarch Tikhon's nominated successors—Metropolitan Kirill (Smirnov), Metropolitan Agafangel (Preobrazhenskii), and Metropolitan Petr (Polianskii)—were all in prison or internal exile within a year of his death. While renowned as a talented theologian and capable administrator, Sergii received only five nominations for consideration as patriarchal candidate in 1917.[5] In free conditions, even a nominated successor to Tikhon would have remained patriarchal *locum tenens* only briefly, until a council of the whole Russian Orthodox Church could meet to elect a new patriarch. As Sergii was merely deputy to Tikhon's third choice of *locum tenens*, his authority was thus tenuous from an Orthodox perspective.

Nevertheless, it is often forgotten that Sergii started out uncontroversially: his pro-Soviet stance marked an abrupt change from his position prior to his arrest in late 1926. For nearly a year after first becoming deputy patriarchal *locum tenens* in late 1925, Sergii was broadly trusted as he battled the latest state-sponsored schism and sought to arrange a patriarchal election by postal vote.[6] The rhetoric of his 1926 draft declaration on the position of the Church toward the new communist state repeated Tikhon's final position by affirming "our sincere readiness to be completely law-abiding citizens of the Soviet Union."[7]

In spelling out the fundamental contradiction between Orthodoxy and communism, Sergii's draft declaration also echoed a 1926 letter to the Soviet government from a group of Orthodox bishops then incarcerated on the far northern archipelago of Solovki. But the Solovki epistle went further by insisting that this contradiction "precludes any intrinsic approximation or reconciliation between the Church and state," and demanding strict separation of the two.[8] Quite unlike Sergii's draft declaration, the epistle also struck a defiant tone: "The Orthodox Church cannot [...] claim that religion is not restricted in any way in the Soviet Union. [...] It will not tell the whole world this shameful lie, which can be inspired only by hypocrisy, servility, or complete indifference to the fate of religion." Unlike Sergii, these bishops were not prepared to compromise.

It is unknown what pressures Metropolitan Sergii faced while under arrest. Yet despite negative personal consequences, it is now known that Tikhon's preferred caretakers of the Church—Metropolitan Kirill (Smirnov), Metropolitan Petr (Polianskii) and Archbishop Serafim (Samoilovich)—all resisted inducement to cooperate with the OGPU secret police, successor to the Cheka. While Sergii was under arrest in early 1927, the OGPU offered the leadership of the Church to Metropolitan Kirill—also then in prison—on condition that he remove hierarchs disliked by the Soviet government as if this were his own choice. Kirill refused, and received three years' exile in Siberia. At the end of 1926—also during Sergii's arrest—Metropolitan Petr refused to renounce his position as *locum tenens* at the OGPU's instigation, presumably in Sergii's favor. "Never and in no circumstances will I abandon my service," Petr told the OGPU. "I will be faithful to the Orthodox Church unto death." He stayed in prison for the remaining eleven years of his life.[9]

By contrast, Metropolitan Sergii was released after four months, with police authorization for a synod of eight named hierarchs.[10] Soon afterward, they added their signatures to Sergii's final July 1927 declaration on the position of the Church toward the new state. This document marked a watershed in the Russian Orthodox Church's relationship with the Soviet Union, and signaled the future path of collaboration.

1927–1940: Repression from Within

The 1927 declaration's slippery pledge "to recognize the Soviet Union as our civil homeland, whose joys and successes are our joys and successes, and whose misfortunes are our misfortunes" is renowned as its most controversial point. Yet the document also contains lines that dilute the fundamental contradiction between Orthodoxy and communism unambiguously: "We must show in deeds as well as words that not only people who are indifferent or traitors to Orthodoxy can be faithful Soviet citizens and loyal to the Soviet authorities, but its most fervent adherents." To the consternation of the bishops imprisoned on Solovki, the declaration also expressed "gratitude to the Soviet government for such attentiveness to the spiritual needs of the Orthodox population."[11]

The 1927 declaration's principal function, however, was to allow the Soviet authorities to use Metropolitan Sergii as a tool to crush the Church from within, mere disagreement with it being treated by the state as counterrevolutionary. Within months of the document's publication, for example, top OGPU antireligious official Evgenii Tuchkov reported from Leningrad: "We will influence Sergii so that he bans some opposition bishops from serving." Soon afterward, Sergii indeed banned two auxiliary bishops of Leningrad diocese who staunchly opposed the declaration.[12] Their arrests followed.

Metropolitan Sergii's subsequent pronouncements cemented this tactic. In a February 1930 interview in the Soviet daily *Izvestiia (News)*, Sergii claimed that clerics were being repressed not due to their faith, but for opposing the government.[13] Anatolii Svenitsitskii—nephew to a Moscow priest who opposed Sergii—recalls in his 2009 memoirs that it was this interview, not the 1927 declaration, that moved his parents to stop attending parishes where prayers were offered for Metropolitan Sergii and the Soviet authorities. "After reading [the interview] my father said, 'What a disgrace!' A long silence fell over our dinner table."[14]

Also of concern to his opponents, Metropolitan Sergii's collaborationism entailed violations of the Church's canonical order. On becoming Church administrator in late 1925, Sergii acted as a conventional deputy, consulting patriarchal *locum tenens* Metropolitan Petr even in his distant prison. Following his own period of arrest, however, Sergii no longer attempted to consult Petr, despite taking such weighty decisions as forming a synod and issuing the 1927 declaration.[15] Later, even when Metropolitan Petr was known to be alive, Sergii assumed privileges associated with his status of first hierarch, such as the title "His Beatitude" in 1934.[16]

One reason why Metropolitan Sergii's course of action continues to be positively received in Russia is that the influential nature of Church opposition to him only fully emerged there following the Soviet collapse. Previously, contemporary criticism such as that of the Solovki bishops could be published officially only abroad.[17] Even as Mikhail Gorbachev's reformist policies were gathering steam in 1988, a Soviet-published Church history insisted that opposition to Sergii had been due to "misunderstanding" his line on Church affairs. Once access to Soviet state archives was granted in the early 1990s, however, it transpired that the three most authoritative hierarchs in the Church—those nominated by Patriarch Tikhon as his preferred successors—had been staunchly critical of Sergii's stance. Thus, metropolitans Petr, Kirill, and Agafangel all rejected Sergii's leadership decisions after the 1927 declaration as uncanonical, while continuing to regard him as the Church's canonically appointed leader. The similar nuance of their positions was remarkable considering their high degree of isolation from one another due to Soviet repression.[18]

Discovered only in the early 1990s, a December 1929 letter from imprisoned Metropolitan Petr expressed deep regret that Sergii "did not endeavor to turn to me with your plans for directing the Church [...] it is grievous for me to enumerate all the details of my negative attitude toward your leadership." Petr also entreated Sergii to "correct the error you have committed, which has placed the Church in a humiliating position [...] I equally request that you annul other undertakings exceeding your authority."[19] While able to receive correspondence for a further eight months, Petr received no response.[20]

In February 1929, Metropolitan Kirill wrote that, by creating a "so-called Synod" while merely deputy to the patriarchal *locum tenens*, Sergii had "undermined the lawful continuation of authority in the Orthodox Church." Consequently, stated Kirill, he could not "in conscience conform to any of his ecclesiastical instructions." When Kirill broke communion with Sergii in the hope of returning him "from the path of usurping Church authority," Sergii's response—further jeopardizing Kirill, who was already under civil arrest—was to place him under an ecclesiastical ban in March 1930.[21]

Metropolitan Agafangel likewise rejected Sergii's policy as set out in the 1927 declaration. With the auxiliary bishops of his Iaroslavl diocese, he protested in February 1928 that, according to Sergii's program,

> the cornerstone rests not upon utmost care to guard the true faith, but upon completely unnecessary servility to the "external," which does not leave any room for an important condition for building Church life according to Christ's teaching and the gospels—freedom.

The Iaroslavl bishops then explained that they would administer their diocese independently, in accordance with a Tikhon-era Church decree.[22] Sergii's response was to bring ecclesiastical sanctions against the group, but they refused to alter their position. Agafangel died aged seventy-four in late 1928; the other signatories were all under arrest by late 1929.

Prominent hierarchs also bluntly challenged Metropolitan Sergii with the charge that his collusion was fuelling Soviet repression. In early 1928, for example, Bishop Damaskin (Tsedrik) asked Sergii if he had never considered

> that by dividing the clergy with your Declaration into "legalized" and "not legalized," subjecting the latter to unjust accusations of counterrevolutionary activity, you are placing the whole exiled Church, the few bishops still free, and a considerable portion of other priests under the constant attack of the suspecting Soviet authorities? [...] Did the thought never enter your head that you enjoy "freedom and peace" due to the slow death of our senior hierarchs whom the authorities find disagreeable? If such a thought crossed your mind but once—how can you sleep soundly, stand calmly before the holy altar?[23]

There was no response.

After 1940: A Shift in Soviet Policy

Whatever their justification, Metropolitan Sergii's hopes for a legalized, functioning Church in return for servility to the atheist Soviet state proved misplaced. Within a decade of Agafangel's death, the other hierarchs so far named here had all either perished in prison or been executed. Sergii's written demands to the Soviet authorities for an improvement in Church fortunes were mostly ignored.[24] He was even forced to dissolve his own synod in 1935, to stop consecrating bishops in 1936, and faced arrest himself in 1937.[25] On the eve of World War Two, there were no more than 350 Orthodox churches and not a single monastery open on the vast territory of the Soviet Union. In the Russian Empire of 1917, there had been 78,000 Orthodox churches and 1,250 monasteries.[26]

Yet at this point of annihilation, Soviet policy toward the Church shifted. This was for purely tactical reasons: In annexing territories on its western border in 1939–1940, the Soviet Union acquired some 3,000 functioning Orthodox churches and 64 monasteries. The Kremlin sought to enhance Soviet influence over these areas by permitting the appointment of three Russian Orthodox hierarchs to their dioceses in 1940. In the wake of the Nazi invasion of 1941, the Soviets were obliged to behave yet more leniently wherever they recaptured these areas, for the Nazis had reopened Orthodox churches there as a way to curry favor with the local population, and it was politically risky to close them again.[27] Joseph Stalin was also seeking to win greater war support from his Western allies, who were alarmed by reports of religious persecution. The semblance of a functioning Orthodox Church for the outside world required a modicum of reality, prompting Stalin to legalize the skeleton that remained of Sergii's ecclesiastical administration.

The Church was fully coopted into this deception. In 1942 it published *The Truth about Religion in Russia*, assuring English-speaking readers that "the Church cannot complain about the authorities," and repeating the lie that churchmen had been put on trial since the 1917 October Revolution "solely because, screening themselves with cassock and cross, they carried on anti-Soviet work."[28] As plans hastened for the 1943 Tehran Conference with US President Franklin Roosevelt and UK Prime Minister Winston Churchill, Stalin met personally with Sergii and the only other two metropolitans at liberty. He granted them permission to make arrangements for the Church to resume a limited legal existence as the Moscow Patriarchate.[29]

As part of the switch from the Church's brutal elimination to its slow suffocation, Stalin made collusion the cornerstone of his religious policy. The state called the shots from the outset. At a May 1944 meeting between Metropolitan Sergii and Georgii Karpov—chair of the new Council for the Affairs of the Russian Orthodox Church—it was Karpov who had the last word on episcopal appointments.[30]

In the postwar period, inducements to collaborate did not generally involve violence. By the late 1960s, the KGB could maintain control over the Church structure simply by hampering the careers of those who refused to collaborate and vetoing independent-minded seminary applicants.[31] While outspoken Church criticism of collaboration with the atheist Soviet regime resurfaced around this time, earlier repression meant that there were fewer clerics alive and willing to voice it. Archbishop Vasilii (Krivoshein) of Brussels proved a rare voice critical of state-sponsored regulations barring priests from leading their own parishes at the Church's 1971 Local Council in Moscow. Metropolitan Iosif of Alma-Ata thanked him afterward, admitting, "We are cowed. We cannot speak." Judging that open criticism of state restrictions would result only in his dismissal and so prove futile, Iosif sought instead "to work quietly for the Church."[32]

The problem with acquiescing to close Soviet control in the hope of preserving the Church as an institution, however, was that this resulted in a perversion of its Christian message. As the dissident writer Solzhenitsyn pointed out in his 1972 "Lenten Letter" to Patriarch Pimen:

> By what reasoning is it possible to convince oneself that the planned destruction of the spirit and body of the church under the guidance of atheists is the best way of preserving it? Preserving it for whom? Certainly not for Christ. Preserving it by what means? By falsehood? But after the falsehood by whose hands are the holy sacraments to be celebrated?[33]

For the slow Soviet suffocation of the Church was continuing steadily: by the mid-1970s there were some seven thousand churches and sixteen monasteries functioning in the USSR, a significant drop after a brief surge to approximately fourteen thousand churches and one hundred monasteries in the wake of World War Two.[34] Yet the Church was not just silently resisting, but defending its fate. In late 1974 a leading hierarch, Metropolitan Pitirim of Volokolamsk, gave an interview to Soviet news agency Novosti in which he flouted Orthodox doctrine by describing Church charitable activity as redundant, and religious instruction to children as "spiritual and moral aggression against their conscience and personality." Not coincidentally, both activities were banned in the USSR. Archbishop Vasilii of Brussels was again the lone voice of reproach:

It is one thing to submit out of necessity, quite another to justify such bans, to praise them. [...] In response they say, "It's easy to teach us from abroad, don't you know that it's impossible to speak the truth under Soviet rule." That's true, I respond, but in that case it would have been better to stay silent than to give such an interview.³⁵

Revelations from the Archives

How was such servility secured? Soon after Pitirim's interview, two major leaks to the West of classified information provided insights into the mechanisms of collaboration. One was a 1974 report by the Council for Religious Affairs (CRA)—the body now charged with controlling religious life—that classified senior Orthodox hierarchs according to their perceived degree of loyalty to the Soviet state. The second consisted of CRA transcripts of separate 1960s meetings with the future Patriarchs Pimen and Aleksii II.³⁶

In the 1974 report, the CRA divided the episcopate into three categories: those sincerely loyal to the socialist order and not actively promoting Orthodoxy; those outwardly loyal but in fact promoting Orthodoxy; and those who had defied state restrictions on Church activity. Prominent in the first group were Patriarch Pimen, the future Patriarch Aleksii II, and Metropolitan Pitirim, who gave the *Novosti* interview.³⁷

In the transcripts of 1960s meetings between CRA officials and then-metropolitan Pimen and Archbishop Aleksii, Pimen is in fact mostly reluctant to cooperate. Aleksii, on the other hand, appears scheming: he reports a conversation in which Metropolitan Nikodim of Leningrad strategizes about becoming patriarch; he denounces popular Moscow priest Fr. Vsevolod Shpiller's criticism of Soviet interference; he maintains Pimen "has women" in Moscow. For some hierarchs at least, the institutional distinction between the Soviet state and the Russian Orthodox Church was becoming blurred.³⁸

More insights came at the close of the Soviet era. In late 1991, the last chairman of the KGB revealed that a minority—some 15 to 20 percent—of Orthodox clerics approached by the KGB had refused to cooperate.³⁹ At the same time, dissident Orthodox priest Fr. Gleb Iakunin gained access to KGB files on religion as part of a government commission investigating the circumstances of the failed August 1991 coup. This atmosphere of openness proved short-lived, however: at the request of the newly elected Patriarch Aleksii II, the commission's investigation was curtailed. Yet by matching archival entries with past news items in the Church's official *Journal of the Moscow Patriarchate*,

Iakunin and journalist Aleksandr Nezhnyi were able to identify certain KGB codenames with senior clergy. *Abbat* was identified as Metropolitan Pitirim of Volokolamsk, *Adamant* as Metropolitan Iuvenalii of Krutitsy and Kolomna, *Antonov* as Metropolitan Filaret of Kiev, and *Drozdov* as Patriarch Aleksii II himself.[40] One archival entry noted that *Drozdov* was even awarded a KGB certificate of honor for his service in 1988.[41]

The archival records outlined how KGB infiltration of the Church could devastate the vocations of clerics inside the Soviet Union. One 1983 archival entry describes how monks at Pskov-Pechory Monastery sent complaints to Patriarch Pimen regarding the brutality of their Abbot Gavriil (Stebliuchenko). They were dealt with by KGB agents conducting "educational work," culminating in the removal of some of the monks from the monastery.[42] This was an effective way of stifling growth in the few monasteries permitted to function in the USSR: during Gavriil's thirteen years as abbot, some sixty monks left Pskov-Pechory.[43]

The bulk of the material on the Orthodox Church uncovered by Iakunin, however, relates to foreign affairs from 1967 onward. *Antonov*, for example, performed "espionage and counterespionage tasks" at the ecumenical Christian Peace Conference in Poland in February 1969, while *Abbat* attended events such as the March 1980 installation of Archbishop of Canterbury Robert Runcie for KGB purposes of "information and counterpropaganda."[44]

The focus on activity abroad is itself suggestive of Soviet influence. Little questioned by Western Christians eager for closer relations with Russian Orthodox, the Moscow Patriarchate entered the main international ecumenical body, the World Council of Churches (WCC), in 1961.[45] This went against Orthodox wishes: In 1948 Metropolitan Nikolai (Iarushevich)—head of the new Department for External Church Relations (DECR)—had insisted that the ecumenical movement was "not in accord with the ideals of Christianity and the aims of the Church of Christ as they are understood by the Orthodox Church." But he was abruptly replaced in 1960 by Metropolitan Nikodim (Rotov), who proclaimed the Church's readiness to begin negotiations to join the WCC. Nikodim's appointment came just weeks after top Soviet antireligious official Vladimir Kuroedov had told colleagues that the Russian Orthodox Church must enter the WCC, "to further the influence on believers abroad, to step up the fight against the Vatican."[46]

Given Iakunin's limited archival access, it is difficult to assess how far his findings are representative, or to what extent the reports' compilers exaggerated their success at Church manipulation with a view to impressing superiors. The data uncovered on the activity of Church representatives abroad, at least, is not particularly sinister-sounding; denunciations of Western ecumenists would hardly lead to their profound personal suffering.

More troubling, however, was the un-Christian denial of truth entailed by service of the Soviet foreign agenda: the records uncovered by Iakunin show that several agents in Church delegations abroad were responsible for repudiating reports of religious persecution in the USSR. Church initiatives could also be so twisted in a Soviet direction that their original intent was lost. In one archival entry, the KGB agreed to Patriarch Pimen's request for a 1987 commemoration of the sixtieth anniversary of the Moscow Patriarchate's restoration, so long as

> the tribune of this event will be used to promote the peaceful foreign policy of the Communist Party of the Soviet Union and the Soviet government, the Soviet way of life, the democratic nature of the socialist system, freedom of conscience in the Soviet Union, and to condemn the aggressive policy of imperialist states.

Further revelations on Church collaboration emerged from the Mitrokhin Archive, part of whose content was made public in a 1999 English-language book and a 2007 digital archive. Its compiler, Vasilii Mitrokhin, was a retired KGB archivist who defected to Britain in the early 1990s. With him, he brought extensive notes he had been able to copy in the 1970s from archives while transferring them from the KGB's Lubianka site in central Moscow to the city's outskirts.[47]

In the minor portion of the Mitrokhin Archive concerned with the Russian Orthodox Church, there is likewise a focus on activity abroad. Many of the clerics it names as KGB agents received multiple postings outside the USSR, notably in German-speaking areas. They include three successive priest-editors of the German-language Moscow Patriarchate journal *Stimme der Orthodoxie (Voice of Orthodoxy)* from 1971–1987, who between them served parishes in Baden-Baden, Berlin, Leipzig, Potsdam, and Vienna.

Unlike Iakunin's findings, many of Mitrokhin's notes give identities as well as KGB codenames. Some are unsurprising: KGB agent *Kuznetsov* is identified as Aleksei Buevskii, a layman who worked at the DECR from its 1946 foundation until his death in 2009. During the Soviet era, Buevskii accompanied all major Church delegations abroad. According to one insider, "nothing was published on external affairs in the *Journal of the Moscow Patriarchate* without his approval."[48]

Some of Mitrokhin's notes suggest classic espionage. Agent *Voronov*, identified as Fr. Arkadii Tyshchuk, was posted to St. Nicholas Cathedral in New York from 1977–1982. There, he was tasked with identifying possible recruits among parishioners, including those employed registering births, marriages, and deaths. Codenamed *Patriot*, Fr. Viktor Petliuchenko was similarly sent to Canada in the early 1970s and tasked with researching parish registers. This data would have been of interest to the Soviet regime as a source for identities of KGB "illegals"—deep-cover secret agents—in North America.[49]

Further items from the Mitrokhin Archive suggest that agents' activity could knowingly harm others. Within the USSR, *Karpov*—identified as heading Sverdlovsk diocese in 1982 and therefore Archbishop Platon (Udovenko)—is reported as having followed the regional KGB's directions to replace "politically immature" priests. *Vladimir*—named by Mitrokhin as Fr. Lev Tserpitskii—was sent to study in Rome in 1975; there he informed the KGB that a fellow agent was visiting "some kind of English college" without telling his handler and showing "heightened interest in the programs of *Voice of America, Deutsche Welle, Radio Free Europe*." A monk recruited by the KGB as *Esaulenko* in 1970 is named as Iosif Pustoutov, who spent time in Western Europe before being appointed Moscow Patriarchate representative to the Christian Peace Conference in Prague in 1976. Pustoutov gave evidence against Fr. Gleb Iakunin at his trial in 1980, alleging harmful international repercussions from his Christian Committee for the Defense of Believers' Rights in the USSR.[50]

Another identity, however, highlights the complexities that could lie behind such cases. Mitrokhin names Fr. Vasilii Fonchenkov as *Drug* ("friend" in Russian), a KGB recruit who infiltrated Iakunin's Committee in 1979. *Drug*, according to Mitrokhin's notes, "was involved in the cultivation of specific individuals [in the Church], carried out his assignments conscientiously and showed initiative."[51] Like other clerics identified as KGB agents, Fonchenkov had a high-flying Church career, holding posts at Zagorsk Theological Academy, the DECR, and a parish in East Berlin.[52]

Yet Iakunin was astounded upon reading this when extracts from Mitrokhin's coauthored 1999 book were published in Russian online in 2010. In reality, wrote Iakunin, "'Friend' Fonchenkov was not such an un-friend to us as the Chekists presumed"; he had warned Fr. Gleb of his future arrest and procured for him the 1974 CRA report discussed above. Iakunin regarded this "mini-Church-Chekist 'Wikileaks'" as one of the most important episodes in his "fight for the freedom of the Russian Orthodox Church."[53]

1990s Inaction on Collaboration: A Missed Opportunity?

The 1991 investigative commission featuring Iakunin had ruled out a state-directed purge of the Russian Orthodox Church. Instead, it recommended, "it would be better if the believers themselves were to find a means of ridding themselves of the anti-constitutional elements that were introduced."[54] The spotlight inevitably fell on the newly elected Patriarch Aleksii II. Aleksii had already offered a general apology in June 1991:

> Before those people [...] to whom the compromises, silence, forced passivity or expressions of loyalty permitted by leaders of the church in those years caused pain, before those people, and not only before God, I ask forgiveness, understanding and prayers.[55]

This paved the way for a bombshell admission in 1992. Archbishop Khrizostom of Vilnius, assigned to the least reliable hierarch category of the 1974 CRA report, made a public confession of collaboration: "I signed things, I had regular meetings, I made reports [...] I was obliged to sign a statement that I would pass information to the KGB." Khrizostom also insisted that he "was never an informer, I never denounced anyone," but in doing so, his revelations grew even more astonishing. If he had ever spoken ill of people, Khrizostom explained, it was primarily "of enemies of the church, of those very KGB agents who had been infiltrated into the church. [...] There are in our church real KGB men who have pursued meteoric careers."

Here, Archbishop Khrizostom singled out then-metropolitan Mefodii of Voronezh:

> He is a KGB officer, an atheist, a vicious man foisted on us by the KGB. The synod was unanimously against consecrating such a man as a bishop, but we were forced to take this sin upon ourselves; and then, what a rapid career he had! He became a metropolitan, and for nearly ten years he controlled the church money. [...] And he never liked independent, honest priests, he failed to defend them, he just persecuted them.[56]

Mefodii has never refuted this claim. He was awarded the Order of Friendship "for many years' conscientious labor" by President Putin—himself with a KGB background—in September 2002.[57] Protesting the award in an open letter to Putin, Fr. Georgii Edelshtein—temporarily banned from serving as a priest by his archbishop in 1987 for renovating a church without state permission—countered Khrizostom's suggestion that the Church could not have acted otherwise:

> To this day there is a myth in our society that our hierarchs were "compelled" or "forced" into active collaboration with the militant atheists [...] unfortunately, not one hierarch has yet explained how and with what they were

"compelled" and "forced" when no gun, forced labor or Solovki threatened anyone any longer."[58]

Despite insisting that KGB contact had been unavoidable, Archbishop Khrizostom did call upon the 1992 Bishops' Council to make "some kind of statement about the need to purify ourselves from all this. Moreover, the more access we have to information and documents, the more deeply and fully we should deal with these questions."[59]

In response, the Council formed a Commission for Investigation into the Activities of the Security Services within the Russian Orthodox Church. But the initiative was stillborn.[60] Writing in 2003, Fr. Georgii Edelshtein lamented that for the past eleven years he had appealed repeatedly both orally and in writing to the Commission's chair—the head of his own diocese, Archbishop Aleksandr of Kostroma—to say at least a few words about the Commission's work. "His answer: only eloquent silence."[61] In 2000, then–patriarchate spokesman Fr. Vsevolod Chaplin told this author that the Commission had not been active in recent years, having already completed its inquiry, and that a report containing the results had not been released.[62] Kostroma diocese did not respond to the author's repeated requests for information about the Commission during a 2003 visit to the region.

Archbishop Aleksandr has since displayed little appetite for critical assessment of Church-Soviet relations. During a 2014 visit to his previous diocese, Metropolitan Aleksandr, now of Astana, presented a Church award to Mikhail Kuznetsov, CRA plenipotentiary for the Kostroma region from 1977–1991, in recognition of his "efforts to develop Church-state dialogue [...] in his post he did everything to preserve Church life, supported parishes, paid close attention to the needs of the diocese."[63] Fr. Georgii Edelshtein has quite different recollections of Kuznetsov: "a good person but in his profession he did only one thing for many years—being nasty to the Church. It was he, the plenipotentiary, who, without blushing, lied to my face that there was no vacancy in the diocese, when in eight churches there had not been a service for a number of years for lack of priests."[64]

Since 1992 there have been no senior calls within the Moscow Patriarchate for lustration: the demotion of pro-Soviet clerics. Archbishop Khrizostom had suggested that the Church should take measures to deal with "those who had acted unworthily [...] as was the case, for example, with the former Bishop of Khabarovsk, Gavriil."[65] As noted above, Bishop Gavriil (Stebliuchenko) was the abbot of Pskov-Pechory Monastery from 1975–1988. The author is not aware of archival evidence that Gavriil was a KGB agent. However, he retained his post despite numerous complaints of physical brutality and heavy drinking, and even a formal dismissal by Patriarch Pimen in 1978, leading to speculation that he enjoyed Soviet protection at the very least.[66]

Despite a three-year ecclesiastical ban on then-bishop Gavriil of Khabarovsk in 1991 after further complaints, he continued his Church career, heading dioceses until his retirement as an archbishop in 2011. In 2001, President Putin presented Gavriil with the state Medal of Honor, "for greatly contributing to civil peace and the revival of spiritual-moral traditions."[67]

At the same time, Putin presented the Medal of Honor to the long-standing DECR official Buevskii, named in Mitrokhin's archive as *Kuznetsov*. Other clerics publicly identified by Mitrokhin as KGB agents similarly continued to advance their Church careers beyond the Soviet collapse. *Karpov* rose to head the diocese of Feodosi in Crimea,[68] *Vladimir*—the diocese of Novgorod.[69] *Patriot* was deputy chair of DECR from 1991–1999 before becoming dean of Odessa cathedral.[70] *Esaulenko* continued to serve parishes in Germany.[71] *Drug*—defended by Iakunin—took a somewhat different path, leaving the Moscow Patriarchate to serve as a priest with the émigré Russian Orthodox Church Outside of Russia (ROCOR) in Austria until his death in 2006.[72] The fact that the Moscow Patriarchate proved so reluctant to address the impact of atheist control over clerical appointments when it became free to do so in itself confirms that the Soviet regime succeeded in molding its institutional culture to a significant degree.

New Millennium—New Direction?

Parallel developments of a radically different nature within the Patriarchate since the Soviet collapse illustrate the profoundly complex nature of collusion's impact, however. In 1989, the Church canonized Patriarch Tikhon; in 1997, patriarchal *locum tenens* Metropolitan Petr. In the summer of 2000, more than a thousand further Orthodox victims of the Soviet state were canonized as New Martyrs and Confessors, including many who had suffered due to their opposition to Metropolitan Sergii. The list of new saints included Sergii's most authoritative critics introduced above: Metropolitan Kirill (Smirnov), Metropolitan Agafangel (Preobrazhenskii), Archbishop Serafim (Samoilovich), and Bishop Damaskin (Tsedrik). Metropolitan Sergii himself was conspicuously absent.

In June 1991 Patriarch Aleksii had suggested that Sergii "wanted to save the Church" through his 1927 declaration. Yet he also admitted that falsehood ran through that document, categorizing it as "regrettable, mistaken." In keeping with his further claim that "Metropolitan Sergi's Declaration has disappeared entirely into the past and we are no longer guided by it,"[73] Aleksii championed the 1994 foundation of a memorial complex at Butovo, a shooting range near Moscow where 20,000 people were executed in 1937–1938, including many since canonized as New Martyrs.[74] Despite his similar reputation as a Soviet loyalist, senior Metropolitan Iuvenalii of Krutitsy and Kolomna also actively supported moves to canonize New Martyrs and Confessors, being chair of the Synodal Commission for Canonization until his retirement in 2011.

In another move away from Metropolitan Sergii's path of servility, the Church's 2000 *Foundations for a Social Concept* asserted the principle of civil disobedience: "If the authority forces Orthodox believers to apostatise from Christ and His Church and to commit sinful and spiritually harmful actions, the Church should refuse to obey the state."[75] These developments were all attempts to reach out to ROCOR, with whom relations had been bitter precisely due to the Patriarchate's collusion with the Soviet regime. Operating independently in emigration, ROCOR used the very term "Sergianism" as a synonym for Moscow Patriarchate servility in the wake of the 1927 declaration. It canonized numerous New Martyrs of the Soviet regime in 1981.

In the run-up to formal reconciliation between these two parts of the Russian Church in May 2007, dialogue resulted in a joint statement on the issue of collaboration:

> It is necessary to define what is permissible and what is impermissible in the relationship between the Church and state, especially a state which pursues the goal of the utter destruction of the Church and the faith of Christ. Orthodox Christians came to a clear understanding of the inadmissibility of the absolutization of government authority. It is unacceptable, in particular, to use the texts of Holy Scripture (for example, Romans 13:1–5) in a way which does not correspond with the interpretation and spirit of the Holy Fathers. Earthly and temporal powers of the state are recognized as imperative to the degree that they are used to support good and limit evil.[76]

Nine decades on, the Church's official position was thus once again in alignment with Patriarch Tikhon's 1918 application of Romans 13 to the new Bolshevik regime: "Any authority permitted by God would receive our blessing if it truly were 'God's servant' [working] for the good of those subordinate and very 'afraid' not of good deeds but of ill."[77]

Both parties also repudiated the 1927 declaration, in which Metropolitan Sergii had interpreted Romans 13 as requiring sincere loyalty to the Soviet Union.[78] The use of the term *podvig* (spiritual feat) to describe Sergii's actions in the official Russian translation of one joint document disturbed some within ROCOR, however.⁷⁹ "Of course I cannot call his service a 'spiritual feat,'" Bishop Gabriel of Manhattan remarked. "The Church cannot act in the way that Metropolitan Sergii did, no matter what the circumstances."⁸⁰ Fr. Mikhail Lyuboshchinsky of ROCOR's parish in Hamilton, Canada pointed to the lasting spiritual damage caused by Sergii's pro-Soviet position:

> Continuing justification of "Sergianism" is an attempt to establish a new dogma—"the admissibility of forced sin in order to save the Church." [...] The Lord God, seeing that I believe in Him inwardly and deny, oppose sin, will forgive me this sin. In that case, it starts to appear that "forced" sin is not sin at all. [...] The concept of "forced" sin makes a person unable to see, to understand, what he needs to repent for, and he will perish without repentance.

For Fr. Mikhail, it was not just the individual at stake, but Russia herself:

> "Sergianism" is [...] the use of the Church to justify and support evil, leading to a drop in the Church's authority and so to the destruction of the Church, an increase in evil in society and consequently the destruction of the state. Until such time as we, the Russian people, understand this, until we direct all our efforts toward the fight against evil in ourselves and toward love for one another, there will be no rebirth of Russia!⁸¹

After 2000: Moscow Patriarchate Revisionism

ROCOR's concern was not misplaced. While the Moscow Patriarchate has still not proposed his formal canonization, material on Sergii produced under its auspices since 2000 has bordered on the hagiographical. Patriarch Aleksii II's foreword in *Watchman of the Lord's House*, a weighty 2003 biography of Metropolitan Sergii, argues that Sergii could be fully included "among those confessors of Christ who have spent long in captivity and suffered greatly at the hands of the Church's persecutors." It also refutes the suggestion that his activity "was characterized by compromise with state power." The biography goes on to dismiss critics of the 1927 declaration—including Metropolitan Kirill (Smirnov), now identified as a New Martyr—as "deaf to any explanation."⁸²

A Patriarchate-approved documentary broadcast on national Russian television on the eve of Orthodox Easter 2006 similarly cast Metropolitan Sergii as an "angel of the Russian Church." In one scene, Moscow parish priest Fr. Sergii (Pravdoliubov)—whose family includes several New Martyrs—told how he opposed the 1927 declaration until revered elder monk Fr. Ioann

(Krestiankin) sent him a shoebox containing Metropolitan Sergii's epitrachelion (stole) and epimanikia (cuffs). "This was given to me as a silent rebuke: 'What right do you have to judge a patriarch? Just try putting it on, what a load, what responsibility for the Church!'"[83]

Defense of Sergii typically takes this form, perceiving opposition to his rapprochement with the atheist regime as a personalized attack against the metropolitan himself. Here, Sergii's resistance to Soviet power prior to late 1926 is overlooked. And even if intolerable secret police pressure is regarded as mitigating the collusion that followed his arrest, this does not alter the fact that his stance was ultimately determined by the Soviet state, which should render Orthodox support for his policy impossible. This too was observed at the time: in November 1927 Archbishop Ilarion (Troitskii)—canonized a New Martyr in 2000—wrote that whether or not Sergii is praised as "a true helmsman of the Russian Church" is irrelevant, as the damaging nature of his action indicates that the Church's *de facto* steward is top Soviet antireligious official Evgenii Tuchkov.[84]

One alarming recent consequence of whitewashing Metropolitan Sergii's stance in this way is the revision of Stalin's antireligious policy. When retrospectively viewed with approval, the 1927 declaration is considered successful, and the state persecution that continued after it is airbrushed out. Thus, the 2003 biography of Sergii notes that his eighteen years of "bearing the cross of directing the Church" saw "churches restored, monasteries and seminaries opened."[85] In his 1999 study *The Way of the Cross of Patriarch Sergi*, former CRA official Mikhail Odintsov similarly maintained that Stalin's 1943 "concordat" with the Church "was upheld by both sides for the whole subsequent decade, allowing us to regard this period as a time of 'religious revival' in Russia."[86] When Anatolii Svenitsitskii similarly suggested that there was a thaw in Church relations from 1943–1953 in his 2009 memoirs, his editors were moved to point out in a footnote that more than one hundred Orthodox priests continued to be executed annually from 1944 to 1946, and not a single church was opened on the territory of the USSR from 1948–1953.[87]

In line with this tendency, Church—and so public—attention to the New Martyrs and Confessors of the Soviet era has waned since the mass canonizations of 2000. Partly, this is because the Putin regime has hampered even Church researchers' access to KGB and other relevant archives. Fr. Damaskin Orlovskii—a pioneer of such research in the 1990s—lamented in 2009 that the state's removal of previously unclassified archival material was complicating assessment of candidate New Martyrs.[88] In 2013, Fr. Vladimir Vorob'ev of St. Tikhon's Orthodox University in Moscow—another pioneer—remarked that the Church's Synodal Commission for Canonization had practically ceased work due to restricted archival access.[89]

By 2015, the Moscow Patriarchate was seeking to "balance" sentiment approving and disapproving of the Soviet record. That April, Patriarch Kirill blessed the foundation stone of a church in Southern Butovo—just a few miles from the 1930s execution site of so many New Martyrs—"in memory of members of the state security organs [such as the KGB] who died while performing their duty."[90] Over the following months, the debate over "Sergianism" resurfaced. Prominent Moscow priest Fr. Aleksei Uminskii lamented to independent newspaper *Novaia gazeta* (New gazette) that the Church officially speaks about Sergii's 1927 declaration "in soft tones—'By this he saved the Church,'" but remains silent about the document itself, "truly disgusting, shameful, where the Church was forced to recognize its martyrs as criminals."[91]

Another prominent Moscow priest, Fr. Maksim Kozlov, countered that the 1927 declaration was not a product of collaborationism or servility, but a compromise chosen precisely "to save the Church," and that Metropolitan Sergii had suffered through personal humiliation rather than martyrdom.[92] In response, Church historian Fr. Georgii Mitrofanov pointed out that—as demonstrated above—recent historical research has found senior hierarchs canonized as New Martyrs to have been highly critical of Sergii's actions. Surely, asked Fr. Georgii, "Fr. Maksim would not dare to accuse Metropolitans Kirill and Petr, Archbishops Serafim and Damaskin—who denounced Sergii—of using 'typical liberal journalistic clichés and judgments,' as he does Fr. Aleksei [Uminskii]?"[93]

In the same polemic, Fr. Aleksei echoed the New Martyr hierarchs' concerns by insisting there were

> things in history that should be called by their proper names. Otherwise, the false Sergian attitude to power is legitimized [...] and this introduces the possibility of staying silent when we should speak. Or of the Church voicing whatever ideology is currently advantageous to the government. It all originates in those times [the period of Sergii's leadership].[94]

At this time the Kremlin was indeed recasting Russia's twentieth-century history in terms it found advantageous: as a positive, all-encompassing continuum rather than a fundamental clash of moral systems. In his 2012 Federal Assembly address, President Putin maintained that "Russia did not begin in 1917, or even in 1991 [...] we have a common, continuous history spanning over one thousand years, and we must rely on it to find inner strength and purpose in our national development."⁹⁵ Putin had led the effort to "balance" the Bolshevik agenda and its victims. In 2007 he made a solemn visit to the Soviet execution site at Butovo,⁹⁶ but as early as 2001 opposed the removal of Lenin's embalmed remains from Red Square, arguing that, since many Russians associated their lives with Lenin, this "would indicate to them that they had worshipped false values."⁹⁷

Moves to Rehabilitate Stalin

Putin has latterly also sought to "balance" conflicting assessments of Stalin, urging that he be praised for Soviet industrialization and victory in World War Two as well as criticized for the Great Terror.⁹⁸ Officially, the Moscow Patriarchate was resolutely opposed to even partial rehabilitation of Stalin as recently as 2010, when DECR representative Fr. Filipp Ryabykh insisted:

> An inhumane system was created under Stalin, and nothing can justify it: not industrialization, not the atom bomb, not the preservation of state borders, not even victory in the Great Patriotic War [World War Two], for these were all the achievements not of Stalin, but our multinational people. The regime created by Stalin relied upon terror, violence, suppressing individuality, lies and denunciation.⁹⁹

Yet creeping rehabilitation of Stalin is now also taking place within the Church, shadowing the tendency to defend Metropolitan Sergii's collaborationist path. Here, there are stylistic echoes of the Stalin era: Reminiscent of Metropolitan Sergii's 1943 prayer "for the authorities headed by our God given leader," Patriarch Kirill described Putin's years of rule as "a miracle of God" in a high-profile February 2012 meeting.¹⁰⁰ More substantially, the Patriarchate-endorsed 2003 biography of Sergii speculates that Stalin's motive for restoring the Church's legal status in 1943 may have been "awakening fear of God." It cites the following anecdote recalled by Sergii's personal assistant: After the metropolitan returned from his momentous wartime meeting with the Soviet leader, he kept repeating in a low voice, "How kind he is!" When the assistant pointed out that Stalin was an atheist, Sergii's response was, "If someone is kind, then God lives in his soul."¹⁰¹

Such sentiment appears widespread. In the summer of 2015, prominent nationalist Aleksandr Prokhanov took a religious "icon" featuring Stalin on a tour of southwest Russia. After photographs emerged on social media of the image being blessed by an Orthodox priest at an air force base in Saratov, the local metropolitanate swiftly released a statement condemning the image, and explained that the priest concerned—ordained only a year previously—"displayed blatant incompetence and spiritual immaturity."[102] Nearby Belgorod diocese similarly tried to distance itself from the image, present during various World War Two victory commemorations.[103] Photographs of related events, however, showed Metropolitan Ioann of Belgorod—hardly an immature cleric—content to appear on discussion panels alongside the "icon" on at least two occasions.[104] In November 2015, the website of Kainsk Orthodox diocese in Siberia featured an article arguing that Stalinists had espoused core Russian values such as "justice, the primacy of truth before the law, of spirituality above materialism." This was quickly removed when it drew broad attention.[105]

In central Moscow, meanwhile, Church and state efforts to promote the "balanced" view of Stalin came together at *Orthodox Rus: My History; From Great Upheavals to Great Victory*, a late 2015 exhibition organized by the Patriarchate and sponsored by the state.[106] Joined by President Putin for the opening of the exhibition, Patriarch Kirill declared:

> The successes of one or other state leader that lie at the source of the rebirth and modernization of the nation must not be placed in doubt, even if that leader was distinguished by evil deeds [...] the negative aspects should not grant the right to exclude all that was positive, and vice versa.[107]

One particular exhibit outraged Orthodox journalist Viktor Sudarikov. The quotation "Stalin saved Russia, demonstrated what she means to the world. Therefore I, as an Orthodox Christian and Russian patriot, bow low before Stalin" was placed beside a photograph of Archbishop Luka Voino-Iasenetskii, canonized among the New Martyrs and Confessors in 2000. This was juxtaposed with an image of the communist revolutionary Leon Trotsky and a correctly attributed quotation: "Stalinism is a clot of all the deformities of the historical state, its malign caricature, a revolting grimace." In Sudarikov's ensuing social media discussion, several Church historians demonstrated that the pro-Stalin quotation had been falsely attributed to Archbishop Luka. Yet prominent Moscow priest Vladimir Vigilianskii was still prepared to defend the exhibit's "balance." "There are indeed conflicting statements, but that is the nature of our history and society," he argued on Sudarikov's Facebook page, pointing out that "an entire hall" in the exhibition had been devoted to the New Martyrs.

The false quotation was removed within days. Yet within weeks, the dismissal of two prominent Patriarchate representatives with divergent views indicated that space for open debate on the impact of Church-Soviet collaboration was shrinking. After they were dismissed from the Patriarchate in December 2015, both were outspoken. Previously editor of the *Journal of the Moscow Patriarchate*, Sergei Chapnin expressed concern that the Church was lauding Stalin as a great Soviet leader "without any external pressure. [...] The Church was practically destroyed by Stalin, and now it recognizes his services to the nation." If Russia failed to reject its Soviet legacy in favor of its prerevolutionary heritage, Chapnin suggested, it would remain in a situation of "hybrid religiosity," with revived Orthodox and Soviet traditions. This would lead to "a post-Soviet civil religion that exploits Orthodox tradition, but is essentially not Orthodoxy [...] a new version of 'Orthodoxy without Christ.'"[108]

As the Patriarchate's main spokesperson, Fr. Vsevolod Chaplin had earlier rejected the notion that Church collaboration with the Soviet state required special examination due to that regime's atheist agenda, instead maintaining that it was morally no different than in other historical circumstances: "This sin was not confined to the Soviet period: it happened under the tsars, it happens now (both in Russia and the West)."[109] Following his dismissal, however, Fr. Chaplin admitted that the communist legacy was still weighing upon the Church: "A lot has remained from Soviet times when priests were too afraid to speak frankly to the people in power, to criticize them. This whole phenomenon is in the spirit not even of yesterday but of the day before yesterday."[110]

Defenders of the Russian Orthodox Church's Soviet record have deflected calls for its critical evaluation by dismissing them as morally unacceptable attacks against particular clerics. Yet as Soviet repression recedes from living memory, the unresolved issue of Church collaboration with the atheist regime is increasingly no longer a question of the lustration of individuals. Few in today's Moscow Patriarchate held authoritative positions in the Soviet era: of some 180 diocesan hierarchs in Russia, only five headed dioceses before 1991.[111] Rather than seeking personal repentance in an effort to secure justice, the task of the Church has become mere establishment of historical truths: how Orthodox integrity was compromised in the interests of institutional survival, and how collusion was tenaciously resisted, particularly by prominent New Martyrs and Confessors.

There are two possible outcomes. The first is more plausible: Given the relative success of Soviet efforts to remold the Church, the dwindling voices of those who resisted, and the limited traction in Putin's Russia of Church historians' studies of the Soviet era, there is little popular awareness of the moral relativism inherent in the hybrid Soviet Orthodox religiosity lamented by Sergei Chapnin. It can thus be expected to thrive. The second possible outcome is a renewed public examination of the impact of historical compromises with Soviet atheism upon the integrity of the Russian Orthodox Church. Precedent suggests otherwise, but even Fr. Vsevolod Chaplin—long a pillar in the Patriarchate establishment—now admits this Soviet legacy within the Church "cannot go on for long."[112]

11

THE USEFUL GOD

Religion and Public Authority in Post-Soviet Russia

James W. Warhola

The Soviet regime made its disposition to religion clear from the outset: religion was viewed as a negative, retrogressive force. How has the historical experience of the Soviet struggle against religion shaped the political environment of post-Soviet Russia? This chapter explores the long-term consequences of the Soviet regime's attempt to contain, overcome, and eventually eliminate religion from public and private life. The antireligious dimension of the Bolshevik experiment is widely viewed in Russia today as ill-conceived, ill-advised, and regrettable. Significantly, this view is shared by the Putin administration, the Russian Orthodox Church (ROC) itself, and much but not all of the general public. Although a certain nostalgia for some elements of the USSR persists in contemporary Russia, the antireligious character of Soviet governance is *not* one of those elements. Rather, the post-Soviet government has increasingly turned to religious leaders and institutions to buttress its authority at home and to project influence abroad.

The role of religion in contemporary Russian governance is complex and ambiguous. On the one hand, the Russian Orthodox Church has reiterated its commitment to prerevolutionary *symphonia* as an ideal,[1] but on the other hand both the ROC and the Russian government (and the general populace, for that matter) appear to be more or less at peace with the formally stated, Western-derived principles of a secular state and freedom of religion. Nonetheless, the realization of those principles remains highly problematical, in part due to the Soviet legacy and also due to the fact that a "secular state" can take various forms.² Russia's version is distinctively different from most in the Western world.³ Thus, numerous questions emerge: how did the Soviet struggle against religion shape the political environment of post-Soviet Russia? How have post-Soviet patterns of religiosity shaped the contours of public life, particularly the religious dimension of public life? And finally, how has the post-Soviet government disposed itself to religion in general and religious institutions in particular?

Religion and Politics: Then and Now

Under the leadership of the Communist Party, the USSR managed to achieve a number of tasks that it set out for itself. Such successes included the development of a system of mass education, the construction of reasonably modern infrastructures of communication and transportation, and significant advances in scientific research. Other tasks proved to be long-term catastrophic failures including the attempted inculcation of a broadly shared sense of *Soviet* identity as opposed to ethnic and national particularism; development of an economic system suited to the late-modern era of globalization and primacy of innovation; and most directly germane to this chapter, the diminution and eventual extirpation of religion from public and private life. The historical momentum of Russia's prerevolutionary and Soviet experience continues to shape the contours of the interplay of politics and religion today. Some have referred to a "Sovietization" of politics in Russia;⁴ perhaps paradoxically, the domain of religion is one in which the post-Soviet governments have both sharply departed from Soviet policy and practices, and in other respects have come to mimic the Communist Party's disposition to religion and particularly to persons and institutions it finds objectionable.

Recent scholarship has shed significant, useful light on the complex interplay of politics and "lived religion" in the USSR, and particularly on the manner in which the antireligious policies and practices of the Communist Party unwittingly created conditions for the energizing of religiosity and the shaping of its character. Wanner offers:

> Soviet efforts to promote atheism via waves of antireligious campaigns that suppressed public expression of religion, especially in its institutional forms, did not, as they were intended, eliminate belief in and appeals to the supernatural. Rather, the Soviet state's efforts to secularize Soviet society yielded substantial momentum that fueled religious change by shifting the objects and foci of religious expression. ... Religious practice in the USSR and efforts to secularize

Soviet society were mutually constituting and shaped the ongoing possibilities for individual and collective self-definition throughout the Soviet period.[5]

This chapter explores the manner in which the Soviet experience has shaped the interplay of religion and politics under the Vladimir Putin and Dmitrii Medvedev presidential administrations. Four areas are examined: (1) the post-Soviet governments' engagement with religion to redress what they perceived as a moral bankruptcy and civilizational decoupling[6] due to seventy-four years of atheistic propaganda undertaken in the name of "communist construction"; (2) the use of religion to buttress a sense of regime legitimacy, to bring about national cohesion, to forge a stronger national identity at home, and to augment Russian influence abroad; (3) control of religion in order to manage its effect on society as a whole (and particularly on civil society), and especially to keep religion from generating social capital that could pose a credible political challenge to the regime that the Putin administration has deliberately created; (4) control of the more explicitly seditious manifestations of religiosity, largely but not exclusively in the form of Islamist jihadism. Of these four areas, the first two involve *positive* dimensions of religion as it pertains to public authority, whereas the latter two pertain to the control of *negative* manifestations of religiosity as it challenges the state. All four exist within the echoes and shadows of the Soviet experiment.

(1) Religion as a Remedy for Moral Bankruptcy and Civilizational Decoupling Due to the Soviet Experiment

Since the dissolution of the USSR, there has been more or less steadily increasing governmental encouragement of religion as an antidote to the moral bankruptcy, corruption, and decoupling from "traditional values" resulting from decades of "forced atheization" by the Communist Party.[7] This encouragement has been done with some delicacy, given various considerations, including the multi-religious nature of society in the Russian Federation, the fact that more or less nominal religious identification far exceeds formal public religious practice, and the dangers involved in colluding too closely with a potentially rival social institution. Regarding the last point, the post-Soviet Russian state has followed the convention inherent in the Byzantine roots of its church-state relations, according to which the governing state apparatus, and not the Church, maintains a clear and rarely disputed upper hand.[8]

Under President Putin there has been a clear pattern of colluding with the Russian Orthodox Church and other major religious institutions, and for at least three reasons. First and perhaps most significantly, religion has been conscripted for redress of the perceived moral decay and resultant social malaise in order to strengthen the fabric of society in a manner different from that of the failed experiment of Soviet communism. The "Moral Code of the Builder of Communism" (*Moral'nyi kodeks stroitelia kommunizma*), issued by the Communist Party at the Twenty-Second Party Congress 1961, may have purchased a degree of political capital for its purposes of ruling over the country, but neither it nor its relentless propagation by the party did much to inculcate the virtues necessary to overcome the corruption, criminality, and moral vacuity that characterized the USSR in its death throes.[9] The chaos of the 1990s did more to reveal and perhaps exacerbate this acuity than to redress it. Some began to talk of the inevitable waning of Russia itself into continued decay and global irrelevance. Jeffrey Tayler's "Russia is Finished" in the May 2001 edition of *The Atlantic Monthly* described matters thus:

> Given that Russia is surviving on human, material, and military reserves accrued during the Soviet years, and that Putin has put forward plans that will only worsen his country's plight, we can draw but one conclusion: Russia is following the path of Mobutu's Zaire, becoming a sparsely populated yet gigantic land of natural resources exploited by an authoritarian elite as the citizenry sinks into poverty, disease, and despair.[10]

Numerous utterances by newly elected President Putin suggest that he largely agreed with the diagnosis but had a very different vision of Russia's trajectory of recovery, for which purpose the Russian Orthodox Church and other major religious institutions would have an important role. Significantly, it was at this time that the Church issued the "Basis of the Social Concept" (August 2000). This document presents the Church as the major institution by which society would be morally guided, Russian civilization would be properly grounded, and Russia would thus resume her rightful place in global affairs—all goals very consistent with the Putin administration's determination to halt and reverse the moral and civilizational decay stemming from the vacuity and bankruptcy of Soviet ideology and practice. In an interview for *Time* magazine in 2007, the following exchange occurred:

> Question: "One of the old stereotypes that Americans have about Russia, and certainly the Russia of the U.S.S.R., is that it was a godless country. You have talked about your own faith. What role does faith play in your own leadership and what role should faith play in government and in the public sphere?

> Putin: First and foremost we should be governed by common sense. But common sense should be based on moral principles first. And it is not possible today to have morality separated from religious values. I will not expand, as I don't want to impose my views on people who have different viewpoints."[11]

Those "religious values" of course need to be articulated and fostered within society through some means, and for that purpose, religious institutions would be essential.[12] The "dangerous God" lurking under the Soviet project and slowly eroding it would be replaced, not by Mark Lilla's "Stillborn God" who had reached a dead end in the morally decayed West,[13] but with a deity more in line with Russia's centuries-long legacy of deep and complex intertwining of government, church, and society. Faith in such a deity could and would restore social Russia's spiritual vitality drained by Soviet atheism and also thwart the West's decadence from undermining Russian moral and spiritual vitality—if accessed properly. And that required a certain disposition of the state toward religion.[14]

The second major reason for colluding with religious institutions, paradoxically, has been to keep them from gaining too much power in and of themselves. To avoid that, these institutions would need to be kept under the constraints of the state itself, and also thereby kept from having too much power over society. The goal, as it had been in the Orthodox lands at least since the promulgation of the *Corpus Iuris Civilis* by Byzantine Emperor Justinian from 529–534 CE (and arguably from Emperor Constantine's Council of Nicea in 325 CE), has been to *sustain the primacy of the state over religious institutions and over all other organized elements within society*. Such an arrangement was viewed as the divinely ordained ordering of authority on earth, and in this respect the moral and telic *cul-de-sac* of Soviet communism provided a remarkably easy segue to the type of *statism* that had characterized Russia for centuries.

After more than twenty-five years of antireligious policies and practices by the Soviet regime, by the 1940s it was clear that religion would not wither away anytime soon. Thus in May 1944 Joseph Stalin established the Council for the Affairs of Religious Cults to monitor and control religion, and prevent the wartime *rapprochement* with the Orthodox Church from allowing it too much leeway and influence over society. This Council was succeeded in 1965 by the Council for Religious Affairs, which in turn was abolished by Boris Yeltsin in 1991. No such national cabinet-level council has been reinstated since. Nonetheless the presidencies of Yeltsin, Putin, Medvedev and again Putin have all adopted a number of measures to manage religious affairs to a degree that simply would not pass constitutional muster in most Western countries adhering to the principles of the Council of Europe, of which Russia has been a member since 1996, to say nothing of the human rights standards of the European Union.[15] Much of the containment of religion and keeping it within bounds acceptable to the ROC and the Putin administration is handled at the level of regional and local government.[16] Thus while the major religious institutions—first and foremost the ROC but also the two major Muslim organizations (*Council of Russian Muftiates* and the *Central Spiritual Board of Muslims*) and the Chief Jewish Rabbinate—play a critical role in the moral grounding and guidance of society, the state clearly maintains the upper hand, not infrequently in a manner echoing the practices of the Soviet regime.[17]

The third reason for the Putin administration's collusion with the ROC and other major religious institutions has been to keep them in a cooperative, more or less harmonious disposition to each other. If the USSR's "dangerous God" was to be duly regarded and channeled as a force for social and political good in the post-Soviet era, then the inherent danger of inter-confessional disharmony would need to be contained if not stymied altogether. This required not only a certain solicitous attitude and disposition toward religious institutions on the part of the government, but would also call for formal institutional channels through which such inter-confessional harmony would be fostered. The Putin administration has done both, and done so in a way that in retrospect suggests that the lessons of the failed Soviet experiment in controlling and hopefully extirpating religion were neither lost nor forgotten.

At higher levels of organized religious institutions, the achievement of inter-confessional harmony and cooperation appears to have succeeded.[18] For example, on February 8, 2016, Talgat Tajuddin, supreme mufti of the Central Spiritual Muslim Board of Russia, commented on the upcoming meeting between the ROC patriarch and Pope Francis in Cuba, referring to the patriarch "as an excellent spiritual leader" who "possesses rich experience in inter-faith dialogue":

> The kind relations between mainstream religions in Russia set an example for the whole world and the fact that these religions exist is due to the huge role of Patriarch Kirill who had worked to strengthen them during his time as head of the Department for External Church Relations, and particularly as the leader of the Church. The fact that Patriarch Kirill has behind him a huge experience in dialogue will allow him to make this meeting with the pope truly historical and will have a beneficial effect on the situation of Christians and their relations with each other.[19]

Yet on other levels, inter-confessional harmony has proven particularly challenging for a number of reasons, not all of which are necessarily echoes of the Soviet period.[20] The emergence of jihadist Islam in particular has complicated matters (explored below). Here it suffices to note that the interrelations among the major religious institutions in Russia and their respective relations with the national and regional governments is complex, variegated, and handled with a certain finesse and even delicacy arguably uncharacteristic of Soviet practice. In Russia the lines of religious affiliation generally run along ethno-national lines—ethnic Russians overwhelmingly identify themselves as Russian Orthodox regardless of their individual degree of practiced religiosity, and most but not all of the 15 to 20 percent of Russian Federation citizens who are Muslims are ethnically non-Russians. Thus with the post-Soviet regime's conscription of religion and implicit encouragement of it for purposes of moral fortification of society, it is imperative that the communities of the faithful get along at the institutional and communal levels. In this regard post-Soviet Russian governments have completely switched from the approach of the Communist Party, which saw religion as a regressive divisive force and thus to be combatted, toward one of cooptation and collaboration. But has the regime's implicit encouragement of socially positive religiosity made religion a more vibrant force in society? This appears to be very much an open question with ambiguity abounding.

The question of whether or not a religious "revival" occurred or is now occurring in Russia is to some degree a semantic one. On the one hand, there can be little question that interest in religious matters and even participation in religious events increased considerably in and around the time of the collapse of the USSR.[21] Since then, however, levels of religiosity as measured by such indicators as church attendance and the like have become much more similar to those of Western Europe than to the United States or much of the developing world. On the other hand, the post-Soviet government's willingness and ability to engage religion for social and political purposes does not so much depend on citizens' degree of religious practice as it does on citizens' regard for the reputation of the institutions and their trust of them.[22] In post-Soviet Russia the Russian Orthodox Church in particular has been consistently reckoned as one of the most trusted and well-reputed institutions in Russian society, a well-known and understood fact by governments.

Patriarch Kirill established the *Interreligious Council of Russia* in 2004, the same year that President Putin announced the intention to establish a 126-member *Public Chamber* composed of representatives from all major sectors of society.[23] The purpose of this latter body is ostensibly to encourage civil society—including a vibrant but controlled subsystem of religious organizations. The current Chamber has eight religious leaders among its members.[24] Opinion in the West is mixed about the efficacy of the Public Chamber in actually representing the various sectors of society, as opposed to their being coopted and used by the regime through the Chamber; the consensus, however, is that it is more the latter than the former.

Close but guarded affinity of the state with the Russian Orthodox Church and major Muslim associations for purposes of perceived moral fortification of society would also have the roundabout effect of diminishing the influence of the Western world on Russian society. This has clearly been a goal of the Putin administration, and in this respect it has permitted and encouraged closely cooperative relations among the major faith groups in addition to inundating the regime-controlled media with a sharply negative depiction of the Western world and especially the United States.[25] In actual fact the relationships among the Russian government, major Russian religious institutions, both of their Western counterparts, and the general population of Russia itself is complex. Nonetheless a clear indicator of the seriousness with which the Putin administration takes this aspect of Russian social and political life is evident in his state of the nation addresses. His 2013 address devoted particular attention to the question of the perceived degraded moral condition of the Western world, and Russia's need to remain grounded in "traditional values" in order to remain socially and politically strong and durable:

> We know that there are more and more people in the world who support our position on defending traditional values that have made up the spiritual and moral foundation of civilisation in every nation for thousands of years: the values of traditional families, real human life, including religious life, not just material existence but also spirituality, the values of humanism and global diversity.[26]

An intended consequence of moral fortification of society and civilizational grounding has been to foster national cohesion and augmentation of national identity—the dearth of both of which figured directly in the dissolution of the USSR. The Yeltsin and Putin regimes have determined that a similar fate would not befall the Russian Federation, and for that purpose religion was a critical component.

(2) Governmental Use of Religion to Buttress Regime Legitimacy, National Cohesion and National Identity, and to Project Russian Influence Abroad

The closely related issues of territorial integrity, national cohesion, and national identity have all been of acute concern to each presidential administration in the post-Soviet Russian Federation. Under president Putin, these concerns were arguably even more pronounced than during the Yeltsin years, given Russia's economic debilitation during the 1990s, its reduced status and role in global affairs, and especially the re-ignition of the Chechen conflict in 1999. The Putin administration was determined to strengthen the Russian state as a prerequisite to redress these conditions. A conglomeration of policies and practices emerged that can be summarized as the "reassertion of vertical authority" and the augmentation and projection of Russian influence on the global stage. For these purposes, religion has played an increasingly important role.

The bitter Soviet experience of failed national cohesion, traceable to a fictive *druzhba narodov* (friendship of the peoples), has not been lost on the post-Soviet leadership. At this point in the post-Soviet experience there can be little question about the regime's use of various dimensions of religion to help foster national cohesion and to a lesser degree, a sense of national identity. Tellingly, only several months after the inauguration of Vladimir Putin as president in May of 2000 the Russian Orthodox Church issued "*The Basis of the Social Concept*" (adopted August 2000). It offers the following:

> Christian patriotism may be expressed at the same time with regard to a nation as an ethnic community and as a community of its citizens. The Orthodox Christian is called to love his fatherland, which has a territorial dimension, and his brothers by blood who live everywhere in the world. This love is one of the ways of fulfilling God's commandment of love to one's neighbour which includes love to one's family, fellow-tribesmen and fellow-citizens.
>
> **The patriotism of the Orthodox Christian should be active. It is manifested when he defends his fatherland against an enemy, works for the good of the motherland, cares for the good order of people's life through, among other things, participation in the affairs of government. The Christian is called to preserve and develop national culture and people's self-awareness.**
> (emphasis in the original)[27]

The degree to which the overall population of the Russian Federation is animated by such religious sentiments is not clear; on the one hand, abundant evidence exists to indicate that most ethnic Russians consider themselves to be Orthodox, at least nominally; most have a positive view of the Russian Orthodox Church as an institution; and most describe themselves as patriotic citizens. On the other hand, Russians' active religious participation (e.g., church attendance) is strikingly low, even by European standards.[28] How these sentiments are all interrelated, however, is also far from clear. The matter of Russian identity is complex and multidimensional, beginning with the rudimentary fact that in Russian language even the adjective "Russian" has two forms, *Russkii* and *Rossiiskii*, signifying generally cultural and political aspects, respectively. There can be little dispute that Orthodoxy is commonly and broadly viewed as an integral part of being Russian in the cultural (*Russkii*) adjectival sense, though not necessarily in the political/citizenship (*Rossiiskii*) sense.

Compounding the matter is the fact that even though Orthodoxy is a universal faith, it manifests itself organizationally and institutionally along national lines (Russian Orthodox, Serbian Orthodox, Greek Orthodox, and so on), unlike Islam, Roman Catholicism, and most but not all branches of Protestantism. Viacheslav Karpov and his colleagues coined the term "ethnodoxy" to signify "a collectively held belief system that rigidly links a group's ethnic identity to its dominant faith".[29]

> We theorize this phenomenon at three levels: macro (the interplay between religion and ethnonational identities), micro (construction of ethnoreligious identities and imagined communities viewed from a social identity theory perspective), and meso (the nature and functions of popular ideologies and religiosities). Subsequently, ethnodoxy is conceptualized as an ideal-typical syndrome of six component beliefs. We further operationalize and verify the concept using representative national survey data from Russia. Findings show ethnodoxy's extent, coherence, dimensionality, and associations with religious and ethnic intolerance.[30]

The problem of course is that religion in this regard can easily degrade from being a force that augments patriotism to spawning a society fractured along religious lines; this in turn underscores the critical role of religious leaders in maintaining harmony both among themselves and in their respective flocks. As noted above, the post-Soviet Russian state abolished the Council for Religious Affairs but certainly has not been indifferent to the interactions among the leaders of the major religious institutions in Russia.[31]

Much has been written in the past few years about the increasingly close cooperation of the Russian Orthodox Church and the Russian state in the projection of Russian influence abroad.[32] Although this approach to foreign policy has roots in the Soviet period, the extent and degree to which it has become used by both institutions to augment and project Russian influence in the world appears to be well beyond that which was practiced in the USSR, both in scale and in degree of sophistication. Van Herpen in particular has explicated in considerable detail the manner in which this pattern has emerged, the strategies and tactics used by both the ROC and the Foreign Ministry, and the effects of this collaboration in terms of Russian "soft power" in global affairs.[33] In this regard the "dangerous God" haunting the USSR has become not only a divine force for the fortification of society and the state, but also a fulcrum by which Russian influence is projected abroad.

The post-Soviet Russian state's disposition to religion has involved more than the positive aspects of colluding with it to buoy the moral center of gravity of society and to augment the state's efforts at promoting social cohesion, important as these two aims have been. The Russian state has also sought to control two aspects of religion that directly confront and challenge its authority: the potential for religion to generate an unwelcome social capital and resultant civil society, and more gravely, to spawn outright sedition in the form of insurgency. The manner in which each of these has manifested in post-Soviet Russia has roots in the Soviet Union's dealings with religion, and accordingly warrants a closer look.

(3) Control of Religion as Potential Generator of Social Capital and Civil Society

The connection between vibrant religiosity and social capital has been scrutinized in depth, particularly the tendency for Protestantism in its various manifestations to generate the type and degree of social capital that contribute to the eventual emergence of liberal democracy. Some view Protestantism as having inadvertently and unwittingly spawned modern liberal democracy; as having spearheaded the spread of conditions leading to the spread of democracy in the late-modern world; and as playing a critical role in the consolidation of democracy where it sprouted in the tumultuous global conditions of the "third wave" of democratization.[34] Regardless of whether the Putin regime was aware of this demonstrated connection between Protestantism and Western-style liberal democracy, in fact all three Putin presidencies have behaved as if they knew perfectly well that religion can and often does generate the type of social capital that in turn gives rise to a sufficiently vibrant civil society so as to pose a direct political challenge to a given state's more or less unbridled scope of authority. Notably, assassinated opposition leader Boris Nemtsov mentioned that Russia's prospective democratization in the 1990s was problematical because there were "not enough Protestants." The latter days of the USSR demonstrated clearly the capacity of religion's "dangerous God" to subtly and often indirectly challenge state authority and undermine it, and the shadow of this experience is hardly lost on the post-Soviet leadership.[35]

There is of course nothing novel in the late-modern world about the force of religion to undermine the authority of tyrannical government or even to seek to impose restraints upon unbridled state power. Such had been the experience of the Christian religion in the West at least since the time of the enunciation of the Two Swords doctrine in 494 CE by way of Pope Gelasius's challenge to Byzantine Emperor Zeno's *Henoticon* of twelve years earlier. Briefly, Emperor Zeno's *Henoticon* edict had the practical effect of formally subjugating church to state, which prompted Pope Gelasius's remonstrance in the form of the *Duo sunt* doctrine: "there are two [swords]," effectively placing even the Byzantine emperor under the pastoral authority of the vicar of Christ in Rome.[36] This critical historical juncture put the Eastern church and thus Orthodox civilization on a different historical path from that of the Western church and thus also thereby all of Western civilization. The precise, practical meaning of the *Duo sunt* doctrine became the subject of intense dispute in the high Middle Ages. Nonetheless the core notion of distinct spheres of religious authority (*sacerdotium*) and secular authority (*imperium*) remained intact, with the former superior to the latter, even though the precise content of that superiority was often the focal point of conceptual dispute that turned increasingly violent as the medieval period gave way to the early modern world.[37]

Among other differences between the Orthodox East and the Latin West was an increasingly vibrant intellectual discourse in the latter about limits to state authority, rights, and prerogatives of citizenship from the twelfth century onward.[38] Nor was it accidental that the major thrust of political theorizing that led to the emergence of modern concepts of constitutionalism, limited government, and human rights derived largely from Protestant thought or thought heavily influenced by Protestantism.[39] The Russian state followed a considerably different developmental path, with a form of *etatism* that included a sympathetic yet collusive cooptation of religion that was discarded in the USSR and brought back with a vengeance in the post-Soviet manifestation.[40] Religion-based dissent is neither more welcomed nor much more tolerated now than then.

Aside from the matter of religion serving as unintended generator of social capital, the Putin administration's dual-track policy of both using and controlling religion is presented with an especially thorny dilemma in the North Caucasus region. There, a certain latitude has been granted to Kremlin-appointed governor Ramzan Kadyrov to rule over Chechnia more or less unhampered by Moscow, yet the control that the Putin administration is able to exercise over religious matters there seems questionable.[41] While the Kadyrov regime has clamped down on the most immediate jihadist threats, it may be sowing the seeds for further troubles in the not too distant future, and in any case represents a force that the Putin administration both needs for control of the region, yet finds difficult to accept precisely because it cannot practically control it there.[42]

Geraldine Fagan's 2013 book *Believing in Russia: Religious Policy after Communism* provides a masterful description of the nature, types, and degree of involvement in religious affairs by the Russian state at the national, regional, and local levels. The picture emerging from her account is one in which public authority at all three of these levels intrudes into organized religious bodies in a manner that would be very often legally and constitutionally unacceptable in the liberal democracies of the Western world. Far from troubling Russian officials, this distinction is defended and in fact touted as an example of Russia's having developed and retained a strong state in the face of actual and potential sedition, all the while enabling the legitimate, recognized religious organizations to work their beneficent effect upon society. The religious organizations and movements that are not recognized as legitimate, however, have also evoked a close eye and sharp response from the Putin administration; that aspect is explored below.

(4) Containment and Control of Religion as a Source of Outright Sedition

Much has been written about the apparent resurgence of religion as a force in global politics in the latter part of the twentieth century, particularly as it has manifested itself in violence.[43] Such violence has sometimes emerged as broad-scale, religion-based demand for change, as in the case of the Iranian Revolution; in other cases, conflicts that did not begin as religion-based at the outset eventually took on a decidedly religious inflection, as in the case of the Chechen wars in Russia, or even more dramatically, in the emergence of ISIS waging full-scale war to erase the political boundaries of the Middle East and establish a caliphate.[44] The Russian case represents essentially the latter of these two types.

The insurgency in Chechnya bedeviling the Russian government since the early 1990s did not begin as an Islamist jihadi revolt, but increasingly became one by about 1997.[45] Even after the Kremlin's claimed pacification of Chechnia by 2005, the jihadist sedition not only continued but spread throughout the North Caucasus region of the Russian Federation. The overarching goal had also morphed, from Chechen independence from Russia to a grander plan of erasing the Russian-drawn borders and establishing a Muslim caliphate. As such the conflict represents a serious and persisting religion-based threat to the regime and has drawn an equally serious response from the Putin administration. Unlike the Soviet regime, which could simply suppress any and all religious movements, groups, or individuals threatening the state with sedition, the Putin administration has faced the more delicate and nuanced task of balancing the positive manifestations of religiosity described above (i.e., to buoy the country's moral center of gravity and buttress regime legitimacy) with the more or less inevitable tendency of religion to either contain or to spawn radical, anti-system elements.[46]

This aspect of post-Soviet policies and practices of the Russian national government have been aimed almost exclusively at Islamic jihadism in its various manifestations. Most but not all of the jihadist resistance to the Russian government concerned first the status of Chechnia, and then as the Chechen conflict morphed into a more broadly, regionally based insurgency, the resistance has taken the form of attempts to wrench Muslim majority territories of the Russian Federation from Moscow's control, and establish some type of Muslim caliphate. Given that the proportion of the population of the Russian Federation is about 15 to 18 percent Muslim (at least nominally) and exhibits the highest rates of population growth of any religion-based subgroup of the country's overall population, this matter is particularly grave and acute. The fact that the south central and southwestern flanks of the country are bordered by Muslim majority countries with jihadist movements of their own makes this issue as much a foreign policy matter as it is a domestic issue. Accordingly, the Putin presidency has taken a number of steps to make religion in various ways and forms a critical aspect of its foreign policy. Some of these represent clear echoes from Soviet policy and practices, and others are more innovative. These bear a closer examination before concluding this chapter.

It is no coincidence—*eto ne sluchaino*, as Russians are fond of saying—that the determination to augment the power of the Russian state by way of "reasserting vertical authority" occurred within the context of the re-ignited Chechen conflict in late 1999 and into 2000. Vladimir Putin was appointed prime minister in August of 1999 and stepped into the role of acting president upon the resignation of Boris Yeltsin on the last day of that year. It is also no coincidence that a closer collusion with religious institutions, and in particular the Russian Orthodox Church, began to emerge more or less simultaneous with the spreading of the Chechen conflict, as a jihadist movement, beyond Chechnia proper and into the surrounding regions of the North Caucasus. Accordingly, the Putin administration has trod a delicate line between suppression of jihadist sedition at home and simultaneously engaging Russia's significant Muslim minority to be loyal, patriotic citizens. The general approach has been to concoct a mixture of close collaboration with the two major Muslim organizations of Russia, and employment of them and the ROC to project "soft power" abroad by presenting Russia as an exemplar of harmony, peacefulness, and stability. As Van Herpen summarizes:

The ROC has proved to be the Kremlin's soft power instrument *par excellence*. With Putin's help the ROC succeeded in bringing the Orthodox Church Outside Russia (ROCOR) back into Moscow's fold, giving the Moscow Patriarchate—in close cooperation with the Kremlin—a grip on the appointment of priests in foreign countries, including the United States, the United Kingdom, and France. Priests are expected to support the conservative and often openly reactionary version of Orthodoxy propagated by the Moscow Patriarchate. The Russian Orthodox Church is also acting as the Kremlin's mouthpiece in international organizations such as the UN, UNESCO, the OSCE, and the Council of Europe, where it is attacking universal human rights in the name of "traditional values."[47]

More recently, with the Russian military ventures in Crimea and in Syria, religious institutions have predictably offered their more or less unbridled succor and support. The *Middle East Monitor* summarized the matter well:

The Russian Orthodox Church's public affairs department quoted the Church's Patriarch Kirill blessing the Russian forces' fight in Syria, saying: "Russia took a responsible decision to use military forces to protect the Syrian people from the woes brought on by the tyranny of terrorists," adding that the "Orthodox people have noticed many acts of violence against Christians in the area."

Russia Today quoted the head of the Church's Public Affairs Department, Vsevolod Chaplin, saying: "The active position of our country has always been connected with protection of the weak and oppressed, like the Middle East Christians who are now experiencing a real genocide. Any fight against terrorism is moral; we can even call it a holy fight."[48]

Again, while this approach represents among other things an echo of the Soviet regime's instrumental use of religion for foreign policy purposes, the manner, scope, sophistication, and degree of collaboration all appear to be far more advanced than that undertaken by the Soviet regime, whose "dangerous God" was arguably even less utile than today, and certainly more of a potential challenge to the fabric of the project of "communist construction." Thus the "dangerous God" despised by Marx and his disciples has become politically useful for the post-Soviet political regime in Russia.

Summary and Conclusions

The Soviet experience in aggregate, and especially the Communist Party's determination to "build communism" by way of creating a thoroughly secularized society, has shaped the landscape of both politics and religion in post-Soviet Russia. The inclination to begin looking to religion to bolster the legitimacy of public authority perhaps began most openly with the 1988 celebration of one thousand years of Christianity in Russia, marking the millennium of the baptism of Rus' by Prince Vladimir in May of 988 CE. That inclination grew stronger through the Yeltsin years and has become even more pronounced under the presidency of Vladimir Putin. Regarding the intersection of religion and public authority, his presidency has been marked by the use of religion to buoy the moral center of gravity of society, to foster national cohesion and to a lesser degree a sense of national identity, and yet to control religion as a potential challenge to the authority and power of the state, and perhaps most resembling the USSR's experience, to intently monitor and throttle religion when and where it manifests as a source of blatant sedition. The "dangerous God" of the USSR is no more, and the Western world's liberal but "Stillborn God" described by Mark Lilla poses no threat to the regime; the traditional Russian deity has been very much invited to collude and cooperate with the post-Soviet state, however.

The positive side of post-Soviet Russia's experience with religion has been the lesson learned from its episodic and often cruel repression: it is both unnecessary in most cases and counterproductive for purposes of state. Though not quite the sort of *volte-face* away from religious persecution displayed by Emperor Constantine in the early fourth century, the post-Soviet national governments of Yeltsin, Putin, Medvedev, and once again Putin in 2012 have all adopted a roughly analogous disposition, such that to understand the present state of religious affairs in Russia at all, one must comprehend the Soviet experience and the shadows that it casts over the country to this day.

AFTERWORD

Whether in Words or Deeds, Known and Unknown

Roy R. Robson

In September 1953, *nastavnik* (preceptor) I. U. Vakon'ia felt vexed. It was no easy job to lead a large Old Believer community in the USSR, especially one that had once enjoyed independence but now reported to the Latvian SSR's Council for Religious Affairs. Rather than fighting Soviet bureaucracy, Vakon'ia had decided to report secretly to the governmental Council on the inner workings of Riga's large Old Believer community. He was not alone in choosing to collaborate with the Soviet state. In April 1952, the high council of Latvian Old Believers had used its annual Paschal greeting to blame "idol-worshiping American-Anglo Imperialism" for the bloodshed in Korea, Mali, Vietnam, and Greece. The next month, Riga's *nastavniki* gained notoriety by attending the "Conference in Defense of Peace of All Churches and Religious Associations in the USSR," convened by the Russian Orthodox patriarch. The Old Believers lugged a large placard from Riga to Zagorsk that proclaimed—in Old Church Slavonic—the support of the "Old Ritualist Church in the Latvian SSR in the Struggle for Peace." Vakon'ia gave an impassioned speech to the conference, further raising his profile.

By September, though, Vakon'ia had become worried that fellow *nastavnik* P. F. Fadeev would not attend the follow-up peace conference to be held on September 21 in Riga. The two had become embroiled in a struggle for leadership of "the twenty," the community's lay council mandated by Soviet law. Fadeev's absence at the conference might have brought attention to a fight between "conservatives" (including Fadeev and two others) and "progressives" (led by

Vakon'ia). The previous year, Vakon'ia's faction had taken over the Council of Twenty. By September 1953, however, Vakon'ia wrote to condemn Fadeev and his "friends in conservatism and in the struggle against progress" who hoped to supplant Vakon'ia's supporters with their own conservative cohort. Valkon'ia pushed for the condemnation of his rival, persuading the committee to decry Fadeev's "terror,"[1] and thwart a "putsch attempt." Even so, Fadeev's not showing up for the peace conference could have hurt Vakon'ia's status and threatened the Latvian SSR Council for Religious Affairs' support for the Old Believers.

Nastavnik Vakon'ia's situation illustrated the complications and difficulties confronting believers every day in the Soviet Union. Consider the following: the Riga community had been forced to accept the Soviet committee of twenty as its governing body. Having done so, however, the community quickly assimilated Soviet legal norms into its traditional structure, and rival *nastavniki* used it to further their own agendas. For the conservatives, the Council of Twenty offered a tool to maintain ritual purity and to limit interaction with both the Soviet state and Latvian society. The Council of Twenty represented something rather different for Vakon'ia and the self-styled "progressives." To them, the Twenty provided a way to replicate Old Believers' traditional egalitarianism while also currying favor with the Soviet government.

It is not known why Vakon'ia had decided to become an informant, but the archives hint that members of the community were on to him. He complained that a fellow *nastavnik* had called him a "smart aleck dictator," and a councilwoman observed that "if one *nastavnik* is a drinker, then the other [Vakon'ia] is a fraud."[2] Also unknown are the precise deliberations that led to the Riga Old Believers' embrace of the peace movement. To be sure, Old Believers could argue for peace on solid Christian theological footing. It would have been difficult to resist pressure from the Council for Religious Affairs. Yet archives also show how Vakon'ia personally profited: he alone among the Old Believers received a visa to Shimizu, Japan for the Second World Religion Congress. Then, in 1954, Vakon'ia's daughter applied to an institute for experimental medicine. Before accepting her as a student, the director pointedly inquired whether Vakon'ia was one of the "progressive servitors" of his cult. In reply, Vakon'ia furnished the requisite biography that highlighted his work at the peace conferences.[3]

Generations of scholars had no access to the archival files that detailed the events described here. Instead, scholars on both sides of the Iron Curtain often fell prey to Cold War assumptions. For Western scholars, the horror of Soviet religious persecution further supported the tendency toward simplification. Rather than nuanced analysis, Western scholars often portrayed true believers fighting communist dupes; Soviet academics described monarchist revanchists undermining progressive servitors. Yet life in the Soviet was not so easily defined; it was a difficult, messy affair for most Christians. Where, for example, did the line blur between truly supporting peace and mindlessly parroting Soviet propaganda? How did believers use Soviet law to their own advantage? Vakon'ia once reported that some on the Council of Twenty concluded that Soviet officials would not "meddle in our internal affairs, we are the complete masters!"[4]

This volume of essays illustrates how broadly and deeply scholars can now analyze the trajectory of Soviet militant atheism, the ongoing power of Christian words and imagery, and the everyday life of Russian Christians. Some authors in the volume, especially Michael Bourdeaux, remind us of the heroic struggle to support and publish the works of Soviet religious dissidents. Others, such as John Burgess, show us the political ramifications of celebrating liturgy. We have read thoughtful biographies of dissidents and have recalled the sea of kerchiefed babushkas, quietly standing in churches during the Brezhnev years. We try to place ourselves in the Gulag camps, and wonder if we too could find grace in a slice of sunlight breaking through a cell window. We now more clearly understand how poets and novelists might weave the language of Christianity into their samizdat publications.

As I read through this volume, three phrases repeatedly jump to mind. The first comes from Dominic Erdozain's essay on *Doctor Zhivago*: words are also deeds. These essays show us the role of words not as descriptors, but also as feats of courage and persecution. Theory-obsessed Bolsheviks understood this, but Western scholars have not always appreciated the power of poetry, prose, and prayer. Likewise, I find myself coming back the title of Geraldine Fagan's essay: "there are things in history that should be called by their proper name." Paradoxically, this volume often argues how difficult a task that can be. How, for example, do we interpret Fr. Dmitrii Dudko's public admission of guilt for anti-Soviet slander, when he had actually worked for believers' rights *within* the bounds of the Soviet Constitution? And finally, these two phrases bring to mind the prayer of St. Macarius, repeated often during Orthodox Lenten services: "forgive my sins ... known or unknown, in word and deed, in thought and by all my senses." Were *Nastavnik* Vakon'ia's words and deeds those of a sinner or a leader, a snitch or a defender of his community? This volume sheds light on documents, events, and people nearly unknown in the broad scholarship of Christianity. Taken together, the essays provide powerful analysis and remembrance of the words and deeds of the USSR's experiment in militant atheism.

November 8, 2016
Lansdowne, PA

CONTRIBUTORS

DOMINIC ERDOZAIN is a Research Fellow at King's College London and an Honorary Research Fellow at the Institute for Advanced Studies in the Humanities at the University of Queensland. He has written widely on religious change and secularization, including most recently, *The Soul of Doubt: The Religious Roots of Unbelief from Luther to Marx* (Oxford University Press, 2015).

SCOTT LINGENFELTER is Visiting Professor of History at Grand Valley State University. He has traveled to Russia several times and was there during the aborted coup of 1991. He is the author of *Between Tradition & Modernity: Sergei Bulgakov, Russian Orthodoxy, and Progressive Reform in Late Imperial Russia* (2013) and of the Russian history text *Russia in the 21st Century*.

JULIE DEGRAFFENRIED is Associate Professor of Russian and East European History in the Department of History at Baylor University. Her book *Sacrificing Childhood: Children and the Soviet State in the Great Patriotic War* was published by University Press of Kansas in 2014.

MICHAEL BOURDEAUX is the founder of the Keston Institute and the author of many books on religion in the USSR. In 1984 Bourdeaux received the Templeton Prize for Progress in Religion. In 1996 the Archbishop of Canterbury awarded him a Lambeth Doctorate of Divinity. He retired in 1999 but continues a worldwide program of lecturing and writing.

WALLACE L. DANIEL is Distinguished University Professor of History at Mercer University in Macon, Georgia. Prior to joining the Mercer faculty in 2008, he was Ralph L. and Bessie Mae Lynn Professor of History at Baylor University. He has written widely on church, state, and society in Soviet Russia and has recently completed a much-anticipated biography of Father Aleksandr Men, the renowned parish priest in Russia, who was murdered in 1990.

JOSEPHINE VON ZITZEWITZ is Leverhulme Early Career Fellow in the Department of Slavonic Studies, Faculty of Modern and Medieval Languages, University of Cambridge. She holds a doctorate from Oxford where she spent the last five years working as a Stipendiary Lecturer and Junior Research

Fellow in Russian. Her book, *Poetry and the Leningrad Religious-Philosophical Seminar 1974–1980: Music for a Deaf Age*, was published by Legenda in 2015.

LAUREN TAPLEY earned a PhD at Baylor University in 2015 for her dissertation on "Human Rights and Religious Dissidents in the Brezhnev Era: The Effect of the Human Rights Movement on the Activism of Religious Dissidents." She also holds a BA and MA in History from Baylor University with a minor in Russian and concentrations in European intellectual history and Russian history.

JOHN P. BURGESS has taught at Pittsburgh Theological Seminary since 1998. His publications include *Encounters with Orthodoxy: How Protestant Churches Can Reform Themselves Again* (Westminster John Knox Press, 2013) and *The East German Church and the End of Communism* (Oxford University Press, 1997).

XENIA DENNEN is a graduate of St. Anne's College, Oxford and the London School of Economics and Political Science. Dennen helped found the Keston Institute and its journal. She has chaired the Keston Institute Council since 2002, and is currently involved in producing the multivolume *Encyclopaedia of Religious Life in Russia Today*.

GERALDINE FAGAN is a graduate of Hertford College, Oxford. She spent twelve years in Russia as a journalist covering religious affairs and is the author of *Believing in Russia—Religious Policy after Communism* (Routledge, 2013).

JAMES W. WARHOLA is Professor of Political Science in the Political Science Department at the University of Maine, where he has previously served as department chair. He has published widely on religion, politics, and ethnicity in late- and post-Soviet Russia.

NOTES

Notes to Introduction: The Rhythm of the Saints

1. Nikolai Mikhailovich Zernov, *The Russian Religious Renaissance of the Twentieth Century* (London: Darton, Longman & Todd, 1963), 88–89.

2. Harvard historian Richard Pipes estimates that "300,000 clergymen" alone were killed by the Soviet regime. Alexander Yakovlev: *The Man Whose Ideas Delivered Russia from Communism* (DeKalb: Northern Illinois University Press, 2015), 67; John Burgess writes that "several hundred thousand Church leaders were martyred in the USSR, compared to the approximately 3,500 Christians who died in the persecutions of the early centuries of Christianity." "The suffering that the Russian Orthodox Church endured under communism," he writes, "was of historically unprecedented dimensions." "Retrieving the Martyrs in Order to Rethink the Political Order: The Russian Orthodox Case," *Journal of the Society of Christian Ethics* 34, no. 2 (2014): 195, doi:10.1353/sce.2014.0035; for a sociologist's analysis of the Soviet campaign against religion, see Paul Froese, *The Plot to Kill God: Findings from the Soviet Experiment in Secularization* (Berkeley: University of California Press, 2008); for a harrowing account of the methods of execution visited on clergy, see Alexander N. Yakovlev, *A Century of Violence in Soviet Russia*, trans. Anthony Austin (New Haven, CT: Yale University Press, 2002), 156–68.

3. David Priestland, *Stalinism and the Politics of Mobilization: Ideas, Power, and Terror in Inter-War Russia* (Oxford: Oxford University Press, 2007), 293.

4. A particular influence on the editor is Philip Boobbyer, *Conscience, Dissent, and Reform in Soviet Russia* (New York: Routledge, 2005).

5. Keston College, *Religious Prisoners in the USSR* (Keston, England: Greenfire Books, 1987), 51. Quoted in Froese, *The Plot to Kill God*, 8.

6. Irina Ratushinskaya, *Grey Is the Color of Hope* (New York: Knopf, 1988), 296.

7. Boobbyer, *Conscience, Dissent, and Reform*, 100, 84–85.

8. Zernov, *Russian Religious Renaissance*, xiii.

9. Alexander N. Yakovlev, *The Fate of Marxism in Russia* (New Haven, CT: Yale University Press, 1993), 102.

10. Aleksandr Kyrlezhev, "The Postsecular Age: Religion and Culture Today," *Religion, State and Society* 36, no. 1 (2008): 22, doi:10.1080/09637490701809654.

11. See the discussion of Strelnikov in Pasternak's *Doctor Zhivago* (New York: Pantheon Books, 1991) and my essay on Pasternak below.

12. Yakovlev, *The Fate of Marxism in Russia*, 17, 28, 27.

13. Boobbyer, *Conscience, Dissent, and Reform*, 130.

14. Koenraad de Wolf, *Dissident for Life: Alexander Ogorodnikov and the Struggle for Religious Freedom in Russia* (Grand Rapids, MI: Eerdmans, 2013), 57.

15. Yakovlev, *The Fate of Marxism in Russia*, 35.

16. Albert Katz Weinberg, *Manifest Destiny: A Study of Nationalist Expansionism in American History* (Baltimore, MD: The Johns Hopkins Press, 1935), 411.

17. Diarmaid MacCulloch, *A History of Christianity: The First Three Thousand Years* (London: Allen Lane, 2009), 163.

18. Ludwig Feuerbach, *Thoughts on Death and Immortality: From the Papers of a Thinker, along with an Appendix of Theological-Satirical Epigrams* (Berkeley: University of California Press, 1980); Ludwig Feuerbach, *The Essence of Christianity*, trans. George Eliot, 2nd ed. (London: John Chapman, 1854); Karl Marx, *Karl Marx: Selected Writings* (Oxford: Oxford University Press, 2000), 72.

19. A request Ogorodnikov declined because he was not a priest. Wolf, *Dissident for Life*, 234.
20. Michael Bourdeaux, *Gorbachev, Glasnost, and the Gospel* (London: Hodder & Stoughton, 1990), 189.
21. Arthur Koestler, *Darkness at Noon* (New York: Simon and Schuster, 2015), 178.
22. Yakovlev, *A Century of Violence*, 64.
23. Boobbyer, *Conscience, Dissent, and Reform*, 178.
24. Ibid., 200.
25. Ibid., 186-201 and throughout.
26. "RUSSIA: Putin Signs Sharing Beliefs, 'Extremism,' Punishments," Forum 18 News Service, July 8, 2016, http://www.forum18.org/archive.php?article_id=2197.
27. Boobbyer, *Conscience, Dissent, and Reform*, 212.

Notes to Chapter 1: Empowering the Faithful

1. "[M. V.] Rodzianko's Memoirs," in *Documents of Russian History, 1914-1917*, ed. Frank Alfred Golder (New York: Century, 1927), 119.
2. A sampling of the literature in English would include Catherine Evtuhov, *The Cross and the Sickle: Sergei Bulgakov and the Fate of Russian Religious Philosophy* (Ithaca, NY: Cornell University Press, 1997); Vera Shevzov, Russian Orthodoxy on the Eve of Revolution (New York: Oxford University Press, 2004); Chris Chulos, *Converging Worlds: Religion and Community in Peasant Russia, 1861-1917* (DeKalb: Northern Illinois University Press, 2003); Nadieszda Kizenko, *A Prodigal Saint: Father John of Kronstadt and the Russian People* (University Park: Pennsylvania State University Press, 2000); Page Herrlinger, Working Souls: Russian Orthodoxy and Factory Labor in St. Petersburg, 1881-1917 (Bloomington, IN: Slavica Press, 2007); Jennifer Hedda, *His Kingdom Come: Orthodox Pastorship and Social Activism in Revolutionary Russia* (DeKalb: Northern Illinois University Press, 2008); and Arthur Repp, "In Search of an Orthodox Way: The Development of Biblical Studies in Late Imperial Russia" (PhD diss., University of Illinois at Chicago, 1999). Several fine review articles have appeared as well. Among them, "Orthodox Christianity in Russia and Eastern Europe: New Directions in Eastern Orthodox History," *Canadian Slavonic Papers* 57, nos. 1-2 (2015): 1-5, introduced by Scott Kenworthy (whose work on monasticism could be added here); an extremely insightful review by Chris Chulos in *Kritika: Explorations in Russian and Eurasian History* 10, no. 1 (Winter 2009): 184-93; Ian Thatcher, "Communism and Religion in Early Bolshevik Russia: A Discussion of Work Published Since 1989," *European History Quarterly* 36, no. 4 (2006): 586-98; and Heather Coleman, "Atheism versus Secularization? Religion in Soviet Russia, 1917-1961," *Kritika* 1, no. 3 (Summer 2000): 547-58.
3. M. A. Babkin, *Rossiiskoe dukhovenstvo i sverzhenie monarkhii v 1917 godu: Materialy i arkhivnye dokumenty po istorii Russkoi pravoslavnoi tserkvi* (Moscow: Indrik, 2006), document 327, p. 238. An English translation can be found in Jonathan Daly and Leonid Trofimov, eds., *Russia in War and Revolution, 1914-1922: A Documentary History* (Indianapolis, IN: Hackett Publishing, 2009), 82. For references to "Ecclesiastical Revolution" and "Red Easter," see Pavel G. Rogoznyi, "The Russian Orthodox Church during the First World War and Revolutionary Turmoil, 1914-1921," in *Russian Culture in War and Revolution, Book 1: Popular Culture, the Arts, and Institutions*, ed. Murray Frame et al. (Bloomington, IN: Slavica Press, 2014), 352.
4. Catherine Evtuhov, "The Church's Revolutionary Moment: Diocesan Congresses and Grassroots Politics in 1917," in Frame el al., *Russian Culture*, 384-402.
5. Boleslaw Szczesniak, ed. and trans., *The Russian Revolution and Religion: A Collection of Documents concerning the Suppression of Religion by the Communists, 1917-1925* (Notre Dame, IN: University of Notre Dame Press, 1959), 235-41. The collection is drawn from P. V. Gidulianov, *Otdelenie tserkvi ot gosudarstva v SSSR: Polnyi sbornik dekretov, vedomstvennykh, rasporiazhenii i opredelenii Verkhsuda RSFSR i drugikh Sovetskikh Sotsialisticheskikh Respublik: USSR, BSSR, ZSFSR, Uzbekskoi i Turkmenskoi* (Moscow: Iuridicheskoe Izdatel'stvo, 1926).
6. Gidulianov, *Otdelenie tserkvi ot gosudarstva*, 34-35.
7. Ibid., 35-36.

8. Ibid., 37–39.
9. Ibid., 40–46.
10. Ibid., 96–98, "Letter of U.S. High Commissioner in Constantinople (Rear-Admiral Mark L. Bristol) to the Secretary of State concerning the Russian Church Abroad," October 10, 1922, document 49.
11. For a persecution narrative, see Dimitry Pospielovsky, *A History of Soviet Atheism in Theory, and Practice, and the Believer, vol. 1, A History of Marxist-Leninist Atheism and Soviet Antireligious Policies* (New York: St. Martin's Press, 1987). For recent tallies, see Gregory L. Freeze, "From Dechristianization to Laicization: State, Church, and Believers in Russia," *Canadian Slavonic Papers* 57, nos. 1–2 (March–June 2015): 6–34 (the figure on p. 10).
12. "Decree of the CSO [Committee of Soviet Organizations] of the Baikal Region on the Separation of School and Church (26 February 1918)/Document 1," in *Religion in the Soviet Union: An Archival Reader*, ed. and trans. Felix Corley (New York: New York University Press, 1996), 17–18; "Memorandum of the Bureau of the Baikal Regional Committee for People's Education to the Commissar of Internal Affairs of Baikal Region on the Taking of Measures to Put into Practice the Decree on the Separation of the Church from the State and the School from the Church (8 April 1918)/Document 2," ibid., 19; "Decree of the Nerchinsk Extraordinary Investigation Commission on the Arrest of the Priest Znamensky for a Counter-Revolutionary Speech" (28 April 1918)/Document 3," ibid., 20.
13. Bohdan Bociurkiw, "The Formulation of Religious Policy in the Soviet Union," *Journal of Church and State* 28, no. 3 (1986): 431. See also Philip Walters, "A Survey of Soviet Religious Policy," in *Religious Policy in the Soviet Union*, ed. Sabrina Ramet (Cambridge: Cambridge University Press, 1993), 3–30.
14. Szczesniak, *The Russian Revolution and Religion*, document 11, p. 49.
15. Quoted in Jonathan W. Daly, "Storming the Last Citadel: The Bolshevik Assault on the Church, 1922," in *The Bolsheviks in Russian Society: The Revolution and the Civil Wars*, ed. Vladimir Brovkin (New Haven, CT: Yale University Press, 1997), 237, from "Lenin to Molotov, 9–21 April 1921," *Leninskii sbornik* 35 (1945): 233.
16. For a definitive look at the church confiscations, see Daly, "Storming the Last Citadel," 235–68. For a contemporary European perspective, see Francis McCullagh, *The Bolshevik Persecution of Christianity* (London: John Murray, 1924). On the pogroms, see "Report of the U.S. Commissioner in Riga, April 21, 1922," in Szczesniak, *The Russian Revolution and Religion*, document 28, pp. 70–71.
17. "To Comr. Stalin, Secretary of the CC of the RCP," 10 April, 1923, in Corley, *Religion in the Soviet Union*, document 15, pp. 36–37. On Catholics under the Soviet regime, see Dennis Dunn, *The Catholic Church and Russia: Popes, Patriarchs, Tsars, and Commissars* (Burlington, VT: Ashgate, 2004).
18. Sean McMeekin, *History's Greatest Heist: The Looting of Russia by the Bolsheviks* (New Haven, CT: Yale University Press, 2009), 211, 212, 219. See also McCullagh, *The Bolshevik Persecution of Christianity*, 12.
19. Freeze, "From Dechristianization to Laicization," 7.
20. Ibid., 10.
21. Quoted in Freeze, "From Dechristianization to Laicization," 11, from *Derzhavnyi archive Zhytomyrskoi oblasti* (DAZhO), f. 5-18920, op. 2, d. 5870, l. 67 (protocol, November 20, 1922).
22. Ibid., 12.
23. Ibid., 7.
24. Heather Coleman, *Russian Baptists and Spiritual Revolution, 1905–1929* (Bloomington, IN: Indiana University Press, 2005), 156. Note especially Coleman's comprehensive bibliography. For a recent study of the theology and influence of a leading Evangelical, especially the impact of Keswick spirituality, see Gregory L. Nichols, *The Development of Russian Evangelical Spirituality: A Study of Ivan V. Kargel, 1849–1937* (Eugene, OR: Pickwick Publications, 2011).
25. KPSS v rezoliutsiiakh i resheniiakh c"ezdov, konferentsii i plenumov TsK (Moscow: Gospolitizdat, 1954), 2:52, quoted in Szczesniak, *The Russian Revolution and Religion*, 22.
26. Marc Raeff, *Russia Abroad: A Cultural History of the Russian Emigration, 1919–1939* (New York: Oxford University Press, 1990). On the YMCA, see Matthew Miller, *The American YMCA and*

Russian Culture: The Preservation and Expansion of Orthodox Christianity, 1900–1940 (Lanham, MD: Lexington Books, 2013).

27. Nikolai Berdiaev, *The Russian Revolution* (London: Sheed & Ward, 1931), 60. For insights on Berdiaev and church and revolution in Russia, see James Cracraft, "Church and Revolution in Russia," *Modern Greek Studies Yearbook* 12–13 (1996–1997): 21–34.

28. Berdiaev, *The Russian Revolution*, 46.

29. Besides his two massive trilogies, published in exile (and now translated into English), Bulgakov's *Dva grada: Issledovaniia o prirode obshchestvennykh idealov* (St. Petersburg: Izd-vo Russkogo khristianskogo gumanitarnogo instituta, 1997) is the best collection of his early work. Why his anthropology "symphony" has been reduced to one of its movements (sophiology) is a debate for another time.

30. Dominic Erdozain, *The Soul of Doubt: The Religious Roots of Unbelief from Luther to Marx* (New York: Oxford University Press, 2015), 7–8. Also Philip Boobbyer, *Conscience, Dissent, and Reform in Soviet Russia* (London: Routledge, 2005). On secularization more generally, see David Nash, "Reconnecting Religion with Social and Cultural History: Secularization's Failure as a Master Narrative," *Cultural and Social History* 1, no. 3 (2004): 302–25; Timothy Larsen, *The Slain God: Anthropologists and the Christian Faith* (Oxford: Oxford University Press, 2014) and *Crisis of Doubt: Honest Faith in Nineteenth-Century England* (Oxford: Oxford University Press, 2006); Charles Taylor, *A Secular Age* (Cambridge, MA: Harvard University Press, 2007).

31. Rogoznyi, "The Russian Orthodox Church," 372, quoting O. Iu. Vasil'eva, comp., *Russkaia pravoslavnaia tserkov' i kommunisticheskoe gosudarstvo, 1917–1941: Dokumenty i fotomaterialy*, ed. Ia. N. Shchapov (Moscow: Bibleisko-Bogoslovskii Institut Sv. Apostola Andreia, 1996), 1005.

Notes to Chapter 2: Combating God and Grandma

1. Thanks to Michael Bourdeaux, Wallace Daniel, Dominic Erdozain, April French, Adina Johnson, and Larisa Seago for helpful comments and suggestions. Thanks also to the Keston Center for Religion, Politics, and Society at Baylor University where initial thoughts about this essay were shared at the 2016 Keston Lecture.

2. Karl Marx, Introduction to *A Contribution to the Critique of Hegel's Philosophy of Right* (1844), ed. Andy Blunden and Matthew Carmody, Marxists.org, at https://www.marxists.org/archive/marx/works/1843/critique-hpr/intro.htm; Vladimir Lenin, "Religion and Socialism (1905)," *Collected Works* (Moscow: Progress Publishers, 1965), 10:83–87, Lenin Internet Archive, https://www.marxists.org/archive/lenin/works/1905/dec/03.htm.

3. For an overview of the field, see essays in *The Journal of the History of Children and Youth* 1, no. 1 (Winter 2008). Pivotal works on Russia, children, and childhood history include Lisa Kirschenbaum, *Small Comrades: Revolutionizing Childhood in Soviet Russia, 1917–1932* (London: Routledge-Falmer, 2001) and Catriona Kelly, *Children's World: Growing Up in Russia, 1890–1991* (New Haven, CT: Yale, 2007).

4. Felix Corley, *Religion in the Soviet Union: An Archival Reader* (New York: New York University Press, 1996), 13.

5. See, for example, Marcia J. Bunge, "The Child, Religion, and the Academy: Developing Robust Theological and Religious Understandings of Children and Childhood," *The Journal of Religion* 86, no. 4 (October 2006): 549–79, and Marcia J. Bunge and Don S. Browning, eds., *Children and Childhood in World Religions: Primary Sources and Texts* (New Brunswick, NJ: Rutgers University Press, 2009).

6. Lewis H. Siegelbaum, "Introduction: Mapping Private Spheres in the Soviet Context," in Siegelbaum, ed., *Borders of Socialism: Private Spheres of Soviet Russia* (New York: Palgrave Macmillan, 2006), 1–3.

7. Corley, *Religion in the Soviet Union*, 3.

8. "Programma Rossiiskoi sotsial-demokraticheskoi rabochei partii, 1903," in *Zakonodatel'stvo o religioznykh kul'takh: Sbornik materialov i dokumentov* (Moscow: Iuridicheskaia literatura, 1971), 20–21.

9. First quote from William Husband, *"Godless Communists": Atheism and Society in Soviet Russia, 1917–1932* (DeKalb: Northern Illinois University Press, 2000), 47; second quote from "Ob otdelenii tserkvi ot gosudarstva i shkoly ot tserkvi, dekret Soveta Narodnykh Komissarov ot 23 ianvaria 1918 g.," in *Zakonodatel'stvo o religioznykh kul'takh*, 54.

10. Cathy Frierson and Semyon Vilensky, *Children of the Gulag* (New Haven, CT: Yale University Press, 2010), 26–28.

11. Frierson and Vilensky, *Children of the Gulag*, 73–74.

12. Examples of letters from priests' children, all of which reference numerous siblings, ibid., 74.

13. Kelly, *Children's World*, 30, 522–24; Husband, *"Godless Communists,"* 80. Nichols and Stavrou state that the Russian Orthodox Church (ROC) operated 46 percent of primary schools in Russia in 1905. Robert L. Nichols and Theofanis George Stavrou, *Russian Orthodoxy under the Old Regime* (Minneapolis: University of Minnesota Press, 1978), 7.

14. "Decree of the Communist State Organization of the Baikal Region on the Separation of School and Church, 26 February 1918," in Corley, *Religion in the Soviet Union*, 17.

15. Glennys Young, *Power and the Sacred in Revolutionary Russia: Religious Activists in the Village* (University Park: Pennsylvania State University Press, 1997), 75.

16. Susan Reid, "The Meaning of Home: 'The Only Bit of the World You Can Have to Yourself,'" in Siegelbaum, *Borders of Socialism*, 152.

17. Kirschenbaum, *Small Comrades*, 161. Gorky's beehive analogy in the next sentence is quoted in Kirschenbaum, 162.

18. Herschel Alt and Edith Alt, *Russia's Children: A First Report on Child Welfare in the Soviet Union* (New York: Bookman Associates, 1959), 94.

19. Literally: the 1900 Civil Code gave parents absolute rights and control over their children. Kelly, *Children's World*, 27.

20. Ibid., 62.

21. Catriona Kelly, "'Shaping the Future Race': Regulating the Daily Life of Children in Early Soviet Russia," in *Everyday Life in Early Soviet Russia: Taking the Revolution Inside*, ed. Christina Kiaer and Eric Naiman (Bloomington: Indiana University Press, 2006), 257.

22. Liubov Denisova, *Rural Women in the Soviet Union and Post-Soviet Russia*, trans. Irina Mukhina (New York: Routledge, 2010), 165.

23. Kelly, *Children's World*, 371.

24. Kelly, "'Shaping the Future Race,'" 259.

25. Kelly, *Children's World*, 76. She points out the "emboldened, politicized" children in the 1920s literature of Mikhail Zoshchenko, Vera Inber, and Evgenii Zamiatin, in Kelly, "'Shaping the Future Race,'" 273–74.

26. Husband, *"Godless Communists,"* 80.

27. Sonja Luehrmann, *Secularism Soviet Style: Teaching Atheism and Religion in a Volga Republic* (Bloomington: Indiana University Press, 2011), 208.

28. Kelly, "'Shaping the Future Race,'" 256. Trotsky's quote from 1923.

29. Ia. A. Karpovskii, quoted in David E. Powell, *Antireligious Propaganda in the Soviet Union: A Study of Mass Persuasion* (Cambridge, MA: The MIT Press, 1975), 72. Karpovskii: "Children are not born atheists or believers, they become one or the other under the influence of their environment or upbringing."

30. Corley, *Religion in the Soviet Union*, 50.

31. Husband, *"Godless Communists,"* 80; "RSFSR NKVD, 22 Sept. 1923 letter to Yaroslavsky, head of CSCS, from Ia. Peters, GPU East Division," in Corley, *Religion in the Soviet Union*, 40.

32. Powell, *Antireligious Propaganda*, 37; Husband, *"Godless Communists,"* 80; "Letters on Method" from Narkompros, 1926, in Kelly, "'Shaping the Future Race,'" 267.

33. Quoted in David E. Fishman, "Judaism in the USSR, 1917–1930: The Fate of Religious Education," in *Jews and Jewish Life in Russia and the Soviet Union*, ed. Yaacov Ro'i (Essex, England: Frank Cass, 1995), 252.

34. Fishman, "Judaism in the USSR," 251–53. The *haderim* went underground for a few years, funded by the American Jewish community, then disappeared entirely.

35. Denisova, *Rural Women,* 165, 73.

36. Ibid., 133.

37. Husband, *"Godless Communists,"* 80, 82.

38. Ibid., 84–85.

39. Young, *Power and the Sacred,* 76; Husband, *"Godless Communists,"* 84–85.

40. Young, *Power and the Sacred,* 164–65; William C. Fletcher, *A Study in Survival: The Church in Russia, 1927–1943* (New York: Macmillan, 1965), 46.

41. "Commission to Establish Separation of Church and State Protocol no. 102, 27 June 1928," in Corley, *Religion in the Soviet Union,* 60.

42. "O religioznykh ob"edineniiakh, postanovlenie VTsIK i SNK RSFSR ot 8 aprelia 1929 g.," in *Zakonodatel'stvo o religioznykh kul'takh,* 83–97.

43. Irina Korovushkina Paert, "Memory and Survival in Stalin's Russia: Old Believers in the Urals during the 1930s–50s," in *On Living Through Soviet Russia,* ed. Daniel Bertaux, Paul Thompson, and Anna Rotkirch (London: Routledge, 2004), 198.

44. Paert, "Memory and Survival," 198.

45. Frierson and Vilensky, *Children of the Gulag,* 156–62.

46. Nathaniel Davis, *A Long Walk to Church: A Contemporary History of Russian Orthodoxy,* 2nd. ed. (Boulder, CO: Westview Press, 2003), 12–13.

47. Fletcher, *A Study in Survival,* 114; Yaacov Ro'i, *Islam in the Soviet Union: From the Second World War to Gorbachev* (New York: Columbia University Press, 2000), 353.

48. Miriam Dobson, "Child Sacrifice in the Soviet Press: Sensationalism and the 'Sectarian' in the Post-Stalin Era," *Russian Review* 73, no. 2 (April 2014): 243.

49. Denisova, *Rural Women,* 135.

50. A four-month campaign from July to November 1954 was followed up by an extended, lengthy campaign beginning in 1959. See "O krupnykh nedostatkakh v nauchno-ateisticheskoi propaganda i merakh ee uluchsheniia, postanovlenie TsK KPSS ot 7 iiulia 1954 g." and "Ob oshibkakh v provedenii nauchno-ateisticheskoi propagandy sredi naseleniia, postanovlenie TsK KPSS of 10 noiabria 1954 g.," in *Zakonodatel'stvo o religioznykh kul'takh,* 34–39, 40–45.

51. See, for example, "Otchetnyi doklad tsentral'nogo komiteta XXII s"ezdu partii" and "O meropriiatiiakh po usileniiu ateisticheskogo vospitaniia naseleniia," in *Zakonodatel'stvo o religioznykh kul'takh,* 46, 47–51.

52. Constantin Prokhorov, "The State and the Baptist Churches in the USSR (1960–1980)," in *Counter-Cultural Communities: Baptistic Life in Twentieth-Century Europe,* ed. Keith G. Jones and Ian M. Randall (Eugene, OR: Wipf & Stock, 2008), 13; Corley, Religion in the Soviet Union, 184–85; Denisova, Rural Women, 137; Luehrmann, *Secularism Soviet Style,* 207.

53. Quoted from *Izvestiia* in Donald A. Lowrie and William C. Fletcher, "Khrushchev's Religious Policy, 1959–1964," in *Aspects of Religion in the Soviet Union, 1917–1967,* ed. Richard H. Marshall (Chicago: University of Chicago Press, 1971), 145.

54. Joshua Rothenberg, "The Legal Status of Religion," in Marshall, *Aspects of Religion,* 87; "Kostroma Plan of Work for CAROC and CARC, 1964," in Corley, *Religion in the Soviet Union,* 236.

55. Powell, *Antireligious Propaganda,* 43.

56. Peter H. Juviler, "The Family in the Soviet System," *The Carl Beck Papers in Russian and East European Studies,* no. 306 (1984): 13.

57. Moor, "Okhraniaite detei ot tsepkikh lap baptistskikh i evangelistskikh proidokh" [Protect your children from the tenacious clutches of the of the Baptist and Evangelical scoundrels], *Bezbozhnik u stanka* 5-6 (1928), cover. Moor's illustration also appeared as a poster.

58. N. B. Terpsikhorov, "Religiia—iad; beregi rebiat" [Religion is poison; protect the children], 1930. Poster Collection, RU/SU 650A, Hoover Institution Archives, Stanford University.

59. See, for example, Travin, "—Babushka, a chto s Serezhei?," in *My—ateisti!, comp.* Boevoi Karandash (Leningrad: Izd. Khudozhnik RSFSR, 1979), 2; Kaminskii, "Pro papu, mamu, vaniu i

prikhodiashchuiu nianiu," in *Oruzhiem satiry po sueveriiat i predrassudkam, comp.* Boevoi Karandash (Leningrad: Izd. Khudozhnik RSFSR, 1985), 15; Zhelobinskii, "On ne 'protiv' i ne 'za,' prosto on otvel glaza," in Boevoi Karandash, *Oruzhiem*, 1.

60. I. V. Trunev, "Sekta" [Sect], 1975. Keston Poster ID 06keston-pos-00031. Keston Center for Religion, Politics, and Society, Baylor University.

61. V. A. Travin, "Sveta Bozh'ego ne vidish'..." [You cannot see God's light], 1975, Keston Poster ID 06keston-pos-00034, Keston Center for Religion, Politics, and Society, Baylor University.

62. See, for example, Donald J. Raleigh, *Soviet Baby Boomers: An Oral History of Russia's Cold War Generation* (Oxford: Oxford University Press, 2012), 43; David Mace and Vera Mace, *The Soviet Family* (Garden City, NY: Doubleday, 1963), 251; Kelly, *Children's World*, 376; Victoria Semenova and Paul Thompson, "Family Models and Transgenerational Influences: Grandparents, Parents, and Children in Moscow and Leningrad from the Soviet to the Market Era," in Bertaux et al., On Living Through Soviet Russia, 136.

63. Semenova and Thompson, "Family Models," 129; Ariela Lowenstein, "Solidarity and Conflicts in Coresidence of Three-Generational Immigrant Families from the Former Soviet Union," *Journal of Aging Studies* 16, no. 3 (2002): 229, 231.

64. A definite tendency toward nuclear families was evident in the Soviet era, but the extended, three-generation household was so common that the authors call it a unique feature of Russian society. Sergey Afontsev, Gijs Kessler, Andrei Markevich, Victoria Tyazhelnikova, Timur Valetov, "The Urban Household in Russia and the Soviet Union, 1900–2000: Patterns of Family Formation in a Turbulent Century," *The History of the Family* 13, no. 2 (2008): 192.

65. Semenova and Thompson, "Family Models," 128–29.

66. Ro'i, *Islam*, 441–42.

67. Afontsev et al., "The Urban Household," 189, 191.

68. Mace and Mace, in The Soviet Family, 257, state that in 1931, at least 10 percent of infants and perhaps as many as 20 percent could be accommodated in nurseries; Alt and Alt, Russia's Children, 101, gives a figure of 12–15 percent for the late 1950s; Yulia Gradskova states that up to 65 percent of children were placed by the mid-1980s in Gradskova, "'Supporting Genuine Development of the Child': Public Childcare Centers versus Family in Post-Soviet Russia," in *And They Lived Happily Ever After: Norms and Everyday Practices of Family and Parenthood in Russia and Eastern Europe*, ed. Helen Carlbäck, Yulia Gradskova, and Zhanna Kravchenko (Budapest: Central European University Press, 2012), 169.

69. Afontsev et al., "The Urban Household," 184–85.

70. Dobson, "Child Sacrifice," 246–50.

71. See, for example, Denisova, *Rural Women*, 133.

72. Semenova and Thompson, "Family Models," 130, on kids "educating" their grandmothers about urban life.

73. Reid, "The Meaning of Home," 145, 147; Juviler, "The Family in the Soviet System," 38; Salvatore Imbrogno, "Changes in the Collective Family in the Soviet Union: A Comparative Perspective," *International Social Work* 29, no. 4 (1986): 336–37; Deborah A. Field, "Irreconcilable Differences: Divorce and Conceptions of Private Life in the Khrushchev Era," *Russian Review* 57, no. 4 (October 1998): 600.

74. Lowrie and Fletcher, "Khrushchev's Religious Policy," 143.

75. Ro'i, *Islam*, 510–11.

76. Raleigh, Soviet Baby Boomers, 42; Paert, "Memory and Survival," 207; Constantin Prokhorov, "Russian Baptists and Orthodoxy, 1960–1990: A Comparative Study of Theology, Liturgy, and Traditions" (PhD diss., University of Wales International Baptist Theological Seminary, 2011), 142.

77. Kelly, *Children's World*, 390.

78. Field, "Irreconcilable Differences," 601–2.

79. Wallace Daniel, *Russia's Uncommon Prophet: Father Aleksandr Men and His Times* (DeKalb: Northern Illinois University Press, 2016), 167.

80. Kelly, *Children's World*, 528; Powell, *Antireligious Propaganda*, 60.

81. Field, "Irreconcilable Differences," 600.

82. On student maltreatment, see Alexander Veinbergs, "Lutheranism and Other Denominations in the Baltic Regions," in Marshall, *Aspects of Religion*, 410; Michael Bourdeaux and Katherine Murray, *Young Christians in Russia* (London: Lakeland, 1976), 139, 147–49, 153; Corley, *Religion in the Soviet Union*, 319–20; Powell, *Antireligious Propaganda*, 103; Prokhorov, *Russian Baptists*, 288. Mikhail Men', on the other hand, recalls teachers in his village school as understanding and fairly tolerant of his beliefs. Daniel, *Russia's Uncommon Prophet*, 167.

83. Sheila Fitzpatrick and Robert Gellately, eds., *Accusatory Practices: Denunciation in Modern European History, 1789-1989* (Chicago: University of Chicago Press, 1997).

84. Corley, *Religion in the Soviet Union*, 72, 171; Luehrmann, *Secularism Soviet Style*, 100, on parents having to make up an answer to "what is that?" questions about a church; children's letters in Deborah Hoffman, ed., *The Littlest Enemies: Children in the Shadow of the Gulag* (Bloomington, IN: Slavica, 2008), 125, discuss the NKVD center at Danilov. The NKVD, or People's Commissariat for Internal Affairs, functioned as the Communist Party's police.

85. See fig. 2 and fig. 4.

86. Raleigh, *Soviet Baby Boomers*, 42; Paert, "Memory and Survival," 211; Corley, *Religion in the Soviet Union*, 23.

87. Denisova, *Rural Women,* 141.

88. Ibid., 137.

89. Prokhorov, *Russian Baptists*, 265–66, 291; Paert, "Memory and Survival," 210–11.

90. Evdokia Alekseevna Shevchuk, oral history interview by April French, May 4, 2015, Iskitim (Novosibirsk oblast). April French, "Evangelicals and Education in Late Soviet Siberia: Children as Sites of Conflict between Believing Parents and the Party/State Apparatus," unpublished paper presented at ASEEES National Convention, November 2015, 15.

91. Frierson and Vilensky, *Children of the Gulag*, 142; Corley, *Religion in the Soviet Union*, 75; Ro'i, *Jews and Jewish Life*, 259; Fletcher, *A Study in Survival*, 88.

92. Frierson and Vilensky, *Children of the Gulag*, 29.

93. Hoffman, *The Littlest Enemies*, 33.

94. Kirschenbaum, *Small Comrades*, 174.

Notes to Chapter 3: Persecution, Collusion, and Liberation

1. For more reflections on this subject see Michael Bourdeaux, *Opium of the People* (London: Faber and Faber, 1965), 107–8.

2. Michael Bourdeaux, *Opium of the People* (London: Faber & Faber, 1965), 56.

3. Michael Bourdeaux, *Patriarch and Prophets: Persecution of the Russian Orthodox Church Today* (London: Macmillan, 1969), 17–20 gives the details.

4. Ibid., 17

5. *Bakinski Rabochi* [Baku worker], June 19, 1963, quoted in Michael Bourdeaux, *Patriarch and Prophets: Persecution of the Russian Orthodox Church today* (London: Macmillan, 1969), 23

6. Though much later an East-West Relations Advisory Committee was set up by the British Council of Churches in London, of which I remained a member until it was dissolved with the advent of Mikhail Gorbachev's *perestroika* twenty-five years later.

7. *Literaturnaia gazeta*, August 23, 1956, quoted in Bourdeaux, *Patriarch and Prophets*, 129

8. Alexander Solzhenitsyn, *One Day in the Life of Ivan Denisovich* (London: Penguin, 1963), 25.

9. Translation in Bourdeaux, *Patriarch and Prophets,* 154–55.

10. Archbishop Ermogen quotes this in his deposition to the patriarch of Moscow of November 1967. See Bourdeaux, *Patriarch and Prophets*, 239.

11. Ibid., 239.

12. Ibid., 242.

13. Bourdeaux, *Patriarch and Prophets*, contains many related texts. See especially 164–77.

NOTES TO CHAPTER 4   239

14. A substantial portion of these long texts is published in Bourdeaux, *Patriarch and Prophets*, 189–223, as well as the main reactions to the documents, 223–38.
15. Ibid., 195.
16. Ibid., 189.
17. This text—in full—is printed in Bourdeaux, *Religious Ferment in Russia: Protestant Opposition to Soviet Religious Policy* (London: Macmillan, 1968), 105–13.
18. Bourdeaux, *Patriarch and Prophets*, 191.
19. *Ibid.*, 193.
20. Ibid., 198.
21. Ibid., 199.
22. Ibid., 226–27.
23. Ibid., 255–303.
24. Bourdeaux, *Patriarch and Prophets*, 263–64.
25. "With Love and Anger," ibid., 275–88.
26. *Religion in Communist Lands*, no. 4 (1979): 234–37.
27. Michael Bourdeaux *Risen Indeed: Lessons in Faith from the USSR* (London: Darton, Longman & Todd, 1983), 32.
28. Ibid., 33.
29. Ibid., 35.
30. For a detailed discussion of the "Nairobi document" and its aftermath, see Jane Ellis, *The Russian Church: A Contemporary History* (London: Routledge, 1986), 355–368
31. Ibid.
32. Ibid.
33. See Ellis, ibid.
34. Michael Bourdeaux, *Gorbachev, Glasnost, and the Gospel* (London: Hodder & Stoughton, 1990), 9–10, gives a fuller account of these events.
35. *Religious Liberty in the Soviet Union: WCC & USSR—A Post-Nairobi Documentation*, published in English and German by the three institutes together.
36. Erich Weingärtner, *Human Rights on the Ecumenical Agenda* (Geneva: Commission of the Church on International Affairs, 1983).
37. *Pravda*, February 26, 1986. Quoted in Michael Bourdeaux, *The Gospel's Triumph Over Communism* (Minneapolis, MN: Bethany House Publishers, 1991), 36.
38. "Celebration of the Millennium of the Baptism of Rus," press release no.1, Moscow Patriarchate, 1988, p. 5.
39. Bourdeaux, *Gorbachev, Glasnost, and the Gospel*, 58.
40. From a typescript of the speech as circulated by the Moscow Patriarchate and quoted in Bourdeaux, *Gorbachev, Glasnost, and the Gospel*, 61.
41. A fuller account of these events, as witnessed by the present author, is in Bourdeaux, *Gorbachev, Glasnost, and the Gospel*, 61–63.
42. See BBC script of program broadcast on Radio 4, September 7, 2008.

Notes to Chapter 4: "I am a fighter by nature"

1. Elena Volkova, interview by author, September 12, 2015, Moscow.
2. Gleb Pavlovich Iakunin, *Khvalebnyi primitiv iurodivyi v chest' Boga, mirozdan'ia, rodiny: Poema*, with an introductory essay by Elena Volkova (Moscow: Biblioteka PravLit, 2008).
3. Ibid., 16.
4. Gleb Pavlovich Iakunin, "Ot avtora," in Iakunin, *Khvalebnyi primitiv iurodivyi*, 10.
5. Ibid.
6. Ibid., 11.
7. Fr. Aleksandr Men made this distinction between magic and faith the subject of the second volume of his *History of Religion: Istoriia religii: V poiskakh puti, istiny, i zhizni*, vol. 2, *Magizm i*

Edinobozhie: Religioznyi put' chelovechestva do epokhi velikikh Uchitelei [History of religion: *In search of the way, the truth, and the life,* vol. 2, *Magic and monotheism: The religious path of humanity up to the epoch of the great teachers*] (1971; repr., Moscow: Izd-vo Sovetsko-Britanskogo sovmestnogo predpriiatiia "Slovo," 1992).

    8. Iakunin, *Khvalebnyi primitiv iurodivyi*, 85–89. Iakunin's criticisms of the institutional Church—its corruption, its silence, refusal to stand up on behalf of religious believers, and its tight relationship with the regime—spoke to what had led religious believers away from the official Church. As Gregory L. Freeze has convincingly argued, "The Soviet regime sought to secularize by dechurching, but the net effect was not to dechristianize but to laicize, to free popular Orthodoxy from clerical control and to lay the ground for a dechurched religious revival in post-Soviet Russia." Gregory L. Freeze, "From Dechristianization to Laicization: State, Church, and Believers in Russia," *Canadian Slavonic Papers* 57, nos. 1 and 2 (March–June 2015): 7.

    9. Elena Volkova, "Poeticheskii manifest Pravoslavnoi reformatsii," in Iakunin, *Khvalebnyi primitiv iurodivyi*, 6.

    10. Ibid.

    11. Feliks Svetlov and Zoia Krakhmal'nikova, "Obrashchenie. Tat'iana Velikanova i o. Gleb Iakunin arestovany!," Moscow, November 1979, Arkhiv Samizdata, in Baylor University's Keston Archive, SU/Ort/8/2, Iakunin file.

    12. See Nigel Wade's excellent article, "Dissident Priest Jailed," in the *Daily Telegraph*, August 29, 1980, in Keston Archive, SU/Ort 8/2, Iakunin file.

    13. Ibid. Article 7 of the Helsinki Accords states, "The participating States will respect human rights and fundamental freedoms, including the freedom of thought, conscience, religion or belief, for all without distinction as to race, sex, language or religion." Thirty-five nations, including the Soviet Union, signed the Helsinki Accords. "Helsinki Accords, Article 7," August 1, 1975, https://berkleycenter.georgetown.edu/quotes/helsinki-accords-article-7.

    14. Wade, "Dissident Priest Jailed."

    15. For details of the courtroom and proceedings, see, "The Trial of Gleb Yakunin," *A Chronicle of Current Events* 58, no. 3 (November 1980), http://chronicle6883.wordpress.com/2016/01/12/58-3-the-trial-of-gleb-yakunin/; Inokentii, "Rasprava," September 1980, in Keston Archive, SU/Ort/8/2, Iakunin file, and, in the same file, "Protsess nad sviashchennikom G. Iakuninym/Po vospominaniiam rodnykh i znakomykh."

    16. "Father Gleb Yakunin's Trial," House of Commons Hansard Archive, UK Parliament, HL Deb, October 6, 1980, vol. 413, cc 176–8WA, http://hansard.millbanksystems.com/written_answers/1980/oct/06/father-gleb-yakunin-trial.

    17. Lubentsova presided over the trials of the Red Square "demonstrators" in 1968; Vladimir Bukovskii in 1972; and Iurii Orlov in 1978. In all three trials, she handed down severe sentences. "Trial of Gleb Yakunin."

    18. Ibid. Archimandrite Iosif, who testified, he said, as a private citizen, maintained that Iakunin had spread abroad false information "about the conditions of religious believers in the Soviet Union." Archimandrite Iosif referenced the appeal written by Iakunin and Lev Regelson to the World Council of Churches, in 1975, which is discussed later in this article. "With deep regret," Archimandrite Iosif said, "I must say that the slanderous letter produced a certain negative reaction among some of the participants at the Assembly, as there were some delegates who were ill-informed about the true situation of the Russian Orthodox Church in the Soviet Union." TASS, "Interview with Archimandrite Iosif: Reply to Western Propaganda," September 19, 1980, in Keston Archive, SU/Ort 8/2, Iakunin file.

    19. "Trial of Gleb Yakunin"; "Protsess nad sviashchennikom G. Iakuninym."

    20. Caroline Cox, *Cox's Book of Modern Saints and Martyrs* (New York: Continuum, 2006), 92.

    21. "Trial of Gleb Yakunin"; "Protsess nad sviashchennikom G. Iakuninym."

    22. Anatolii Levitin-Krasnov, "Sud'ba Iakunina i Kapitanchuka pod ugroznoi," *Russkaia mysl'*, January 1, 1978, p. 2, in Keston Archive, SU/Ort/8/2, Iakunin file.

    23. *Bulletin of the Swedish Mission*, no. 3 (1979), p. 2, in Keston Archive, SU/Ort 8/2, Iakunin file.

24. According to Anatolii Levitin-Krasnov, the documents the KGB confiscated related to the case of Vladimir Poresh, one of the main representatives of the study group that Aleksandr Ogorodnikov created in 1974. Poresh was arrested in August 1979. Anatolii Levitin-Krasnov, "KGB Search Linked to Poresh Investigation," October 4, 1979, in Keston Archive, SU/Ort 8/2, Iakunin file.

25. "Trial of Gleb Yakunin," *Chronicle of Current Events*.

26. Elena Volkova, interview by author, September 12, 2015, Moscow; Zoia Afanas'evna Maslenikova, *Zhizn' ottsa Aleksandra Menia* (Moscow: Izd-vo Pristsel's, 1995), 117–19.

27. Mitrofan Vasil'evich Lodyzhenskii, *Sverkhoznaniia i puti ego dostizheniiu: Indusskaia redzhaiogo i khristianskoe podrizhnichestvo*, vol. 1 of *Misticheskaia trilogiia* (Petrograd: Ekaterininskaia tipografiia, 1915). Lodyzhenskii (1852–1917), Russian theologian and theosophist, wrote a three-volume study of Christian mystics and mysticism in Western and Eastern religions at the beginning of the nineteenth century. The first volume explores mysticism in Eastern Christianity and its relationship to what he calls higher consciousness.

28. See, for these and other details of Gleb Iakunin's early childhood, Anatoli Levitin-Krasnov, "Father Gleb Yakunin and Lev Regelson," in *Letters from Moscow: Religion and Human Rights in the USSR*, ed. Jane Ellis (San Francisco: H. S. Dakin, 1978), 1–3.

29. Gleb Pavlovich Iakunin, interview by author, May 10, 2007, Moscow.

30. Ibid. Iakunin did not mention the identity of these fellow students, but Maslenikova describes the circle of friends in the institute that formed a close relationship around Aleksandr Men. They included, in addition to Iakunin, Viktor Alekseev and Oleg Drobinskii. See Maslenikova, *Zhizn' ottsa Aleksandra Menia*, 119.

31. Gleb Pavlovich Iakunin, interview by author, May 10, 2007, Moscow.

32. Ibid.

33. Ibid. Iakunin's conviction that the patriarchate did not represent the true Orthodox Church likely began at this time. As he would later write, "The Orthodox Church, founded in Rus' in 988, after 1927 existed only in the catacombs and in exile abroad." (Gleb Iakunin, *Istoricheskii put' pravoslavnogo talibanstva* [Moscow: Tip. IPO profsoiuzov Profizdat, 2002], 12).

34. These facts on Iakunin's early church service are drawn from Levitin-Krasnov, "Father Gleb Yakunin and Lev Regelson," 3; and Aleksii, metropolitan of Tallinn and Estonia, "Spravka osnovanii lichnogo dela, imeiushchegosia v Moskovskoi Patriarkhii," January 12, 1976, in Keston Archive, SU/Ort/8/2, Iakunin file.

35. Gleb Pavlovich Iakunin, interview by author, May 10, 2007, Moscow; Aleksandr Men', *O sebe: Vospominaniia, interv'iu, besedy, pis'ma* (Moscow: Zhizn' s Bogom, 2007), 111.

36. N. I. Eshliman and Gleb Yakunin, "An Open Letter to His Holiness, the Most Holy Patriarch of Moscow and All Russia," November 21, 1965, in *Patriarch and Prophets: Persecution of the Russian Orthodox Church Today*, ed. Michael Bourdeaux (New York: Praeger, 1970), 194–221, and "To the Chairman of the Presidium of the Supreme Soviet of the Union of Soviet Socialist Republics," in the same volume, 189–94.

37. Mikhail Vital'evich Shkarovskii, *Russkaia Pravoslavnaia Tserkov' v XX veke* (Moscow: Veche, Lepta, 2010), 272–75; Dimitry Pospielovsky, *Russkaia pravoslavnaia tserkov' v XX veke* (Moscow: Respublika, 1995), 349–53; Jane Ellis, *The Russian Orthodox Church: A Contemporary History* (1986; repr., New York: Routledge, 1988), 292–95.

38. Eshliman and Yakunin, "To the Chairman of the Presidium," 189–93.

39. Eshliman and Yakunin, "Open Letter to His Holiness," 203, 211.

40. Ibid., 209, 218–19.

41. Ibid.

42. Ibid., 211.

43. Ibid., 211–12.

44. Ibid., 227.

45. "The Resolution of His Holiness Patriarch Aleksi I," May 13, 1966, communicated through the office of the metropolitan of Krutitsy and Kolomna, diocesan bishop of Moscow, in Bourdeaux, *Patriarch and Prophets*, 226–27.

46. See Eshliman's obituary, "Nikolai I. Eshliman, Russian Priest Dies at 57," Special to the *New York Times*, June 14, 1985, in Keston Archive, SU/Ort 8/2, Iakunin file.

47. Fr. Gleb Iakunin, interview by author, May 10, 2007, Moscow.

48. Ibid.

49. Anonymous, "Father Gleb Yakunin," in Keston Archive, SU/Ort 8/2, Iakunin file.

50. Such events include the trial of Iulii Daniel and Andrei Siniavskii in Moscow in 1966, the suppression of the reform movement in Czechoslovakia in the summer of 1968, and workers' protests and strikes in Poland in 1976.

51. Nikolai Aleksandrovich Berdiaev, *Filosofiia svobody* (Moscow: Tip. A. I. Mamontova, 1911).

52. Elena Volkova, interview by author, September 12, 2015, Moscow.

53. Berdiaev is a central figure in Russia's religious renaissance that evolved from the writings of such leading writers as Fedor Dostoevsky, Vladimir Solov'ev, Aleksei Khomiakov, and Vasilii Rozanov. (See Alexander Schmemann's comments in *Ultimate Questions: An Anthology of Modern Russian Religious Thought* [Crestwood, NY: St. Vladimir's Seminary Press, 1977], 241). As students in Irkutsk, both Men and Iakunin read and studied their ideas. In different, but sometimes complementary ways, Berdiaev's conception of freedom influenced both young men. They became convinced that for the Church to have an effective voice in Russia's future, it had to be reformed.

54. Nikolai Aleksandrovich Berdiaev, *Self-Knowledge*, quoted in Nicolas Zernov, *The Russian Religious Renaissance of the Twentieth Century* (New York: Harper & Row, 1963), 153.

55. Berdiaev, *Filosofiia svobody*, iv, 17, 28, 61. Freedom, in this sense, is not unbridled license to act in any desired manner, but is guided by one's understanding of the Gospels and by the prophetic teachings of Jesus Christ.

56. Ibid., iii, 11, 61–62.

57. In his discussion of freedom, Berdiaev referenced Dostoevsky's "The Grand Inquisitor" in his novel *The Brothers Karamazov*. The Grand Inquisitor reproached Christ: "You desired the free love of man, that he should follow you freely, seduced and captivated by you" (ibid., 213). I have used the translation of the passage from Fedor Dostoevsky, *The Brothers Karamazov*, trans. and annotated Richard Pevear and Larissa Volokhonsky [New York: Farrar, Straus and Giroux, 1990], 255). In this passage, Berdiaev writes, Dostoevsky clearly showed the meaning of Christian freedom: "Man must carry the burden of freedom in order to be saved. Christianity offers freedom in Christ. Salvation through the use of compulsion is impossible and useless" (Berdiaev, *Filosofiia svobody*, 213–14).

58. Berdiaev was a member of the Russian Orthodox Church, but he did not unreservedly embrace its actions. He was dismayed by the subservient attitude to political power found in the large majority of priests and by the lack of courage of Church leaders, who did not stand up to the governing authorities. The Church, he maintained, must not submit to the government, or become part of the government, without losing its most precious gift, its internal freedom. "In the Church community, there is no place for compulsion, this kind of force is alien to the Church" (Berdiaev, *Filosofiia svobody*, 223). Berdiaev retained the right, as an independent person, to criticize the leaders of the Church for their subservience. He saw present-day religious life as filled with idolatry and the failure to remain true to what he called the "divine principle in life" (Ibid., 17; Nikolai Berdiaev, *The Destiny of Man* [New York: Harper, 1960], 134).

59. Gleb Yakunin, "Open Letter to Serafim, Metropolitan of Krutitsy and Kolomna," February 18, 1974, in Yakunin and Regelson, *Letters from Moscow*, 21.

60. Gleb Iakunin and Lev Regelson, "Obrashchenie k khristianam Portugalii," April 3, 1975, in Keston Archive, SU/Ort 8/2, Iakunin file. An English translation of the letter may be found in Yakunin and Regelson, *Letters from Moscow*, 29–31. Their appeal referenced the Most Holy Mother of God's foretelling, in Fatima, of the October 1917 Russian Revolution and the tragedies that soon followed.

61. Iakunin and Regelson, "Obrashchenie k khristianam Portugalii."

62. Ibid.

63. Iakunin wrote several other letters between the communication to the Church in Portugal and the next letter discussed below. They include Iakunin's "Politburo Ts.K.KPSS—Oktrytoe pis'mo," April 19, 1975, in Keston Archive, SU/Ort 8/2, Iakunin file, and in Yakunin and Regelson, *Letters from*

Moscow, 32-33. In it, Iakunin responded to the Soviet practice of the *subbotnik* or "Red Saturday," a day of voluntary labor required of the citizen on Lenin's birthday, April 22. In 1975, the *subbotnik* happened to fall on Easter Sunday. The required labor service on Easter would offend millions of believers, and Iakunin requested it be moved either to May 1 or November 7. Another letter was written by Gleb Yakunin, Viktor Kapitanchuk, and Lev Regelson, an "Appeal for the Glorification of Russian Martyrs in the USSR," May 25, 1975, in Yakunin and Regelson, *Letters from Moscow*, 34-40. The appeal encouraged the patriarch and church leaders to make preparations for the glorification of martyrs who had perished in the early years of the USSR. The authors proposed such glorification for Patriarch Tikhon, who had courageously supported the freedom of the Church and its separation from the Soviet government. The writers also underscored the sacrifices of six additional church leaders, who had died in the early Soviet period, and they criticized the government's support for church leaders, including Metropolitan Sergei, who in 1925 had compromised the Church.

64. Gleb Iakunin and Lev Regelson, "Obrashchenie k delegatam V Assembleia Vsemirnogo Soveta Tserkvei," October 16, 1975, Arkhiv Samizdata, no. 2380, in Keston Archive, Ort/SU/8/2, Iakunin file. An English language translation may be found in Yakunin and Regelson, *Letters from Moscow*, 41-50, and in *Religion in Communist Lands* 4, no. 1 (1976): 9-14. For accounts of the Appeal's reception by the Assembly, see David Kelly, "Nairobi: A Door Opened," *Religion in Communist Lands* 4, no. 1 (1976): 4-8, and Ellis, *Russian Orthodox Church*, 358-60.

65. Ellis, *Russian Orthodox Church*, 355.

66. Iakunin and Regelson, "Obrashchenie k delegatam V Assembleia."

67. Iakunin and Regelson cite psychiatrist Robert Coles's description of people in psychiatric hospitals, "Obrashchenie k delegatam V Assembleia."

68. Ibid.

69. See, for example, Ellis, *Russian Orthodox Church*, 350-61.

70. Iakunin and Regelson, "Obrashchenie k delegatam V Assembleia." In their use of the word "conscience," Iakunin and Regelson had in mind its moral and spiritual essence and its association with those qualities. See Philip Boobbyer's interesting discussion of this term (*sovest'*) and its distinction from the common Bolshevik usage of the terms "revolutionary conscience" and "consciousness" (*soznatel'nost'*), in *Conscience, Dissent, and Reform in Soviet Russia* (New York: Routledge, 2005), 27-28, 43.

71. Iakunin and Regelson, "Obrashchenie k delegatam V Assembleia."

72. "The Final Act of the Conference on Security and Cooperation in Europe," August 1, 1975, 14 I.L.M. 1292 (Helsinki Declaration), University of Minnesota, Human Rights Library, http//www1.umn.edu/humanrts/osce/basics/finact75.htm.

73. Peter Slezkine, "From Helsinki to Human Rights Watch: How an American Cold War Monitoring Group Became an International Human Rights Institution," *Humanity* 5, no. 3 (Winter 2014): 347.

74. "The Final Act."

75. Slezkine, "From Helsinki to Human Rights Watch," 348. See the interpretations by political leaders in the United States and the Soviet Union, in Patrick G. Vaughan, "Zbigniew Brzezinski and the Helsinki Final Act," in *The Crisis of Détente in Europe: From Helsinki to Gorbachev, 1975-1985*, ed. Leopoldo Nuti (New York: Routledge, 2009), 11-25, and, in the same volume, Svetlana Savranskaya, "Human Rights Movement in the USSR after the Signing of the Helsinki Final Act, and the Reaction of Soviet Authorities," 26-40; Sarah B. Snyder, *Human Rights Activism and the End of the Cold War: A Transnational History of the Helsinki Network* (Cambridge: Cambridge University Press, 2011), 28-29.

76. Slezkine, "From Helsinki to Human Rights Watch," 348-49; Ludmila Alexeyeva [Liudmila Alekseeva], *Soviet Dissent: Contemporary Movements for National, Religious, and Human Rights*, trans. Carol Pearce and John Glad (Middletown, CT: Wesleyan University Press, 1985), 335-37.

77. The Moscow Group's formal name was the "Public Group to Promote Fulfillment of the Helsinki Accords in the USSR" (Obshchestvennaia gruppa sodeistviia vypolneniiu khel'sinskikh soglashenii v SSSR). Its membership included, in addition to Orlov, Sakharov's wife Elena Bonner, Liudmila Alekseeva, Aleksandr Ginzburg, Anatolii Marchenko, Anatolii Shcharanskii, Petro Grigorenko, and

others ("Ob obrazovanii obshchestvennoi gruppy sodeistviia vypolneniiu Khel'sinkskikh soglashenii v SSSR, Moskovkaia khel'sinksksia gruppa," http://www.mhg.ru/history/14454FE).

78. Ibid.

79. Gleb Iakunin, interview by author, May 10, 2007, Moscow.

80. The Christian Committee for the Defense of Believers' Rights in the USSR (CCDBR), "Deklaratsiia ob obrazovanii i tseli komiteta," in Keston Archive, SU/12/11 4/1, file 1 of 2. In creating the Committee, the founders underscored their obligation to defend members of all denominations, because, the founders maintained, the Orthodox Church historically had enjoyed a privileged position in the Russian state, and they hoped to atone for the past abuses that the Church had inflicted on other denominations. In addition, while the Committee members apparently had wanted to create an interdenominational organization, they had decided for pragmatic reasons that their membership should be unidenominational. They made this decision, Jane Ellis writes, "chiefly, because it would be difficult to keep up communications with various groups of believers over long distances." Jane Ellis, "The Christian Committee for the Defence of Believers' Rights in the USSR," *Religion in Communist Lands* 11, no. 4 (1980): 279.

81. Iakunin, Khaibulin, and Kapitanchuk's response to the newly written Soviet Constitution of 1977 made very clear what they saw as the contradictions in communist theory. The Constitution, they wrote, "describes a Communist society as being one in which the best strivings of man are allowed to exist, but religious ideals, and ideals of spiritual and moral union of man with God and man with man through God are excluded." Gleb Iakunin, Varsonofii Khaibulin, and Viktor Kapitanchuk, "K predstoiateliam i episkopam khristianskikh tserkvei," July 3, 1977, in Keston Archive, SU/12/11, file 4/L.

82. Ibid.

83. Ibid.

84. Ibid.

85. Ibid. In addition, Iakunin, Khaibulin, and Kapitanchuk wanted an official party admission of the "fundamental incompatibility of religion and communism," and they proposed that the new Constitution guarantee the existence of religion under communism (ibid).

86. V. A. Kuroedov, *Religiia i tserkov' v sovetskom obshchestve*, 2nd ed. (Moscow: Politizdat 1984), 3-4.

87. Ibid., 18.

88. Gleb Yakunin, "Statement by a Member of the CCDBR in the USSR," in *Christian Committee for the Defence of Believers' Rights in Russia: A Selection of Documents in Translation*, vol. 13 of Dokumenty khristianskogo komiteta zashchity prav veruiushchikh v SSSR, ed. Alan Scarfe, trans. Maria Belaeffa (Glendale, CA: Door of Hope Press, 1982), 58.

89. Gleb Iakunin, interview by author, May 10, 2007, Moscow.

90. For example, see the case of Grigorii Vladimirovich Mitasov, an Orthodox Christian and a resident of Krasnoiarsk, in *Selection of Documents*, 58; and the cases of S. A. Redin and family, in Riazan; Galina Afanas'evna Ivashura in Lisichansk, Voroshilovgrad District; Tatiana Ivanovna Sorokhina, a Baptist-Pentacostal, in Taganrog, in *Selection of Documents*, 119-20, 121-22, 142-43. See also the case of Lidiia Zhdanovskaia, the wife of Anatolii Levitin-Krasnov and Gleb Iakunin's aunt, "The Relatives of Orthodox Priest Searched," in *Informationsdiest*, November 1979, p. 5, in Keston Archive, SU/Ort/8/2, Iakunin file.

91. Gleb Iakunin, Varsonofii Khaibulin, Viktor Kapitanchuk, and Vadim Shcheglov, "Soobshcheniia," in *Dokumenty khristianskogo komiteta zashchity prav veruishchikh v SSSR*, vol. 2 (San Francisco: Washington Research Center, 1978), 166.

92. Gleb Iakunin, Viktor Kapitanchuk, and Vadim Shcheglov of the CCDBR, and Vsevelod Kuvakin of the Committee for the Defense of Workers' Rights, "Zaiavlenie dlia pechati," May 29, 1978, in *Dokumenty khristianskogo komiteta*, 2:170. Originally published in samizdat, the appeal dealt with the case of the Jewish believer Iosif Begun, who was brought to trial in 1978.

93. Aleksandr Argentev, "Letter to Pimen, Most Holy Patriarch of Moscow and All Russia," written from Psychiatric Clinic No. 14, Moscow, July 21, 1976, in Keston Archive, SU/12/11.1, Individual Clergy file: Fr. Nikolai Eshliman, Fr. Nikolai Gainov, and Fr. Gleb Iakunin.

94. Ibid.

95. Argentev wrote to Patriarch Pimen, "Your holiness, be so good as to speak out for me! If it is impossible to speak out, then give your blessing, even silently, to my martyrdom for the faith" (ibid).

96. Anatolii Levitin-Krasnov, "Sud'ba Iakunina i Kapitanchuka pod ugrozoi," *Russkaia mysl'*, January 1, 1978, p. 2.

97. Boris Roshchin, "Svobody religii i klepki," *Literaturnaia gazeta*, April 13 and 20, 1977; "Freedom of Religion and the Slanderers," in Yakunin and Regelson, *Letters from Moscow*, 78–83.

98. Iakunin, the author maintained, acts not out of religious, but out of political motives. These intentions, he said, had always characterized Iakunin's behavior, dating back to his earlier letters in 1965. "Failures don't upset him," Roshchin wrote; Iakunin had simply moved on to a larger global arena. "He slanders the Soviet Union indefatigably" (Roshchin, "Svobody religii i klepki," *Literaturnaia gazeta*, April 20, 1977).

99. Ellis, *Russian Orthodox Church*, 422. On the same day as Iakunin's arrest, the KGB also arrested Tat'iana Mikhailovna Velikanova, a mathematician and a leading figure in the human rights movement. Velikanova served as an editor of *A Chronicle of Human Events*. Svetlov and Krakhmal'nikova, "Obrashchenie."

100. After a decade in which he voiced strong criticism of the Soviet government and, in the late 1970s, supported Fr. Gleb Iakunin, Dudko's "confession" came as a surprise to his many followers. On Dudko, see Dmitrii Dudko, "Paskhal'noe prevetsvie o. Dmitriia Dudko," *Russkaia mysl'*, May 5, 1977, p. 2; Janice A. Broun, "A Knock on the Door," *Scottish Catholic Observer*, August 8, 1977, p. 3; Oliver Bullough, *The Last Man in Russia: The Struggle to Save a Dying Nation* (New York: Basic Books, 2013), 173–78.

101. "Protsess nad sviashchennikom G. Iakuninym."

102. These details were recounted to me by Elena Volkova, a close family friend of Iakunin, interview by author, September 12, 2015, Moscow.

103. Arkhiv Samizdata no. 3779, in Keston Archive, SU/Ort 8/5, Iakunin file.

104. Iakunin was moved to Perm Camp 5 and fed intravenously ten days after he began the fast. *Keston News Service* 137, November 19, 1981, p. 2, in Keston Archive, SU Ort 8/2, Iakunin file; "Priest is Force Fed," *Church Times*, November 24, 1981, in the same file.

105. Nadezhda Mandelstam, *Hope against Hope: A Memoir*, trans. Max Hayward, with an introduction by Clarence Brown (New York: Atheneum, 1970), 333.

106. *Keston News Service* 217, January 24, 1985, p. 13, in Keston Archive, SU/Ort/8/2, Iakunin file; and *Keston News Service* 214, December 6, 1984, pp. 3–4, in the same file.

107. Iakunin, *Khvalebnyi primitiv iurodivyi*, 34–36. On the history of religion, Iakunin is very close to the theological perspectives of Fr. Aleksandr Men. Many lines in the poem refer directly to Fr. Aleksandr's views of history. Fr. Aleksandr held not a static, but a dynamic model of world history, one in "which the whole cosmos is in movement," constantly evolving toward something different from what existed earlier (Aleksandr Borisov, "Dukhovnyi realizm otssa Aleksandra Menia," in *Tserkovnaia zhizn' XX veka: Protoierei Aleksandr Men' i ego dukhovnye nastavniki; Nauchnaia konferentsiia, 2006, Sergiev Posad*, ed. M. V. Grigorenko, Menevskie chteniia 2006 [Sergiev Posad: Izdanie prikhoda Sergievskoi tserkvi v Semkhoze, 2007], 167). The evolutionary process by which history moves forward is a major thesis of Men's magnum opus *History of Religion*; in the writing of his poem Iakunin shares a similar perspective. Christianity, according to Men, was still in its infancy. Given the long period of time since the beginning of human civilization, Christianity was a latecomer; in terms of morality, human beings are still Neanderthals: "Many words of Christ are still incomprehensible to us even now," Men wrote, "because we are still Neanderthals in spirit and morals; because the arrow of the Gospels is aimed at eternity; because the history of Christianity is only beginning" (Alexander Men, "Christianity for the Twenty-First Century," in *Christianity for the Twenty-First Century: The Life and Work of Alexander Men*, ed. Elizabeth Roberts and Ann Shukman [London: SCM Press, 1996], 185. The original text is in Men', *Byt' khristianom* [Moscow: Anno Domini, 1992], 19–320). Christianity, therefore, is incomplete; people who claim to have a complete knowledge of the truth are misguided, because it, too, is in process. Iakunin's poem

underscores this view. He is extremely critical of those high-minded, conservative clerics, whose main desire is to preserve the past.

108. Ibid., 40. In one of the most powerful parts of his poem, Iakunin identifies the shortcomings, or what he calls "sins," of the Church. He explores these deficiencies through two different approaches to Christianity found in Fedor Dostoevsky's novel *Brothers Karamazov*. In his chapter on the monastery, Dostoevsky portrayed the monk Ferrapont as a dark, misanthropic, inward-looking, and otherworldly figure, who practiced a particularly rigorous form of asceticism. His counterpart, the monk Zosima, is humble and compassionate and reaches out to people, whom he attracts in large numbers. In his critical view of the Russian Church in the twentieth century, Iakunin describes the Church's practices as Ferrapontism:

> The Ferraponts disdain the whole world,
> To hate the world is instilled in Orthodoxy.
> Everything temporal—is ash, vanity of vanities.
> (Iakunin, *Khvalebnyi primitiv iurodivyi*, 79)

109. Ibid., 118-19.
110. Ibid., 111.
111. Ibid.
112. Ibid., 97.
113. Ibid., 10, 32-33, 46. Pierre Teilhard de Chardin (1881-1955) is a universally prominent French Jesuit theologian, geologist, and paleontologist. His *The Human Phenomenon* (*Le phénomène humain*, originally published in 1955) was translated into Russian in 1965. Teilhard's writings had a large influence on Aleksandr Men, as well as on Iakunin. See Wallace Daniel, *Russia's Uncommon Prophet: Father Aleksandr Men and His Times* (DeKalb: Northern Illinois University Press, 2016), 183-84, 190-92. Iakunin tells his readers that he was also influenced by the writings of the Russian geochemist Vladimir Ivanovich Vernadskii (1863-1945). Iakunin, *Khvalebnyi primitiv iurodivyi*, 10. Vernadskii, of Russian and Ukranian parentage, is identified as one of the founders of biochemistry, geochemistry, and radiation. He was an important contributor to the idea of the noosphere, which Teilhard de Chardin introduced in 1922. The noosphere is the theory of human cognition, whose emergence through human evolution Vernadskii viewed as transforming biological life.

114. Lev Regelson, "Letter to the Soviet Government on the Expulsion of Solzhenitsyn," February 17, 1974, in Yakunin and Regelson, *Letters from Moscow*, 12-20; Yakunin et al., "Appeal for the Glorification of Russian Martyrs"; Iakunin and Regelson, "Obrashchenie k delegatam V Assembleia"; Iakunin, *Khvalebnyi primitiv iurodivyi*, 93, 111, 117.

115. Gleb Iakunin, interview by author, May 10, 2007, Moscow.

116. Gleb Yakunin, "Open Letter to the Politburo of the Central Committee of the Communist Party of the Soviet Union," April 19, 1975, in Keston Archive, SU/Ort 8/2, Iakunin file.

117. L. Sergeeva, "Litsom k Rossii: Interv'iu E. A. Vagina," *Posev*, no. 10 (October 1976): 53. Evgenii Aleksandrovich Vagin, a leading literary critic, emigrated from Russia in August 1976. A founder and participant in a major unofficial group that connected democracy and religion, he was arrested in 1967 and spent eight years in prison. At the time of his arrest, he, along with several other colleagues in the Institute of Russian Literature in the Academy of Sciences, were preparing a scholarly collection of the works of Fedor Dostoevsky (see Sergeeva's editorial comments, p. 52).

Notes to Chapter 5: "An inward music"

1. Philip Boobbyer, *Conscience, Dissent, and Reform* (New York: Routledge, 2005), 70.
2. Ibid., 132-33.
3. Ibid., 132.
4. Ibid., 162.

5. Thomas F. Remington, "Alexander Yakovlev and the Limits of Reform," in *The Fate of Marxism in Russia*, by Alexander Yakovlev (New Haven, CT: Yale University Press, 1993), xii.
6. Ibid., 55.
7. James H. Billington, *The Icon and the Axe: An Interpretive History of Russian Culture* (New York: Knopf, 1966), 555.
8. Irving Howe, "Boris Pasternak's 'Doctor Zhivago' Should Inspire Reverence," *New Republic*, September 8, 1958, https://newrepublic.com/article/115305/boris-pasternaks-doctor-zhivago-reviewed.
9. Boris Pasternak, *Doctor Zhivago* (New York: Pantheon Books, 1991), 518, 459–60, 461.
10. Ibid., 248–50, 298.
11. Ibid., 146–47.
12. Ibid., 146–47, 518.
13. Ibid., 136, 223, 224, 182.
14. Ibid., 137, 196, 461, 139.
15. Ibid., 114, 404.
16. Ibid., 407, 284–85, 139.
17. Ibid., 139, 251.
18. Ibid., 258–59.
19. Karl Marx and Friedrich Engels, *The Communist Manifesto*, ed. Gareth Stedman Jones (London: Penguin, 2002), 222–25.
20. Pasternak, *Doctor Zhivago*, 127.
21. Marx and Engels, *Communist Manifesto*, 239–40.
22. Pasternak, *Doctor Zhivago*, 339, 301.
23. Ibid., 180.
24. Ibid., 457.
25. Ibid., 483.
26. Ibid., 507.
27. Ibid., 250, 299, 402.
28. Ibid., 349.
29. Ibid., 370.
30. I am grateful to Philip Boobyer for this observation. *Conscience, Dissent, and Reform*, 69.
31. Pasternak, *Doctor Zhivago*, 121.
32. Ibid., 49–50.
33. Ibid., 285, 297, 184.
34. Ibid., 90.
35. Ibid., 526.
36. Ibid., 343, 142, 141, 233.
37. Ibid., 335–36.
38. Ibid., 66, 65, 121–22.
39. Ibid., 9–10.
40. Ibid., 42.
41. Ibid., 43.
42. Ibid., 122–23.
43. Ibid., 412–13.
44. Ibid., 415, 461, 395.
45. For a discussion of this position see Guy de Mallac, "Pasternak and Religion," *The Russian Review* 32, no. 4 (1973): 361–62, doi:10.2307/127580.
46. Ibid., 368, 361, 360.
47. Guy de Mallac, *Boris Pasternak: His Life and Art* (Norman: University of Oklahoma Press, 1983), 9.
48. Boris Pasternak, *Safe Conduct: An Autobiography, and Other Writings* (New York: New Directions, 1958), 91.
49. Pasternak, *Doctor Zhivago*, 503.

50. Billington, *The Icon and the Axe*, 555.
51. Ibid., 556.
52. Pasternak, *Doctor Zhivago*, 261.
53. Zernov, *The Russian Religious Renaissance of the Twentieth Century* (New York: Harper & Row, 1963), 311.
54. Boobbyer, *Conscience, Dissent, and Reform*, 57, 77.
55. Koenraad de Wolf, *Dissident for Life: Alexander Ogorodnikov and the Struggle for Religious Freedom in Russia* (Grand Rapids, MI: Eerdmans, 2013), 54, 55.
56. Pasternak, *Doctor Zhivago*, 519.

Notes to Chapter 6: "The pearl of an unreasonable thought"

1. D. Ia. Severiukhin and Viacheslav Dolinin, eds., *Samizdat Leningrada: 1950e–1980e gody; Literaturnaia entsiklopediia* [Leningrad samizdat: 1950s-1980s. A literary encyclopaedia] (Moscow: NLO, 2003) is a useful reference work, also featuring introductory essays. See especially "Neofitsial'naia kul'tura i religioznoe dvizhenie" [Unofficial culture and the religious movement], 34–36. Stanislav Savitskii's study of Leningrad's underground devotes part of a chapter to the unofficial poets' spiritual quest: Stanislav Savitskii, *Andegraund: Istoriia i mify leningradskoi neofitsial'noi literatury* [Underground: The history and myths of Leningrad's unofficial literature] (Moscow: NLO, 2002). Leonid Borodin's novel *Rasstavanie* [The parting] (Frankfurt: Posev, 1984) describes the interest in Orthodoxy among the Moscow unofficial intelligentsia in the 1970s.

2. Elena Shvarts, "O bezumii v poezii" [On madness in poetry], in *Sochineniia*, 5 vols. (St. Petersburg: Pushkinskii Fond, 2002–2013), 3:270.

3. For the significance of religious philosophy for Symbolism, see P. Gaidenko, *Vladimir Solov'ev i filosofiia Serebrianogo veka* [Vladimir Solov'ev and the philosophy of the Silver Age] (Moscow: Progress-Traditsiia, 2001). For a discussion of the specifically aesthetic aspects of the religious renaissance in the early twentieth century, see the work of Viktor Bychkov, especially *Russkaia teurgicheskaia estetika* [Russian theurgic aesthetics] (Moscow: Ladomir, 2007).

4. For an overview of writers, not only Russians, who worked with biblical imagery throughout the centuries, see Aleksandr Men', *Bibliia i literatura* [The Bible and literature] (Moscow: Zhizn' s Bogom, 2009).

5. Anton Nesterov, "Germenevtika, metafizika i 'drugaia kritika,'" [Hermeneutics, metaphysics and new criticism] *Novoe literaturnoe obozrenie* 61 (2003): 75–97.

6. Viktor Krivulin, "Peterburgskaia spiritual'naia lirika" [Petersburg's spiritual lyric poetry], in *Istoriia leningradskoi nepodtsenzurnoi literatury, 1950e–1980e gody*, ed. B. Ivanov and B. Roginskii (St. Petersburg: Dean, 2000), 99–110.

7. Mikhail Berg, "Neofitsial'naia leningradskaia literatura mezhdu proshlym i budushchim [Leningrad's unofficial literature between past and future], 2005, accessed April 19, 2016, http://www.mberg.net/prbud/.

8. Mikhail Epshtein describes metarealism as "not the relative similarity of things, but the complicity of different worlds." See *Postmodern v russkoi literature* [The postmodern age in Russian literature] (Moscow: Vysshaia shkola, 2005), 154.

9. Vladislav Kulakov, "Po obrazu i podobiu iazyka: Poeziia 80-kh godov" [After the image and likeness of language: the poetry of the 80s], *Novoe literaturnoe obozrenie* 32 (1998): 202–14 (204).

10. Olga Sedakova, "Muzyka glukhogo vremeni" [Music for a deaf age], *Vestnik novoi literatury* 2 (1990), 257–63 (258).

11. Brodsky was fascinated with the symbolism of Christmas and continued to write Christmas poems throughout his life. They are collected in the bilingual volume *Nativity Poems* (New York: Farrar, Straus, and Giroux, 2001).

12. "For us, culture in its broadest historical aspect was that very freedom and height of the spirit denied to us by the Soviet system. [...] We all emerged from some kind of protest movement,

which was not so much political as aesthetic or spiritual resistance." Olga Sedakova and Slava I. Yastremski, "A Dialogue on Poetry," in *Poems and Elegies*, by Olga Sedakova, ed. Slava I. Yastremski (Lewisburg, PA: Bucknell University Press, 2003), 11-20 (15).

13. Olga Sedakova, "Russkaia poeziia posle Brodskogo: Vstuplenie k Stanfordskim lektsiiam" [Russian poetry after Brodsky: Introduction to the Stanford lectures], in *Sobranie socheneniia*, vol. 3, *Poetica* (Moscow: Universitet Dmitriia Pozharskogo, 2010), 504-14 (508).

14. Sedakova, "Neprodolzhitel'nye nachala russkoi poezii" [The short beginnings of Russian poetry], in *Sobranie socheneniia*, 3:429-36 (432).

15. The Latin verb "religare" means "to tie, fasten, bind (one thing to another)."

16. See Per-Arne Bodin, *Eternity and Time: Studies in Russian Literature and the Orthodox Tradition* (Stockholm: Amqvist & Wiksell International, 2007), 185.

17. Pasternak himself wrote in a letter to Jacqueline de Proyart: "I've always felt the unity of everything that exists as one, the totality of everything that lives and breathes, happens and appears, of all of existence, all of life." Translation mine. Quoted in Bodin, *Eternity and Time*, 192. Bodin traces Pasternak's concept of linkage back to Vladimir Solov'ev, Leo Tolstoy, Anton Chekhov, and Johann Wolfgang von Goethe.

18. Boris Pasternak, *Doctor Zhivago* (Moscow: Troika, 1994), 37. Translation mine.

19. See Bodin, *Eternity and Time*, 186.

20. For a discussion of the "Christian" poems, see Per-Arne Bodin, *Nine Poems from Doktor Zhivago: A Study of Christian Motifs in Boris Pasternak's Poetry* (Stockholm: Amqvist & Wiksell International, 1976).

21. The Leningrad poet Sergei Stratanovskii (born 1944) made the barren fig tree the central image of his Christology, detailed in: "Pritcha o smokovnitse" [The parable of the fig tree], *Zvezda* 10 (2012): 211-22. The collection *Smokovnitsa [The fig tree]* (2010) brings together the religious poetry Stratanovskii wrote during four decades.

22. Pasternak, *Doctor Zhivago*, 420-21.

23. Ibid., 441.

24. Poetry as sacrifice (and the poet as a Christ figure) are the themes of "Gamlet" [Hamlet], the first poem of the Zhivago cycle.

25. For figures on the Orthodox church in the late Soviet Union, see Nathaniel Davis, *A Long Walk to Church: A Contemporary History of Russian Orthodoxy* (Boulder, CO: Westview, 1995).

26. Sergei Stratanovskii explores this phenomenon in a series of essays on religious motifs in the poetry of his contemporaries, published in the journal *Volga* in 1993. For a verbatim statement to this effect, see Stratanovskii, "Religioznye motivy v sovremennoi russkoi poezii: Stat'ia pervaia" [Religious motifs in contemporary Russian poetry: essay one], *Volga* 4 (1993): 158-61 (158).

27. The most complete collection of Sedakova's work to date, including her poetry, translations, and many of her essays, is Olga Sedakova, *Sobranie socheneniia*, 4 vols. (Moscow: Universitet Dmitriia Pozharskogo, 2010). Her website, http://www.olgasedakova.com, contains excerpts from articles and essays, poems, and also many interviews. Sedakova maintains a Facebook feed and regularly publishes lectures and readings on YouTube.

28. For a statement to this effect see: Ol'ga Sedakova, "Eshche raz o detstve, poezii, muzhestve ... Otvety Elene Stepanian" [Once again about childhood, poetry and courage... answers of Elena Stepanian], in *Sobranie socheneniia*, 2 vols. (Moscow: En Ef K'iu/Tu Print, 2001), 2:194-205 (194).

29. "Sestre" [To my sister] in *Stikhi*, by Ol'ga Sedakova (Moscow: Gnozis-Carte Blanche, 1994), 9.

30. Sedakova, "Zametki i vospominaniia o raznykh stikhotvoreniiakh, a takzhe pokhvala poezii" [Notes and recollections of various poems, and also in praise of poetry], in *Sobranie socheneniia*, 3:13-98 (27).

31. Her love for the multifaceted motif of the garden, which alternatively carries notions of the hereafter ("Legenda deviataia" [The ninth legend]), earthly paradise ("Neuzheli, Mariia" [Indeed, Mariia]), but also enigmatic darkness ("Proshchanie" [Farewell]) and terror ("Pobeg bludnogo syna" [The flight of the prodigal son]), was possibly inspired by Dante's description of the deserted Garden

of Eden in the second part of his *Divine Comedy (Purgatory)*, cantos 28–31. The garden also features in "Moi slukh nagatove" [My ears are primed], "Legenda sed'maia: Smert' Aleksandra Rimskogo Ugodnika" [The seventh legend: the death of Saint Alexander of Rome], "Proshchanie" [Farewell], "Strannoe puteshestvie" [A strange journey], "Pobeg" [The flight], "Veter proshchaniia" [The wind of farewell], and "Utro v sadu" [Morning in the garden].

32. Sedakova, *Sobranie socheneniia*, (Moscow: Universitet Dmitriia Pozharskogo, 2010) vol. 1, *Stikhi*, 381–83.

33. Ibid., 59.

34. In other poems, namely "Iz pesni Dante" [From the songs of Dante] and "Varlaam i Iosaff" [Varlam and Josaff], the gardener stands for God.

35. Noted by Mikhail Epshtein in *Postmodern v russkoi literature*, 150.

36. Sedakova has confirmed that the poem refers to the scene by the tomb on Easter morning when Mary Magdalene mistakes the risen Christ for the gardener (John 20). See Valentina Polukhina, Robert Reid, and Olga Sedakova, "'Collective Analysis of Ol'ga Sedakova's 'The Wild Rose,'" *Essays in Poetics* 22 (1997): 237–57 (242).

37. See Epshtein, *Postmodern v russkoi literature*, 146–51 and 203–8; Stephanie Sandler, "Mirrors and Metarealists: The Poetry of Ol'ga Sedakova and Ivan Zhdanov," *Slavonica* 12 (2006): 3–23.

38. Noticeable is his fascination with the figure of Judas ("Plach Iudy" [Judas crying]; "Vzgliad" [Gaze]). In the poem "Kreshchenie" [Baptism] fallen leaves are baptized.

39. Ivan Zhdanov, *Mesto zemli* [The place of the earth] (Moscow: Molodaia gvardiia, 1991), http://www.vavilon.ru/texts/prim/zhdanov1.html/.

40. The same technique is employed in "Portret otsa" [Portrait of my father], where the point of view changes several times until it becomes that of a plowed field.

41. Kulakov, "Po obrazu i podobiu iazyka," [After the image and likeness of language] 204, 207.

42. Other poems from the same collection that include the poppy are "Portret otsa" [Portrait of my father], "Neon," "Voda v glazakh ne tonet" [Water doesn't drown in the eyes], "Gde sorok sorokov" [Where there is a multitude].

43. Other poems that feature the cross are "Do Slova" [Until the word] and "Kak dushu vneshniuiu" [Like an outward soul].

44. Many artists have explicitly turned the cross into a tree from which new life grows, for example the German priest and painter Sieger Koeder.

45. Another list of surprising redefinitions can be found in "Voda v glazakh ne tonet." [Water doesn't drown in the eyes]

46. Zhdanov, *Mesto zemli* [The place of the earth].

47. See the biographical entry on Krivulin in Severiukhin and Dolinin, *Samizdat Leningrada*, 229–30.

48. A brilliant example of Krivulin's scholarly mind is the article "Dvadtsat' let noveishei russkoi poezii" [Twenty years of modern Russian poetry], written under the pseudonym A. Kalomirov and published in *Severnaia pochta* 1, no. 2 (1979). The article traces the development of poetic language since the 1960s and establishes firm links between the prerevolutionary twentieth-century Russian poetic tradition and 1970s unofficial poetry.

49. V. Krivulin, *Okhota na mamonta [Hunting for mammoths]* (St. Petersburg: BLITs, 1998), 8.

50. For a retrospective account of the moment that Krivulin says turned him into a different, real poet, see Viktor Krivulin, "'Poeziia—eto razgovor samogo iazyka': Interv'iu s V. Kulakovym," ["Poetry is the conversation of language itself": and interview with V. Kulakov] *Novoe literaturnoe obozrenie* 14 (1995): 223–33 (226). A very similar version features in *Okhota na mamonta*, 7. This account strongly resembles Brodsky's reminiscences of reading great poets of the past, specifically Anna Akhmatova and W. H. Auden. See the interview with Iuz Aleshkovskii in Valentina Polukhina, ed., *Iosif Brodskii: Bol'shaia kniga interv'iu* (Moscow: Zakharov, 2000). See also Solomon Volkov, *Dialogi s Iosifom Brodskim: Literaturnye biografii* (Moscow: Nezavisimaia gazeta, 1998), 159.

51. The intertextual relationship between "P'iu vino arkhaizmov" and Mandel'shtam's poem has been analyzed in great detail by Clint B. Walker in his essay "The Spirit(s) of the Leningrad Underground," *The Slavic and East European Journal* 43, no. 4 (1999), 674–98.

52. Viktor Krivulin, *Stikhi*, 2 vols. (Leningrad: Beseda, 1988), 1:108-9.

53. For a perceptive study of Krivulin's concept of the poetic word, see Ol'ga Sedakova, "Ocherki drugoi poezii. Ocherk pervyi: Viktor Krivulin" [Sketches on the other poetry. Sketch 1: Viktor Krivulin], in *Sobranie socheneniia*, 2 vols., 2:684-704.

54. Krivulin, *Stikhi*, 1:110.

55. Blindness, the mouth/eating and the soles of the feet are metaphors Krivulin uses frequently. For a reading, see Tat'iana Goricheva et al., *"P'iu vino arkhaizmov—": O poezii Viktora Krivulina ["I drink the wine of archaisms: on the poetry of Viktor Krivulin]* (St. Petersburg: KOSTA, 2007).

56. As claimed by Pavel Kriuchkov in his obituary of Shvarts, entitled "Blizhe angel'skaia rech'" ["Closer the angels' speech "]. She was buried according to Orthodox ritual. https://foma.ru/blizhe-zangelskaya-rech.html.

57. "Interv'iu s Elenoi Shvarts" (1990), in *Iosif Brodskii glazami sovremennikov: Kniga pervaia (1987-1992) [Joseph Brodsky through the eyes of his contemporaries: volume 1]*, ed. Valentina Polukhina (St. Petersburg: Zvezda, 2006), 226-46 (236).

58. Dunja Popovic, "Symbolic Injury and Embodied Mysticism in Elena Shvarts's 'Trudy i Dni Lavinii,'" *The Slavic and East European Journal* 51, no. 4 (2007): 753-71 (744).

59. Scholars of late Soviet literature have repeatedly used the paradigm of holy foolishness to unlock the meaning of unfamiliar imagery, especially imagery with a religious component. A study directed exclusively at the main group discussed here is Marco Sabbatini's, "The Pathos of Holy Foolishness in the Leningrad Underground," in *Holy Foolishness in Russia: New Perspectives*, ed. Priscilla Hunt and Svitlana Kobets (Bloomington, IN: Slavica, 2011), 337-52.

60. A standard work on holy foolishness is S. A. Ivanov, *Blazhennye pokhaby: Kul'turnaia istoriia iurodstva* [Blessed indecencies: A cultural history of holy foolishness] (Moscow: Iazyki slavianskikh kul'tur, 2005); also Per-Arne Bodin, *Language, Canonization, and Holy Foolishness: Studies in Postsoviet Russian Culture and the Orthodox Tradition* (Stockholm: Stockholm University, 2009).

61. Michel Foucault has argued that before the Enlightenment, madness was regarded as a (different) way of speaking the truth. See *History of Madness*, trans. Jonathan Murphy and Jean Khalfa (1961; repr., London: Routledge, 2006).

62. Elena Aizenshtein, "Sokrovennoe, v slezakh, edva prosheptannoe slovo" [The innermost word, whispered quietly, under tears], *Neva* 5 (2013): 175-97.

63. Shvarts, *Sochineniia*, 1:38-39.

64. Ibid., 2:77-82 (79-80).

65. Poems that exemplify this approach include several from the "Trudy i dni Lavinii" [The days and works of Laviniia] cycle: no. 19 ("Obrezanie serdtsa" [The circumcision of the heart]), no. 49, no. 61 ("Bez vdokhnoven'ia i truda" [Without inspiration and labour]); as well as "Tkan' serdtsa rassteliu Spasitel'iu pod nogi" [I spread the fabric of my heart under my Saviour's feet], "Ia rodilas' s ladon'iu gladkoi" [I was born with an unlined hand], "Bashnia, v nei kletki" [A tower with cells inside], "Martovskie mertvetsy" [Corpses in March].

66. "Tri osobennosti moikh stikhov" [Three particularities of my poems], *Sochineniia*, 4:276-78 (277).

67. The scene of David dancing is in 2 Samuel 6:14.

68. "5 etazh—vverkh" [5th floor—upstairs] of the cycle "Lestnitsa s dyriavymi ploshchadkami" [Staircase with hole-ridden landings], *Sochineniia*, 1:69-93 (79).

69. His article "Khristianstvo i gumanizm" [Christianity and humanism] appeared in "37," no. 7-8 (1976).

70. A large number of poems refer to his friend and mentor Asya Lvovna Maizel ("Asya Lvovna"); others who feature frequently are Elena Shvarts ("Lena") and Olga Sedakova ("Olia Sedakova").

71. Vasilii Filippov, *Izbrannye stikhotvoreniia, 1984-1990* (Moscow: Novoe literaturnoe obozrenie, 2002), 88.

72. "Chital Afanasia Aleksandriiskogo" ["I was reading Afanasy of Alexandria"], ibid., 136-37.

73. Ibid., 122-24.

74. "Kuriu 'Shipku' i vdykhaiu akvamarin dnia" [I smoke a 'Shipka' and breathe out the day's aquamarine], ibid., 41. See also the poem that begins with the lines "Prosvetliaetsia razum pod stikhami Eleny Shvarts" [My mind becomes clear under Elena Shvarts's poems].

75. See the biographical entry on Kuprianov in Severiukhin and Dolinin, *Samizdat Leningrada*, 241.

76. Strictly speaking, any artwork aspiring to the label "Christian" ought to communicate the message inherent in scripture, with little scope for the individual artist's opinion. For an exposition of this position, see "The Meaning and Language of Icons," in *The Meaning of Icons, by Leonid Ouspensky and Vladimir Lossky* (Crestwood, NY: St. Vladimir's Seminary Press, 1999), 25–49.

77. For a detailed discussion of how artistic and religious practice become conflated in the work of two underground poets, see Josephine von Zitzewitz, "Viktor Krivulin and Aleksandr Mironov: The Quest for Sacred Language in 1970s Russian Poetry," *Modern Languages Review* 107, no. 3 (2012): 872–93.

78. Viktor Krivulin, "Peterburgskaia spiritual'naia lirika vchera i segodnia," in Ivanov and Roginskii, *Istoriia leningradskoi nepodtsenzurnoi literatury*, 99–110 (102).

Notes to Chapter 7: "I hasten to establish a common language with you"

1. "Interview Given by Metropolitan Filaret of Kiev and Galich to a Novosti Press Agency Correspondent," *Journal of the Moscow Patriarchate*, no. 5 (1976): 5.

2. Dimitry Pospielovsky, *The Russian Church under the Soviet Regime, 1917–1982* (Crestwood, NY: St. Vladimir's Seminary Press, 1984), 2:310–13. Metropolitan Nikolai Iarushevich, one of the church leaders to meet with Stalin in 1943, served as the chief spokesman for Stalin's peace campaigns beginning in 1948. Pospielovsky asserts that Stalin's peace campaigns were motivated by the still inferior military power of the Soviet Union vis-à-vis the United States. At this point the Soviet Union still did not possess the technology of the atomic bomb.s

3. Quoted in Jane Ellis, *The Russian Orthodox Church: A Contemporary History*. (London: Croom Helm Ltd., 1986), 209.

4. Quoted in William Taubman, *Khrushchev: The Man and His Era* (New York: Norton, 2003), 271–72.

5. The Thaw represented a brief period during Khrushchev's leadership in which thousands of political prisoners were released, the policy of "peaceful coexistence" with other nations was ushered in, and Khrushchev allowed for a brief blossoming of the "arts."

6. Ludmilla Alexeyeva and Paul Goldberg, *The Thaw Generation: Coming of Age in the Post-Stalin Era* (Boston, MA: Little, Brown and Company, 1990), 4.

7. Dissident Liudmila Alekseeva provides a firsthand account of her students attacking her, claiming that she lied to them about Stalin ruling the country as a great leader. She also writes that it was during the Thaw that she and other intellectuals "search[ed] for an alternative system of beliefs" to make their own. Alexeyeva and Goldberg, *The Thaw*, 4.

8. The importance of these early meetings are described in detail by scholar Philip Boobbyer in *Conscience, Dissent, and Reform in Soviet Russia* (New York: Routledge 2005). He explains that in the late Stalinist period, close friends formed circles to talk about various topics. Boobbyer terms these circles "micro-communities" and claims that they "represented a zone of private loyalty that the state could not always reach," 57.

9. Valerii Chalidze, *To Defend These Rights: Human Rights in the Soviet Union* (New York: Random House, 1974), 60.

10. Lev Timofeev, ed., "Dissident s parlamentskim mandatom," *Referendum, zhurnal nezavisimykh mnenii: Izbrannye materialy*, no. 35 (1990): 175.

11. Quoted in Boobbyer, *Conscience, Dissent, and Reform*, 76.

12. Ludmilla Alexeyeva [Liudmila Alekseeva], *Soviet Dissent: Contemporary Movements for National, Religious, and Human Rights* (Middletown, CT: Wesleyan University Press, 1985), 267. Alekseeva claims that the ideas of the international human rights movement did not initially influence

Soviet dissidents and intellectuals because they were poorly informed about it. Rather, she suggests that the shock of the Secret Speech in affirming what many intellectuals already believed to be true combined with the cruelty and lawlessness of the Soviet system inspired Soviet dissidents and activists to demand constitutional observation by the government and an end to totalitarianism.

13. Joshua Rubenstein, *Soviet Dissidents: Their Struggle for Human Rights (Boston, MA: Beacon Press, 1980)*, 9.

14. Pasternak famously won the Nobel Prize for Literature in 1958 but renounced the award under intense Soviet pressure and threats of forced emigration.

15. Rubenstein, *Soviet Dissidents*, 10–16.

16. Alexeyeva, *Soviet Dissent*, 13–14.

17. Vladimir Bukovsky, *To Build a Castle: My Life as a Dissenter* (New York: Viking Press, 1979), 116–26. Bukovskii provides a thorough account of the origins of the Maiakovskii Square readings and the significance of the meetings for future Soviet dissidents.

18. Ibid., 119.

19. Ibid., 119–20.

20. Beginning in the late 1950s, many of the Russian intelligentsia began to enter the Russian Orthodox Church. This revival is known as the *Russkoe religioznoe vozrozhdenie* (Russian religious renaissance).

21. During an interview conducted on March 28, 2014, at the Keston Center in Waco, Texas by the author, Orthodox dissident Aleksandr Ogorodnikov stated that Western literature was very difficult to find and often dissidents did not have regular access to it. As Liudmila Alekseeva also mentioned, traditional Russian novels that championed the defense of the "ordinary Russian" had a great deal of influence on the human rights dissidents.

22. "The Church in the Soviet Union," interview with Anatolii Levitin Krasnov, *Russkaia mysl'*, December 5, 1974, 5. According to many scholars, including Jane Ellis, 40 million is an accurate number of regularly attending worshippers; she estimated in the 1970s that the number of people who regarded themselves as Orthodox, including those who attended worship and those who did not, was as high as 50 million, roughly 15 percent of the population. Ellis, *Russian Orthodox Church*, 174.

23. *Chronicle of Current Events*, no. 5 (December 31, 1968), http://www.memo.ru/history/diss/chr/.

24. Michael Bourdeaux, *Patriarch and Prophets: Persecution of the Russian Orthodox Church Today (New York: Praeger, 1970)*, 339–40.

25. Sergi Zheludkov, "Fr. Sergi Zheludkov writes to Pavel Litvinov," in Bourdeaux, *Patriarch and Prophets*, 339–40.

26. Bohdan R. Bociurkiw, "Political Dissent in the Soviet Union," *Studies in Comparative Communism: An Interdisciplinary Journal* 3, no. 2 (April 1970), 95.

27. *Chronicle of Current Events*, no. 8 (June 30, 1969), http://www.memo.ru/history/diss/chr/.

28. Anatolii Levitin-Krasnov, "A Light in the Little Window," 3, in Baylor University's Keston Archive, SU/Ort/2, Levitin-Krasnov file.

29. Gleb Yakunin and Lev Regelson, "Letter to Dr. Philip Potter," in *Letters from Moscow: Religion and Human Rights in the USSR* (San Francisco, CA: H. S. Dakin Company, 1978), 65.

30. Yakunin and Regelson, "Press Conference at the Apartment of Dmitri Dudko," in *Letters from Moscow*, 85–87. The letter to which Iakunin responded was written in 1977 and accused Gleb Iakunin, Aleksandr Ogorodnikov, Lev Regelson, and Dmitrii Dudko of deceiving people in the West by feigning religious activity and falsely attacking Soviet authorities for persecuting religion and religious believers. The complete text of Roschin's letter can be found in *Letters from Moscow*.

31. Yakunin and Regelson, "Press Conference," in *Letters from Moscow*, 85.

32. Igor Shafarevich, "Does Russia Have a Future?," in *From under the Rubble*, ed. Alexander Solzhenitsyn et al. (Boston, MA: Little, Brown, 1975), 287, 290–92.

33. *Chronicle of Current Events*, no. 26 (July 5, 1972), 270. In numerous essays, letters, petitions, and reports, Sakharov emphasizes the importance of freedom of conscience, even though he remained an atheist until his death.

34. *Russkaia mysl'*, September 11, 1971.
35. *Chronicle of Current Events*, no. 20 (July 2, 1971), 236.
36. Andrei Sakharov, "O Zaiavleniia Evgeniia Barabanova," September 19, 1973, in Keston Archive, SU/Ort 2, Barabanov file.
37. "Znachitel'noe ozhivlenie nezavisimoi Russkoi obshchestvennosti," *Posev* (October 1974): 6–7.
38. *Chronicle of Current Events*, no. 31 (May 1, 1975), 159–60.
39. Alexeyeva, *Soviet Dissent*, 252. Dissident Sergei Kovalev worked as a prominent biologist at Moscow State University before resigning due to his work with the Initiative Group for the Defense of Human Rights. The most comprehensive book about his life and his work with human rights in the Soviet Union and post-Soviet Russia is Emma Gilligan's *Defending Human Rights in Russia: Sergei Kovalyov, Dissident and Human Rights Commissioner, 1969–2003* (New York: Routledge, 2004).
40. *Chronicle of Current Events*, no. 20 (September 1, 1971), 234–35.
41. Andrei Tverdokhlebov, *Andrei Tverdokhlebov: V zashchitu prav cheloveka* (New York: Khronika, 1975), 92–114.
42. *Chronicle of Current Events*, no. 32 (July 17, 1974), 10–11.
43. Leopold Labedz, ed., *Solzhenitsyn: A Documentary Record* (Bloomington: Indiana University Press, 1973), 64.
44. Michael Bourdeaux, ed., "Peter Vins Rearrested," *Keston News Service* 49, 1978, p. 1.
45. Xenia Dennen, "The Dissident Movement and Soviet Christians," 23, unpublished manuscript (July 23, 2014).
46. *Chronicle of Current Events*, no. 37 (September 30, 1975), 7.
47. Andrei D. Sakharov, *Alarm and Hope* (London: Collins and Harvill Press, 1979), 46–47.
48. Bociurkiw, "Political Dissent," 82. The Initiative Group included Orthodox intellectuals such as Anatolii Levitin-Krasnov, Tatiana Velikanova, and Natalia Gorbanevskaia.
49. Alexeyeva, *Soviet Dissent*, 292.
50. *Chronicle of Current Events*, no. 56 (April 30, 1980), 9–10. *Initsiativniki*: A group of schismatic Russian Baptists who formed in 1960 after the All-Union Council of Evangelical Christian Baptists (AUCECB) adopted the New Statutes and Letter of Instructions, which sought to curtail religious activity in the Soviet Union. The Initsiativniki initially sought to reform the New Statutes and the AUCECB, but eventually broke away completely and formed their own union—the Council of Churches of Evangelical Christian Baptists (CCECB). The group engaged in public dissent against the Soviet state, openly evangelized to young people, held outdoor meetings, and Sunday school classes for children. The group still exists in Russia today and has reported some incidents of persecution by the Russian government. Their churches were not officially recognized in the Soviet period and therefore, never received registration. Their communities are still not registered today in Russia.
51. *Ibid.*, no. 19 (April 30, 1971), 169.
52. Quoted in *Chronicle of Current Events*, no. 19 (April 30, 1971), 209.
53. *Ibid.*, no. 22 (November 10, 1971), 21.
54. *Ibid.*, 24.
55. Moscow Helsinki Group, "Zaiavlenie chlenov Obshchestvennoi gruppy sodeistviia vypolneniiu Khel'sinkskikh soglashenii v SSSR po povodu obyskov, provedennykh 4–5 ianvaria 1977 g. u chlenov Gruppy, doprosov i drugikh repressii," January 7, 1977, http://www.mhg.ru/history/14AE131.
56. Moscow Helsinki Group, "Repressii protiv religioznykh semei," June 17, 1976, http://www.mhg.ru/history/1458985.
57. *Chronicle of Current Events*, no. 34 (December 31, 1974), 26–27.
58. David Kowalewski, "Protest for Religious Rights in the USSR: Characteristics and Consequences," *Russian Review* 39, no. 4 (October 1980): 435.
59. Alexeyeva, *Soviet Dissent*, 15–16.
60. Dmitrii Dudko, *Our Hope* (Crestwood, NY: St. Vladimir's Seminary Press, 1977), 130.
61. Dudko, *Our Hope*, 46–47.

62. Janice A. Broun, "Russia's Don Quixote," *New Blackfriars* 55, no. 649 (June 1974): 277. Interestingly, Georgii Vins wrote in his autobiography that his father Petr Vins served his prison sentence with ten Orthodox priests in Svetlaia Bay in the early 1930s. According to Georgii, the priests behaved "very warmly and sympathetically" toward Petr and "got him a job as an orderly in the hospital."

63. Gerd R. von Doemming, "Appeals for Civil Rights Filmed by Soviet Dissidents," *Radio Liberty Research*, September 21, 1971, p. 3, in Keston Archive, SU/Ort/2, Levitin-Krasnov file.

64. "Demand This Man's Release, Baptists Are Urged," *Baptist Times*, October 10, 1974, p. 7, in Keston Archive SU/Ort/2, Levitin-Krasnov file.

65. Aleksandr Ogorodnikov and Vladimir Poresh, *Obshchina*, no. 2, 1978.

66. Anatoli Levitin-Krasnov, "Father Gleb Yakunin and Lev Regelson," in *Letters from Moscow*, 3.

67. Gleb Yakunin and Nikolai Eshliman, *A Cry of Despair from Moscow Churchmen* (New York: Synod of Bishops of the Russian Orthodox Church Outside of Russia, 1966), 9–17.

68. Yakunin and Eshliman, *A Cry of Despair*, 42–53.

69. Elizabeth Roberts and Ann Shukman, eds., *Christianity for the Twenty-First Century: The Life and Work of Alexander Men* (London: SCM Press, 1996), 9–11.

70. Ibid., 12.

71. Ibid., 32, 66.

72. Ibid., 71.

73. *Ibid.*, 24.

74. *Chronicle of Current Events*, no. 43 (December 31, 1976), 43–44.

75. Moscow Helsinki Group, "Desiat' let spustia," August 16, 1978, http://www.mhg.ru/history/1555EF8.

76. Moscow Helsinki Group, "Zaiavlenie chlenov," January 7, 1977, http://www.mhg.ru/history/14AE131; Moscow Helsinki Group, "Repressii protiv," June 17, 1976, http://www.mhg.ru/history/1458985. Orlov, like Ginzburg, also collected documents from various religious groups and often appealed on their behalf, especially as a member of the Moscow Helsinki Group. When Orlov was arrested in 1978, many believers petitioned for his release including Vladimir Shelkov, the leader of the unregistered Seventh-Day Adventists in Russia.

77. Yakunin and Regelson, "Appeal to the Delegates of the 5th Assembly of the World Council of Churches, Nairobi, Kenya," in *Letters from Moscow*, 45–46.

78. Ellis, *The Orthodox Church*, 369–72. According to Jane Ellis's close study of the appeal, the tone of the document suggests that it was drafted by an Orthodox believer. Ellis writes, "This ecumenical venture, therefore, was most probably a venture by . . . Orthodox who reached out to members of other denominations," 369-372.

79. Yakunin and Regelson, "Letter to Dr. Philip Potter, General Secretary of the World Council of Churches," in *Letters from Moscow*, 57.

80. Gleb Iakunin et al., *Dokumenty khristianskoi komiteta zashchity prav verulushchikh v SSSR*, vol. 3 (Moscow, 1976), 283.

81. Khailo Family, "Appeal," in *Dokumenty khristianskoi komiteta zashchity prav veruiushchikh v SSSR*, vol. 1 (Moscow, 1977), 122–23. In his letter, Khailo explains that his oldest son was arrested and imprisoned, whereas two of his other sons were moved to special schools because they received religious education at home, effectively denying Khailo his parental rights.

82. "Urgent Communication," in *Dokumenty khristianskoi komiteta zashchity prav veruiushchikh v SSSR*, vol. 2 (Moscow, 1977), 202–3. This communication from the Initsiativniki Baptists to the Committee was written on December 25, 1977, and discusses the increased persecution against members of their denomination as a result of the new Soviet Constitution. They list names of members arrested and literature seized. Interestingly, at the end of the letter, they ask the Committee to send the Council of Prisoners' Relatives copies of petitions created so that they may sign "on behalf of all who now endure persecutions and sorrows," 202-203.

83. Rostislav Galetsky, "A Chronicle: Nina Fedorovna Mikhel," *Dokumenty khristianskoi komiteta*, 1:23–27. Galetsky writes that in addition to receiving the fine, Nina Mikhel was in danger of losing her children because of the religious education they received at home.

84. Gleb Iakunin, "Letter to Pope Paul VI," *Russkaia mysl'*, September 1, 1977, 5.

85. Michael Bourdeaux, *Risen Indeed: Lessons of Faith in the USSR* (Crestwood, NY: St. Vladimir's Seminary Press, 1983), 22.

86. *Chronicle of Current Events*, no. 45 (May 25, 1977), 306–7.

87. Lev Regelson, "Appeal to the Participants of the Belgrade Conference," in *Dokumenty khristianskoi komiteta*, 152–54.

88. Iakunin, "Appeal," in *Dokumenty khristianskoi komiteta zashchity prav veruiushchikh v SSSR*, vol. 4 (Moscow, 1978), 451.

89. Bourdeaux, *Risen Indeed*, 22–23. Iakunin was sentenced for anti-Soviet activity under Article 70 of the Soviet Criminal Code. Viktor Kapitanchuk, a member of the Christian Committee since its creation, was also arrested and testified against Iakunin during his trial after recanting his "harmful" activities. Lev Regelson, Iakunin's friend and fellow dissident, also testified against him after recanting his activities following his arrest. Interestingly, Regelson was released after his own trial, in view of his "sincere repentance," and stated to the Western press that he was "prepared to go to prison for the faith, but not for human rights." Following Iakunin's arrest, no. 54 of the *Chronicle of Current Events* listed several items confiscated from Iakunin's home including Baptist and Adventist correspondence and literature, the work of philosopher Solov'ev and other Orthodox philosophy, and materials in connection with human rights cases, in particular the case of Viacheslav Kondratevich Zaitsev, a doctor of philological sciences who was forcibly confined to a psychiatric hospital.

90. Ellis, *Russian Orthodox Church*, 443–44.

91. *Chronicle of Current Events*, no. 55 (January 31, 1980), 10.

92. Sakharov, *Alarm and Hope*, 36.

93. Ibid., 103–4. This statement was signed by human rights activists Leonid Borodin, Vladimir Osipov, Nikolai Ivanov, and others and called on the world public, Amnesty International, and the International Red Cross to speak out on the conditions that political prisoners in the USSR were confined to in prisons and labor camps. Iurii Galanskov was sentenced to seven years in a labor camp in 1968, after what became known as the "trial of the four." Galanskov was one of the earliest participants in the Soviet human rights movement and authored or co-authored many early *samizdat* works including *The White Book* and *Phoenix*.

94. Levitin-Krasnov, "A Light in the Little Window," 8–11, in Keston Archive, SU/Ort/2, Levitin-Krasnov file.

95. Aleksandr Ogorodnikov and Vladimir Poresh, "Declaration of Seminar's Principles," *Obshchina*, no. 2, 1978.

96. Yakunin and Regelson, "Letter to Dr. Philip Potter," in *Letters from Moscow*, 54.

97. Yakunin and Regelson, "Letter to the Reverend David Hathaway," in *Letters from Moscow*, 69.

98. Yakunin, "Appeal to the Delegates of the 5th Assembly," in *Letters from Moscow*, 45.

99. Iakunin et al., "Open Letter," November 11, 1977, in *Dokumenty khristianskoi komiteta*, 1:37–38.

100. Levitin-Krasnov, "A Light in the Little Window," 10, in Keston Archive, SU/Ort 2, Levitin-Krasnov file.

101. Natalya Gorbanevskaya, *Red Square at Noon* (London: Andre Deutsch Limited, 1972), 31–36.

102. *Chronicle of Current Events*, no. 27 (October 15, 1972), 298.

103. Ibid., no. 23 (January 5, 1972), 66.

104. Ibid., no. 42 (October 8, 1976), 174. Several artists and poets affiliated with groups advocating for the freedom of creativity and expression in the Soviet Union took credit for the slogans, but no conclusive evidence was found as to who created them.

105. Lev Regelson, *Dokumenty khristianskoi komiteta*, 1:152.

106. Levitin, "Appeal," in Keston Archive, SU/Ort/2, Levitin-Krasnov file.
107. Evgenii Barabanov, "Statement," in Keston Archive, SU/Ort/2, Barabanov file.

Notes to Chapter 8: The Orthodox Liturgy as Political Resistance

1. *The Journals of Father Alexander Schmemann, 1973–1983*, trans. Juliana Schmemann (Crestwood, NY: St. Vladimir's Seminary Press, 2000), 50.
2. Ibid., 78.
3. Ibid., 25.
4. Ibid., 24.
5. Alexander Schmemann, *Great Lent: Journey to Pascha*, rev. ed. (1969; repr., Crestwood, NY: St. Vladimir's Seminary Press, 1974), 132.
6. Alexander Schmemann, *For the Life of the World*, rev. ed. (1963; repr., Crestwood, NY: St. Vladimir's Seminary Press, 1973), 124.
7. Ol'ga E. Kaz'mina, *Russkaia Pravoslavnaia Tserkov' i novaia religioznaia situatsiia v Rossii* (Moscow: Moskovskii gosudarstvennyi universitet, 2009), 57.
8. Scott M. Kenworthy, *The Heart of Russia: Trinity-Sergius, Monasticism, and Society after 1825* (New York: Oxford University Press, 2010), 366.
9. Reinhold Niebuhr, *The Nature and Destiny of Man* (New York: Charles Scribner's Sons, 1947), 2:269.
10. Jon D. Levenson, *The Love of God: Divine Gift, Human Gratitude, and Mutual Faithfulness in Judaism* (Princeton, NJ: Princeton University Press, 2016), 10.
11. Alexander Schmemann, *Introduction to Liturgical Theology*, trans. Asheleigh Moorhouse, 3rd ed. (1966; repr., Crestwood, NY: St. Vladimir's Seminary Press, 1986).
12. Hans-Christian Diedrich, *"Wohin sollen wir gehen . . .": Der Weg der Christen durch die sowjetische Religionsverfolgung* (Erlangen: Martin-Luther Verlag, 2007), 63.
13. Kenworthy, *Heart of Russia*, 312.
14. Vladimir Vorob'ev, ed., *Postradavshie za veru i tserkov' Khristovu, 1917–1937* (Moscow: Pravoslavnyi Sviato-Tikhonovskii gumanitarnyi universitet, 2012), 200.
15. As quoted in Nathaniel Davis, *A Long Walk to Church: A Contemporary History of Russian Orthodoxy* (Boulder, CO: Westview Press, 2003), 3.
16. Kenworthy, *Heart of Russia*, 326.
17. For these events, see Davis, *A Long Walk to Church*, 7–8.
18. As quoted in A. V. Kuraev, *Osnovy pravoslavnoi kul'tury* (Moscow: Prosveshchenie, 2010), 60–61.
19. Davis, *A Long Walk to Church*, 9–10.
20. Diedrich, *"Wohin sollen wir gehen,"* 79–82.
21. N. A. Krivosheeva, "Novomucheniki Russkoi Pravoslavnoi Tserkvi—Chleni Pomestnogo Sobora 1917-18 gg.," in *Proslavlenie i pochitanie Sviatikh* (Moscow: XVII International Educational Christmas Lectures, February 17, 2009), 56–58.
22. Diedrich, *"Wohin sollen wir gehen,"* 67.
23. See Diedrich, *"Wohin sollen wir gehen,"* 142–46; and Gregory L. Freeze, "Von der Entkirchlichung zur Laisierung: Staat, Kirche und Gläubige in Russland," in *Politik und Religion: Zur Diagnose der Gegenwart*, ed. Friedrich-Wilhelm Graf and Heinrich Meier (Munich: C. H. Beck, 2013), 103.
24. Diedrich, *"Wohin sollen wir gehen,"* 133–34.
25. Ibid., 142.
26. Aleksei Beglov, *V poiskakh "bezgreshnykh katakomb": Tserkovnoe podpol'e v SSSR* (Moscow: Arefa, 2008).
27. Davis, *A Long Walk to Church*, 55, 172.
28. The importance of maintaining traditions of icon painting also testifies to the continuing power of the Church's liturgical vision during these years. See Irina Yazykova, *Hidden and Triumphant:*

The Underground Struggle to Save Russian Iconography, trans. Paul Grenier (Brewster, MA: Paraclete, 2010), 91–118.

29. Vorob'ev, *Postradavshie za veru*, 266.

30. See Beglov, *V poiskakh "bezgreshnykh katakomb."*

31. "Zhitie sviashchennomuchenika Sergeia Mecheva," *Klenniki.ru*, http://klenniki.ru/srrg-mech-life; and "Mechevskaia obshchina," June 16, 2010, *Klenniki.ru*, http://klenniki.ru/mechev-obchin.

32. "Mechevskaia obshchina."

33. *Father Arseny, 1893–1973: Priest, Prisoner, Spiritual Father*, trans. Vera Bouteneff (Crestwood, NY: St. Vladimir's Seminary Press, 2002), 12.

34. *Father Arseny*, 65.

35. Viktor Mamontov, "Serdtse pustyni: Zhizneopisanie archimandrita Serafima (Tiapochkina)," *Pravoslavnaia Obshchina* 49, http://pravoslavni.ucoz.ru/news/arkhim_viktor_mamontov_serdce_pustyni/2011-06-01-464.

36. O. Vsevolod Shpiller, *Stranitsy zhizni v sokhranivshikhsia pis'makh* (Moscow: Reglant, 2004), 566.

37. Schmemann, *For the Life of the World*, 13.

38. As quoted in Trevor Beeson, *Discretion and Valour: Religious Conditions in Russia and Eastern Europe* (Philadelphia, PA: Fortress, 1982), 77–78.

39. Vorob'ev, *Postradavshie za veru*, 276.

40. See M. V. Shkarovskii and D. P. Anashkin, eds., *Pravoslanoe tserkovnoe soprotivlenie v SSSR (1927–1938)* (Moscow: ROSSPEN, 2013). Some émigré parishes, not acknowledging Nicholas's death, continued to commemorate him.

41. Kenworthy, *Heart of Russia*, 345.

42. Vladimir Vorob'ev, "Predislovie," in *Kifa: Patriarshii mestobliustitel' sviashchennomuchenik Petr, Mitropolit Krutitskii (1861–1937)* (Moscow: Pravoslavnyi Sviato-Tikhonovskii gumanitarnyi universitet, 2012), 8.

43. See John P. Burgess, "Retrieving the Martyrs in Order to Rethink the Political Order: The Russian Orthodox Case," *Journal of the Society of Christian Ethics* 34, no. 2 (Fall/Winter 2014): 177–201.

Notes to Chapter 9: "And I will tell of the best people in all the earth"

1. Viktor E. Frankl, *Man's Search for Meaning* (London: Rider, 2004).
2. Simone Weil, *Waiting on God* (London: Fontana, 1959), 84.
3. Ivan S. Turgenev, "Zhivye moshchi," in *Zapiski okhotnika* (Moscow: GIKhL, 1954), 364–77.
4. Irina Ratushinskaya, *No, I'm Not Afraid* (Newcastle upon Tyne: Bloodaxe, 1986), 132.
5. Irina Ratushinskaya, *Grey is the Colour of Hope*, trans. Alyona Kojevnikov (Hodder & Stoughton: London) 1988.
6. *Shtrafnoi izolyator*
7. Ibid., 193.
8. Isaiah Berlin, *Enlightening: Letters 1946–1960*, ed. Henry Hardy and Jennifer Holmes (London: Pimlico, 2011), 541.
9. Ratushinskaya, *Grey is the Colour of Hope*, 234.
10. "'The Living Poet': A Reading by Irina Ratushinskaya," BBC broadcast, May 3, 1987.
11. Ratushinskaya, *Grey is the Colour of Hope*, 146.
12. Ibid., 243–44.
13. Ibid., 186–87.
14. A memoir by Ilya Nykin in Ratushinskaya, *No, I'm Not Afraid*, 23.
15. Jonathan Luxmoore's interview with Ratushinskaya, September 1990, in *The God of the Gulag* by Jonathan Luxmoore (Leominster, UK: Gracewing, 2016), 2:157.
16. Ratushinskaya, *Grey is the Colour of Hope*, 25.
17. Ibid., 212.
18. Ibid., 65.

19. Ibid., 160.
20. Ibid., 74.
21. Ibid., 102
22. Ibid., 182.
23. Ibid., 248.
24. "Someone is thinking of me now," interview with Ratushinskaia conducted by Keston College staff, *Frontier* (Keston College), March–April 1987, pp. 12–14.
25. Ratushinskaya, *No, I'm Not Afraid*, 14–15.
26. Ibid., 132.
27. Ibid., 136.
28. Ratushinskaya, *Grey is the Colour of Hope*, 67.
29. Ibid., 69.
30. Ibid., 186.
31. Ibid.
32. The author, Xenia Dennen, was one of the founders with Michael Bourdeaux of Keston College, and is now its chairman.
33. Author's interview (May 2016) with Alyona Kojevnikov who observed, "the translation of *Grey* [sic] took one month from start to finish, as Irina, who was staying in my house, would write one chapter every day while I was at work, and I would translate it the same evening."
34. Ibid.
35. Ibid.
36. Ibid.
37. Ibid.
38. Ibid.
39. Ibid.
40. "Believe me, it was often thus," poem by Irina Ratushinskaia, quoted in "Someone is thinking of me now," interview with Ratushinskaia conducted by Keston College staff, *Frontier*, (Keston College), March–April 1987, p. 13.
41. *The Unknown Homeland,* trans. Marite Sapiets (London: Mowbrays, 1978).
42. Ibid., 110–11.
43. Ibid., 141.
44. Ibid., 247.
45. E. V. Chicherina, *U Boga vse zhivyi: Vospominaniia o Danilovskom startse Arkhimandrite Georgii (Lavrove)* (Moscow: Danilovskii blagovestnik, 1996).
46. Ibid., 110.
47. Serafim Chetverukhin, *Tolmachi: Vospominaniia ob otse* (Moscow: Nauka, 1992). The word *tolmach* in the seventeenth century meant an interpreter or translator, and became the name of an area in Moscow where *tolmachi* lived, and where a church dedicated to St. Nikolai was built. Fr. Il'ia Chetverukhin served as priest in charge of this church for ten years.
48. Ibid., 73.
49. Ibid., 76.
50. Ibid., 81.
51. V. S. Bobrinskaia, *Zapiski sviashchennika Sergiia Sidorova* (Moscow: Pravoslavnyi Sviato-Tikhonovskii gumanitarnyi institut, 1999).
52. Ibid., 276.
53. Ibid., 277–78.
54. Ibid., 280–81.
55. Michael Bourdeaux, *Patriarch and Prophets: Persecution of the Russian Orthodox Church Today* (London: Macmillan, 1969), 68–69.
56. O. V. Kosik, *Molitva vsekh vas spaset: Materialy k zhizneopisaniiu Sviatitelia Afanasia, Episkopa Kovrovskogo* (Moscow: Pravoslavnyi Sviato-Tikhonovskii bogoslovskii institut, 2000), 133 (Archpriest Vasilii Arkhangel'skii's reminiscences).

57. Ibid., 67 (N. V. Trapani's reminiscences).
58. Ibid., 144 (N. S. Fioletova's reminiscences about Bishop Afanasii's final days).
59. Ibid., 95-98.
60. Ibid., 95.
61. Ibid., 147 and 159.
62. Andrei Amalrik, *Will the Soviet Union Survive until 1984?* (New York: Harper & Row, 1970). The Russian edition was published by the Herzen Foundation, Amsterdam, in 1969.
63. The Keston Center website: http://www.baylor.edu/kestoncenter.

Notes to Chapter 10: "There are things in history that should be called by their proper names"

1. Nathaniel Davis, *A Long Walk to Church: A Contemporary History of Russian Orthodoxy* (Boulder, CO: Westview Press, 1995), 213.
2. Felix Corley, *Religion in the Soviet Union: An Archival Reader* (Basingstoke: Macmillan, 1996), 25.
3. Ia. N. Shchapov, ed., *Russkaia Pravoslavnaia Tserkov' i kommunisticheskoe gosudarstvo: 1917-1941; Dokumenty i fotomaterialy* (Moscow: Bibleisko-Bogoslovskii institut sv. apostola Andreia, 1996), 23-24.
4. M. E. Gubonin, ed., *Akty Sviateishego Tikhona, Patriarkha Moskovskogo i vseia Rossii, pozdneishie dokumenty i perepiska o kanonicheskom preemstve vysshei tserkovnoi vlasti 1917-1943* (Moscow: Pravoslavnyi Sviato-Tikhonovskii bogoslovskii institut, 1994), 280-81, 288, 296-98, 307, 361-63.
5. Sergei Firsov, "Kompromiss vo imia spaseniia," *NG-Religii*, May 26, 2004, http://www.ng.ru/ng_religii/2004-05-26/7_compromise.html.
6. Aleksandr Mazyrin, *Vysshie ierarkhi o preemstve vlasti v Russkoi Pravoslavnoi Tserkvi v 1920-x-1930-x godakh* (Moscow: Pravoslavnyi Sviato-Tikhonovskii gumanitarnyi universitet, 2006), 12, 246.
7. Gubonin, *Akty Sviateishego Tikhona*, 473-75.
8. Ibid., 500-507; Dimitry Pospielovsky, *The Russian Church under the Soviet Regime, 1917-1982* (Crestwood, NY: St Vladimir's Seminary Press, 1984), 1:144-46.
9. Mazyrin, *Vysshie ierarkhi*, 61, 266-67; Damaskin (Orlovskii), *Mucheniki, ispovedniki i podvizhniki blagochestiia Russkoi Pravoslavnoi Tserkvi XX stoletiia: Zhizneopisaniia i materialy k nim* (Tver: Bulat, 2001), 2:361.
10. Gubonin, *Akty Sviateishego Tikhona*, 498.
11. Ibid., 509-13.
12. Mazyrin, *Vysshie ierarkhi*, 19-20.
13. Gubonin, *Akty Sviateishego Tikhona*, 682-86.
14. Anatolii Svenitsitskii, *Nevidimye niti: Tserkov', sobytiia, liudi* (Moscow: Izd-vo Moskovskoi Patriarkhii, 2009), 112-13.
15. Mazyrin, *Vysshie ierarkhi*, 345.
16. Ibid., 357-58; Gubonin, *Akty Sviateishego Tikhona*, 703.
17. Lev Regel'son, *Tragediia Russkoi Tserkvi 1917-1945* (Moscow: Izdatel'stvo Krutitskogo Podvor'ia/Obshchestvo liubitelei tserkovnoi istorii, 2007), 4.
18. Mazyrin, *Vysshie ierarkhi*, 40-41, 392-93.
19. Ibid., 380, Gubonin, *Akty Sviateishego Tikhona*, 681-82.
20. Mazyrin, *Vysshie ierarkhi*, 352, 387.
21. Ibid., 73, 80, 83.
22. Church decree 362 of November 20, 1920, urged dioceses to govern themselves if cut off from higher ecclesiastical authority or if it ceased to exist. Gubonin, *Akty Sviateishego Tikhona*, 573-74; Mazyrin, *Vysshie ierarkhi*, 67.
23. "Freedom and peace" apparently refers to the 1927 Declaration's promise for "peaceful and quiet lives" [1 Timothy 2:2] for Orthodox obedient to the Soviet authorities. Mazyrin, *Vysshie ierarkhi*, 352-53.

24. M. I. Odintsov, *Russkie patriarkhi XX veka* (Moscow: RAGS, 1999), 1:272.

25. Mazyrin, *Vysshie ierarkhi*, 174, 182, 193.

26. Shchapov, *Russkaia Pravoslavnaia Tserkov'*, 298; Sergei Firsov, "Stalinskii konkordat," *NG-Religii*, September 3, 2003, http://www.ng.ru/ng_religii/2003-09-03/6_konkordat.html.

27. Innokentii (Pavlov), "Povorotnyi punkt istorii ili propagandistskaia aktsiia?," *Portal-Credo*, September 10, 2003, https://www.portal-credo.ru/site/?act=fresh&id=132.

28. Nicholas (Yarushevich), Gregory Petrovich Georgievsky, and Alexander Pavlovich Smirnov, eds., *The Truth About Religion in Russia, Issued by the Moscow Patriarchate (1942)* (London: Hutchinson & Co., 1944), 21.

29. Odintsov, *Russkie patriarkhi XX veka*, 283–91.

30. Ibid., 310.

31. Jane Ellis, *The Russian Orthodox Church: A Contemporary History* (London: Routledge, 1986), 111–14.

32. Ibid., 223–24, 237.

33. Ibid., 304.

34. M. V. Shkarovskii, *Russkaia Pravoslavnaia Tserkov v XX veke* (Moscow: Veche/Lepta, 2010), 429–30.

35. Vasilii, "Neskol'ko slov ob interv'iu Arkhiepiskopa Volokolamskogo Pitirima," *Vestnik Russkogo khristianskogo dvizheniia*, no. 114 (1974): 268–70.

36. Davis, *A Long Walk to Church*, 95.

37. Ellis, *The Russian Orthodox Church*, 215–17.

38. "KGB, Moskovskaia patriarkhiia i polozhenie Russkoi Pravoslavnoi tserkvi," *Glasnost'*, no. 13 (1988): http://grigoryants.ru/zhurnal-glasnost/glasnost-13/#8; Ellis, *The Russian Orthodox Church*, 224–26.

39. Yevgeni Polyakov, "The Activities of the Moscow Patriarchate during 1991," *Religion, State and Society* 22, no. 2 (1994): 152.

40. Davis, *A Long Walk to Church*, 95; Jane Ellis, *The Russian Orthodox Church: Triumphalism and Defensiveness* (Basingstoke: Macmillan, 1996), 133–36.

41. Patriarch Aleksii II's identity as "Drozdov" was further corroborated by archival records in Estonia in 1996. See Felix Corley, "Russia: The Patriarch and the KGB," *Keston News Service*, September 21, 2000.

42. Corley, *Religion in the Soviet Union*, 369.

43. Nikolai Mitrokhin and Sof'ia Timofeeva, *Episkopy i eparkhii Russkoi Pravoslavnoi Tserkvi* (Moscow: Panorama, 1997), 112.

44. Corley, *Religion in the Soviet Union*, 375. Iakunin also found material concerned with collaboration by other faith communities in the USSR.

45. Ellis, *The Russian Orthodox Church*, 53–69.

46. Gerhard Besier, Armin Boyens, and Gerhard Lindemann, *Nationaler Protestantismus und Ökumenische Bewegung: Kirchliches Handeln im Kalten Krieg (1945–1990)* (Berlin: Duncker & Humblot, 1999), 40–44.

47. Christopher Andrew and Vasili Mitrokhin, *The Sword and the Shield: The Mitrokhin Archive and the Secret History of the KGB* (New York: Basic Books, 1999), 486–507; "The Mitrokin Archive—A Note on Sources," 2004, Wilson Center Digital Archive, http://digitalarchive.wilsoncenter.org/document/112821; "By the Church Gates, Folder 1: The Chekist Anthology," June 2007, Wilson Center Digital Archive, http://digitalarchive.wilsoncenter.org/document/113349.

48. Andrew and Mitrokhin, *The Sword and the Shield*, 488; "Skonchalsia stareishii sotrudnik Otdela vneshnikh tserkovnykh sviazei A. S. Buevskii," Official Website of the Moscow Patriarchate, April 9, 2009, http://www.patriarchia.ru/db/text/611117.html; Ellis, *The Russian Orthodox Church*, 266; Avgustin (Nikitin), *Tserkov' plenennaia: Mitropolit Nikodim (1929–1978) i ego epokha* (St. Petersburg: St. Petersburg University, 2008), 261.

49. Andrew and Mitrokhin, *The Sword and the Shield*, 497–98.

50. "By the Church Gates"; Andrew and Mitrokhin, *The Sword and the Shield*, 496.

51. Andrew and Mitrokhin, *The Sword and the Shield*, 495–96; "By the Church Gates."
52. Ellis, *The Russian Orthodox Church*, 380–81.
53. "Dokument: Dobroe slovo ob agente 'Drug.'" Pis'mo sviashchennika Gleba Iakunina glavnomu redaktoru 'Portala-Credo.Ru' Aleksandru Soldatovu," *Portal-Credo*, January 18, 2011, http://www.portal-credo.ru/site/?act=news&id=81918.
54. Ellis, *The Russian Orthodox Church*, 141.
55. Davis, *A Long Walk to Church*, 89.
56. Mikhail Pozdnyayev, "'I Cooperated with the KGB ... but I Was Not an Informer': An Interview with Archbishop Khrizostom of Vilnius and Lithuania," *Religion, State and Society* 21, nos. 3–4 (1993): 347–49.
57. "O nagrazhdenii gosudarstvennymi nagrazhdeniiami Rossiiskoi Federatsii," presidential decree (*ukaz*) no. 1019, September 29, 2002, http://www.kremlin.ru/acts/bank/18541.
58. "Dokument: Obrashchenie chlena Moskovskoi Khel'sinskoi gruppy, klirika Kostromskoi eparkhii RPTs MP sviashchennika Georgiia Edel'shteina, k prezidentu RF V. V. Putinu," *Portal-Credo*, May 28, 2003, http://portal-credo.ru/site/?act=news&id=10684&type=view.
59. Pozdnyayev, "'I Cooperated with the KGB.'"
60. Evgenii Komarov, "FSB podtianula RPTs k svoemu 'pi-aru,'" *Novye Izvestiia*, March 12, 2002, http://www.rusglobus.net/komar/index.htm?church/fsb.htm&1.
61. "Dokument: Obrashchenie chlena."
62. Author's interview with Fr. Vsevolod Chaplin, February 18, 2000, Moscow.
63. Andrei Kuraev, "Budni i tiagoty tserkovnoi zhizni," *Livejournal*, March 29, 2014, http://diak-kuraev.livejournal.com/646226.html.
64. Georgii Edel'shtein, *Zapiski Sel'skogo Sviashchennika* (Moscow: RGGU, 2005), 121–22.
65. Pozdnyayev, "'I Cooperated with the KGB.'"
66. Mitrokhin and Timofeeva, *Episkopy i eparkhii*; Tikhon (Shevkunov), *Everyday Saints and Other Stories* (Moscow: Pokrov, 2012), 117–39; Georgii Edel'shtein, "O knige arkhimandrita Tikhona (Shevkunova) 'Nesviatye sviatye' (chast'1)," *Livejournal*, January 30, 2013, http://g-edelstein.livejournal.com/8267.html.
67. "Gavriil (Stebliuchenko)," *Drevo*, https://drevo-info.ru/articles/6040.html#1; "Ukaz Presidenta Rossiiskoi Federatsii o nagrazhdenii gosudarstvennymi nagradami Rossiiskoi Federatsii," Archive of the Official Site of the Moscow Patriarchate, April 11, 2001, https://mospat.ru/archive/2001/04/nr104112/.
68. "Platon, mitropolit Feodosiiskii i Kerchenskii (Udovenko Vladimir Petrovich)," Official Website of the Moscow Patriarchate, http://www.patriarchia.ru/db/text/77113.html.
69. "Lev, mitropolit Novgorodskii i Starorusskii (Tserpitskii Nikolai L'vovich)," Official Website of the Moscow Patriarchate, http://www.patriarchia.ru/db/text/38914.html.
70. "Prepodavateli Odesskoi Dukhovnoi Seminarii," Odessa Theological Seminary website, http://www.odseminary.orthodox.ru/prepod_ods.htm.
71. "Iosif (Pustoutov)," Russkoe Pravoslavie Charitable Foundation website, http://www.orthorus.ru/cgi-bin/ps_file.cgi?3_2535.
72. "Svetloi pamiati prot. Vasiliia Fonchenkova," The Russian Orthodox Church outside Russia (ROCOR) German diocese website, October 10, 2006, http://rocor.de/vestnik/2006/4/svetloj-pamyati-prot-vasiliya-fonchenkova.html.
73. Ellis, *The Russian Orthodox Church*, 127–28.
74. Kirill Milovidov, "Butovskii poligon: Lekarstvo ot kommunizma," *Neskuchnyi Sad*, May 31, 2013, http://www.nsad.ru/articles/butovskij-poligon-lekarstvo-ot-kommunizma.
75. "The Basis of the Social Concept," ch. 3, pt. 5, The Russian Orthodox Church: Department for External Church Relations website, http://www.mospat.ru/en/documents/social-concepts/iii/.
76. "On the Relationship Between the Church and State," ROCOR website, June 21, 2005, http://www.synod.com/synod/engdocuments/enmat_churchandstate.html.
77. Gubonin, *Akty Sviateishego Tikhona*, 151.

78. "On the Joint Work of the Commissions of the Moscow Patriarchate and the Russian Orthodox Church Outside of Russia," ROCOR website, June 21, 2005, http://www.synod.com/synod/engdocuments/enmat_aboutwork.html.

79. "Commentary on the Joint Document of the Commissions of the Moscow Patriarchate and the Russian Orthodox Church Outside of Russia Entitled 'On the Relationship between Church and State,'" ROCOR website, June 21, 2005, http://www.synod.com/synod/engdocuments/enmat_commentary.html; "Kommentarii k sovmestnomu dokumentu Komissii Moskovskogo Patriarkhata i Russkoi Zarubezhnoi Tserkvi 'Ob otnosheniiakh Tserkvi i gosudarstva,'" ROCOR and Moscow Patriarchate websites, June 21, 2005, http://www.synod.com/synod/documents/mat_kommentariy.html; http://www.patriarchia.ru/db/text/26049.html.

80. Gavriil (Chemodakov), "Bol'shei chaste nashei pastvy neponiatno, chto izmenilos', pochemu vdrug seichas takoe otnoshenie k MP, budto drugogo vzgliada na nee nikogda ne bylo," *Portal-Credo*, June 24, 2005, http://portal-credo.ru/site/?act=authority&id=340.

81. "'Moskovskiie Novosti': 'Sobornye golosa. Velikaia kniaginia Mariia Vladimirovna Romanova spetsial'no dlia 'MN,'" *Interfax*, May 19, 2006, http://www.interfax-religion.ru/print.php?act=print_media&id=3550.

82. Sergei Fomin, *Strazh Doma Gospodnia: Patriarkh Moskovskii i vseia Rusi Sergii (Stragorodskii)* (Moscow: Pravilo Very, 2003), 4–5, 246–47.

83. *Angel russkoi tserkvi protov ottsa vsekh narodov*, NTV, April 22, 2006, https://www.youtube.com/watch?v=BxcMLerggjM.

84. Shchapov, *Russkaia Pravoslavnaia Tserkov'*, 237–39.

85. Fomin, *Strazh Doma Gospodnia*, 2.

86. Odintsov, *Russkie patriarkhi XX veka*, 202.

87. Svenitsitskii, *Nevidimye nity*, 144.

88. "Gosstruktury zatrudniaiut rabotu Sinodal'noi komissii po kanonizatsii sviatykh," *Newsru*, February 17, 2009, http://www.newsru.com/religy/17feb2009/geheimnisse.html.

89. "Predstavitel' RPTs: Zakrytost' rossiiskikh arkhivov tormozit protsess kanonizatsii sviatykh," *Newsru*, May 16, 2013, http://www.newsru.com/religy/16may2013/archive.html.

90. "Sviateishii Patriarkh Kirill sovershil chin osviashcheniia zakladnogo kamnia v osnovanie khrama sv. Feodora Ushakova v stolichnom raione Iuzhnoe Butovo," Official Website of the Moscow Patriarchate, April 15, 2015, http://www.patriarchia.ru/db/text/4042225.html.

91. Marina Tokareva, "Otets Aleksei (Uminskii): 'U Tserkvi net tseli bor'by so zlom,'" *Novaia Gazeta*, August 28, 2015, http://www.novayagazeta.ru/arts/69720.html.

92. Maksim Kozlov, "'Novaia Gazeta.' Patriarkh Sergi Stragorodskii: 'S takim pis'mom i na strashnyi sud ne strashno!,'" *Interfax*, October 25, 2015, http://www.interfax-religion.ru/?act=print&div=18921.

93. Georgii Mitrofanov, "Spasutsia li prebyvaiushchie v sergianstve veruiushchie?," *Novaia gazeta*, November 11, 2015, http://www.novayagazeta.ru/arts/70690.html.

94. Tokareva, "Otets Aleksei."

95. "Address to the Federal Assembly," December 12, 2012, Russian presidential website, http://en.kremlin.ru/events/president/news/17118. See also Igor Torbakov, "The Russian Orthodox Church and Contestations over History in Contemporary Russia," *Demokratizatsiya* 22, no. 1 (2014): 156–57.

96. "V den' pamiati zhertv politicheskikh repressii Vladimir Putin posetil Butovskii memoral'nyi kompleks," Russian presidential website, October 30, 2007, http://kremlin.ru/events/president/news/43148.

97. "Stenograficheskii otchet o rashirennoi press-konferentsii dlia rossiiskikh i inostrannykh zhurnalistov," Russian presidential website, July 18, 2001, http://www.kremlin.ru/events/president/transcripts/21291.

98. "Spetsial'naia programma 'Razgovor s Vladimirom Putinym: Prodolzhenie,'" Government of the Russian Federation, December 3, 2009, http://2009.moskva-putinu.ru/.

99. "Zamestitel' predsedatelia OVTsS igumen Filipp (Riabykh): 'Voinu vyigral nash mnogonatsional'nyi narod, vedomyi svoei liubov'iu k Otechestvu,'" ROC Department of External Church Relations, May 6, 2010, http://www.mospat.ru/ru/2010/05/06/news17638/.

100. "Poslanie Patriarkha Sergiia k 26-i godovshchine Sovetskogo gosudarstva," *Zhurnal Moskovskoi Patriarkhii*, no. 3 (November 1943): 4; "Vladimir Putin vstretilsiia v Sviato-Danilovom monastyre s predstaviteliami religioznykh konfessii Rossii," Slavic Centre for Law and Justice, February 9, 2012, http://www.sclj.ru/massmedia/detail.php?ELEMENT_ID=3883.

101. Fomin, *Strazh Doma Gospodnia*, 700–702.

102. "Saratovskaia mitropoliia izvinilas' za torzhestvennoe osviashchenie ikony so Stalinym," *Obshchestvennoe Mnenie Saratov*, June 16, 2015, http://om-saratov.ru/novosti/16-June-2015-i25540-saratovskaya-mitropoliya-izvin.

103. "Otvet Belgorodskoi mitropolii na publikatsiiu o 'sovershennom bogosluzhenii pered ikonoi Stalina,'" Belgorod and Starooskol diocese website, May 29, 2015, http://beleparh.ru/index.php/novosti/21-sluzhenie/5887-otvet-belgorodskoj-mitropolii-na-publikatsiyu-o-sovershennom-bogosluzhenii-pered-ikonoj-stalina.

104. "Delegatsiia Brianskogo otdeleniia Izborgskogo kluba priniala uchastie v rabote plenuma Soiuza pisatelei Rossii, posviashchennogo 70-letiiu Velikoi Pobedy," *Borodino 2012–2045*, May 23, 2015, http://www.borodino2012-2045.com/новости /23896.html.

105. Aleksandr Samsonov, "Bol'sheviki spasli russkuiu tsivilizatsiiu," Kainsk diocesan website, November 7, 2015, http://kainsk-eparhia.ru/bolsheviki-spasli-russkuyu-civilizaciyu/.

106. Andrei Desnitskii, "Pravoslavnyi stalinizm: Pochemu v RPTs poliubili Stalina," Moscow Carnegie Centre, December 24, 2015, http://carnegie.ru/commentary/2015/12/24/ru-62352/io7t.

107. "'Glava gosudarstva i Predstoiatel' Russkoi Pravoslavnoi Tserkvi otkryli vystavku 'Pravoslavnaia Rus' v Moskve," Official Website of the Moscow Patriarchate, November 4, 2015, http://www.patriarchia.ru/db/text/4263139.html.

108. Leonid Smirnov, "'Tserkov' budet meniat'sia v storonu prostoty," *Rosbalt*, January 5, 2016, http://www.rosbalt.ru/moscow/2016/01/05/1476536.html.

109. Vsevolod Chaplin, "Gazeta 'Pravoslavnaia Moskva': 'Loskutki,'" *Interfax*, August 7, 2006, http://www.interfax-religion.ru/?act=print&div=4084.

110. Tom Balmforth, "In Russia, an Outspoken Priest Falls from Grace," *RadioFreeEurope/RadioLiberty*, March 28, 2016, http://www.rferl.org/content/russia-chaplin-interview-putin-kirill-orthodox-church-conservatism/27639946.html.

111. Patriarch Kirill (Gundiaev) of Moscow and all Rus', Metropolitan Varnava (Kedrov) of Cheboksary and Chuvashia, Metropolitan Iuvenali (Poiarkov) of Krutitsy and Kolomna, Metropolitan German (Timofeev) of Volgograd and Kamyshin, Metropolitan Isidor (Kirichenko) of Ekaterinodar and Kuban.

112. Balmforth, "In Russia, an Outspoken Priest Falls from Grace."

Notes to Chapter 11: The Useful God

1. The concept of *symphonia* evolved in Byzantium in the fifth century CE and was formally enunciated as doctrine by Byzantine emperor Justinian in the *Corpus Iuris Civilis* (Body of civil law) in 533 CE. The thrust of *symphonia* was a cooperative, formally non-dominant relation between church and state in which each operated in its respective divinely ordained spheres. *Symphonia* presumed the official status of Christianity as the established, governmentally sanctioned, and protected religion, according to Emperor Theodosius's Edict of Thessalonika promulgated in 380 CE.

2. Alfred Stepan, "The Multiple Secularisms of Modern Democratic and Non-Democratic Regimes", in Craig Calhoun, Mark Juergensmeyer, and Jonathan Van Antwerpen, eds., *Rethinking Secularism* (New York: Oxford University Press, 2011), 118–184.

3. Alfred Stepan, "Religion, Democracy, and the 'Twin Tolerations,'" *Journal of Democracy*, 11, no. 2 (October 2000): 37–57; Michael Walzer, *The Revolution of the Saints: A Study in the Origins of Radical Politics* (Cambridge: Harvard University Press, 1965).

4. Ol'ga Kryshtanovskaya and Stephen White, "The Sovietization of Russian Politics," *Post-Soviet Affairs* 25, no. 4 (2009), 283–309.

5. Catherine Wanner, ed., introduction to *State Secularism and Lived Religion in Soviet Russia and Ukraine* (New York: Oxford University Press, 2012), 2.

6. "Civilizational decoupling" in this case means the Communist Party's insistence that the success of "communist construction" depended upon a radical break, not only with Russia's tsarist political and economic institutions, but more fundamentally with the entire set of ideas and principles from which Russia's variant of Judeo-Christian civilization derived. In this respect the Communist Party attempted a wholesale cultural revolution.

7. The phrase "forced atheization" has tended to be used in post-Soviet Russia more often than the term "secularization" to describe the Communist Party's intentions and goals.

8. The doctrine of *symphonia,* noted above, called for an essentially equal co-governance of society by the state and the officially established Christian Church; in practice, however, the emperor clearly had the upper hand, and beginning with the cases of Emperors Constantine and Theodosius (among others), unapologetically so. Joseph Canning, *A History of Medieval Political Thought,* 300–1450, 2nd ed. (New York: Routledge, 1996), 1–39.

9. The *Moral Code of the Builder of Communism* was the following (with point #2, clearly derived from the New Testament [2 Thessalonians 3:10], representing an indulgence from the overall project of "civilizational decoupling" noted above):

1. Devotion to the cause of communism, love of the socialist motherland and of the socialist countries.
2. Conscientious labor for the good of society: he who does not work, neither shall he eat.
3. Concern on the part of everyone for the preservation and growth of public property.
4. High sense of public duty; intolerance of actions harmful to the public interest.
5. Collectivism and comradely mutual assistance: one for all and all for one.
6. Humane relations and mutual respect between individuals: man is to man a friend, a comrade, and a brother.
7. Honesty and truthfulness, moral purity, unpretentiousness and modesty in social and private life.
8. Mutual respect in the family, concern for the upbringing of children.
9. Irreconcilability toward injustice, parasitism, dishonesty, careerism, and profiteering.
10. Friendship and brotherhood among all peoples of the USSR, intolerance of national and racial hatred.
11. Intolerance toward the enemies of communism, peace, and freedom of nations.
12. Fraternal solidarity with the working people of all countries, and with all peoples.

10. Jeffrey Tayler, "Russia is Finished: The Unstoppable Descent into Social Catastrophe and Strategic Irrelevance," *The Atlantic Monthly* (May 2001), 52.

11. "Person of the Year 2007—Putin Q & A: Full Transcript," *Time* (2007); accessed 4 February 2016, http://content.time.com/time/specials/2007/personoftheyear/article/0,28804,1690753_1690757_1695787-3,00.html.

12. Helge Blakkisrud, "Blurring the boundary between civic and ethnic: The Kremlin's new approach to national identity under Putin's third term," *The New Russian Nationalism: Imperialism, Ethnicity and Authoritarianism 2000–15,* ed. Pål Kolstø and Helge Blakkisrud (Edinburgh: Edinburgh University Press), 258.

13. Mark Lilla, *The Stillborn God: Religion, Politics, and the Modern West* (New York: Alfred A. Knopf, 2007).

14. Sociologist Vyacheslav Karpov has referred to a process of "desecularization" in Russia, spurred by the Putin administration for a number of reasons of social and political expediency; see "The Social Dynamics of Russia's 'Desecularization'": A Comparative and Theoretical Perspective," *Religion, State, and Society* (September 2013), 1–30.

15. Jim Murdoch, "Protecting the Right to Freedom of Thought, Conscience, and Religion under the European Convention of Human Rights," Council of Europe Human Rights Handbooks (Strasbourg: Council of Europe, 2012), 6, 17, 39, 59, accessed January 17, 2017, http://www.coe.int/t/dgi/hr-natimplement/Source/documentation/hb09_rightfreedom_en.pdf.

16. Geraldine Fagan, *Believing in Russia: Religious Policy After Communism* (New York: Routledge, 2013); 53–68, 155–171; see also John Garrard and Carol Garrard, *Russian Orthodoxy Resurgent: Faith and Power in the New Russia* (Princeton and Oxford: Princeton University Press, 2008), 101–140.

17. Fagan, *Believing in Russia*, 172–200; see also *Forum 18 News Service*: "Russia: Religious Freedom Survey, January 2017," January 13, 2017, accessed January 17, 2017, http://www.forum18.org/archive.php?article_id=2246.

18. James W. Warhola, "Coexistence or Confrontation? The Politics of Interaction between Orthodoxy and Islam in Putin's Russia: Culture, Institutions, and Leadership," *Religion, State, and Society* 6, no. 4 (Fall 2008): 343–359.

19. "Patriarch-Pope Meeting to Benefit Christians in Islamic Countries—Mufti Tajuddin," February 8, 2016, *Interfax—Religion*, http://www.interfax-religion.com/?act=news&div=12723. See also Daniel P. Payne, "Spiritual Security, the Russian Orthodox Church, and the Russian Foreign Ministry: Collaboration or Cooptation?," *Journal of Church and State* 52, no. 4 (November 2010): 712–27.

20. Alicja Curanović, "Weaknesses of the Post-Soviet Religious Model: The Kremlin and "Traditional" Religions in face of Interethnic Tensions in Russia," *Politics and Religion* 7, no 4, (December 2014): 788–817; James W. Warhola, "Dilemmas of the Modern Secular State: The Case of Russia under Putin," *Forum on Public Policy* 4, no. 1 (2008): 111–122.

21. This matter has been pursued in great depth and breadth; pertinent investigations can be found in John and Carol Garrard, *Russian Orthodoxy Resurgent: Faith and Power in the New Russia* (Princeton, NJ: Princeton University Press, 2008); Zoe Knox, *Russian Society and the Orthodox Church: Religion in Russia after Communism* (NY: Routledge, 2005); and Kimo Kaariainen and Dmitry Furman, *Starye tserkvi, novye veruiushchie: Religiia v massovom soznanii postsovetskoi Rossii* (St. Petersburg: Letniy Sad, 2000).

22. In the 2012-2013 Levada Center Annual report, surveys done in October 2012 indicated that 50 percent considered the Church "quite trustworthy," by far the modal response; 29 percent considered it "not quite trustworthy," and only 10 percent considered it "not trustworthy at all." Twelve percent indicated, "difficult to answer." These figures remained generally stable from 1997 onward, and if anything show increased trust of the ROC. Source: http://www.levada.ru/sites/default/files/2012_eng.pdf, p. 140, accessed February 2, 2016.

23. James Richter, "Putin and the Public Chamber," *Post-Soviet Affairs* 25, no. 1 (2009): 39–65.

24. "The Civic Chamber of the Russian Federation", official website (2016); accessed March 18, 2016, https://www.oprf.ru/en/about/.

25. Marcel H. Van Herpen, *Putin's Propaganda Machine: Soft Power and Russian Foreign Policy* (Maryland: Rowman and Littlefield, 2016), 127–176; Robert C. Blitt, "Russia's 'Orthodox' Foreign Policy: The Growing Influence of the Russian Orthodox Church in Shaping Russia's Policies Abroad," *University of Pennsylvania Journal of International Law* 33, no. 2 (2011): 363–460.

26. Vladimir Putin, "Presidential Address to the Federal Assembly," (Moscow: The Kremlin, December 12, 2013), accessed February 11, 2016, http://en.kremlin.ru/events/president/news/19825.

27. "Basis of the Social Concept, II. Church and Nation," sec. 3, The Russian Orthodox Church: Department for External Relations (official website), accessed January 17, 2017, https://mospat.ru/en/documents/social-concepts/ii/.

28. "Russians Return to Religion, But Not to Church," *Pew Research Center: Religion and Public Life*, May 10, 2014, accessed January 18, 2017, http://www.pewforum.org/2014/02/10/russians-return-to-religion-but-not-to-church/.

29. Vyacheslav Karpov, Elena Lisovskaya, and David Barry, "Ethnodoxy: How Popular Ideologies Fuse Religious and Ethnic Identities," *Journal for the Scientific Study of Religion* 51, no. 1 (2013): 638–655.

30. Karpov et al., "Ethnodoxy," abstract.

31. Curanović, "Weaknesses of the Post-Soviet Religious Model," 802–811; Geraldine Fagan, *Believing in Russia: Religious Policy After Communism*, (NY: Routledge, 2013), 95-120; Warhola, "Dilemmas of the Modern Secular State," 347–353.

32. Alicja Curanović, *The Religious Factor in Russian Foreign Policy* (NY: Routledge, 2012); Robert C. Blitt, "Russia's "Orthodox" Foreign Policy: The Growing Influence of the Russian Orthodox Church in Shaping Russia's Policies Abroad," *University of Pennsylvania Journal of International Law* 33, no. 2 (2011): 363–460; and Daniel P. Payne, "Spiritual Security, The Russian Orthodox Church, and the Russian Foreign Ministry: Collaboration or Cooptation?" *Journal of Church and State* 52, no. 4 (November 2010): 712–727.

33. Marcel H. Van Herpen, *Putin's Propaganda Machine: Soft Power and Russian Foreign Policy* (Lanham, Maryland: Rowman & Littlefield, 2016), 129–176.

34. Steve Bruce, "Did Protestantism Create Democracy?" *Democratization* 11, no. 4 (August 2004): 3–20; Robert D. Woodberry and Timothy S. Shah, "The Pioneering Protestants," *Journal of Democracy* 15, no. 5 (April 2004): 47–61; and Roland F. Tusalem, "The Role of Protestantism in Democratic Consolidation Among Transitional States," *Comparative Political Studies* 42, no. 7 (July 2009): 882–915.

35. James W. Warhola, "Religion and Modernization in Gorbachev's Soviet Union: An Indirect Challenge to Secular Authority," in Matthew C. Moen and Lowell Gustafson, eds. (Philadelphia: Temple University Press, 1992), 268–291.

36. Joseph Canning, *A History of Medieval Political Thought, 300–1450* (London: Routledge, 1996), 6–29.

37. Such disputes became more frequent, more sophisticated, and more historically influential as the controversies of the twelfth to thirteenth century Renaissance became manifest in highly influential works such as John of Paris's *On Royal and Papal Power* (1302), Dante's *De Monarchia* (1313), and especially Marsilius of Padua's *Defensor Pacis* (1324). The late medieval process of state formation in Russia does not appear to have been affected nor even influenced by these crucially important currents in Western political thought, all of which had the effect of calling for limited government and a socially constrained state.

38. James W. Warhola, "Revisiting the Russian 'Constrained Autocracy': 'Absolutism' and Natural Rights Theories in Russia and the West," in Christopher Marsh and Nikolas K. Gvosdev, eds., *Civil Society and the Search for Justice in Russia* (Lanham, Maryland: Lexington Press, 2002), 19–39.

39. Michael Walzer, *The Revolution of the Saints: A Study in the Origins of Radical Politics* (Cambridge: Harvard University Press, 1965); Robert D. Woodberry and Timothy S. Shah, "Christianity and Democracy: The Pioneering Protestants," *Journal of Democracy* 15, no. 2 (April, 2004): 47–60; and Robert D. Woodberry, "The Missionary Roots of Liberal Democracy," *The American Political Science Review* 106, no. 2 (May, 2012), 244–274.

40. Allen C. Lynch, *How Russia is Not Governed: Reflections on Russian Political Development* (New York: Oxford University Press, 2005).

41. Valeri Dzutsati, "Kadyrov Tests Moscow's Strategy in the North Caucasus," *Eurasia Daily Monitor* 13, no. 26 (February 8, 2016), accessed February 8, 2016, http://www.jamestown.org/programs/edm/single/?tx_ttnews % 5Btt_news % 5D=45078&tx_ttnews % 5BbackPid % 5D=27&cHash=67a6b4e3dc5aca9be4ff3dc90b86f4b6#.VrleZ7w4np5.

42. Dzutsati explains the matter well and is worth citing at length: "Moscow has supported 'traditional Islam' in the North Caucasus in its attempt to hold back and eliminate the Salafist type of Islam in the region. Salafists are often equated with the insurgency; but perhaps most importantly, the Salafists are not under control of the authorities—something the Russian government does not tolerate. In fact, the very reason for the popularity of the Salafists may be that they are relatively independent of the government. Thus, Moscow should presumably support Kadyrov's crusade against the 'wrong'

Islam. However, if Moscow supports Kadyrov and his crusaders, it will expand his influence, along with that of Sufism. Ironically, the North Caucasian regional governors, especially Ingushetia's Yevkurov, find themselves in the position of endorsing the pan-Islamist teaching of Salafism rather than the local-based Sufism, because the latter is used by Kadyrov to undermine their authority. It is unclear what position Moscow will take. On the one hand, Moscow probably has no interest in seeing the expansion of Kadyrov's influence beyond Chechnya but, at the same time, is afraid of a religious teaching it does not control. Intentionally or not, Kadyrov put Moscow in the position that its influence in the North Caucasus will be undermined whatever move it takes." Dzutsati, "Kadyrov Tests Moscow's Strategy."

43. Mark Juergensmeyer, *Global Rebellion: Religious Challenge to the Secular State* (Berkeley: University of California Press, 2008); Pippa Norris and Ronald Inglehart, *Sacred and and Secular: Religion and Politics Worldwide* (New York: Cambridge University Press, 2004).

44. Much of the upper leadership of ISIS (the Islamic State of Iraq and Syria) was drawn from the ranks of the former military establishment of Saddam Hussein's regime, and exhibited very little if any religion-based motive or goal per se. Jessica Stern and J. M. Berger, *ISIS: The State of Terror* (New York: HarperCollins, 2016).

45. James Hughes, *Chechnya: From Nationalism to Jihad* (Philadelphia: University of Pennsylvania Press, 2007).

46. Alicja Curanović, "The Post-Soviet Religious Model: Reflections on Relations between the State and Religious Institutions in the CIS Area," *Religion, State, and Society* 41, no. 3 (October, 2013): 330–351; see also James W. Warhola and Alex Lehning, "Political Order, Identity, and Security in Multinational, Multi-Religious Russia," *The Nationalities Papers* 35, no. 5 (November 2007): 945–968.

47. Van Herpen, *Putin's Propaganda Machine*, 268.

48. "Russian church's declaration of holy in Syria sparks calls for jihad," *Middle East Monitor* (October 2, 2015), accessed January 18, 2017, https://www.middleeastmonitor.com/news/middle-east/21407-russian-churchs-declaration-of-holy-in-syria-sparks-calls-for-jihad.

Notes to Afterword: Whether in Words or Deeds, Known and Unknown

1. Latvijas Valsts arhīvs (The State Archives of Latvia), fond 1448, opis' 1, delo 91, list 79–79 ob.
2. Ibid., f. 1448, op. 1, d. 92, ll. 9, 58.
3. Ibid., l. 60–60 ob.
4. Ibid., l. 2–2 ob.

INDEX

Abolition of Confessional and National Restrictions, 18
Adventists, 152–153
Afanas'ev, Iurii, 11
Alexander the Second, 51
Alekseev, Viktor, 79
Aleksii I, 60, 65, 81–82
Aleksii II (Patriarch), 95, 150, 195–196, 199, 201–202
Alexeeva, Liudmila, 140, 148
All-Russian Church Council of 1917–1918, 16–17
All-Russian Communist Party, 23
Amalrik, Andrei, 185
American Relief Administration, 25
Amnesty International, 154, 176
And Quiet Flows the Don, 98
Andropov, Yuri, 68, 70
Antireligious Commission, 22
Argentev, Aleksandr, 90–91
Arkhangelskii, Vasilii, 184
Aronzon, Leonid, 118
Aschberg, Olof, 26
Aseev, Nikolai, 99
Atheism, 27, 33, 47, 49–50, 56, 142, 206, 212
  militant, 30, 56, 91
Atlantic Monthly, The, 213

Babushkas, 56
  childcare and, 45–46
  demonizing of, 10, 18, 32–50
  religious instruction and, 41–50
Baptists, 41, 60, 67, 142,
  Initsiativniki, 145, 147–148, 152–154
Barabanov, Evgenii, 145–146, 152, 157
Barats-Kokhan, Galina, 174
Basis of the Social Concept, The, 218
Baylor University, 186
BBC, 52, 155, 172
  Russian Service, 71
Begun, Iosif, 90, 153
Belgrade Conference, 153, 157
Believing in Russia: Religious Policy after Communism, 222
Bellavin, Vasilii Ivanovich, 17

Berdiaev, Nikolai, 7, 30–31, 84–85, 92, 94, 151
  exile, 84
Bieliauskiene, Jadvyga, 174
Blok, Aleksandr, 3, 118
Bobrinskaia, Vera, 182–183
Bogoraz, Larisa Daniel, 140, 156
Bolsheviks/Bolshevism, 5, 10–11, 23, 30, 32, 95, 167–169
  collapse of, 8
  confiscation of church property, 18–21, 24–28, 35, 38
  decrees, 18, 21
  goals, 8, 206
  public support, 13–14
  religious policies, 12–31, 161–163, 166
  revolution, 17–18, 21, 29
  secular education and, 33, 37
Bolshoi Chorus and Orchestra, 72
Bolshoi Theatre, 72
Bonch-Bruevich, Vladimir, 18, 29
Boobbyer, Philip, 9, 98, 115
Boomerang, 141
Bordeaux, Michael, 6, 10–11, 51–73, 184
Boris (Saint), 95
Boris and Gleb Orthodox Church, 15–16
Borovoi, Vitalii, 56–57
Brezhnev, Leonid, 59–68, 83
Briand, Aristide, 21
Bristol, Mark I., 20
British Council of Churches, 68
British Museum, 26
British War Stock, 26
Brodskii, Iosif 115, 118, 129, 131, 175
Brothers Karamazov, 4
Budkiewicz, Konstantin, 25–26
Buevskii, Aleksei, 197
Bukovskii, Vladimir, 9, 141, 147
Bulgakov, Sergei, 17, 31, 94
Bulletin of the Council of Prisoner's Relatives, 148
Burgess, John, 7, 158–86
Butyrskaia Prison, 180, 183

Caesaropapism, 7
Café Saigon, 135
Carter, Jimmy, 147

INDEX

Cathedral of Christ the Savior, 54
Catherine the Great, 28
Catacomb churches, 80–81
Central Committee, 24
    Agitation and Propaganda Department, 22
Chalidze, Valerii, 146, 148
Chaplin, Vsevolod, 200, 208–209, 224
Chapnin, Sergei, 208
Chechnia, 221–223
Chernenko, Konstantin, 68
Chetverukhin, Il'ia, 181–182
Chetverukhin, Serafim, 181–182
Chetverukhin, Sergei, 181
Chicherin, Georgii, 25–26
Chicherina, Elena, 180–181
Childhood,
    activism and, 39
    atheism and, 33
    conceptions of, 36
    education of, 32–33, 54
    family and, 41–50
    grandmas and, 41–50
    historians of, 33
    ideals of, 33–34
    New Soviet Children, 41
    physical spaces of, 48
    post-Stalin Soviet view of, 40
    religion and, 32–50
    removal of, 39–40
    roles of children, 34
    Soviet authorities and, 35–41
    state's creation of a Soviet, 36
Chronicle of Current Events, 145–146, 148, 153
Chronicle of the Catholic Church in Lithuania, 145, 148
Churches Commission on International Affairs (CCIA), 68
Christ the Savior Cathedral, 163
Christian Committee for the Defense of Believers' Rights (CCDBR), 67, 77–78, 87, 90, 96, 151–152, 198
Christian Peace Conference, 198
Christian Seminar, 6, 64, 78
Chronicle, 72
Church of Hagia Sophia, 159
Church of St. Nikolai, 165–166
Church of St. Peter and St. Paul, 59
"Church on the Blood," 51
Churchill, Winston, 193
Cieplak, Jan, 25, 30
Civil War, 21, 31, 35, 161
Clergy

    disenfranchisement of, 20, 39, 49
    dissent, 52–68
    execution, 23, 25, 53
    exiled, 30, 39, 84, 90
    imprisonment, 20–21
    persecution, 52–68, 162–163
Cocktail, 141
Cold War, 87, 155, 176, 228
"Thaw," 140
Combes, Emile Justin Louis, 20–21
Combes legislation, 20
Comintern, 26
Commissariat of Education, 32
Commissariat of Enlightenment, 22, 37
Commissariat of Internal Affairs, 22
Commissariat of Justice, 20, 22
Commission on Juvenile Affairs, 153
Committee of the United Clergy (KODM), 17
Communism, 11, 30, 33, 36–37, 69
    religion under, 4, 23
    Ten Principals of the Moral Codex of the Builder of, 160, 213
Communist Manifesto, 106–107
Communist Party, 71, 99, 186, 211, 224–225
    goals of, 88
    Nineteenth Conference, 186
    Twenty-Second Party Congress, 213
    Twenty-Seventh Party Congress, 69
Communist Youth League (Komsomol), 40
Conference in Defense of All Churches and Religions, 226
Constantine (Emperor), 225
Constituent Assembly, 14
Convent of the Dormition, 180
Corley, Felix, 35
Corpus Iuris Civilis, 214
Council for Russian Orthodox Church Affairs (CROCA), 60–61
Council for Religious Affairs (CRA), 59, 195, 204, 214
Council for the Affairs of Religious Cults, 46, 214
Council of Ministers, 150
Council of Prisoners' Relatives, 153
Council of Religious Cults, 40
Cultural Revolution, 39
Czechoslovakia, Soviet invasion of, 5

Daily Worker, 53
Dakin, Henry, 67
Daniel, Iulii, 63, 115–116, 145, 156
Daniel, Wallace, 4, 6, 74–96

INDEX

Danilov Monastery, 48, 70, 73, 180
Darkness at Noon, 8
Davis, Nathaniel, 39
De Pressensé, Francis, 21
De Proyart, Jacqueline, 114
Decree on Abolishment of Military Chaplain Service, 18-19
Decree on Freedom of Conscience, Church and Religious Organizations. *See* January Decree
Decree on Separation of Church from State, and of School from Church. *See* January Decree
  "Concerning Execution of," 20
deGraffenried, Julie, 9-10, 32-50
Dennen, Xenia, 7, 170-186
Department for Agitation and Propaganda, 22
Deutsche Welle, 155, 198
Discretion and Valour, 68
Dobrovolskii, Aleksandr, 142
Doctor Zhivago, 1, 97-116, 141
  art of living in, 109-116
  "Chudo," 122
  demystifying the Revolution in, 100-109
  epilogue, 100
  Gordon, 101, 114
  Ivan Ivanovich, 111-112
  Larisa Feodorovna Guishar (Lara), 8, 101, 104, 106, 108, 110, 113-115
  "Na strastnoi" (During Holy Week), 121-122
  Nikolai Nikolaievich "Uncle Kolia," 97, 111-113
  Pamphil Palykh, 108
  Pasternakian Christ in, 114-115
  poetry in, 100, 110, 120-123
  Samdeviatov, 102
  Sima, 113-114
  Strelnikov, 102, 105-109
  Yurii Zhivago, 100-108, 110-114, 115
Dostoevsky, Fyodor, 4, 98, 102
Dudintsev, Vladimir, 141
Dudko, Dmitrii, 64-66, 81, 142, 145, 148-150, 152
  arrest and imprisonment, 66, 91-92
  birth and childhood, 65
  education, 65

Ecclesiastical Revolution, 16
Edelshtein, Georgii, 199-200
Eighth Party Congress, 10
  Article 13, 23
Eisenstadt, Moshe, 37

Ellis, Jane, 85-86
Enemies of the people, 39
Engels, Friedrich, 106-107
Enlightenment, Russian, 5, 101
Episcopal Church of Scotland, 66
Ermogen of Kaluga (Archbishop), 58-59, 62, 150
Esenin-Volpin, Aleksandr, 146
Eshliman, Nikolai, 59-61, 81-84, 150
  death, 83
  letters, 81-83, 86
Evangelicals, 28-29, 41
Evsektsiia, 37-38
Evtushenko, Evgenii, 98

Fadeev, P.F., 227-228
Fagan, Geraldine, 6-7, 187-209, 222
Famine, 7, 13, 24-25, 35
Fedorovskii Cathedral, 163
Feuerbach, Ludwig, 7, 31
Fioletova, Nina, 185
Filaret of Kiev and Galicia (Metropolitan), 139, 196
Filippov, Vasilii, 117, 134-137
Final Act of the Conference on Security and Cooperation in Europe, 87
  Concluding Act, 87
Fonchenkov, Vasilii, 198
Foundations for a Social Concept, 202
Francis (Pope), 215
Frankl, Viktor, 170-171
Fraternal Leaflet, 148
Freedom For All Denominations, 95
French, April, 48
Frontier, 178, 186
Fundamentals of Legislation of the USSR and Union Republics of Marriage and Family ("Fundamentals"), 40

Gabriel of Manhattan (Bishop), 203
Galanskov, Iurii, 141-142, 145, 154
Galetskii, Rostislav, 153
Gavrilova, Akulina, 114-115
Gelasius (Pope), 221
Genoa debt conference, 26
Georgievna, Iraida, 77, 80, 83, 92
Geraschenko, Igor, 171, 176
Ginzburg, Aleksandr, 141-142, 144-146, 148, 156
Glasnost, 11, 70, 140
Glaube in der 2 Welt Institute, 67
Gleb (Saint), 95
Glemp of Warsaw (Cardinal), 73

272 INDEX

Gokhran collection, 26
Gorbachev, Mikhail, 40–41, 51, 63, 66, 70, 95, 158, 176, 186
   lessening of religious restrictions, 68–73, 191
Gorbachev, Raisa, 72
Gorbanevskaia, Natalia, 5, 145–146, 156
Gorky, Maxim, 36
Gorky Institute of World Literature, 116
Grandmaison, Evgenii, 181
Granin, Daniil, 9
Great Reforms, 16
Great Terror of 1936–1938, 28, 163, 206
Greek Orthodox Church, 72
Grey Is the Colour of Hope, 176
Grigorenko, Petro, 143
Gromyko, Andrei, 72
Gubonin, M.E., 185
Gulag, 4–5, 8, 54, 85, 98, 100, 163, 178
   dismantling of, 166
   faith and resistance in, 170–186
   forgotten heroes of, 179–185
Gulad Archipelago, 85

Hackel, Sergei, 71
Hebly, Hans, 67–68
Helsinki Accords, 66–67, 87, 151
Helsinki Final Act, 87
Henoticon, 221
Herald of Salvation, 148
Herzen, Aleksandr, 31
Hitler, Adolph, 163
Holloway, Richard, 66
Holy Trinity-St. Sergius Monastery, 162, 168
Hoover, Herbert, 25
House, Francis, 57
Human Rights Committee, 146
Human Rights Day, 145
Human Rights on the Ecumenical Agenda, 68
Human rights movement, 5, 74, 86–92, 95
   ecumenism and collaboration, 147–154
   human dignity and freedom, 154–157
   Orthodox Christian dissidents and, 138–157
   religious freedom and, 141–146

Iakir, Petr, 145
Iakovlev, Aleksandr, 5, 8
Iakunin, Gleb, 4, 6, 8, 59–61, 66–67, 74–96, 155, 195, 197, 201
   arrest and imprisonment, 68, 91–94, 154
   birth, 79
   education, 80–81

"Eulogy of a Simple-Minded Fool of God," 75–76, 94–95
   human rights activism, 86–92, 95–96, 144, 146, 149–152, 156
   letters, 83–86, 96, 151–152
   mother, 79–80
   poetry, 74–76, 92–95
   priesthood, 81–83
   priesthood, suspension from, 83–86
   release from prison, 69
   trial, 77–79
Iakunina, Klavdiia Iosifovna, 79–80
Iaroslavksii, Emelian, 22, 37
Ilichov, L.F., 55–56
Initiative Group for the Defense of Human Rights in the USSR, 145, 147
Inter-Academic Institute for Missiological and Ecumenical Research. 67
"Instruction to the Orthodox Church against Government Acts," 19
Ioann of Belgorod (Metropolitan), 207
Islam, 4, 18, 34, 39, 46, 86, 212, 215, 217
Iurkiv, M.M., 90
Iuvenalii of Krutitsy and Kolomna (Metropolitan), 71, 196, 202
Ivanov, Viacheslav, 94
Izvestiia (News), 191

January Decree, 18–22, 27–28, 32, 35, 37–38, 53
Jaures, Jean, 21
Jehovah's Witnesses, 54
John Paul II, 40
Joint Services School for Linguists, 53
Journal of the Moscow Patriarchate, 54, 71, 139, 195, 208
Judaism, 4, 24–25, 34, 49–50, 63, 69, 86, 90, 131
Justinian (Emperor), 214

Kadyrov, Ramzan, 221
Kafka, Franz, 170–171
Kalanta, Romas, 156
Kalinin, Mikhail, 29
Kapitanchuk, Viktor, 78, 87, 89, 91, 151
Karpov, Georgii, 194
Karpov, Viacheslav, 219
Kazmina, Olga, 160
Kelly, Catriona, 37
Kerensky, Alexander, 13
Keston College, 174, 176–178, 186
   Center for Religion, Politics, and Society, 186
Keston News Service, 176

KGB, 6, 65–66, 68, 76–77, 85, 91–92, 177, 183, 195, 200–201, 205
  archives, 95
  infiltration of the Church, 195–198
Khaibulin, Hierodeacon Varsonofii, 78, 87, 89, 151
Khailo, Vladimir Pavlovich, 152
Khrizostom of Vilnius, 199–200
Khrushchev, Nikita, 10, 39–40, 47, 51, 55–56, 62, 138–139, 164, 166, 185
  censorship, relaxation of, 140–141
  foundations of Soviet dissent and, 139–141
  "Secret Speech," 139, 141
Kirillov, Vladimir, 118
Kirsanov, Vladimir, 182
Koestler, Arthur, 8
Kojevnikov, Alyona, 176–178
Kopelev, Lev, 49–50
Kosygin, Aleksei, 150
Kovalev, Sergei, 140, 145
Kozlov, Maksim, 205
Kowalewski, David, 148
Krasin, Viktor, 145
Krestiankin, Ioann, 203–204
Krivoshein, Vasilii, 194–195
Krivulin, Viktor, 117, 129–131, 134
  "Neopalimaia kupina" (The burning bush), 130–131
Krupskaia, Nadezhda, 37
Kulakov, Vladislav, 118
Kuprianov, Boris, 136
Kuroedov, Vladimir, 196
Kuroyedov, V.A., 59
Kuznetsov, Mikhail, 200

L'Humanite, 53
Lashkov, Vera, 142
Latvian SSR Council for Religious Affairs, 226–227
Lavrov, Georgii, 180
Law on Religious Associations, 38–39, 53
Lazareva, Natalia, 172, 174
League of Atheists, 22
League of Militant Godless, 22
Lefortovo Prison, 92
Lenin, Vladimir, 5, 18, 29, 33, 37, 84, 100, 106–107, 162, 166, 206
  Eighth Party Congress, 10
  execution of priests, 23, 25, 53
  Tenth Party Congress, 10, 23
Leningrad Theological Academy, 56

Lert, Raissa, 5–6
Levenson, Jon, 161
Levitin, Anatolii, 63–64, 142, 146–147, 149–150, 155, 179
  "A Light in the Little Window," 143, 155–156
  trial, 144–146, 151
Liberty Loan Bonds, 26
Lilla, Mark, 214, 225
Lingenfelter, Scott, 9–31
Literaturnaia gazeta, 57, 91
Lithuanian Catholic Church, 69
Litvinov, Pavel, 142–143, 156
Loyalty oaths and tests, 29, 54
Lubentsova, Valentina, 77
Lunacharskii, Anatolii, 37
Lutherans, 28, 54
Lyuboshchinsky, Mikhail, 203

MacCulloch, Diarmaid, 6
Maiakovskii, Vladimir, 99, 118
Mandel'shtam, Nadezhda, 93, 129–131
  "V Peterburge soidemsia snova" (We'll meet again in Petersburg), 130
Mandel'shtam, Osip, 98–99
Manifesto of Man, 141
Marchenko, Anatolii, 142–143
Marx, Karl, 31, 33, 100, 106–107
Marxism, 17, 106
  Christianity/religion and, 5, 7
  environment and, 36
Mechev, Aleksei, 165
Mechev, Sergei, 165
Medvedev, Dmitrii, 212, 214, 225
Medvedev, Roi, 146
Mefodii of Voronezh (Metropolitan), 199
Men, Aleksandr, 7, 47, 73, 79–81, 164
  death, 73
  education, 80
  human rights activism, 150–151
Men, Mikhail, 47
Mendelevich, Iosef, 148
Mennonites, 28
Merton, Thomas, 114
Metamorphosis, 170–171
Methodists, 54
Middle East Monitor, The, 224
Miracles, reports of, 28
Mitrofanov, Georgii, 205
Mitrokhin Archive, 197–198, 201
Moor, Dmitri, 42
Moscow City Court Building, 77

INDEX

Moscow Helsinki Monitoring Group, 87, 91, 148, 151
Moscow Patriarchate, 55, 62, 66–68, 80, 89, 153, 193, 197, 205
  Revisionism, 203–206, 208
Moscow University, 116, 174
My Testimony, 142
Nauka i religiia (Science and Religion), 55

Nazis, 54, 193
Nestor, 72
New Economic Policy (NEP), 18, 23, 26
New Martyrs and Confessors, 71, 163, 201–205, 207–208
"New Soviet Man," 30–32, 160
Nezhnyi, Aleksandr, 196, 200
Nicholas II, 13–14, 168
Niebuhr, Reinhold, 160
Nikitin, Sergei, 181
Nikolai (Metropolitan), 56–57
Ninth Congress of Soviets, 99
NKVD operations, 39, 48
Not By Bread Alone, 141
Novaia gazeta (New gazette), 205
Novosti, 195

Obolensky, Dmitri, 71
Obshchina (Community), 64, 155
October Revolution of 1917, 3, 102, 162–163, 167–168, 193
Odessa University, 171
Odintsov, Mikhail, 204
Ogorodnikiv, Aleksandr, 6–8, 64–65, 149, 155
Okhapkin, Oleg, 117
On Freedom of Conscience, 18
One Day in the Life of Ivan Denisovich, 58, 141
Orlov, Iurii, 87, 144, 151
Orlovskii, Damaskin, 204
Orthodox Church outside Russia (ROCOR), 224
Orthodox Rus: My History, From Great Upheavals to Great Victory, 207
Osipov, Aleksandr, 56, 147
Our Hope, 65
Our Lady of Kazan, 51–53
Oxford University, 59

Pacifism, 29
Paganism, 76
"Parasitism," 90
Parliamentary Committee for Freedom of Conscience, 95
Pasternak, Boris, 1, 5–8, 97–116, 124, 131, 141–142
  childhood, 99
  funeral, 115
  poetry, 100, 110, 120–123
Pasternak, Leonid, 99
Patriarch and Prophets, 184
Paul VI, 145
Payne, Ernest, 67
PEN International, 176
Pentecostals, 48, 67, 90–147, 152, 154
Perestroika, 5, 11, 70, 186
Perm oblast, 181
Perm 35, 93
Perm 37, 92–93
Peter the Great, 14
Petliuchencko, Viktor, 197
Philosophy of Freedom, 84
Phoenix, 141
Pimen of Krutitsy and Kolomna (Metropolitan), 62, 65, 70, 90–91
Pimen (Patriarch), 167, 194–195, 197, 201
Pitirim of Volokolamsk (Metropolitan), 194–196
Pochaev Monastery, 60
Podgornyi, Nikolai, 60–61, 81
Poetry
  Futurist, 118
  Metarealism, 126
  politics and, 98–100
  religion and, 117–137
  Symbolist, 118
  underground, 9, 123
Polianskii, Petr, 168, 189–191, 201, 205
Politburo, 25, 31, 87, 96
Poresh, Vladimir, 6, 64
Portret, 126
Posad, Sergiev, 162
Possessed, 102
Potter, Philip, 144
Pravda, 85
Pravdoliubov, Sergii, 203–204
Preobrazhenskii, Agafangel, 189, 191–192, 201
Prokhanov, Aleksandr, 206–207
Propaganda, 86
  antireligious, 34, 46–47, 52–68
  anti-babushka, 41–50
Prose Poems, 58
"Protect the children from the tenacious clutches of the Baptist and Evangelical scoundrels, 42
Pskov-Pechory Monastery, 196, 200
Public Chamber, 216–217
Pussy Riot, 96
Provisional Government, 13, 15, 17, 25
  Council of Ministers, 15

INDEX

Putin, Vladimir, 11, 74, 95, 199, 201, 207, 209, 212–225
   2012 Federal Assembly Address, 205–206

Rachmaninov, Sergei, 99
Radio Free Europe, 198
Ratushinskaia, Irina, 4, 7–8, 171–172, 179–180
   education, 171–172
   faith and compassion, 173–175
   imprisonment, 4, 171–176, 179
   labor camp brutality, 172–173
   memoir, 4–5
   poetry, 175–176
   residency at Northwestern University, 178
   release, 69, 176–178
Reagan, Ronald, 69–70, 176
Red Easter, 16
Regelson, Lev L'vovich, 66, 85, 144, 151
   arrest, 91
   letters, 85–86, 152–153, 157
   trial, 92
Reid, Susan, 36
"Religion is Poison; Protect the Children," 41, 43
Religion, State and Society, 186
Religious-Philosophical Seminar, 129, 134
Renovationists, 24, 28, 167
Rilke, Rainer Maria, 99
Robson, Roy R., 226–228
Rodzianko, Mikhail, 13
Roman Catholic Church, 25, 51, 54
Roshchin, Boris, 91, 144
Rossel, Jacques, 66
Rotov, Nikodim, 57, 62, 195–196
Rublev, Andrei, 162
Rudenko, Roman, 150
Russian Soviet Federative Socialist Republic (RSFSR) Criminal Code
   Article 70, 77, 172
   Article 198, 90
   Article 227, 40
Russian Empire, 28, 76
   collapse of, 31
Russian Orthodox Church, 4, 34, 48, 51–73, 73, 74, 95, 142, 186
   Baikal regional party committee and, 21–22
   collaboration with the Soviet state, 6–7, 54–55, 79, 82, 90, 147–154, 187–209, 212–213
   Commission for Investigation into the Activities of the Security Services, 200
   confiscation of church property, 18–20, 24–28, 35, 38
   confiscations, resistance to, 24, 28
   Council for the Affairs of, 56, 194
   destabilizing of, 11, 21
   dissidents within, 5–6, 138–157, 187–190
   education and, 32–50
   execution of priests, 11, 25
   General Assembly, 145
   Holy Synod, 15, 24, 62
   incorporation into the Russian Empire, 28
   liturgy as alternative worldview, 159–161
   liturgy as political threat, 161–164
   liturgy as political resistance, 158–186
   liturgy as solace and strength, 164–166
   liturgy, muting the, 166–168
   Nizhnii Novgorod, 16–17
   Old Believers, 27, 39, 227
   parish revival, 16, 27
   postwar revival, 39
   renewed *sobornost* (spiritual harmony), 16
   repression from within, 190–192
   schism within, 24
   Stalin's concessions to, 10, 53, 193–194
   Synod of Bishops, 56, 58, 62
   Synodal Commission for Canonization, 205
   Vladimir Putin and, 11, 210–225
Russian Orthodox Church, Organization, Situation, Activity, 55
Ruskombank (Russian Bank of Commerce), 26
Russian Red Cross, 49
Russian Revolution, 1
Ryabykh, Filipp, 206

Safe Conduct, 115
Sakharov, Afanasii, 184–185
Sakharov, Andrei, 69, 74, 87, 90, 116, 144–147, 154
Samizdat, 63–65, 67, 129, 131, 141–142, 147
Samoilovich, Serafim, 166, 189, 201, 205
Schmemann, Alexander, 159–161, 167–168
Second World Religion Congress, 227
"Sect," 41, 44
Sedakova, Olga, 9, 118–119, 122, 123–126, 131
   "Dikii shipovnik" (The wild rose), 124–126
   "Elegiia smokovnitsy" (Elegy to the fig tree), 124–1256
Serafim of Krutitsy and Kolomna (Metropolitan), 85
Sergii of Sarov (Saint), 95
Severnaia pochta, 129
Shafarevich, Igor, 144, 146, 152
Shcharanskii, Anatolii, 69, 144
Shipley, Stephen, 52
SHIZO (Small Zone), 171–175
Sholokhov, Mikhail, 98

Shpiller, Vsevolod, 166–167, 195
Shvarts, Elena, 9, 118–119, 131–136
　"Chernaia Paskha" (Black Easter), 133–134
　"Igra v priatki" (A game of hide and seek), 132, 134
　"Moisei is kust, v kotorom iavilsia Bog" (Moses and the bush in which God appeared), 132–133
　"Tantsuiushchii David" (Dancing David), 134
Sidorov, Sergii, 182–183
Siniavskii, Andrei, 63, 115–116, 145
Smirnov, Kirill, 62, 71, 168, 189–190, 192, 203, 205–207, 216
Smolensk Cathedral, 58
Socialist Revolutionaries (SRs), 14
"Solemn Act," 72
Solov'ev, Aleksii, 168
Solov'ev, Vladimir, 94, 151
Solovki, 53
Solzhenitsyn, Alexander, 7–8, 58, 85, 98, 116, 167, 194
　human rights activism, 141–142, 146
Solzhenitsyn Fund, 146
Soviet Constitution, 20, 88–89
　Committee on, 60–61
Soviet Council for Religious Affairs, 68, 70, 219
Soviet Union, 66
　antireligious/religious policies, 26–27, 30–31, 32–50
　collapse of, 7, 11, 13, 185–186, 212
　imperial decrees, 17–18
　religion and children, 35–41
Soviet Writers' Congress, 146
Spanish Inquisition, 52
Spinoza, Baruch, 31
St. Catherine, 51
St. Nicholas Cathedral, 197
St. Tikhon's Orthodox University, 204
Stalin, Joseph, 3, 10, 26, 39, 53, 70, 74, 98–99, 115, 165–166, 193–194, 204, 214
　crimes, recognition of, 71–72, 107
　death, 55, 100
　education, 54
　moves to rehabilitate legacy, 206–209
Starchik, Petr, 151
Stimme der Orthodoxie (*Voice of Orthodoxy*), 197
Stragorodskii, Sergii, 53, 168, 117, 188–194, 201–206
　biography of, 206
Strel'tsov, Arsenii, 165

Stebliuchenko, Gavriil, 196, 200–201
Sudarikov, Viktor, 207
Svenitsitskii, Anatolii, 191, 204
Syntax, 141

Tajuddin, Talgat, 215
Tapley, Lauren, 5, 138–157
Tayler, Jeffrey, 213
Taylor, Charles, 31
Tehran Conference, 193
Tenth Party Congress, 10, 23
Terpsikhorov, N.B., 41, 43, 48
Thatcher, Margaret, 178
Thirteenth Party Congress, 29 37, 129
Tikhon (Patriarch), 17, 19–20, 24, 54, 168, 188, 191, 201–202
　arrest, 25, 164
Tolmachi: Reminiscences about My Father, 181
Tolstoy, Leo, 98–99
Travin, V.A., 44–45, 48
Treaty of Brest-Litovsk, 18
Treaty of Rapallo, 26
Troitskii, Ilarion, 204
Trotsky, Leon, 24–25, 31, 37
Trunev, I.V., 41, 44
Truth About Religion in Russia, The, 193
Truth-telling, 8–9
Tschuy, Theo, 68
Tsedrik, Damaskin, 192, 201, 205
Tserpitskii, Lev, 198
Tsvetaeva, Marina, 118
Tuchkov, Evgenii, 204
Turgenev, Ivan, 170–171
Tverdokhlebov, Andrei, 146, 155–156
Twenty-Second Party Congress, 40
Two Swords Doctrine, 221
Tyshchuk, Arkadii, 197

Udovenko, Platon, 198
Uminskii, Aleksii, 205
Union of Soviet Writers, 99
United School of Labor, 37
United States State Department, 20
Universal Declaration of Human Rights, 155–156
University of Marburg, 99
Unknown Homeland, The, 179–180

V. I. Lenin All-Union Young Pioneer Organization. See Young Pioneers
Vakon'ia, I.U., 226–227

Van Herpen, Marcel, 219-220, 223-224
Vatican, 23, 62, 153
Veche, 147
Velikanova, Tatiana, 145-147, 151, 173
Vigilianskii, Vladimir, 207
Vins, Georgii, 145, 149
Vladimir (Prince), 72, 158, 225
Vladimir Diocese, 184, 185
Vladimir of Kiev (Metropolitan), 21, 163
Vladimir of Rostov and Novocherkassk (Metropolitan), 71
Voice of America, 155, 198
Voino-Iasenetskii, Luka, 207
Volkova, Elena, 76
Voloshin, Maksimilian, 136
Voltaire, 31
Von der Ropp, Eduard, 25
Von Zitzewitz, Josephine, 9, 117-137
Vorob'ev, Vladimir, 169, 204-205
Vorontsova, Vera, 49
Voss, Eugen, 67
Vvedenskii (Metropolitan), 63
Vvedenskii, Aleksandr, 24

Wanner, Catherine, 211-212
Warhola, James, 11, 210-225
Watchman of the Lord's House, 203
Way of the Cross of Patriarch Sergi, The, 204
Weil, Simone, 170
Weinberg, Albert, 6
Weingärtner, Erich, 68
White Book, The, 145
Will the Soviet Union Survive until 1984?, 185
World Christian Peace Congress, 139

World Council of Churches (WCC), 10, 67-68, 86, 139, 144, 196
   Central Committee, 68
   Fifth General Assembly, 66, 152, 155
   Headquarters, 56-57
   Human Rights Advisory Group, 68
   New Delhi, 56
   Resolutions Committee, 67
   Sixth General Assembly, 68,
   Third General Assembly of, 57
World War I, 13, 18, 30, 79, 161
World War II, 10, 22, 26, 39, 53, 65, 71, 99-100, 139, 139, 194, 206-207

Yeltsin, Boris, 95, 214, 217, 225
YMCA, 30
"You Cannot See God's Light," 44-45
Young Pioneers, 38, 40-42, 44, 49
   clubhouses, 48

Zagorsk Theological Academy, 198
Zdebskis, Juozas, 148
Zeno (Emperor), 221
Zernov, Nicolas, 5, 59-60
Zhdanov, Ivan, 126-128
   Kamen plyvet v zemle" (A stone is swimming in the earth), 128
   "Melkii dozd' idet na net" (A drizzle running dry), 126-128
   "More, shto zazhato v kliuvakh ptits" (The sea clutched in the beak of birds), 128
   "Proroki" (The prophets), 127
Zheludkov, Sergei, 142-143, 151
Znamenskii (Father), 22